Emerging Issues in European Economic Diplomacy

Andreas N. Papastamou

Emerging Issues in European Economic Diplomacy

PETER LANG

Berlin - Bruxelles - Chennai - Lausanne - New York - Oxford

Library of Congress Cataloging-in-Publication Data
A CIP catalog record for this book has been applied for at the
Library of Congress.

Bibliographic information published by the Deutsche Nationalbibliothek. The
German National Library lists this publication in the German National Bibliography;
detailed bibliographic data is available on the Internet at http://dnb.d-nb.de.

Cover design by © "Emerging Issues in European Economic Diplomacy"
by Andreas N. Papastamou, 2025.

ISBN 978-3-631-91340-6 (Print)
E-ISBN 978-3-631-91341-3 (E-PDF)
E-ISBN 978-3-631-93051-9 (EPUB)
DOI 10.3726/b22554

© 2025 Peter Lang Group AG, Lausanne
Published by Peter Lang GmbH, Berlin, Germany

info@peterlang.com - www.peterlang.com

Contents

List of Acronyms

ACP	African Caribbean and Pacific States
AIFD	Alternative Investment Funds Directive
ALDE	Alliance of Liberals and Democrats for Europe
BCBS	Basel Committee on Banking Supervision
BfF	Bundesanstalt fuer Finanzdienstleistungen
CAP	Common Agricultural Policy
CCP	Common Commercial Policy
CDM	Clean Development Mechanism
CET	Common External Tariff
CFPS	Common Foreign and Security Policy
CITES	Convention on International Trade in Endangered Species
COP	Committee of the Parties
CRNM	Caribbean Regional Negotiating Machinery
CSP	Country Strategy Programme
CTS	Carbon Trading Scheme
DAC	Development Assistance Committee
DCI	Development Cooperation Instrument
DDA	Doha Development Agenda
DG	Directorate General
EBA	Everything But Arms
EC	European Community
ECB	European Central Bank
ECOFIN	Economic and Financial Affairs Council
EDF	European Development Fund
EEAS	European External Action Service
EEC	European Economic Communities
EFC	Economic and Finance Committee
EIB	European Investment Bank
EMS	European Monetary System
EP	European Parliament
EPA	Economic Partnership Agreement
EPP	European Peoples Party
ESFS	European System of Financial Stability
ESRC	European Systemic Risk Council
EU	European Union

FCCC	Framework Convention on Climate Change
FDI	Foreign Direct Investment
FSA	Financial Services Authority
FSAP	Financial Services Action Plan
FSB	Financial Stability Board
FTA	Free Trade Agreement
GATS	General Agreement on Trade in Services
GATT	General Agreement on Tariffs and Trade
GNP	Gross National Product
GSP	General System of Preferences
HRCFSP	High Representative for Common Foreign and Security Policy
IAIS	International Association of Insurance Supervisors
IASB	International Accounting Standards Board
IMF	International Monetary Fund
IOSCO	International Organization of Securities Commissions
INTA	International Trade Committee
IPA	Instrument for Pre-Accession
LDC	Least Developed Country
NGO	Non-Governmental Organisation
NIC	Newly Industrializing Country
NIEO	New International Economic Order
NIP	National Indicative Programme
ODA	Official Development Assistance
OECD	Organisation for Economic Cooperation and Development
OLP	Ordinary Legislative Procedure
PCD	Policy Coordination for Development
QMV	Qualified Majority Voting
REIO	Regional Economic Integration Organisation
RIP	Regional Indicative Programme
SBCD	Second Banking Coordination Directive
SCA	Sub Committee for Agriculture
SEA	Single European Act
SEM	Single European Market
SFM	Single Financial Market
TEC	Treaty Establishing the European Community
TEU	Treaty on European Union
TFEU	Treaty on the Functioning of the European Union
TPC	Trade Policy Committee
TRIMs	Trade Related Investment Measures

TRIPs	Trade Related Intellectual Property Rights
UN	United Nations
UNCTAD	United Nations Committee on Trade and Development
US	United States (of America)
VER	Voluntary Export Restraint

Preface

Economic diplomacy is of paramount importance for Europe given its position as a major global economic player. International trade, foreign investment, energy, and finance make up the landscape of economic development in Europe. EU member states, as well EU as an international entity engage in economic diplomacy to advance their interests, promote economic growth, and address various global challenges.

Europe is a major exporter and importer of goods and services. Therefore, Economic diplomacy helps negotiate trade agreements, resolve trade disputes, and open up new markets for European businesses. The EU, in particular, has a robust trade diplomacy agenda and has negotiated numerous trade agreements with countries and regions worldwide. At the same time, attracting foreign direct investment (FDI) is vital for economic development. European countries actively engage in economic diplomacy to attract FDI by offering incentives, promoting their business environments, and ensuring legal protections for investors. At the same time, increasingly, the problem of energy security is emerging as a leading factor in international order and prosperity. Energy diplomacy plays a significant role in Europe due to its dependence on energy imports, particularly natural gas and oil. Economic diplomacy helps secure stable energy supplies, diversify energy sources, and manage energy-related geopolitical risks. Economic diplomacy also extends to financial matters, including currency stability, financial regulation, and cooperation with international financial institutions. The European Central Bank (ECB) and European Union institutions often engage in financial diplomacy to safeguard the euro and financial stability. Europe seeks to strengthen its alliances and partnerships with other countries and regions through economic diplomacy. This can include cooperation on economic development projects, infrastructure investment, and regional economic integration.

Economic diplomacy is essential for addressing global challenges such as climate change, sustainable development, and public health crises. European nations often work together to promote common positions and initiatives in international forums. At the same time, economic diplomacy economic diplomacy emerges as a leading factor during political and economic crises. European nations coordinate their efforts to manage financial crises, debt restructuring, and economic recovery, as seen during the European sovereign debt crisis in the early 2010s.

The EU leverages its economic power to shape global governance, advocate for multilateralism, and promote European values and norms. Economic diplomacy contributes to peace and stability by fostering economic interdependence among nations. Economic cooperation and integration are often seen as mechanisms to reduce the likelihood of conflict. it is therefore clear that Economic diplomacy is a multifaceted tool that European countries, both individually and collectively through the EU, use to promote their economic interests, enhance their global standing, and address pressing global challenges. Given Europe's economic significance, its engagement in economic diplomacy has a profound impact on the international economic and political landscape.

The book has six chapters, covering major challenges of economic diplomacy for the European Union:

In the first chapter, entitled *Economic Diplomacy Historical Milestones*, we examine the rich historical tradition of diplomacy, and by extension economic and commercial diplomacy, as it took shape in the imposing royal courts of the powerful states of antiquity. A useful compass for every rationally thinking person and rationally managed organizations, state and non-state.

In the second chapter, entitled *How safe we are? Geopolitical shocks & European Economic Diplomacy*, we "swim in the deep waters" of international security, offering both the theoretical framework and the practical dimension of its problems.

The third chapter, entitled *Ukraine Post-War Reconstruction: the role of European Economic Diplomacy*, is more of an "exercise" of theoretical models, but with an entirely practical dimension to the burning problem of the war in Ukraine. Economic diplomacy emerges once again as the most appropriate means of resolving disputes in a creative way for sustainable development in a region of our planet that has been severely affected by war.

In the fourth chapter, entitled *Trade, Development Aid & Democracy*, we attempt to summarize and update the strategy and instruments that combine economic aid with the difficult task of social and economic development, always in a context of democracy and respect for human rights: perhaps the most difficult task for the European Union if it wants to maintain its rich historical tradition.

The last two chapters, the fifth and sixth, entitled *Economic Diplomacy Studies: organizing postgraduate studies in Economic Diplomacy* and *European Universities: bridges of diplomacy & prosperity*, respectively, focus on the crucial issue of economic diplomacy education: how can postgraduate studies be organized in an effective and timely manner, and what is the contemporary role of universities in bridging diplomacy and prosperity?

If I had been working in a vacuum, I doubt whether anything worthwhile would have ever been produced. So, I am deeply grateful for the interest, advice and criticism of a number of people from the Ministry of Foreign Affairs of Greece where I worked as an economic diplomat for 24 years, as well as to friends in the foreign diplomatic community, and of course to fellow academics from Panteion University of Social & Political Sciences.

It goes without saying that any error or omission is entirely my fault.

It is my expectation that this book will contribute to the debate on the role of economic diplomacy.

Andreas Papastamou, Ph.D.

Department of International, European & Area Studies

Panteion University of Social & Political Sciences
Athens, Greece

1. Economic Diplomacy: Historical Milestones

Economic diplomacy, the use of diplomacy to advance a country's economic interests, has a long and varied history. It has evolved over time, reflecting changes in the global economic landscape and the strategies employed by nations to promote their economic goals.

Ancient Trade and Diplomacy (Pre-Modern Era)

Economic diplomacy has ancient roots, dating back to Ancient Egypt, Mesopotamia – Babylonian and Assyrian Empires, the Silk Road and other ancient trade routes (Dani, 2002; Baipakov & Pidayev, 2011). Ancient economic diplomacy refers to the practices and strategies employed by ancient civilizations to conduct international trade, establish economic relationships with other nations, and promote their economic interests through diplomatic means. While the term "economic diplomacy" may not have existed in the same form as it does today, ancient societies engaged in various forms of economic diplomacy to facilitate trade and ensure their prosperity, thus laying the groundwork for the development of international trade and economic relations in subsequent centuries:

Phoenicians, Egyptians, and Silk Road traders established extensive trade networks and routes that spanned vast distances. Diplomatic envoys and emissaries were often responsible for negotiating access to these routes and securing safe passage for traders (Chandra, 1977; McLaughlin, 2010). "How did the relationship between human societies and their surrounding terrain shape the formation of long-distance trade networks such as the Silk Road?" M.J. Harrower & I.A. Dumitru, wondered in their study, offering insights by digital mapping and computer modelling (Harrower & Dumitru, 2017).

Gifts and tribute were common tools of diplomacy in ancient times. Rulers and leaders exchanged valuable commodities, luxury goods, and other items as a way to establish or maintain friendly relations and secure economic advantages, thus strengthening, voluntarily or involuntarily, cultural relations (Auwers, 2013; Tremml-Werner et al., 2020).

Marriage alliances were used to solidify diplomatic and economic ties between ancient kingdoms and empires. Royal marriages could bring economic benefits, including access to new territories, resources, and trade partners (Schulman, 1979; Cohen & Westbrook, 2000; Melville, 2020).

Diplomats and envoys were dispatched to foreign courts to negotiate trade agreements, establish economic partnerships, and resolve disputes. These missions often involved the exchange of gifts, the negotiation of trade terms, and the signing of treaties or agreements.

Ancient civilizations entered into formal treaties and alliances that included provisions related to trade and economic cooperation. These agreements often specified the terms of trade, tariffs, and mutual assistance in economic matters (Lamber, 1988; Altman, 2010; Lauinger, 2016; Kolb, 2018).

Merchant guilds and associations played a crucial role in ancient economic diplomacy. These organizations, often with the support of their governments, negotiated trade agreements, established trade regulations, and provided a platform for merchants to protect their interests (Sen, 2006; Ptak, 2011).

The introduction and acceptance of a common currency or a standardized system of weights and measures facilitated trade in many ancient societies. This promoted economic diplomacy by reducing uncertainty and enhancing trust in commercial transactions (West, 1923).

Diplomacy in ancient times was not limited to economic matters. Cultural exchanges, including the sharing of knowledge, technology, and artistic traditions, often accompanied economic interactions and helped build goodwill between nations.

Diplomatic efforts were made to secure and protect trade routes from piracy, banditry, and other threats. Nations would form alliances or establish agreements to ensure the safety of their merchants and goods in transit (West, 1923; Amin, 1970; Feldman, 2006; Ptak, 2011; Wizarat, 2014; Charlesworth, 2016).

Control over valuable resources, such as precious metals, minerals, spices, and agricultural products, often required diplomatic negotiations and sometimes even military conquest. "For instance, for many Greek city-states access to timber was a matter of importance if not necessity. And not only for Ancient Greeks. Russell Meiggs in his valuable monograph Trees and Timber in the Ancient Mediterranean World (Oxford 1982), 116, reminds us that one of the reasons for the failure of British ships during the American War of Independence was the weakness of their masts" (Borza, 1987).

Ancient Egypt (3rd Millennium BCE–4th c. CE)

Ancient Egypt relied heavily on the Nile River for agriculture and trade. The river served as a natural trade route, facilitating the exchange of goods within Egypt and with neighboring regions. Egypt had a long history of economic interaction with Nubia (modern-day Sudan), which was rich in resources such as gold, ivory, ebony, and precious stones (O'Connor, 1993; Norbo'tayev, 2022). Thus, maintaining diplomatic relations with neighboring regions, including Nubia (Kush) to secure access to valuable resources like gold, ivory, and exotic goods, was an absolute necessity (Abo-Eleaz, 2023). Diplomatic missions aimed at maintaining trade routes and ensuring the flow of resources. As it is known Ancient Egypt. Diplomatic efforts between Egypt and Nubia often involved the negotiation of trade treaties. These agreements regulated trade routes, established trade privileges, and set terms for the exchange of goods (Cohen, 2000; Cohen & Westbrook, 2000). The first, historically, diplomatic correspondence dates back to the 14th century BC, between Ramses II and the Hittite king Hatusili III in cuneiform tablets in Akkadian, their common language: the famous Eternal Treaty, the Silver Treaty of 1269 BC, after the deadly Battle of ancient Kadesh (Wilson, 1927) a copy of which now adorns the United Nations Offices in New York, donated by the Turkish government, resolved the long-standing (at least two centuries) conflict between the two kingdoms over control of trade from the Indus River valley to the Mediterranean. The oldest diplomatic treaty with a clearly economic object!

Amenhotep III's reign was largely peaceful, as he was involved in military operations only once, in the fifth year of his reign, when he went to Nubia to suppress a rebellion. He was a "master" of diplomacy, securing peace with neighbouring states through economic means, while marrying his sisters and daughters to powerful leaders in the region, making "diplomatic marriages" a means of foreign policy. O'Connor, D. B., & Cline, E. H. (Eds.). (O'Connor & Cline, 2001).

One of the greatest archaeological discoveries of the 20th century, the Mari archives were thoroughly studied, especially by Jack M. Sasson, an Assyrian professor at the Vanderbilt University School of Theology. In his book *From the Mari Archives: An Anthology of Old Babylonian Letters*, published in 2017, he selected 700 administrative documents and correspondence to kings of neighbouring states, scribes and messengers, to reveal startling aspects of the diplomacy of the period in material buried for more than 4,000 years. Sasson's study focuses on six institutions of ancient civilization (Sasson, 2001, 2017):

a. Kingship, which deals with the accumulation of wealth, control of subjects, dynastic marriages, treaty obligations, and the dangers and "nuisances" of governing such a large territory as Ancient Babylon,

b. Administration, from palaces teeming with bureaucrats, musicians and cooks, to the management of provinces and vassal kingdoms,

c. War, military installation and warfare practices,

d. Society, including the institutions of justice and civil transactions

e. Religion: rituals, priesthood function, means of worship, oaths, trials and channels of "communication" with the gods (divination, dreams and prophecy)

f. and Culture: ethnic distinctions, class structure and the cycle of life (birth, childhood, family life, health issues, death and commemoration).

Archaeological excavations have shown that diplomatic missions between Egypt and Nubia included the exchange of gifts as a sign of goodwill and diplomatic engagement. Gifts could range from luxury items to tribute payments. Apparently, economic diplomacy led to cultural exchange between Egypt and Nubia. Along with trade goods, ideas, art, and architectural styles were exchanged, enriching the cultures of both regions (Wang, 2023). Among the diplomatic means, marriages of convenience (diplomatic marriages) were sometimes used to strengthen economic and political ties between Egypt and Nubia. Pharaohs and Nubian rulers would marry into each other's families to solidify relations (Schulman, 1979; Adams, 1984). At certain points in history, Nubia expanded its control into Egyptian territories, including the northern region known as Upper Egypt. This expansion was often the result of political and economic considerations.

Mesopotamia: Babylonian and Assyrian Empires

Modern archaeology has recorded, among hundreds of thousands of texts (from myths and local histories to scientific papers and legal texts, as well as correspondence) and parts of treaties between the city-states of **Mesopotamia**, the Fertile Crescent (today's Iraq, Middle East and eastern Egypt) as it is called by archaeologists, from 2850 BC. It is the oldest evidence of diplomacy known to mankind. The Akkadian or Assyro-Babylonian language, the first diplomatic language of the Middle East, owes its name to the city of Akkad, an important Mesopotamian cultural centre, and used the cuneiform script of its oldest language, Sumerian (Soldt, 2012). The **Babylonian** and **Assyrian** empires in Mesopotamia (2nd and 1st Millennia BCE) engaged in diplomatic relations with neighboring powers to secure access to key trade routes and resources like timber, metals, and agricultural products (Beckman, 1996). Mesopotamia was strategically located at the crossroads of several ancient trade routes, making it a hub for commercial activities. This geographical position gave the Babylonians and Assyrians a significant advantage in trade relations with neighboring regions. Both Babylonians and Assyrians engaged in long-distance trade, which involved the exchange of goods (such as grains, especially barley, textiles, metals like copper and tin, precious stones, timber, and luxury items like perfumes and jewelry) with regions as far away as Anatolia (modern Turkey), the Levant (modern Israel, Palestine,

Lebanon, and Syria), Persia (modern Iran), and the Arabian Peninsula. The exchange of goods often went hand-in-hand with diplomatic treaties and agreements. Babylonians and Assyrians sometimes established formal alliances or trade pacts with neighboring city-states or empires to secure trade routes and protect merchants. Cities like Babylon had bustling marketplaces and bazaars where merchants from different regions converged to trade. These markets served as centers of economic activity and cultural exchange.

To ensure fair trade, Babylonians and Assyrians developed standardized systems of weights and measures. They used various units for different types of commodities, which helped prevent disputes and promote trust among traders. Both civilizations kept detailed cuneiform records of trade transactions. These clay tablets contained information about trade agreements, prices, quantities, and the identities of the parties involved. Such records played a role in resolving disputes and enforcing contracts.

The exchange of diplomatic gifts was common practice. Rulers would send emissaries bearing gifts to establish and maintain friendly relations with neighboring states. These gifts often included valuable items, such as precious metals, textiles, and exotic goods (Bell, 1992). As the Austrian Assyrian scholar Karen Radner wrote: "Assyrian foreign policy was not only about war. Diplomatic marriages with foreign dynasties and the exchange of noble hostages were aimed at protecting international treaties and ensuring peace." (Radner, 2013).

But beyond the official state diplomacy, traders and merchants acted as intermediaries in economic diplomacy. They played a crucial role in connecting the Babylonian and Assyrian economies with those of their neighbors, often requiring negotiation skills and cultural awareness.

Caravan Cities

Caravan cities, such as Palmyra in the Syrian desert, served as hubs for trade and diplomacy along the Silk Road since they frequently hosted diplomatic missions from foreign states, aiming to negotiate trade agreements, secure safe passage for merchants, and establish friendly relations (Rostovtzeff, 1932; Gawlikowski, 1994; Millar, 1998; Dien, 2004). Diplomatic envoys often stayed in caravanserais (roadside inns) within these cities, with the mission of negotiating trade agreements and treaties that determined tariffs, taxes, and trade conditions, ensuring the smooth flow of goods and the protection of merchants. Caravan cities provided currency exchange services, allowing traders to convert their coins and currencies into those accepted in the city or region they were visiting (Rostovtzeff, 2011). This helped facilitate trade and contributed to economic diplomacy. City authorities and local rulers often ensured the safety of traders and their goods, enhancing the reputation of the city as a reliable trading hub. The economic prosperity of caravan cities was closely tied to their role in facilitating trade and diplomacy. The revenue generated from trade, taxation, and services provided the resources needed to maintain and improve infrastructure, making these cities even more attractive to traders and diplomats. These cities were melting pots of diverse cultures and languages since they were known for their tolerance of different religions and cultures (Gawlikowski, 2016). This openness attracted traders and diplomats from various backgrounds, contributing to the cosmopolitan nature of these urban centers. Samarkand, Bukhara, Kashgar, Dunhuang, and Aleppo, among others, not only thrived economically but also played vital roles in fostering diplomatic relations, cultural exchange, and peaceful interactions among the diverse peoples and civilizations of the Silk Road.

Phoenician City-States (8th–4th c. BCE)

The Phoenician city-states engaged in trade across the Mediterranean. Although diplomats and emissaries were sent to secure trade agreements, negotiate commercial treaties, and establish colonies for economic purposes, Phoenician and Greek city-states approaches' and strategies' varied. The Phoenicians, known as skilled seafarers and traders, established colonies and trading posts across the Mediterranean. Their economic diplomacy was largely centered around maintaining control of crucial trade routes and securing access to valuable resources, such as metals and timber (Demetriou, 2023). Phoenician city-states established colonies and trading outposts in various locations, including Cyprus, Carthage (in modern-day Tunisia), and parts of Sicily. These colonies were strategically located to facilitate trade and diplomacy (Jönsson & Hall, 2003). Phoenician city-states, like Tyre and Sidon, engaged in diplomatic negotiations and trade agreements with other Mediterranean powers. These alliances helped protect trade routes and bolstered their economic interests since they included provisions for trade privileges, mutual protection, and the establishment of trading colonies (Demetriou, 2023). Phoenician colonies served as hubs for cultural exchange, where goods, technologies, and ideas were shared among different civilizations. Diplomats and traders played a role in facilitating this exchange (Demetriou, 2018).

Ancient China

The earliest records of Chinese and Indian diplomacy date back to the 1st millennium BC (Bagchi, 2011). By the 8th century BC, the Chinese maintained alliances supported by diplomatic missions, in an organized system of "courtly understanding" between the many (sometimes warring) states that made up the palimpsest of the Chinese empire. A grand tradition with a moral basis, as advised by the philosopher Zhuang Zhou (Zhuangzi, i.e. Master Chuang) a great master of Taoism (Raphals, 1994): "if relations between states are close, then mutual trust can be established through daily interactions, but if relations are distant, then mutual trust can only be established through the exchange of messages. Messages must be carried by messengers (diplomats). Their content may be pleasant for both sides, but they are likely to provoke anger. The faithful transmission of such messages is perhaps the most difficult task, for in the event that the words generate a positive response on both sides, there will be a temptation to exaggerate them with flattery, and if they are unpleasant, there will be a tendency to make them even more caustic. In either case, the truth will be lost. But if truth is lost, mutual trust will also be lost. And if mutual trust is lost, then the messenger himself may be in danger. Therefore, I say to you that it is a wise rule: always tell the truth and never embellish it. In this way, you will avoid great harm to yourself." The Chinese philosopher Zhuang Zhou is considered the "father" of one of the most important principles of economic theory: the spontaneous order (Dale, 2018). Zhuang Zhou reiterated and enriched Lao Tzu's dedication to economic freedom, opposing state interference: "society does not need interference, in fact it should not be governed". "Spontaneous order" would become a basic theory of the French anarchist Proudhon in the 19th century, and of the Nobel Prize-winning economist F. A. Hayek of the famous "Austrian School" in the 20th century (Boettke, 1990; Hodgson, 1994; Boykin, 2010; Luban, 2020)

Eventually, this tradition of equal diplomatic trade between the warring states within China ended with the unification of the country under Emperor Qin in 221 BC and the consolidation of unity under the Han dynasty in 206 BC (Khalimovich et al., 2020). However, the moral tradition continued or as advised by Mencius, perhaps the greatest Chinese philosopher after Confucius: "the best way for a state to exert influence abroad is to develop a moral society worthy of emulation by admiring foreigners and to confidently wait for them to come to China to learn" (Van Norden, 2004). Of course, the pattern of the Chinese conception of international relations repeated itself: with the consolidation of a dynasty's rule, relations with the outside world were limited to three areas:

a. defense of national borders from foreign attacks,
b. receiving envoys from neighbouring states attempting to establish trade relations,
c. and control of foreign merchants at certain ports designated for foreign trade.

Ancient China developed a tribute system in which neighboring states and tribes would send envoys bearing tribute to the Chinese emperor, especially during the Ming and Qing dynasties (Mancall, 1968; Feng, 2009; Wang, 2013). The Tribute System was based on the idea of hierarchical relations, with China at the center as the superior, and other states as vassals or tributaries (Kang, 2010). To maintain favorable economic relations with China, these tributary states were expected to offer symbolic tribute, which often included rare and valuable items like precious metals, exotic animals, and cultural artifacts. While the tribute was primarily symbolic, it provided tributary states with access to the lucrative Chinese market (Zijun, 2019). Tribute missions led by emissaries from tributary states, were received by the Chinese emperor, offering an opportunity for trade, as tribute bearers could engage in commerce with Chinese merchants. Chinese goods, including silk, ceramics, tea, and other luxury items, were highly sought after by tributary states. Thus, the Tribute System provided opportunities for dialogue, negotiation, and the establishment of diplomatic and economic ties, but based on China's dominance: China regulated the types of goods that could be traded, established trade routes and markets, and set tariffs and trade conditions, allowing China to maintain a favorable balance of trade in its favor. By participating in the system, tributary states acknowledged China's political authority and sought protection and recognition from the powerful Chinese empire. This acknowledgment of China's authority had economic implications as well, as it allowed for smoother trade relations, since the Tribute System was flexible and adapted to the specific circumstances of different tributary states. While some states paid tribute regularly and were considered more "loyal" tributaries, others had more sporadic interactions. China adjusted its economic diplomacy accordingly (Lee, 2021). Economic diplomacy in the Tribute System often went hand-in-hand with cultural diplomacy. Tributary states would showcase their cultural achievements and perform rituals of submission to the Chinese emperor. This cultural exchange served to reinforce the hierarchical relationship and build goodwill. The Tribute System gradually declined in the 19th century as Western powers exerted more influence in Asia. China's loss in the Opium Wars and the imposition of unequal treaties led to the abolition of the system. This marked a significant shift in China's economic and diplomatic relations with the world (Tian & Amando Mendes, 2021; Carrai, 2021).

Ancient Greek City-States (8th–4th c. BCE)

However, the tradition that eventually inspired the birth of modern diplomacy in Renaissance Europe, and created the rules of international relations, started in Ancient Greece. Thucydides' work is a standard textbook in most university international relations schools around the world, and the famous "Thucydides' Trap", a term used by the American political scientist Graham T. Allison to describe the potential for warfare when a rising regional power threatens to replace a superpower, is applicable to contemporary great power competition, with US-China relations being a representative example (Allison, 2017; Lee, 2019). The *Iliad* and the *Odyssey* abound with diplomatic references, while the role of the Greek colonies in the whole spectrum of political relations was evident, and even in the broader sense, that is, even of aesthetic and artistic standards, with their influence, social and political, on the then known world undeniable. The exchange of goods and services confirmed the value of commercial – and not only commercial – negotiations, by promoting their skill, while threatening to be annulled in the absence, at least, of political relations (although the desirable one would have been "friendly relations"). The exchange of goods between neighbouring tribes, and also cities, at trade fairs in common religious shrines, and always under the suspension of warlike conditions, contributed substantially to the development of diplomatic institutions. The Olympic Games inaugurated a long tradition of truce and negotiation with respect for all participants, regardless of their disposition and interests, a true transcendence of human nature, in the unique way of the ancient Greeks.

In the 6th c. BC, the amphictyonic leagues maintained interstate assemblies with extraterritorial rights and permanent secretariats. In 2007, the British scholar Simon Hornblower, professor of classics at Oxford and known for his three-volume work on Thucydides, published a paper on the political aspects of the Delphic Amphictyony in the classical period, reaffirming, in contrast to recent work, the political importance of the Delphic Amphictyony not only in the 6th century (self-evident fact), but in the 5th and up to the 4th century, bringing to light important evidence, especially in the 4th century, when we have more records, mainly epigraphic evidence from Athens and Delphi, for the political "exploitation" of the institution of the Amphictyony by Thebes, at least for twenty years, from 360 to 350 BC. (Hornblower, 2007). Moreover, the foundation of the city of Heraclea Trachinia in the valley of Sperchios river by Sparta is obviously linked to the competition for Delphic prestige. Sparta, as early as the middle of the 6th century BC, had formed alliances and by 500 BC had established the famous Peloponnesian Alliance which lasted for about two hundred years (550–366 BC). Athens was forced to join the Alliance in 404 BC, after its defeat in the Peloponnesian War, only to finally leave it in 395 BC with the Corinthian War.

The famous Delos Alliance is also an illustrative example: it began in 478 BC, in the middle of the disastrous, but glorious for us, Persian Wars, from Athens, almost all the Aegean islands (Aegina, Milos and Thera did not participate), most of the cities of Hellespont and Bosporus, some Aeolian cities, most of the cities of Ionia, but also Doric cities of Anatolia and Caria (today's southwestern Asia Minor). The transfer of the Fund from Delos to Athens is linked to the reorganization of the Alliance in 454 BC, by decision of Pericles, under the pretext of protecting it from the Persians. The sequel is well known: the use of the Alliance's funds by Athens for its own benefit led to conflicts between Athens and the less powerful members of the Alliance. By 431 BC, the threat posed by the Alliance to Spartan hegemony, combined with Athens' tight control of the Alliance, caused the Peloponnesian War to erupt. Eventually, the Alliance was dissolved at the end of the war in 404 BC under the leadership of the Spartan Lysander. The economic aspect of diplomacy in all its manifestations (French, 1988).

Polybius' account of the "democratic" Achaean League of Hellenistic times aptly analyses the disastrous course caused by the abuse of hegemony, a potentially useful lesson for the modern era (Mendels, 1979). However, its organizational structure reached into modern times and is thought to have influenced the constitution of the United States and other modern federal states. A high-profile diplomacy course, taught in modern university schools of international relations, but also an unknown episode, indicative of the relationship between political diplomacy and academia in disciplines that are, at first glance, unrelated (but essentially very relevant): in 1898, the French geographer Marcel Dubois (1856–1916), whose book, *Les ligues Étolienne et Achéenne*, (On the Achaean Confederation, Dubois, 1885) occupies a special place in the study of ancient Greek history, was invited to join the "Alliance for the French Homeland" (Ligue de la patrie française) founded by three young university professors (Louis Dausset, Gabriel Syveton and Henri Vaugeois) against "reyfism" and Émile Zola! Dubois not only accepted, but was elected to the steering committee. Thus, the profound scholar of the Achaean Confederation was involved in a political scandal that marked the Third French Republic.

Diplomacy, political power and economic relations, in an inseparable triptych in Ancient Greece, as was shown, among other things, by the policy of Philip of Macedonia. As S. Perlman argued in his lecture at the 4th Conference on

Ancient Macedonia in Thessaloniki in 1983, "Aristotle's reference to the ability of the Greeks to rule other peoples, if they could achieve political unity, could well express a position that was widely discussed in the 4th century B.C. and suggests, without a doubt, the philosopher's approval of Philip II's policy in Greece" (Perlman, 1985).

The presence of numerous independent city-states such as Athens and Corinth, each with its own foreign policy and economic interests, establishing trade networks across the Mediterranean aimed to secure access to resources like grain, metals, and luxury goods from distant regions. Economic diplomacy often involved rivalry among these city-states, as they competed for resources and trade opportunities (Brown, 1947; Adcock & Mosley, 1975). Athens, as the leader of the Delian League, engaged in economic diplomacy with member states. The league's treasury was based on contributions from member city-states, and Athens used its influence to control trade and resources. Diplomatic missions from Greek city-states included the exchange of gifts as a diplomatic gesture. These gifts could be valuable items, artwork, or even tributes to more powerful states (Mosley, 1973).Some Greek city-states formed Amphictyonic Leagues, which were religious and economic organizations. Diplomacy within these leagues aimed to regulate trade and establish codes of conduct. Greek city-states established colonies in regions like southern Italy, the Black Sea, and Asia Minor. These colonies played a significant role in expanding trade and economic influence (Sealey, 1976; Irad, 2013; Zuchtriegel, 2020; Chen et al., 2022). While the Phoenician city-states were known for their maritime dominance and trade networks, Greek city-states emphasized autonomy and often competed with one another. Both engaged in economic diplomacy to secure resources, promote trade, and protect their interests, contributing to the economic vibrancy of the ancient Mediterranean world (Demetriou, 2013; Demetriou, 2018, 2023).

Ancient India (5th c. BCE–5th c. CE)

Ancient India gave a special place to diplomacy, even cultivating a tradition of complex *Realpolitik*, free of moral determinations, that surprises modern scholars. Its systematization was the central theme of *Arthashastra* (*The Science of Material Gain*), one of the oldest books in secular Sanskrit literature, by Kautilya (Chanakya) the erudite advisor to the young Chandragupta, with the aim of overthrowing the Macedonian rule in northern India and establishing the Mauryan dynasty in the late 4th century BC (Jha & Jha, 1998; Waldauer et al., 1996; Tisdell, 2003; Sihag, 2007; Olivelle, 2013). The "diplomatic bible" of the Indian dynasty prioritized the serving of personal interest, focusing on diplomatic maneuvering and espionage in a complex system of six forms of state policy (peace, war, non-alliance, alliances, show of force and double-dealing) with four policy instruments (conciliation, seduction, subversion and coercion). A surprising diplomatic "geometry" with three categories of diplomatic representatives (plenipotentiaries, envoys charged with special missions and royal messengers), one type of consular agent and commercial attaché (similar to the consul in Ancient Greece) charged with managing trade relations and transactions, and two types of spies (informers and saboteurs). *Arthashastra* contained detailed rules on diplomatic immunities and privileges, the commencement and termination of diplomatic missions, and the selection and duties of envoys, with a striking resemblance to modern times: "collecting and sending information to the king, securing the terms of treaties, protecting the king's honor, obtaining allies, fomenting discord between friends of rivals, transporting secret agents and troops into enemy territory, recruiting the enemy's relatives to his own king's side, illegally obtaining gems and other valuable materials for his own king, and showing valor in freeing hostages captured by the enemy."

Ancient India played a central role in both the Silk Road and maritime trade routes. The Silk Road facilitated trade between India and regions like Central Asia, the Middle East, and China (Sen, 2001) while maritime routes connected India with Southeast Asia (Indian traders and settlers established trade links, cultural exchange, and even influenced the political landscape of regions like present-day Indonesia and Malaysia), the Mediterranean, and East Africa. Valuable commodities such as spices, textiles, gemstones, and metals were traded. Indian rulers, particularly during the Maurya, Gupta, and Chola empires, sent diplomatic missions (diplomats known as "amatya" or "duta" represented the Indian rulers) to neighboring states and regions, to establish friendly relations, negotiate treaties (the Edicts of Ashoka, for example, mention treaties with various neighboring states) and promote cultural exchange (Roy, 1981). India had thriving trade relations with the Roman Empire. Roman merchants sought Indian goods like spices, textiles, and gemstones. The Roman historian Pliny the Elder documented the trade between the two regions (Szekely). As in the case of the Athenian Republic and the Roman Empire, the development of standardized coinage systems helped facilitate trade and diplomacy. Coins minted by Indian rulers carried inscriptions in multiple languages, reflecting the multicultural nature of trade and diplomacy in the region. The decline of the ancient Indian empires, particularly the Gupta Empire, led to disruptions in trade and diplomacy. Invasions by Central Asian and Turkic tribes, such as the Huns and the Kushans, also had a significant impact on the region's diplomacy and trade.

The Silk Road (2nd c. BCE-14th c. CE)

The Silk Road, a network of trade routes connecting China to the Mediterranean, was a conduit for both economic exchange and diplomatic relations. Diplomats from the Han Dynasty of China interacted with foreign envoys along the Silk Road, facilitating trade and cultural exchange (Lewis, 2007; Sen, 2014: Qin, 2020). Silk Road diplomacy involved the exchange of diplomatic envoys and missions between the various states and empires along the route. These missions, often tasked with negotiating trade agreements, establishing diplomatic relations, and ensuring safe passage for merchants, served as conduits for cultural exchange. They brought not only goods but also art, literature, religions, and knowledge from one region to another. This cultural diffusion enriched the societies along the route. Diplomatic posts and caravanserais (roadside inns) provided resting places and accommodations for diplomats, merchants, and travelers. These facilities were often protected by local rulers and served as hubs for diplomatic activities (Wilkinson, 2002). Many regions along the Silk Road, such as Central Asia and the Fergana Valley, functioned as intermediaries where diplomats from different civilizations met and conducted negotiations. These intermediaries played a vital role in facilitating diplomacy (Blaydes & Paik, 2021). Diplomatic missions often included the exchange of gifts and tribute. Rulers along the Silk Road would send valuable gifts as a sign of goodwill or to secure favorable trade terms. Tribute payments were made by vassal states to more powerful empires. Diplomats traveling along the Silk Road enjoyed diplomatic immunity, which guaranteed their safety and security during their journeys. This immunity allowed them to cross borders and engage in diplomatic exchanges without fear of harm (Frey & Frey, 1999; Blaydes & Paik, 2021). Silk Road diplomacy led to the negotiation of treaties and agreements between empires and city-states. These treaties often regulated trade, the conduct of diplomats, and issues related to border security. Silk Road diplomacy played a role in the spread of religions, including Buddhism, Christianity, Islam, and others. Diplomats and religious missionaries often traveled together, using diplomacy to gain support for their religious missions (Khalimovich et al., 2020). Silk Road diplomacy contributed to the interconnectedness of the ancient world and facilitated the exchange of goods, cultures, and ideas. It played a vital role in the economic and cultural development of the civilizations along the Silk Road and helped foster a sense of cosmopolitanism in this diverse and dynamic region.

The Roman Empire (27 BCE – 3rd c. CE)

The largest empire that followed was the Roman Empire which made the most of both its military power and its diplomacy, to establish and maintain Pax Romana (Roman Peace) across its vast territory. This peace, which lasted from roughly 27 BCE to 180 CE, allowed for the expansion of trade and the circulation of Roman currency, facilitating economic prosperity and cultural exchange within the empire and beyond (Starr, 1956; Schwarz, 1974; Szekely, 2005; Canepa, 2008; Paterson, 1998). Indeed, one of the key foundations of Roman economic diplomacy was the military expansion of the Roman Empire. Through military conquests and diplomacy, the Romans integrated diverse regions into their empire, creating a vast economic network. The Roman navy ensured safe passage for merchants and protected against piracy, contributing to the security of trade, but, without a credible and well-planned economic policy, military power alone could not bear fruit in the long term. The Roman government introduced standardized coinage, such as the denarius, across the empire – a successful practice already since the years of Philip II of Macedón (West, 1923). This stable currency facilitated trade and economic transactions, both domestically and with foreign regions, but also provided the basis for negotiating diplomatic treaties and agreements, often with neighboring states and allies. These treaties included terms related to trade, mutual protection, and the establishment of diplomatic relations. Roman governors and administrators in the provinces played a role in economic diplomacy. They collected taxes, ensured the efficient functioning of markets, and maintained law and order, fostering economic stability. Like all powerful countries, Roman diplomatic missions and exchanges often involved the giving of gifts and the receipt of tribute. Roman diplomats and emissaries presented valuable items as a sign of goodwill, and tribute could include goods, resources, or financial contributions from vassal states. But nothing could be done without the right infrastructure: the Roman Empire invested heavily in infrastructure, including the construction of roads, bridges, and ports. These investments facilitated the movement of goods, merchants, and diplomats throughout the empire. The formation of economic partnerships and alliances with various regions and trading partners, including those along the Silk Road and in India, facilitated even more the exchange of goods and resources, and led to the exchange of cultures, languages, and technologies across the empire. Diplomatic relations with foreign powers contributed to the blending of cultures within the Roman world, and Roman institutions and practices influenced the economic and political systems of regions within the empire.

Ancient African States

Economic diplomacy in **ancient African** trade empires played a significant role in shaping the economic, political, and cultural landscape of the continent and its interactions with other regions of the world (Jones, 1999). Several prominent African empires engaged in economic diplomacy through trade, alliances, and cultural exchanges:

–   **Aksum**, located in what is now Ethiopia, was a major trading empire from the 1st to the 7th century CE. Economic diplomacy was a cornerstone of Aksum's foreign policy. It established trade links with the Roman Empire, India, and other African kingdoms through the Red Sea and Indian Ocean. The Aksumite state actively promoted trade by minting its own currency and providing a stable and secure environment for merchants (Phillips, 1997; Jones, 1999; Phillipson, 2003, 2012).
–   **Ghana**, not to be confused with the modern country of Ghana, was an ancient empire located in West Africa (approximately 6th to 13th century CE). Ghana controlled the lucrative trans-Saharan trade routes, facilitating trade between North Africa, Europe, and West Africa. Economic diplomacy in Ghana involved regulating trade, imposing taxes on goods passing through its territory, and negotiating alliances with neighboring states (Meyerowitz, 1952; Fage, 1957; Bathily, 1975; Willis, 1975; Munson, 1980).
–   The **Mali** Empire (13th to 16th century CE) succeeded Ghana and became one of the wealthiest empires in the world at its peak. Economic diplomacy in Mali was exemplified by the legendary Mansa Musa, who embarked on a famous pilgrimage to Mecca. During his journey, he distributed gold generously, thereby increasing Mali's reputation and forging diplomatic ties with other Islamic states (Ly-Tall, 1984; Munnik, 1987; Jansen, 2018; Canós-Donnay, 2019; Cartwright & Brink, 2020).
–   Along the East African coast, **Swahili city-states** such as Kilwa, Mombasa, and Zanzibar engaged in extensive trade with the Middle East, India, and China. Economic diplomacy involved establishing trade agreements, facilitating cultural exchanges, and adapting to the customs and languages of their trading partners (Mugane, 2015; Kusimba et al., 2017; Kusimba & Walz, 2021).
–   **Great Zimbabwe** (11th to 15th century CE) was a powerful empire in Southern Africa, known for its impressive stone architecture. Economic diplomacy in Great Zimbabwe involved trade with neighboring regions, including the Swahili coast and the interior of Africa. This trade contributed to the empire's prosperity (Hall, 1905; Pikirayi, 2013; Fontein, 2016).

Throughout ancient Africa, caravan routes and trade fairs were essential hubs for economic diplomacy. These routes and fairs facilitated the exchange of goods, cultures, and ideas among different African kingdoms and with external partners. Economic diplomacy in these ancient African trade empires was not limited to economic transactions; it often included the exchange of knowledge, technology, and religious beliefs. These diplomatic interactions helped shape the history and legacy of Africa and its place in the global trade network.

Middle Ages' Diplomacy

Diplomacy during the Middle Ages was a complex and multifaceted endeavor, shaped by the feudal system, religious influences, and the need to navigate a politically fragmented and often turbulent landscape (Mattingly, 1937; Jucker, 2008; Egenfeldt-Nielsen, 2012; Brough, 2018). It was characterized by a blend of formal and informal methods, with a heavy reliance on personal relationships and alliances among rulers and nobles:

The feudal system was the dominant social and political structure during the Middle Ages in Europe. Kings and monarchs held the highest authority, and they relied on a network of vassals, lords, and nobles to govern their realms. Diplomacy often revolved around the relationships and alliances between these feudal lords (Emerton, 1898; De Wulf, 2008).

One of the most common diplomatic strategies was the use of marriage alliances. Noble families would arrange marriages between their children to solidify political and territorial alliances. These unions were often used to forge peace treaties, secure support in times of conflict, or expand territories (Molho, 1994; Jussen, 2000; Crisp, 2003).

While treaties existed during the Middle Ages, they were less formal and legally binding than modern treaties. They were often sealed with oaths, religious ceremonies, or symbolic acts rather than complex legal documents. These agreements could pertain to borders, trade, military support, or other aspects of governance (Cohen, 2001).

The Catholic Church played a significant role in medieval diplomacy. Popes and bishops were often mediators in conflicts between rulers and could excommunicate or place kingdoms under interdict as a form of diplomatic pressure. Additionally, the Crusades, a series of religious wars, had a profound impact on diplomacy during this time.

Diplomacy often relied on envoys or emissaries who were sent to negotiate on behalf of a ruler or kingdom. These envoys could be priests, knights, or other trusted individuals and would carry messages, gifts, and tokens of goodwill to present to their counterparts.

The code of chivalry, which emphasized honor, loyalty, and courtesy among knights, had an influence on diplomatic conduct. Knights were often involved in diplomatic missions and were expected to adhere to the principles of chivalry even in diplomatic negotiations.

Diplomacy was closely tied to trade and commerce. Medieval cities often engaged in trade with neighboring regions and kingdoms, and diplomacy was essential in negotiating trade agreements, tariffs, and safe passage for merchants (Citarella, 1968; Lieber, 1968; Dahl, 2000).

Spying and espionage were common in medieval diplomacy. Rulers and nobles used spies to gather information about the intentions and activities of rival kingdoms. These spies were often disguised as merchants, diplomats, or travelers (Devries, 2002; MacDonald, 2006; Edgington, 2016).

Neutral third parties, often from neighboring kingdoms or the church, were frequently called upon to mediate disputes and conflicts between rulers. These mediators would attempt to find peaceful solutions to avoid costly and destructive wars.

Despite diplomatic efforts, warfare was still a common feature of medieval politics. Battles and sieges were often the result of failed diplomacy or the pursuit of territorial gains.

The Byzantine Empire (4th–15th c.)

The Byzantine Empire's strategic location at the crossroads of Europe and Asia allowed it to play a crucial role in fostering economic exchanges between the East and West, making diplomacy an essential tool for managing its economic interests and maintaining its influence in the region. Byzantine economic diplomacy encompassed a wide range of diplomatic activities aimed at promoting trade, securing access to essential resources -including grain from Egypt, textiles from the Middle East, and precious metals from the Balkans and Asia Minor, to support the empire's economy – and managing economic relations with neighboring states and distant regions. Byzantine cities like Constantinople served as major commercial centers and hubs for economic diplomacy. Foreign merchants, diplomats, and envoys frequented these cities to engage in trade and diplomatic activities. Meanwhile, Byzantine diplomats and envoys were sent to neighboring regions, including the Sassanian Empire, the Abbasid Caliphate, and various European kingdoms. These missions, enjoying diplomatic immunity, sought to establish and maintain trade agreements, negotiate commercial treaties, and promote economic exchanges. Byzantine emperors used diplomatic gifts and tribute payments as tools of economic diplomacy. Sending valuable gifts to foreign rulers was a way to establish favorable relations and encourage trade. In return, Byzantine emperors received tribute from vassal states and neighboring powers. Byzantine diplomats negotiated trade treaties and alliances with neighboring states and rival powers. These agreements often included provisions related to tariffs, market access, and the protection of merchants and traders. It is worth noting that the Byzantine Empire maintained a diplomatic corps, which included skilled diplomats and ambassadors. These individuals were trained in the art of negotiation and diplomacy and played a crucial role in managing economic relations. One notable example of Byzantine economic diplomacy was the Treaty of 716 CE between the Byzantine Empire and the Umayyad Caliphate, aiming at regulate trade and economic relations between the two powers, allowing for the exchange of goods and merchants (Bibicou, 1959; Wozniak, 1979; Shepard & Franklin, 1992; Diebler, 1995; Drocourt, 2008, 2016, 2018; Moulet, 2019; Drocourt & Malamut, 2020).

Muslim Diplomacy

Muslim diplomacy has a long and complex history that spans over centuries, encompassing various dynasties, empires, and regions across the Islamic world. The practice of diplomacy in the Muslim world has been influenced by Islamic principles, cultural norms, and the political context of different times and places (Knobler, 1996; Drocourt, 2010; Köhler, 2013; Van Gelder & Krstić, 2015):

Islamic principles have played a significant role in shaping Muslim diplomacy. The concept of shura (consultation), for example, encourages consultation and consensus-building in decision-making, which can be reflected in diplomatic negotiations and alliances. Islamic law, or Sharia, has provided a framework for the conduct of diplomatic relations. Diplomats from Muslim-majority countries have often been guided by Islamic legal principles when negotiating treaties, trade agreements, and other diplomatic matters. Muslim rulers, including caliphs and sultans, were responsible for conducting diplomatic relations with neighboring states and foreign powers. They appointed diplomats or envoys, known as "wazirs" or "ambassadors," to represent their interests abroad. Equally, Muslim merchants played a crucial role in medieval trade, and diplomacy was closely tied to commerce. Diplomatic missions were often sent to establish trade agreements, negotiate tariffs, and ensure the safety of Muslim merchants traveling along the Silk Road and other trade routes. And of course we cannot omit the role of Muslim rulers and scholars as mediators and arbitrators in regional and international conflicts. The Islamic tradition of conflict resolution through arbitration was employed to settle disputes between states or warring factions. During times of conflict or conquest, Muslim diplomacy was often intertwined with the concept of "jihad" (struggle or holy war). Diplomatic negotiations might include terms related to the treatment of non-Muslim populations, religious freedoms, and the protection of holy sites. Muslim rulers and leaders frequently entered into treaties and agreements, known as "sulh" or "hudna," with other states or empires. These treaties covered various aspects, including military alliances, borders, and the cessation of hostilities. Religion has always been in the arsenal of diplomacy Muslim leaders used religious diplomacy to strengthen ties with other Islamic states or to promote Islamic interests. This often involved supporting religious institutions, sending scholars as envoys, or establishing religious alliances. And all this within a rich cultural context: Muslim diplomats facilitated cultural exchanges between Islamic civilization and other parts of the world. They played a key role in the transmission of knowledge, sciences, and technologies between the Muslim world and Europe, Asia, and Africa. Diplomats and scholars from the Islamic world contributed to the documentation of their travels and diplomatic missions. Travel accounts, such as those by Ibn Battuta and Ibn Khaldun, provide valuable insights into the diplomatic practices and cultural interactions of their time.

Venetian Diplomacy (9th–15th c.)

Venice, historically known for its maritime and trade prowess, has a rich history of economic diplomacy that dates back to its days as a powerful city-state during the Middle Ages and the Renaissance (Shaw, 2018) establishing a vast network of trade routes extending across the Mediterranean, the Adriatic Sea, and into the Middle East (Pedani, 2000). The city's merchants – such as the Fondaco dei Tedeschi for German traders and the Fondaco dei Turchi for Ottoman merchants – and diplomatic envoys, known as ambassadors or "bailos" (deriving from the Latin term "baiulus", meaning "porter, bearer") to foreign courts and city-states – including Constantinople and Alexandria – negotiated trade treaties ("condotte" or "concessions") with various powers, resolve disputes (Foscari, 1844; Dario, 1992; Nicol, 1992; Dursteler, 2001) and represent Venetian interests in exactly the same way that modern economic diplomacy seeks to promote the economic interests of a state, i.e., by making use of diplomatic contacts and, above all, by gathering reliable information on market conditions (Beverley, 1999). Venice' diplomacy allowed Venetian merchants to access valuable goods and markets across the Mediterranean, such as spices, textiles, and precious metals, thereby maintaining Venice's economic influence (Pirillo, 2016).

However, diplomacy alone was not enough: Venice invested heavily in the protection of its trade routes, maintaining a powerful navy to safeguard Venetian merchant vessels from piracy and other threats. Venice encouraged innovation in shipbuilding, navigation, and finance, which helped sustain its economic diplomacy. The city was at the forefront of developing new maritime technologies and financial instruments, and competed with other maritime powers, such as Genoa and the Ottoman Empire, for control of key trade routes and ports (Lane, 1934; Hocquet, 1995; Dotson, 2001; Greene, 2001). As cited in Clark and Pinder study, "the Arsenale founded in 1104 by Doge Ordelafo Falier, it was certainly operational by the early 13th century, and rapidly became central to the development and security of the Venetian trading empire. Over 3000 workers were employed in the 16th century, and shortly before the Battle of Lepanto against the Ottoman empire in 1571 the yard was launching seven warships a month. At various times between the late 14th and 15th centuries the Venetian trade routes extended from England, Flanders and Portugal in the west, to Constantinople, Tana and Trebizond around the Black Sea in the east. Southwards they included Alexandria and Tripoli in north Africa. Moreover, although Venetian colonisation was more restricted geographically, the city established itself as a dominant force in many towns" (Clark & Pinder, 1999).

In all these ancient civilizations, economic diplomacy often entailed sending envoys, emissaries, and diplomats to negotiate trade agreements, secure access to valuable resources, and establish diplomatic relations with neighboring powers: experienced high officers of the administration or recognized personalities were frequently accompanied by officers of junior status, and all this in a wise proportion, according to the importance and objectives of the mission. These early forms of economic diplomacy laid the foundation for the development of more sophisticated diplomatic practices in later periods. In Ancient Grece these "ambassadors" carried the title of herald (κῆρυξ: in the singular, κήρυκες: in plural) or *angelos*, as frequently employed by Homer.

Colonialism and Mercantilism (16th–18th Centuries)

During the period of colonialism and mercantilism in the 16th to 18th centuries, economic diplomacy took on a very different form compared to the earlier African trade empires. Colonial powers such as Spain, Portugal, England, France, and the Netherlands pursued policies that aimed to extract wealth from their colonies for the benefit of the mother country. Economic diplomacy in this context was primarily focused on exploiting colonial resources, controlling trade, and maximizing economic gain.

Mercantilism was the prevailing economic doctrine of the time, emphasizing the accumulation of precious metals (gold and silver) and the maintenance of a favorable balance of trade. Colonial powers granted monopolies to trading companies, such as the British East India Company and the Dutch East India Company, to control and monopolize colonial trade. Economic diplomacy involved securing these trade monopolies, negotiating trade agreements with other European powers, and protecting the interests of the chartered companies (Mattingly, 1988; Mallett, 2001; Fletcher, 2015; Lazzarini, 2015; Lundell, 2016; Azzolini & Lazzarini, 2017).

A second aspect was the wretched regime forced labor and slave trade: economic diplomacy in colonial contexts often involved negotiating with African, Asian, and Indigenous American leaders for the supply of labor, including the transatlantic slave trade. The exchange of enslaved people was a brutal form of economic diplomacy aimed at providing labor for plantations and mines in the colonies (Perbi, 1992; Eltis & Richardson, 1995; Geggus, 2001; Trade et al., 2005; Postma, 2008; McKee, 2008).

Economic diplomacy frequently involved conflicts and competition among colonial powers for control of profitable colonies and trade routes. This competition often led to diplomatic negotiations, alliances, and even wars. Colonial powers, particularly England, imposed strict trade regulations and navigation acts that required colonial goods to be transported on home-country ships and sold in the home country, and at the same time used treaties, alliances, and diplomatic negotiations to legitimize their territorial expansion and control over new colonies. Treaties with indigenous leaders were sometimes used to gain access to resources and establish colonial footholds. Today we know that the outcome has been disastrous not only for the colonized regions (leading to the exploitation of their resources, the displacement of indigenous populations, and the disruption of traditional economies and social structures), but also for the colonial powers.

Imperialism and Geopolitical Rivalries (19th Century)

Economic diplomacy during the 19th century, a period characterized by imperialism and geopolitical rivalries among the major European powers, played a crucial role in shaping global economic relationships, territorial expansion, and international conflicts. Here are key aspects of economic diplomacy during this period:

European powers, including Britain, France, Germany, and Belgium, engaged in a race for colonial territories in Africa, Asia, and the Pacific. Economic interests, such as access to raw materials and new markets, were a primary motivation for colonial expansion. Economic diplomacy was employed to secure colonial possessions, negotiate territorial claims, and establish trade agreements with local rulers or other colonial powers.

The Opium Wars between Britain and China (1839–1842 and 1856–1860) exemplify economic diplomacy in the context of imperialism. The conflict centered on Britain's desire to trade opium for Chinese tea and other goods. The Treaty of Nanking (1842) and the Treaty of Tientsin (1856) resulted in unequal treaties that granted extraterritorial rights to Western powers in China, opening up Chinese ports and markets to foreign trade (Stinchcombe, 1994; Waley, 2013; Chen, 2017; Keevak, 2017).

The construction of the Suez Canal (completed in 1869) was a pivotal development in 19th-century economic diplomacy. Controlling this key maritime route became crucial for European powers seeking to facilitate trade with Asia. The British acquisition of a controlling interest in the Suez Canal Company in 1875 was an example of how economic interests were intertwined with geopolitical considerations (Hoskins, 1940; Kunz, 1991; Šedivý, 2022; Curli, 2022).

Economic diplomacy played a significant role in the "Scramble for Africa" as European powers competed for control of African territories and resources. Diplomatic negotiations and treaties with African leaders were used to legitimize territorial claims and secure access to valuable resources such as rubber, minerals, and agricultural products. European powers sought to secure preferential access to each other's markets while imposing tariffs on goods from non-colonial sources. The negotiation of trade agreements and tariff arrangements was used as a means of economic leverage and rivalry among European powers (Griffiths, 1986; Chamberlain, 2014; Pakenham, 2015; Michalopoulos & Papaioannou, 2016).

Most importantly, however, was the context of geopolitical rivalries which in turn shaped the European alliances. For example, the Triple Entente (France, Russia, and Britain) and the Triple Alliance (Germany, Austria-Hungary, and Italy) were partly motivated by economic and territorial interests. The competition for economic and strategic advantages in various regions, such as the Balkans, contributed to the tensions leading up to World War I (Schmitt, 1924; Lammers, 1967; Stevenson, 1997; Tomaszewski, 2002; White, 2002).

The 19th-century economic diplomacy was closely intertwined with the imperialistic ambitions and geopolitical rivalries of the major European powers. It involved the pursuit of economic advantages, territorial expansion, and the negotiation of treaties and agreements to advance national interests, often at the expense of colonized regions and non-European nations. These developments laid the groundwork for the complex geopolitical landscape of the 20th century.

Interwar Period and Economic Nationalism (1919–1939)

Following World War I, countries sought to protect their economies through economic nationalism. Tariffs, trade barriers, and economic self-sufficiency became prominent features of economic diplomacy during this era (Burk, 1981). The Treaty of Versailles (1919) which officially ended World War I, imposed reparations and economic penalties on Germany. This economic burden contributed to Germany's economic difficulties during the interwar period (Anievas, 2014; Boemeke et al., 1998; Snap, 2013; Malygina, 2019)

The Great Depression (1929–1939) triggered by the Wall Street Crash of 1929 led to a severe contraction in international trade and investment. Many countries adopted protectionist measures, such as raising tariffs and imposing import quotas, to shield their domestic industries and preserve jobs (Eichengreen & Irwin, 2010).

Economic nationalism was a prominent feature of interwar economic diplomacy. Countries became increasingly focused on protecting their own economic interests, often at the expense of international cooperation. Nationalistic policies included the imposition of tariffs, import substitution industrialization (ISI), and the pursuit of autarky (economic self-sufficiency) (Heilperin, 2010).

The Smoot-Hawley Tariff Act in the United States raised tariffs to historically high levels, exacerbating the global economic downturn by reducing international trade (Hayford & Pasurka, 1992).

To gain an advantage in international trade, some countries engaged in competitive devaluations of their currencies, which further destabilized the global economy. These currency wars created tensions and contributed to the breakdown of the international monetary system.

Economic diplomacy during this period often involved the negotiation of bilateral trade agreements between individual countries. These agreements aimed to secure preferential trade relationships.

In response to currency instability, some countries engaged in barter trade agreements or bilateral clearing arrangements, bypassing the use of international currencies (Gatch, 2008).

Many countries adopted isolationist policies, withdrawing from active engagement in international affairs and focusing on domestic concerns.

Governments implemented various economic recovery programs to combat the Great Depression. These included public works projects, bank reforms, and monetary policy measures (Wallis, 1987; Rosen, 2005).

Economic blocs and regional trading arrangements gained prominence during this period. Notable examples include the Autarky Bloc in Central Europe

(Eichengreen & Irwin, 1995) and the Greater East Asia Co-Prosperity Sphere in Asia (Yellen, 2019).

Economic diplomacy during the interwar period was marked by a retreat from international cooperation, the rise of economic nationalism, protectionist measures, and efforts by countries to protect their domestic industries and economic interests. These trends contributed to the global economic instability of the time and had far-reaching consequences for the international order, ultimately leading to the outbreak of World War II.

Post-World War II and Bretton Woods (1944)

After World War II, economic diplomacy played a central role in the establishment of the Bretton Woods system, which created the International Monetary Fund (IMF), the World Bank, and the General Agreement on Tariffs and Trade (GATT), which later became the World Trade Organization (WTO). These institutions were designed to promote economic stability and cooperation.

The Bretton Woods Conference, held in July 1944 in New Hampshire, United States, brought together representatives from 44 Allied nations (Schuler & Bernkopf, 2014). The Bretton Woods System had two aspects:

- the monetary one with the establishment of fixed exchange rates tied to the U.S. dollar, which was convertible into gold at a fixed rate. This system provided stability to international currencies and facilitated trade and investment,
- and the institutional with the design of a new international monetary and financial system. Two key institutions emerged from the conference: the International Monetary Fund (IMF) and the International Bank for Reconstruction and Development (now part of the World Bank). These institutions were created to promote international monetary cooperation and provide financial assistance for post-war reconstruction and development.

The United States, through the Marshall Plan (1947) officially known as the European Recovery Program, was a major initiative by the United States to provide financial assistance to Western European countries devastated by World War II. It aimed to promote economic recovery, prevent the spread of communism, and strengthen Western European economies as a bulwark against the Soviet Union (Hogan, 1987; DeLong & Eichengreen, 1991).

The Cold War rivalry between the United States and the Soviet Union (1947–1991) marked a whole generation (Seaborg, 1981). Economic alliances and strategies were used as tools to advance their respective interests and ideologies:

– the Soviet Union established its own sphere of influence in Eastern Europe and supported communist governments in countries such as East Germany, Poland, Hungary, and Czechoslovakia. Economic assistance, trade agreements, and financial aid from the Soviet Union were used to solidify the economic ties of these Eastern Bloc countries.

– European countries in the Western bloc, with the support of the United States, engaged in trade diplomacy to strengthen their economies and counter the economic influence of the Eastern bloc. They negotiated trade agreements, reduced tariffs, and promoted economic liberalization to encourage trade among Western European nations and with the United States (Gowan, 1990; Spaulding, 1997).

– The General Agreement on Tariffs and Trade (GATT) was established in 1947 as a multilateral agreement aimed at reducing trade barriers, primarily tariffs, and promoting international trade. It was not a formal international organization but rather a series of negotiations and agreements among member countries. GATT successfully conducted several rounds of negotiations, such as the Kennedy Round and the Uruguay Round, which led to significant reductions in tariffs and the inclusion of non-tariff trade measures in its scope. While GATT played a crucial role in promoting trade liberalization, it had limitations, particularly in addressing trade in services, intellectual property rights, and trade-related disputes (Azevêdo, 2015).

– The Organization for Economic Co-operation and Development (OECD) provided a platform for a more creative economic diplomacy, trade negotiations, and the promotion of economic cooperation (Bainbridge, 2000).

– The creation of the European Coal and Steel Community (ECSC) in 1951 and later the European Economic Community (EEC) in 1957 aimed to promote economic cooperation and prevent further conflict in Europe. Economic diplomats from member states negotiated treaties and agreements to facilitate economic integration, including the common market and the eventual creation of the European Union (EU) (Mason, 2013; Smith, 2016).

– The North Atlantic Treaty Organization (NATO), a military alliance, but it also had economic implications by strengthening economic ties among its member countries (Schmidt, 2001).

The United States and the Soviet Union both engaged in economic diplomacy with other countries through bilateral trade agreements. These agreements often included provisions for economic aid, technology transfer, and access to markets.

Both superpowers used trade embargoes and economic sanctions as tools to exert pressure on countries aligned with the opposing side (Hufbauer et al., 1990; Dobson, 2002). For example, the U.S. imposed an embargo on Cuba (Kaplowitz, 1998; Drain & Barry, 2010) while the Soviet Union placed sanctions on Yugoslavia (Eastwood, 1992).

The Cold War saw proxy wars in various parts of the world, such as the Korean War (Cumings, 2010) and the Vietnam War (Burns et al., 2017). The superpowers provided economic and military support to their respective allies in these conflicts.

The arms race between the United States and the Soviet Union had significant economic implications. Both superpowers invested heavily in military research, development, and production, leading to substantial defense budgets and economic growth in these sectors (Gray, 1971).

Economic espionage and intelligence activities played a role in economic diplomacy during the Cold War. Both sides sought to gather information on each other's economic and technological capabilities (Trahair, 2004; Gaddis, 1989)

The Space Race between the United States and the Soviet Union was not just about scientific achievement but also had economic and military dimensions. Success in space was seen as a symbol of technological and economic prowess (Siddiqi, 2000).

The Cold War was also a battle of ideologies, with the United States promoting capitalism and democracy and the Soviet Union advocating communism. Economic diplomacy was used to showcase the benefits of each system.

During periods of détente, such as in the 1970s, there were efforts to reduce tensions between the superpowers. Economic diplomats from Western and Eastern bloc countries engaged in economic cooperation, trade negotiations, and arms control negotiations during this period (Westad, 1997; Copeland, 1999; Zubok, 2008; Zelizer, 2009). The signing of the Helsinki Accord in 1975 included economic cooperation as one of its key principles (Fascell, 1979; Morgan, 2018).

At the same time, many former colonies gained independence in the post-war period, and economic diplomacy played a role in shaping their relationships with former colonial powers and other nations. New nations sought economic assistance, trade partnerships, and development aid (Head et al., 2010).

The post-war period saw the rise of the oil industry as a significant player in economic diplomacy. Oil-producing nations, particularly those in the

Middle East, used their energy resources as diplomatic leverage in international affairs.

The Bretton Woods System began to unravel in the 1970s due to economic imbalances and the U.S. decision to end the dollar's convertibility into gold. This led to the transition to a system of floating exchange rates (Ghizoni, 2013).

Economic diplomacy in the late 20th century included efforts to address debt crises in developing countries. International institutions and creditor nations negotiated debt relief and restructuring arrangements.

Economic diplomacy in the post-World War II era was characterized by the creation of international institutions, regional economic integration, efforts to promote trade and financial stability, and the complex interactions of economic interests and geopolitical rivalries. On thing is certain: the Bretton Woods Conference and its outcomes played a central role in shaping the international economic order during this period, and this was to determine the terms of the developments of the next decade or as Keynes put it, with his usual bitter humour: "Before committing ourselves definitely to a major monkey-house [a formal conference], I should like to get the preliminary reactions of those monkeys who will be optional guests."

Globalization and Trade Liberalization (Late 20th Century)

The late 20th century saw a surge in economic globalization and trade liberalization. Economic diplomacy focused on negotiations to reduce trade barriers and expand economic cooperation. The Uruguay Round of trade talks led to the creation of the **WTO** in 1995 (Hoekman, 2002).

Trade Liberalization and Multilateral Agreements

The **WTO** was established on January 1, 1995, as a successor to GATT. Unlike GATT, the WTO is a formal international organization with a broader mandate to cover not only trade in goods but also trade in services and intellectual property rights. The WTO aims to provide a more comprehensive and structured framework for international trade rules and dispute settlement, by means of three agreements:

the General Agreement on Trade in Services (GATS)	the Agreement on Trade-Related Aspects of Intellectual Property Rights (TRIPS)	the WTO's Dispute Settlement Body (DSB)

➢ The *General Agreement on Trade in Services* (GATS) (Sauvé, 1995; Marchetti & Mavroidis, 2011)

❖ *Negotiating Trade in Services*: Economic diplomacy involves negotiations among WTO member countries to liberalize trade in services. These negotiations aim to reduce barriers and restrictions on cross-border trade in services, such as financial services, telecommunications, tourism, and professional services. Diplomats and trade negotiators engage in discussions to determine the terms and conditions under which services can be provided and consumed across borders. This includes negotiations on market access, national treatment, and specific commitments related to each service sector.

❖ *Bilateral and Multilateral Negotiations*: Economic diplomacy encompasses both bilateral negotiations between individual countries and multilateral negotiations involving a group of countries within the GATS framework. Bilateral negotiations allow countries to tailor their commitments and liberalization measures to suit their specific interests and needs, while multilateral negotiations aim for more comprehensive and coordinated liberalization across all sectors and participating countries.

❖ *Mode of Supply*: The GATS distinguishes between four modes of supplying services: cross-border supply, consumption abroad, commercial presence, and the presence of natural persons. Economic diplomacy involves negotiations and agreements on the extent to which each mode is opened up for international trade. Diplomatic efforts are crucial in determining how countries are willing to allow foreign service providers to operate within their borders and under what conditions.

❖ *Market Access and National Treatment*: Market access commitments in the GATS specify the conditions under which foreign service providers can access a country's domestic market. Economic diplomacy plays a role in negotiating these commitments, including tariff and non-tariff measures. National treatment commitments require countries to treat foreign service providers on par with domestic providers. Negotiating the scope and extent of national treatment is a key aspect of economic diplomacy within the GATS.

❖ *Exceptions and Safeguard Measures*: Economic diplomacy also involves negotiations on exceptions and safeguard measures. Countries may negotiate specific exceptions or limitations to their GATS commitments to protect certain sectors or address national concerns. Discussions on how and when safeguard measures can be invoked to protect domestic industries or address balance-of-payments problems are important aspects of eco-nomic diplomacy within the GATS.

❖ *Trade-Related Issues*: The GATS addresses trade-related issues, such as transparency, domestic regulation, and the recognition of qualifications and licenses. Economic diplomacy is used to negotiate agreements on these issues, facilitating smoother trade in services.

❖ *Dispute Settlement*: Economic diplomacy is essential in the context of dis-pute settlement under the GATS. If a dispute arises regarding a member country's compliance with GATS commitments, diplomatic efforts may be used to resolve the issue through consultations, mediation, or WTO dispute settlement procedures.

Economic diplomacy is a fundamental component of the GATS, which regulates trade in services among WTO member countries. It involves negotiations, com-mitments, and agreements related to the liberalization of trade in services, as well as dispute resolution and the handling of trade-related issues. Economic diplomats and negotiators play a central role in shaping the rules and regulations governing international trade in services through the GATS.

➤ The **Agreement on Trade-Related Aspects of Intellectual Property Rights** (TRIPS) is a crucial component of the World Trade Organization (WTO) framework, and economic diplomacy, and plays a significant role in its implementation and negotiations. TRIPS is designed to harmonize and enforce intellectual property (IP) protection and regulation on a global scale (Cottier, 2005; Correa, 2020).

❖ *Negotiating IP Standards*: Economic diplomacy was instrumental in the negotiation and drafting of TRIPS during the Uruguay Round of GATT (1986–1994). Diplomats and trade negotiators representing WTO mem-ber countries engaged in extensive discussions to establish common international standards for the protection and enforcement of IP rights. These negotiations addressed various forms of intellectual property, including patents, copyrights, trademarks, trade secrets, and geograph-ical indications.

❖ *Minimum Standards and Flexibilities*: Economic diplomacy within TRIPS involves striking a balance between setting minimum IP protection stan-dards and allowing for certain flexibilities to accommodate the diverse needs and developmental levels of member countries. Negotiators must consider how to accommodate countries with different levels of economic development while ensuring adequate IP protection.

❖ *Transition Periods and Special Provisions*: TRIPS recognizes that some developing countries may need additional time to fully implement its provisions. Diplomatic efforts may be needed to negotiate transition periods and special provisions that allow these countries to gradually conform to TRIPS requirements.

❖ *Enforcement Measures*: Economic diplomacy is crucial in addressing issues related to the enforcement of IP rights. This includes negotiations on the mechanisms and remedies available to protect IP holders, such as civil and criminal procedures and border measures. Negotiators must consider how to strike a balance between protecting IP rights and ensuring access to essential medicines, knowledge, and technology, particularly in public health crises.

❖ *Dispute Settlement and Compliance*: The TRIPS Agreement includes a dispute settlement mechanism within the WTO framework. Economic diplomacy is involved when member countries bring complaints against other countries for alleged violations of TRIPS commitments. Diplomats and negotiators engage in consultations and dispute resolution efforts to resolve IP-related trade disputes. Compliance with TRIPS rulings is another aspect of economic diplomacy.

❖ *Transparency and Technical Assistance*: Economic diplomacy within TRIPS also encompasses discussions on transparency measures, notification requirements, and the exchange of information among member countries. Technical assistance programs may be negotiated and coordinated to help developing countries build the capacity to implement and enforce IP regulations effectively.

❖ *Public Health and Access to Medicines*: Economic diplomacy has been crucial in addressing the public health implications of TRIPS, particularly in ensuring access to affordable medicines. Negotiations have resulted in the Doha Declaration on TRIPS and Public Health, which affirmed countries' rights to use TRIPS flexibilities to protect public health.

❖ *Multilateral and Bilateral Agreements*: Some aspects of TRIPS, such as the protection of geographical indications, have led to additional negotiations and agreements, both within the WTO framework and through bilateral negotiations.

Economic diplomacy plays a significant role in the implementation and ongoing negotiations of the TRIPS Agreement within the WTO. It involves addressing the complex and sometimes conflicting interests of member countries, striking a balance between IP protection and access to essential goods and technology, and resolving disputes related to IP rights. Economic diplomats and negotiators work to ensure that TRIPS serves the interests of both IP holders and the broader global community.

➤ *The WTO's Dispute Settlement Body* (DSB) has the authority to address trade disputes and enforce trade rules more effectively than GATT. "Such disputes may arise with respect to any agreement contained in the Final Act of the Uruguay Round that is subject to the Understanding on Rules and Procedures Governing the Settlement of Disputes (DSU). The DSB has authority to establish dispute settlement panels, refer matters to arbitration, adopt panel, Appellate Body and arbitration reports, maintain surveillance over the implementation of recommendations and rulings contained in such reports, and authorize suspension of concessions in the event of non-compliance with those recommendations and rulings" as stated on the official website of the WTO. Economic diplomacy focused on negotiating trade agreements within the framework of the WTO, reducing tariffs, and eliminating trade barriers (Trachtman, 1999; Bartels, 2001; Iida, 2004; Davey, 2005).

Regional Trade Blocs and Agreements

North American Free Trade Agreement (NAFTA) January 1, 1994	European Single Market 1992 January 1, 1993	Association of Southeast Asian Nations (ASEAN) August 8, 1967 (Bangkok Declaration)	Mercosur (South America) March 26, 1991 (Treaty of Asunción) Protocol of Ouro Preto, 1994

Economic diplomacy involved negotiating and managing these regional trade pacts, which aimed to enhance economic cooperation and market access among member countries.

A. *North American Free Trade Agreement* (NAFTA) established in the late 20th century and represented a significant development in economic diplomacy in North America. NAFTA, which came into force on January 1, 1994, created a trilateral trade bloc among the United States, Canada, and Mexico (Kondonassis & Malliaris, 1996; Goud, 1998; Heindl, 2006).

❖ *Negotiating the Agreement*: The negotiation of NAFTA involved extensive economic diplomacy efforts among the three member countries. Negotiators from each country engaged in protracted discussions to address trade issues, including tariffs, non-tariff barriers, agricultural trade, and dispute resolution mechanisms. Economic diplomats worked to reconcile differences in economic policies, regulatory frameworks, and trade practices among the three nations.

❖ *Trade Liberalization*: NAFTA was designed to promote trade liberalization among its member countries. Economic diplomacy was essential in achieving significant reductions in tariffs and the elimination of many non-tariff trade barriers. The agreement aimed to create a more open and integrated market by gradually phasing out tariffs and promoting the free movement of goods and services across borders.

❖ *Investment Provisions*: NAFTA included provisions to protect and promote foreign direct investment (FDI) among member countries. Economic diplomats negotiated rules to provide a stable and predictable investment environment. These provisions aimed to encourage cross-border investment by providing legal protections and mechanisms for dispute resolution.

❖ *Dispute Resolution Mechanisms*: NAFTA established dispute resolution mechanisms, such as the binational panel process, to address trade disputes among member countries. Economic diplomacy played a role in the negotiation and functioning of these mechanisms. Diplomats worked to ensure that trade disputes were resolved fairly and that member countries complied with the rulings of dispute settlement panels.

❖ *Labor and Environmental Standards*: Economic diplomacy within NAFTA also addressed labor and environmental standards. Negotiators included side agreements, such as the North American Agreement on Environmental Cooperation (NAAEC) and the North American Agreement on Labor Cooperation (NAALC), to address concerns about the impact of trade on labor and the environment. These agreements aimed to promote cooperation and set standards for labor rights and environmental protection.

❖ *Review and Modernization*: Economic diplomacy continued to play a role in the review and modernization of NAFTA. In 2020, the United States-Mexico-Canada Agreement (USMCA), also known as CUSMA in Canada and T-MEC in Mexico, replaced NAFTA after negotiations to update and modernize the agreement. These negotiations required diplomatic efforts to address new trade issues, intellectual property, and other contemporary challenges.

❖ *Benefits and Challenges*: Economic diplomats were tasked with promoting the benefits of NAFTA, such as increased trade, economic growth, and job creation, while addressing challenges and concerns raised by various stakeholders, including labor unions, industries, and environmental groups.

NAFTA represented a significant achievement in economic diplomacy in the late 20th century. It aimed to promote trade liberalization, economic integration, and investment while addressing various challenges and concerns. Economic diplomats played a central role in negotiating, implementing, and modernizing the agreement to benefit the economies of the United States, Canada, and Mexico.

B. The establishment of the **European Single Market** in the late 20th century was a landmark in economic diplomacy, involving European Union (EU) member states. It aimed to create a unified and integrated market within the EU, facilitating the free movement of goods, services, capital, and labor. Economic diplomacy played a crucial role in this process (Gillingham, 2003; Dinan, 2004):

❖ *Negotiating the Single Market*: Economic diplomats from EU member states were actively involved in the negotiation and drafting of the Single European Act (SEA) of 1986, which laid the legal framework for the Single Market. These negotiations required diplomats to reconcile national interests, overcome trade barriers, and coordinate efforts to harmonize regulations and standards across the EU.

❖ *Customs Union and Elimination of Tariffs*: One of the key components of the Single Market was the creation of a customs union. Diplomats negotiated the elimination of customs duties and tariffs on trade among EU member states. The elimination of tariffs played a central role in boosting intra-EU trade and reducing trade barriers.

❖ *Harmonization of Regulations and Standards*: Economic diplomacy played a crucial role in harmonizing regulations and standards across the EU. Diplomats worked to align national regulations and remove non-tariff barriers that hindered trade. Harmonization efforts sought to create a level playing field for businesses operating across the EU and ensure consumer safety and protection.

❖ *Services and Capital Flows*: The Single Market extended beyond goods and included services and capital flows. Diplomats negotiated the liberalization of services and the removal of barriers to the movement of capital within the EU. This involved discussions on financial regulations, banking, insurance, and the mutual recognition of professional qualifications.

❖ *Free Movement of Labor*: Economic diplomacy was also involved in negotiations regarding the free movement of labor within the EU. Diplomats worked on agreements related to workers' rights, social security coordination, and the recognition of qualifications.

❖ *Competition Policy and State Aid*: Diplomats played a role in shaping EU competition policy and state aid rules. Economic diplomacy addressed concerns related to anti-competitive practices, monopolies, and subsidies that could distort the Single Market.

❖ *Enforcement and Dispute Resolution*: Economic diplomacy continued to play a role in enforcing Single Market rules and resolving disputes among EU member states. This included addressing violations of market access, competition rules, and trade practices. The European Commission and the European Court of Justice were key institutions involved in the enforcement of Single Market rules.

❖ *Expanding the Single Market*: Economic diplomacy extended to negotiations with countries outside the EU. The EU engaged in trade negotiations and agreements to expand market access and economic cooperation with non-EU countries while safeguarding the integrity of the Single Market.

The creation of the European Single Market in the late 20th century was a significant achievement in economic diplomacy. It required negotiations, coordination, and diplomacy among EU member states to create a unified and integrated economic space that facilitated trade, investment, and economic growth across the European Union. Economic diplomats played a central role in shaping and implementing the Single Market's rules and principles.

C. The *Association of Southeast Asian Nations* (ASEAN) played a significant role in economic diplomacy in the late 20th century as it sought to promote regional stability, economic development, and cooperation among its member states (Lee, 2006; Narine, 2008).

❖ ASEAN Free Trade Area (AFTA): AFTA, launched in 1992, was a major initiative aimed at creating a single market and production base within ASEAN. It involved negotiations to reduce and eliminate tariffs and trade barriers among member states. Economic diplomats from ASEAN countries were actively involved in the negotiation process to facilitate the gradual reduction of tariffs on intra-ASEAN trade.

❖ ASEAN Investment Area (AIA) initiated in 1998, aimed to encourage foreign direct investment (FDI) within the region by reducing investment barriers and enhancing the investment climate. Economic diplomats played a key role in negotiating agreements and commitments related to investment liberalization among ASEAN member states.

❖ ASEAN Industrial Cooperation (AICO): AICO was established to promote industrial cooperation and specialization among ASEAN member states. It aimed to enhance economic complementarity and encourage joint ventures and technology transfer. Economic diplomats engaged in discussions and negotiations related to industrial cooperation, working to facilitate agreements that would promote economic growth and diversification.

❖ ASEAN Framework Agreement on Services (AFAS) launched in 1995, aimed to promote trade liberalization in services among ASEAN countries. It involved negotiations to open up various service sectors, including finance, telecommunications, and professional services. Diplomats representing ASEAN member states worked to negotiate commitments and agreements that would facilitate the liberalization of services trade.

❖ ASEAN Plus Three (APT): ASEAN engaged in economic diplomacy with its Northeast Asian neighbors (China, Japan, and South Korea) under the APT framework. This cooperation aimed to enhance regional economic integration, financial stability, and cooperation in various sectors. Economic diplomats from ASEAN and the Plus Three countries engaged in discussions and negotiations to strengthen economic ties and address regional challenges.

❖ External Trade Agreements: ASEAN sought to expand its economic cooperation and diplomacy with external partners, negotiating trade agreements and economic partnerships with countries and regions beyond Southeast Asia. Diplomats representing ASEAN were involved in trade negotiations with partners such as the European Union, the United States, and other countries.

❖ The ASEAN Economic Ministers Meetings provided a platform for economic diplomats to discuss regional economic issues, review progress, and negotiate agreements. These meetings allowed ASEAN countries to coordinate their economic policies and address challenges facing the region.

❖ *ASEAN's Response to Economic Crises*: ASEAN faced economic challenges in the late 20th century, including the Asian financial crisis of 1997–1998. Economic diplomacy was crucial in coordinating regional responses, seeking financial assistance, and stabilizing affected economies.

ASEAN's economic diplomacy in the late 20th century was characterized by efforts to promote regional economic integration, trade liberalization, investment facilitation, and cooperation with external partners. Diplomatic negotiations and agreements were essential in achieving these economic objectives and fostering stability and development within Southeast Asia.

D. In the late 20th century, **Mercosur** (Southern Common Market) emerged as a regional trade bloc in South America, and economic diplomacy played a significant role in its development. Mercosur aimed to promote economic integration, trade liberalization, and cooperation among its member countries (Perez de Castillo, 1993; Heymann, 2001; Arieti, 2005, Gardini, 2007, 2010, 2012):

❖ *Founding and Expansion*: Mercosur was officially established in 1991 by Argentina, Brazil, Paraguay, and Uruguay. It was founded with the goal of creating a common market and customs union in the region. Economic diplomacy played a central role in negotiations leading to the accession of new members. For example, Paraguay and Uruguay joined as full members in the 1990s, while Bolivia and Chile became associate members.

❖ *Trade Liberalization*: A key objective of Mercosur was to promote trade liberalization among member countries. Economic diplomats engaged in negotiations to reduce tariffs and trade barriers, facilitating the flow of goods within the bloc. Efforts were made to harmonize trade rules and regulations to create a more integrated market.

❖ *Dispute Resolution*: Economic diplomacy was essential in addressing trade disputes among Mercosur member countries. Diplomats and negotiators worked to resolve conflicts related to trade practices, tariffs, and non-tariff barriers. Mercosur established a dispute settlement mechanism to address trade-related issues.

❖ *Customs Union*: The formation of a customs union was a significant step in Mercosur's economic integration. Diplomats negotiated customs procedures, rules of origin, and the elimination of internal tariffs within the bloc. This customs union aimed to promote the free movement of goods among member countries.

❖ *Common External Tariff* (CET): Mercosur members negotiated a common external tariff, which established a unified tariff schedule for imports from non-member countries. Diplomats played a role in determining the CET rates and ensuring its consistent application.

❖ *Economic and Financial Cooperation*: Economic diplomacy also extended to financial cooperation and coordination among Mercosur countries. Diplomats worked to promote economic stability and financial integration within the bloc.

❖ *Trade Agreements with External Partners*: Mercosur engaged in economic diplomacy with external partners to negotiate trade agreements. Diplomats represented the bloc in negotiations with countries and regions outside South America, seeking to expand market access. Notable trade negotiations included agreements with the European Union and countries in Africa and the Middle East.

❖ *Expansion to Associate Members*: Mercosur expanded its membership to include associate members like Bolivia and Chile. Economic diplomacy was involved in negotiating the terms and conditions of their participation, including trade and cooperation agreements.

❖ *Common Market and Economic Policies*: Diplomats from Mercosur countries engaged in discussions and negotiations related to the harmonization of economic policies, regulatory frameworks, and trade practices to create a more unified and competitive common market.

Economic diplomacy played a central role in Mercosur's development as a regional trade bloc in the late 20th century. It involved negotiations to promote trade liberalization, economic integration, dispute resolution, and cooperation both within the bloc and with external partners. Mercosur's economic diplomats worked to advance the economic interests of member countries and strengthen South America's position in the global economy.

China's Economic Integration

China's economic integration into the global economy during the late 20th century was a transformative process that involved extensive economic diplomacy. China's economic reforms and its accession to the WTO in 2001 marked a significant shift in global economic dynamics. Economic diplomacy with China revolved around its role as a major trading partner, investor, and provider of low-cost manufacturing.

❖ *Opening and Reform* (Late 1970s): China's economic integration began with the opening-up and reform policies initiated by Deng Xiaoping in the late 1970s. These policies involved diplomatic efforts to attract foreign investment, technology, and expertise (Zhu & Webber, 2016). Economic diplomats played an important role in negotiating trade and investment agreements with foreign countries and multinational corporations (Medeiros & Fravel, 2003; Goth, 2004; Warner, 2007).

❖ *Accession to the World Trade Organization* (WTO) (2001): China's accession to the WTO marked a significant milestone in its economic integration into the global economy. It involved lengthy negotiations, concessions, and commitments related to trade liberalization, intellectual property rights, and market access. Economic diplomacy played a crucial role in the negotiations leading to China's WTO accession, as well as in subsequent trade negotiations (Fewsmith, 2001; Potter, 2001; Guohua & Jin, 2001; Mattoo, 2003; Halverson, 2004).

❖ *Foreign Direct Investment* (FDI): Economic diplomacy was essential in attracting foreign direct investment (FDI) into China. Diplomats worked to promote China as a destination for FDI by negotiating investment protection agreements and providing assurances to foreign investors. The establishment of special economic zones and investment-friendly policies were key components of China's FDI attraction strategy (Fenwick, 1984).

❖ *Bilateral Trade Agreements*: China engaged in economic diplomacy to negotiate bilateral trade agreements with various countries and regions. These agreements aimed to expand market access for Chinese goods and services. Notable agreements included the China-ASEAN Free Trade Agreement and the China-Pakistan Free Trade Agreement, among others (Mukhtar & Hongdao, 2017; Shah et al., 2022).

❖ *Trade Surplus and Currency Policies*: China's trade surplus with many countries, particularly the United States, became a subject of economic diplomacy. Negotiations and diplomatic efforts focused on addressing trade imbalances, currency issues, and trade disputes. The exchange rate of China's currency, the Renminbi (RMB), was a key topic in economic diplomacy discussions (Chiu, 2011).

❖ *One Belt, One Road* (OBOR) Initiative: China's OBOR initiative, later renamed the Belt and Road Initiative (BRI), involved economic diplomacy on a massive scale. It aimed to promote economic cooperation, infrastructure development, and trade connectivity across Asia, Europe, and Africa. Economic diplomats engaged with numerous countries to negotiate infrastructure projects, investments, and trade agreements as part of the BRI (Lim et al., 2016; Chan & Song, 2020; Carrai, 2018; Freymann, 2022).

❖ *Free Trade Agreements* (FTAs): China entered into negotiations for various FTAs with regional partners. These agreements sought to promote economic integration and reduce trade barriers. Examples include the China-Australia FTA (Xiang et al., 2017; Qi & Zhang, 2018) and the Regional Comprehensive Economic Partnership (RCEP), which includes China and several ASEAN countries (Cheong & Tongzon, 2013; Basu Das, 2015; Ravenhill, 2016; Flach et al., 2021).

❖ *Development Assistance and Aid Diplomacy*: China expanded its economic diplomacy efforts in the form of development assistance and aid to other developing countries. Through initiatives such as the Forum on China-Africa Cooperation (FOCAC), China provided financial and technical assistance to foster economic cooperation (Shelton & Paruk, 2008; Taylor, 2010; Aiping & Zhan, 2018; Siméon et al., 2022).

China's economic integration into the global economy during the late 20th century and beyond involved extensive economic diplomacy efforts. Chinese economic diplomats negotiated trade agreements, attracted foreign investment, addressed trade imbalances, and played a central role in China's engagement with international economic institutions. China's economic integration had a profound impact on the global economic landscape and contributed to its emergence as a major economic power.

Bilateral Trade Agreements

Economic diplomacy and bilateral trade agreements played a significant role in shaping international trade and economic relations during the late 20th century. These agreements were instrumental in facilitating trade, promoting economic cooperation, and addressing various economic issues.

❖ *Trade Liberalization*: One of the primary objectives of bilateral trade agreements in the late 20th century was trade liberalization. Countries sought to reduce or eliminate tariffs and non-tariff barriers to promote the flow of goods and services across borders. Economic diplomats engaged in negotiations to determine the extent of tariff reductions, phased liberalization, and rules of origin to qualify for preferential treatment (Cagé & Gadenne, 2018).

❖ *Market Access*: Bilateral trade agreements aimed at providing improved market access for each participating country's goods and services. Economic diplomats negotiated terms related to market entry, customs procedures, and trade facilitation measures. Agreements often included provisions for the protection of intellectual property rights, investment, and the removal of trade-distorting measures.

❖ *Rules-Based Trade*: Economic diplomacy in the late 20th century emphasized the establishment of rules-based trade. Bilateral agreements included provisions on dispute resolution mechanisms to address trade conflicts. These mechanisms provided a forum for resolving disputes and enforcing trade rules, contributing to a more predictable and stable trading environment (Osakwe, 2015).

❖ *Specialization and Cooperation*: Bilateral trade agreements often encouraged specialization and cooperation in specific industries or sectors. Diplomatic efforts aimed to identify areas of mutual interest and promote collaboration in research, development, and technology transfer. Such agreements could lead to joint ventures, supply chain integration, and increased competitiveness.

❖ *Reciprocity and Mutual Benefit*: Economic diplomacy in bilateral trade negotiations emphasized reciprocity and mutual benefit. Countries sought to ensure that the terms of the agreement were balanced and offered advantages to both sides. Economic diplomats negotiated concessions and commitments that reflected the interests of their respective countries.

❖ *Geopolitical Considerations*: Bilateral trade agreements sometimes had geopolitical considerations. Economic diplomacy played a role in aligning economic interests with broader geopolitical objectives, such as building alliances and countering regional or global rivals. These agreements could strengthen diplomatic ties and enhance a country's strategic position.

❖ *Bilateral Investment Treaties* (BITs): Economic diplomats also negotiated BITs alongside trade agreements. BITs aimed to protect and promote foreign investment by providing legal safeguards and mechanisms for dispute resolution. These agreements encouraged cross-border investments and contributed to economic cooperation (Dolzer & Stevens, 1995; Vandevelde, 2010).

❖ *Regional and Multilateral Compatibility*: Bilateral trade agreements were often designed to be compatible with regional and multilateral trade frameworks. Economic diplomats worked to ensure that bilateral agreements did not contradict or undermine existing regional or global trade rules. Bilateral agreements sometimes served as building blocks for broader regional trade initiatives.

❖ *Trade Promotion and Export Facilitation*: Bilateral trade agreements included provisions for trade promotion and export facilitation. Economic diplomats negotiated measures to simplify customs procedures, reduce trade costs, and enhance market access for exporters.

Economic diplomacy and bilateral trade agreements in the late 20th century were instrumental in shaping international trade and economic relations. These agreements aimed to liberalize trade, promote economic cooperation, and address various economic issues while considering geopolitical considerations and the broader context of regional and multilateral trade frameworks. Economic diplomats played a central role in negotiating and implementing these agreements to advance the economic interests of their respective countries (Phlipot, 2010).

Trade Disputes and Conflict Resolution

Economic diplomacy indeed played a crucial role in resolving trade disputes and addressing conflicts in the late 20th century. As international trade and economic relations expanded during this period, disputes and conflicts inevitably arose due to differing economic interests, trade practices, and policies. Economic diplomacy was instrumental in mitigating these issues through negotiation, diplomacy, and various dispute resolution mechanisms.

❖ *Negotiation of Trade Agreements*: Economic diplomacy played a central role in negotiating bilateral and multilateral trade agreements. These agreements often included dispute resolution mechanisms, such as arbitration panels, designed to address trade conflicts. Diplomats engaged in dialogue to resolve disagreements over trade practices and policies, seeking mutually acceptable solutions.

❖ *World Trade Organization* (WTO) *Dispute Settlement*: The establishment of the WTO in 1995 provided a structured framework for resolving trade disputes. Economic diplomats from member countries utilized the WTO's dispute settlement system to address trade conflicts. This system involved consultations, mediation, dispute panels, and appellate reviews, all of which required diplomatic efforts to navigate and seek resolution.

❖ *Bilateral and Regional Dispute Resolution*: In addition to the WTO, economic diplomacy was employed in resolving trade disputes through bilateral and regional mechanisms. Bilateral negotiations between countries allowed for direct discussions to find common ground. Regional trade blocs often had their own dispute resolution mechanisms, where economic diplomats played a key role in mediating and facilitating solutions (Sander, 1985; Guzman, 2002; Delikat & Kleiner, 2003; Bowler et al., 2016).

❖ *Negotiating Settlements and Compromises*: Diplomats engaged in negotiation processes aimed at finding settlements and compromises that would address the concerns of all parties involved. Economic diplomacy encouraged dialogue and concession-making to resolve conflicts. Compromise solutions could involve adjustments to trade practices, tariffs, or regulatory measures to alleviate tensions.

❖ *Consultations and Diplomatic Channels*: Diplomats engaged in consultations and diplomatic channels to defuse trade disputes. These discussions allowed countries to express their grievances, exchange information, and seek common ground before resorting to formal dispute resolution mechanisms. Economic diplomacy helped prevent disputes from escalating and provided opportunities for early resolution (Arnopoulos, 1975; Waibel, 2010).

❖ *Conflict Prevention and Mitigation*: Economic diplomacy also played a role in conflict prevention and mitigation. Diplomats worked to build relationships, improve transparency, and establish protocols to reduce the likelihood of trade disputes arising in the first place. By addressing underlying issues and building trust, economic diplomacy contributed to a more stable trade environment (Aggestam, 2004).

❖ *Enforcement of Trade Rules*: Economic diplomats were involved in the enforcement of trade rules and the implementation of dispute settlement rulings. This included ensuring that countries complied with the outcomes of dispute resolution processes. Economic diplomacy efforts aimed to prevent non-compliance and maintain the integrity of the international trading system (Reich, 1996; Conti, 2010).

❖ *Adherence to International Agreements*: Diplomats emphasized the importance of adherence to international agreements, treaties, and trade rules as a means to prevent trade disputes. Economic diplomacy promoted the rule of law and the peaceful resolution of conflicts through established mechanisms.

Economic diplomacy was a critical tool in resolving trade disputes and conflicts during the late 20th century. It provided diplomatic channels for dialogue, negotiation, and compromise, reducing trade tensions and contributing to a more stable and predictable global trade environment. Diplomats played a pivotal role in finding solutions that balanced the economic interests of countries and preserved the rules-based international trading system.

Financial Diplomacy and Exchange Rates

Financial diplomacy in the late 20th century played a significant role in shaping exchange rates, managing currency crises, and fostering international economic cooperation. Several key events and initiatives during this period highlighted the importance of financial diplomacy in managing exchange rates and promoting global financial stability:

❖ *Nixon Shock* (1971): In 1971, President Richard Nixon announced the suspension of dollar-to-gold convertibility, effectively ending the Bretton Woods system. This event highlighted the need for financial diplomacy to navigate the transition to a new international monetary order. Diplomatic negotiations were necessary to establish a new framework for exchange rates and international monetary cooperation (Scott, 2011; Irwin, 2013; Zeiler, 2013; Streltsov, 2019).

❖ *Floating Exchange Rates* (1970s Onward): After the collapse of Bretton Woods, most major currencies adopted floating exchange rates. Financial diplomacy continued to play a role in discussions among countries on managing exchange rate fluctuations and minimizing currency conflicts. Economic diplomats worked to address concerns related to exchange rate volatility and its impact on trade and economic stability (Edwards, 1983; Obstfeld et al., 1985; Reinhart, 2000).

❖ *Plaza Accord* (1985) and *Louvre Accord* (1987): These international agreements exemplified financial diplomacy in addressing exchange rate issues. The Plaza Accord aimed to depreciate the U.S. dollar to reduce the U.S. trade deficit (Henning & Destler, 1988; Frankel, 2015; Green et al., 2015; Bergsten & Green, 2016) while the Louvre Accord sought to stabilize exchange rates after the Plaza Agreement led to an overly weak dollar. Diplomatic efforts were required to negotiate and implement these agreements among major economies (Richter, 1989; Tucker & Madura, 1991; Richter & Schmidt-Mohr, 1992; Esaka, 2000).

❖ *Asian Financial Crisis* (1997–1998): The Asian financial crisis underscored the importance of financial diplomacy in managing currency crises. Economic diplomats worked with countries affected by the crisis to secure financial assistance and stabilize exchange rates. The IMF played a central role in providing support and facilitating diplomatic negotiations to address the crisis (Dean, 2001; Philippi, 2004; Lee, 2017).

❖ *Euro and European Monetary Union* (1999): The creation of the euro and the European Monetary Union (EMU) required extensive financial diplomacy among European Union member states. Negotiations involved setting exchange rates and establishing the institutions responsible for monetary policy. Economic diplomats played a crucial role in coordinating these efforts (Dyson & Featherstone, 1999; Dyson, 1999; Everts, 1999; Risse et al., 1999; Hodson, 2011).

❖ *International Monetary Fund* (IMF) and *Exchange Rate Surveillance*: The IMF conducted exchange rate surveillance to assess the policies and practices of member countries. Economic diplomacy was involved in IMF consultations with member states on their exchange rate policies. These consultations aimed to prevent exchange rate manipulation and address imbalances that could lead to currency conflicts (Young, 1977; Goldstein & Crockett, 1987; Barnett, 1993; Mussa, 1997; Gianviti, 2000; Lee et al., 2008).

❖ *G7 and G20 Summits*: G7 and G20 summits brought together leaders and finance ministers from major economies to discuss global economic and financial issues, including exchange rates. Economic diplomacy was at the forefront of these meetings, which often resulted in statements or agreements on exchange rate policies (Bayne, 1997; Dobson, 2006; Smith, 2011; Bradford & Linn, 2012; Penttilä, 2013; Prodi, 2016; Bouillaud, 2016; Hajnal, 2019; Larionova, 2022).

Financial diplomacy played a crucial role in managing exchange rates and addressing currency-related issues in the late 20th century. Diplomats and policymakers engaged in negotiations, agreements, and coordination efforts to promote exchange rate stability, manage currency crises, and foster international economic cooperation. These diplomatic efforts aimed to maintain a stable global monetary system and facilitate economic growth and trade.

Foreign Direct Investment

Attracting Foreign Direct Investment (FDI) and protecting the interests of multinational corporations became central to economic diplomacy. As globalization and economic integration accelerated during this period, countries recognized the importance of FDI as a catalyst for economic growth, job creation, and technology transfer.

❖ *Investment Promotion and Diplomacy*: Economic diplomats actively promoted their countries as attractive investment destinations. They engaged in diplomatic efforts to highlight investment opportunities, economic stability, and favorable business environments. Diplomats often participated in investment promotion forums, trade missions, and international conferences to showcase their countries to potential investors (Naray, 2008).

❖ *Bilateral Investment Treaties* (BITs): Countries entered into BITs to protect and promote FDI. These agreements provided legal safeguards for foreign investors and established mechanisms for dispute resolution. Economic diplomats played a crucial role in negotiating and implementing BITs, providing assurances to foreign investors and improving the investment climate.

❖ *Regional and Bilateral Investment Agreements*: Economic diplomacy extended to the negotiation of regional and bilateral investment agreements. These agreements aimed to reduce investment barriers, provide preferential treatment to investors, and establish frameworks for cooperation. Diplomats worked to create an environment conducive to cross-border investments and enhance economic ties with specific countries or regions.

❖ *Investment Promotion Agencies* (IPAs): Many countries established IPAs to facilitate FDI. Economic diplomats collaborated with IPAs to coordinate investment promotion efforts, provide information to potential investors, and address investor inquiries. IPAs often worked closely with diplomatic missions to support FDI-related activities.

❖ *Conflict Resolution and Investor Protection*: Economic diplomats played a role in resolving conflicts related to FDI. They engaged in diplomatic negotiations to address investor concerns, regulatory issues, and disputes with host countries. Protecting the rights of foreign investors and ensuring a fair and predictable investment environment were key priorities (Egli, 2006; Matveev, 2015; Gertz, 2018).

❖ *Trade and Investment Agreements*: Economic diplomacy extended to the negotiation of trade and investment agreements. These agreements included provisions to promote and protect FDI, encourage technology transfer, and reduce trade barriers. Diplomats participated in negotiations to ensure that FDI-related provisions met the interests of their countries.

❖ *Investment Promotion Campaigns*: Diplomats engaged in investment promotion campaigns to showcase specific sectors or industries that offered significant investment opportunities. They often collaborated with chambers of commerce, industry associations, and foreign business councils. Investment promotion campaigns aimed to attract investments in areas such as infrastructure, manufacturing, and services (Simonin, 2008; Naray, 2011; Lop, 2017).

❖ *International Investment Forums*: Diplomats attended international investment forums and summits to engage with potential investors, discuss investment policies, and showcase investment projects. These forums provided a platform for economic diplomacy efforts to attract FDI and foster international economic cooperation (Lee & Hocking, 2010; Woolcock & Bayne, 2013; Poulsen & Aisbett, 2016).

❖ *Incentives and Guarantees*: Economic diplomats were involved in negotiations related to investment incentives and guarantees. They worked with governments to offer incentives such as tax breaks, repatriation guarantees, and investment protection to attract foreign capital (Davis, 1999; Hottinger, 2005; Gottardi & Mezzetti, 2022)

Economic diplomacy played a critical role in attracting and facilitating FDI in the late 20th century. Diplomats worked to promote their countries as attractive investment destinations, negotiate investment agreements, protect investor rights, and resolve conflicts. FDI became a significant driver of economic growth and development in many countries, and economic diplomacy was a key enabler of this trend.

Development and Aid Diplomacy

Development and aid diplomacy in the late 20th century were characterized by efforts to promote economic development, poverty reduction, and cooperation between donor countries and developing nations. During this period, various international organizations, donor countries, and development agencies played significant roles in providing financial assistance and technical support to help developing countries achieve their development goals. Here are key aspects of development and aid diplomacy in the late 20th century:

❖ *Official Development Assistance* (ODA): Donor countries, often through their foreign aid agencies, provided ODA to developing nations. ODA included grants, concessional loans, and technical assistance aimed at supporting economic development and improving living standards. The diplomatic efforts of donor countries involved negotiating aid agreements, disbursing funds, and ensuring aid effectiveness (Pamment, 2016; Gulrajani et al., 2020).

❖ *Multilateral Development Organizations*: Diplomacy was critical in the operations of multilateral development organizations like the World Bank and the International Monetary Fund (IMF). These institutions provided financial assistance, policy advice, and technical expertise to developing countries. Diplomats engaged in negotiations related to funding, project approval, and policy conditionality with these institutions (Weiss, 1985, 1986; Mahbubani & Mahbubani, 2022)

❖ *Bilateral Aid Agreements*: Donor countries established bilateral aid agreements with recipient countries, outlining the terms and conditions of assistance. These agreements often addressed specific development sectors, such as healthcare, education, infrastructure, and agriculture. Diplomatic efforts were needed to negotiate and manage these agreements (Hjertholm & White, 2000; Dollar & Levin, 2006; Lancaster, 2008).

❖ *Debt Relief and Forgiveness*: Diplomacy played a role in debt relief initiatives aimed at reducing the debt burden of heavily indebted developing countries. International negotiations and debt restructuring efforts were key components of this diplomacy (Cohen, 1981; Sachs, 1989; Saner, 2006; Bunte et al., 2022).

❖ *Humanitarian Aid*: Diplomatic efforts were crucial in coordinating and delivering humanitarian aid to countries facing natural disasters, conflicts, and humanitarian crises. Diplomats worked with international organizations, relief agencies, and governments to provide timely assistance.

❖ *Trade and Development*: Economic diplomacy linked trade policies to development goals. Negotiations in forums like the General Agreement on Tariffs and Trade (GATT) aimed to ensure that trade policies supported the interests of developing countries, particularly in terms of market access and fair-trade practices.

❖ *Development Goals and Agendas*: Diplomatic efforts contributed to the formulation of international development goals and agendas. The United Nations played a central role in setting goals such as the Millennium Development Goals (MDGs) and later the Sustainable Development Goals (SDGs). Diplomats participated in negotiations to adopt these goals and mobilized support for their implementation.

❖ *North-South Dialogues*: Diplomatic dialogues between developed and developing countries, often referred to as North-South dialogues, addressed various development issues, including trade, finance, technology transfer, and debt relief. These dialogues aimed to bridge the gap between the interests of developed and developing nations (Amuzegar, 1975, 1977; Lateef, 1981; Muller, 1981; Moore, 1984; Zhou, 2001).

❖ *Foreign Aid Coordination*: Donor countries and development agencies engaged in diplomatic coordination efforts to align their aid programs, avoid duplication, and maximize the impact of aid. Coordination was essential to ensure that aid efforts were coherent and complemented each other (Lancaster, 2008; Lawson, 2013; Arel-Bundock et al., 2015).

❖ *Human Development and Capacity Building*: Diplomacy supported efforts to enhance human development and build capacity in developing countries. This included initiatives related to education, healthcare, vocational training, and governance. Technical cooperation and knowledge sharing were key elements of capacity-building efforts (Metzl, 2001; Amadei, 2019; Piros & Koops, 2020).

Development and aid diplomacy in the late 20th century involved a range of diplomatic efforts aimed at promoting economic development, reducing poverty, and addressing global development challenges. Donor countries, international organizations, and diplomatic missions worked together to provide financial assistance, technical support, and policy guidance to developing nations, contributing to the advancement of development goals during this period.

Environmental and Trade Sustainability

Economic diplomacy in the late 20th century increasingly incorporated environmental sustainability and trade sustainability considerations as global awareness of environmental issues grew. Diplomats and international organizations worked to strike a balance between economic growth and environmental protection, as well as to ensure that trade policies supported sustainability goals. Here are key aspects of economic diplomacy related to environmental and trade sustainability during that period:

❖ *Environmental Agreements and Diplomacy*: Diplomats participated in negotiations and diplomatic efforts to address global environmental challenges. Notable agreements include the Montreal Protocol (1987) to protect the ozone layer (Benedick, 1998, 2009; Sarma & Andersen, 2011; Moomaw, 2018; Whitesides, 2020) and the United Nations Framework Convention on Climate Change (UNFCCC) (1992) (Obergassel et al., 2015; Dimitrov, 2015; Victor, 2016; Depledge, 2016; Tänzler, 2018) that laid the groundwork for addressing climate change. Diplomatic missions represented their countries in environmental summits and conferences where international environmental treaties and agreements were adopted.

❖ *Trade and Environment Linkages*: Economic diplomats engaged in discussions on the relationship between trade and environmental sustainability. Trade negotiations considered environmental concerns, including the potential impact of trade on ecosystems and natural resources. The World Trade Organization (WTO) established the Committee on Trade and Environment (CTE) to address trade-related environmental issues, and diplomats participated in CTE discussions (Charnovitz, 1997; Tarasofsky, 1999; Gabler, 2010; Sinha, 2013; Woody, 1995).

❖ *Trade and Sustainable Development*: Economic diplomacy played a role in negotiations that aimed to link trade and sustainable development. This included discussions on integrating social and environmental considerations into trade agreements. The inclusion of sustainable development chapters in trade agreements became more common (Blowers, 1993; Lafferty & Meadowcroft, 2000; Orbie et al., 2016; Yao et al., 2019; Poletti et al., 2021)

❖ *Sustainable Resource Management*: Diplomats engaged in discussions on sustainable resource management, including negotiations related to the Convention on Biological Diversity (CBD) and the sustainable use of natural resources, such as forests and fisheries. Sustainable resource management was a key aspect of international diplomacy for preserving biodiversity (Glowka et al., 1994; Ward, 1995; Johnston, 1997; Swanson, 2013; Le Prestre, 2017).

❖ *Environmental Impact Assessments* (EIAs): Economic diplomacy influenced discussions about incorporating EIAs into trade negotiations. EIAs assessed the potential environmental impacts of trade agreements and projects. Diplomats worked to ensure that EIAs were conducted and that their findings informed trade and investment decisions (Ortolano & Shepherd, 1995; Abdel Wahaab, 2003; Glasson & Therivel, 2013).

❖ *Technology Transfer and Capacity Building*: Diplomats engaged in negotiations to facilitate technology transfer from developed to developing countries to support environmentally friendly practices. Capacity-building efforts aimed to enhance the ability of developing nations to implement sustainable practices. These initiatives were often part of broader international agreements and diplomacy efforts.

❖ *Sanitary and Phytosanitary* (SPS) *Measures*: Economic diplomats were involved in discussions related to SPS measures, which addressed the safety of food and agricultural products. These measures aimed to protect human, animal, and plant health while facilitating trade. Diplomatic negotiations sought to ensure that SPS measures were science-based and not used as disguised trade barriers (Pauwelyn, 1999; Fisher, 2006; Büthe, 2008; Zahrnt, 2011; Pattanshetty & Brand, 2022).

❖ *Trade and Conservation*: Diplomats engaged in discussions about trade in endangered species and conservation efforts. International agreements like the Convention on International Trade in Endangered Species of Wild Fauna and Flora (CITES) regulated the trade in endangered species to protect them from exploitation (Hutton & Dickson, 2000; Zhu & Wei, 2022).

❖ *Consumer Awareness and Labeling*: Diplomats addressed consumer concerns about environmental sustainability through discussions on product labeling and certification schemes. These efforts aimed to provide consumers with information about the environmental impact of products.

❖ *Civil Society Engagement*: Diplomacy efforts included engaging with civil society organizations and environmental NGOs to promote sustainable trade practices and garner public support for sustainability initiatives (Anton, 2022a, 2022b; Andersen, 2022; Burlinova, 2022; Sebastião & de Carvalho Spínola, 2022)

Economic diplomacy in the late 20th century incorporated environmental and trade sustainability considerations, recognizing the need to balance economic growth with environmental protection and social development. Diplomats played a key role in negotiations, agreements, and discussions aimed at addressing environmental challenges and integrating sustainability principles into international trade and economic policies.

Emerging Markets and BRICS

The BRICS grouping (Brazil, Russia, India, China, and South Africa) emerged in the late 20th century as an important platform for economic diplomacy and cooperation among major emerging economies. Although the term "BRIC" was coined in 2001, the groundwork for this grouping was laid in the late 1990s.

❖ *Emergence of BRIC* (Late 1990s): The idea of BRIC as an economic bloc began to take shape in the late 1990s. Initially, it was known as "BRIC" without South Africa, which joined later. Economic diplomats and policymakers from these countries began informal discussions to explore areas of mutual interest, particularly in the economic and financial spheres (Vijayakumar et al., 2010; Wang & Li-Ying, 2014; Sing & Dube, 2014; Chakraborty, 2018).

❖ *Economic Cooperation*: Economic diplomacy among BRIC nations focused on enhancing economic cooperation and facilitating trade and investment. These countries recognized their growing economic influence and the potential for collaboration to promote their interests on the global stage. Trade and investment agreements, as well as diplomatic dialogues, were initiated to deepen economic ties (Iqbal & Rahman, 2016; Ramos, 2018).

❖ *Geopolitical and Economic Goals*: The BRIC nations shared common geopolitical interests and economic goals. They sought to reform international financial institutions like the International Monetary Fund (IMF) and the World Bank to reflect the changing global economic landscape. Economic diplomacy efforts included advocating for greater representation and voting power for emerging economies within these institutions (Toye, 2003; Radulescu et al., 2014; Duggan, 2015; Bond, 2020).

❖ *Annual Summits* (2009 Onward): The BRIC countries started holding annual summits in 2009. These summits provided a platform for leaders and diplomats to discuss economic and geopolitical issues. Economic diplomacy played a central role in these summits, where leaders discussed ways to enhance economic cooperation, promote trade, and address global challenges (Pant, 2013; Singh, 2013; Kirton & Larionova, 2022; Guerrero, 2022; Daldegan & Carvalho, 2022).

❖ *Economic Growth and Investment*: During the late 20th century, each BRIC country experienced significant economic growth. Economic diplomats worked to promote their countries as attractive destinations for foreign investment and trade. Bilateral and multilateral agreements were negotiated to facilitate economic ties and investment flows.

❖ *Development Banks and Initiatives*: Economic diplomacy efforts included the establishment of development banks such as the New Development Bank

(NDB) (Griffith-Jones, 2014; Abdenur & Folly, 2015; Cooper, 2017; Wang, 2019) and the Contingent Reserve Arrangement (CRA) (Biziwick et al., 2015; Cattaneo et al., 2015; Mazenda & Ncwadi, 2016; Würdemann, 2018; Mihajlovic, 2019) within the BRICS framework. These institutions were created to provide financial support for infrastructure development and crisis prevention in member countries.

❖ *Multilateral Diplomacy*: BRIC countries engaged in multilateral diplomacy on various global issues, including climate change negotiations and trade negotiations such as the Doha Round. Their collective weight in international forums allowed them to influence global economic and environmental agendas (Abdenur, 2014; Ferdinand, 2014; Chin, 2015; Troitskiy, 2015; Gowan, 2016; Baciu & Kotzé, 2022).

❖ *Bilateral Trade and Investment Partnerships*: Economic diplomacy extended to bilateral trade and investment partnerships between BRIC countries. These bilateral agreements aimed to boost economic ties and foster collaboration in sectors such as energy, technology, and manufacturing.

❖ *South Africa's Inclusion* (2010): South Africa formally joined the BRIC grouping in 2010, expanding it to BRICS. South Africa's inclusion broadened the geographical and economic diversity of the group (Kahn, 2011; Besada et al., 2013; Besada & Tok, 2014; Chiyemura, 2014; Harrison, 2014; Petropoulos, 2015; Shaw, 2015; Shubin, 2015).

Economic diplomacy played a significant role in the formation and development of BRICS in the late 20th century. These emerging economies recognized the need to cooperate on economic and geopolitical issues to advance their interests in the changing global landscape. The BRICS forum continues to be an important platform for economic diplomacy and collaboration among these nations in the 21st century.

Global Financial Crises: 2008 and After

The global financial crisis of 2008 and its aftermath required international economic diplomacy to address financial stability, regulatory reforms, and economic recovery efforts. The crisis, often referred to as the Great Recession, had profound economic and financial implications worldwide. Economic diplomats, policymakers, and international organizations engaged in a range of diplomatic efforts to address the crisis and stabilize the global economy.

❖ *International Coordination*: Economic diplomats engaged in intense international coordination efforts. Finance ministers and central bank governors from major economies participated in G20 meetings to discuss strategies for addressing the crisis. These high-level diplomatic meetings led to commitments to cooperate on financial regulation, fiscal stimulus packages, and monetary policies to stabilize the global economy (Slaughter, 2013; Woolcock & Bayne, 2013; Cooper, 2014; Slaughter, 2015; Cooper & Cornut, 2019).

❖ *Central Bank Cooperation*: Central banks, such as the Federal Reserve in the United States and the European Central Bank, coordinated monetary policies to provide liquidity to financial markets and prevent a collapse of the banking system. Economic diplomats played a role in facilitating communication and coordination among central banks to ensure their efforts were aligned (Flandreau, 1997; Borio & Toniolo, 2006; Arner et al., 2010).

❖ *Financial Sector Reforms*: Economic diplomats were involved in diplomatic negotiations to reform and strengthen the global financial regulatory framework. The Basel III accord, for example, aimed to enhance the stability and resilience of the banking sector. Diplomats negotiated international agreements to improve transparency, risk management, and regulatory oversight in the financial sector (Blundell-Wignall & Atkinson, 2010; Cosimano & Hakura, 2011; King & Tarbert, 2011; Slovik & Cournède, 2011; Allen et al., 2012; Muñoz & Soler, 2017; Shakdwipee & Mehta, 2017).

❖ *Bilateral and Multilateral Agreements*: Countries engaged in bilateral and multilateral agreements to provide financial assistance to struggling economies and institutions. Diplomatic negotiations led to agreements on financial bailouts and support packages for affected countries. International financial institutions, such as the International Monetary Fund (IMF), played a central role in facilitating these agreements.

❖ *Trade and Protectionism*: Economic diplomats worked to prevent the escalation of trade protectionism in the wake of the crisis. Trade barriers and protectionist measures can exacerbate economic challenges during a crisis. Diplomatic efforts aimed to keep markets open and ensure the continued flow of goods and services across borders.

❖ *G20 Summits* became a critical platform for economic diplomacy during the crisis. Leaders and diplomats from major economies discussed coordinated responses to the crisis, including fiscal stimulus measures and financial system reforms. These summits played a pivotal role in shaping global economic policy during the crisis.

❖ *Global Economic Governance*: Diplomats engaged in discussions about the reform of global economic governance. Calls for increased representation of emerging economies in international financial institutions gained prominence. Reforms aimed to give emerging economies a greater voice in decision-making processes (Saner & Yiu, 2008; Eccleston, 2013; Leguey-Feilleux, 2017; Martin, 2022).

❖ *Debt Relief and Aid*: Diplomatic negotiations resulted in debt relief initiatives for heavily indebted countries. Debt relief aimed to alleviate financial pressures on struggling nations and promote economic recovery. Humanitarian and development aid efforts were also a part of economic diplomacy to support affected populations.

❖ *Financial Stability Forums:* Diplomatic efforts included participation in international forums dedicated to financial stability, such as the Financial Stability Board (FSB) (Arner & Taylor, 2009; Helleiner, 2010a, 2010b; Gadinis, 2012).

These forums sought to identify and address vulnerabilities in the global financial system.

Economic diplomacy played a pivotal role in responding to the global financial crisis of 2008. Diplomats and policymakers engaged in international coordination, negotiations, and agreements to stabilize financial markets, reform the financial sector, and prevent the crisis from spiraling into a deeper global economic downturn. These diplomatic efforts helped mitigate the impact of the crisis and laid the groundwork for financial system reforms in subsequent years.

Economic diplomacy during the late 20th century was characterized by efforts to promote greater economic integration, trade liberalization, and the management of economic interdependencies on a global scale. It involved negotiations, agreements, and diplomatic efforts aimed at fostering economic growth, resolving disputes, and addressing the challenges and opportunities presented by globalization.

The 21st Century

In the 21st century, economic diplomacy has evolved to address issues such as digital trade, intellectual property, climate change, and sustainable development. Economic diplomacy is not limited to trade negotiations but also encompasses investment promotion, economic cooperation agreements, and efforts to attract foreign direct investment.

Modern economic diplomacy faces a range of challenges in an increasingly complex and interconnected global landscape. These challenges arise from various factors, including shifts in economic power, technological advancements, evolving trade dynamics, and the emergence of new issues on the global agenda.

Geopolitical rivalries and conflicts can complicate economic diplomacy efforts. Trade disputes, sanctions, and political disagreements can disrupt economic relations and negotiations: Russia-NATO tensions, cyber-attacks,

US-China relations, anti/de-globalization, climate risk, energy security, COVID-19 Pandemic (Bossman et al., 2023; Cheikh & Zaied, 2023; Fan et al., 2023).

The resurgence of protectionist policies in some countries has led to trade barriers, tariffs, and disputes. Economic diplomats must navigate these challenges to maintain open markets (Dadush, 2009, 2022; Dizioli & van Roye, 2018; Abdul Razaq, 2022; Giordani & Mariani, 2022; Sanskar, 2023).

The digital economy presents new challenges, including digital trade issues, data governance, and intellectual property rights. Economic diplomats must address these complex and rapidly evolving issues (Limna et al., 2022; Rong, 2022; Sama et al., 2022).

The rise of emerging powers, such as China and India, has shifted the global economic landscape. Traditional economic powers must adapt to the changing dynamics and balance their interests (Kenkel & Destradi, 2019; Hopewell, 2022a, 2022b; Martínez, 2022; Kirchberger et al., 2022).

The COVID-19 pandemic exposed vulnerabilities in global supply chains. Diplomats must address these vulnerabilities and promote resilience in supply chains (Fonseca & Azevedo, 2020; Miroudot, 2020; Xu et al., 2020; Free & Hecimovic, 2021; Gurtu & Johny, 2021; Sharma, 2023).

Climate change and sustainability are increasingly important issues in economic diplomacy. Countries are seeking to align economic policies with climate goals, which can be challenging (de Paula, 2021; Özkaragöz Doğan et al., 2021; Shrestha et al., 2022).

Trade negotiations can reach deadlocks due to differing interests and demands. Overcoming these impasses requires diplomatic skill and creativity (Stephen & Parízek, 2019; Singh, 2020; Gheyle, 2022; Narlikar, 2022).

Addressing economic inequality, both within and among countries, is a diplomatic challenge. Diplomats must balance economic growth with social inclusion and equity (Solana, 2020; Prantl, 2022; Livada et al., 2023).

As demand for resources grows, competition for access to energy, minerals, water, and other critical resources intensifies. Diplomacy is needed to manage these resource conflicts (Klimes et at., 2019; Porter, 2019; Bovan et al., 2020; Ruffini, 2020; Nagabhatla et al., 2021).

The use of economic sanctions as a diplomatic tool can have unintended consequences. Diplomats must assess the effectiveness and impact of sanctions carefully (Lohmann, 2019; Peksen, 2019; Hufbauer & Jung, 2020; Yazdi-Feyzabadi et al., 2020; Hufbauer & Jung, 2021; Morgan et al., 2023).

Economic diplomats must address cybersecurity threats that can disrupt economic activities, compromise intellectual property, and undermine trust in digital trade (Attatfa et al., 2020; Zwarts et al., 2022; Alexandra-Cristina, 2023).

Public opinion and civil society organizations increasingly influence economic diplomacy. Diplomats must engage with diverse stakeholders and consider public sentiment (Graz & Hauert, 2019; Huijgh, 2019; Nye, 2019; Hucker, 2020; Roederer-Rynning & Greenwood, 2020; Goldsmith et al., 2021; Kholmuradovich, 2022).

Negotiating and implementing complex trade agreements, such as megaregional agreements, can be challenging due to their diverse provisions and multiple stakeholders (Buri & Polanco, 2020; Friel et al., 2020; Orsini et al., 2020; Conconi et al., 2021; Gereffi et al., 2021).

The COVID-19 pandemic highlighted the importance of health diplomacy and its intersection with economic interests. Diplomats must address health emergencies while safeguarding economic stability (Chattu & Chami, 2020; Javed & Chattu, 2020; Chattu et al., 2021; Kickbusch & Liu, 2022).

The effectiveness and relevance of existing global economic governance structures are being questioned. Diplomats must adapt and reform these institutions to address emerging challenges (Henry, 2019; Weiss & Wilkinson, 2019; Kim, 2020; Korosteleva & Flockhart, 2020; Roger, 2020; Linsenmaier et al., 2021).

To address these challenges, modern economic diplomats must be adept at multidisciplinary diplomacy, engage in strategic negotiations, build coalitions, and leverage international organizations and forums. They must also incorporate economic and trade considerations into broader foreign policy objectives to promote economic growth, stability, and global cooperation.

The Case of Europe

European economic diplomacy in the 21st century has been shaped by the evolving dynamics of the European Union (EU) as a major economic bloc and global player. European economic diplomacy encompasses a wide range of activities, from trade negotiations and investment promotion to financial regulation and development cooperation.

- *Trade Negotiations*: The EU is one of the world's largest trading entities, and trade negotiations are a central aspect of its economic diplomacy. The EU negotiates trade agreements with various countries and regions to promote market access for European goods and services. Key trade agreements include:

  ❖ the *Comprehensive Economic and Trade Agreement* (CETA) *with Canada* (Meunier & Nicolaidis, 2019; Morita, 2020; Fileva, 2021; Neuwahl, 2021)
  ❖ the *EU-Japan Economic Partnership Agreement* (Alvstam & Kettunen, 2019; Felbermayr et al., 2019; Pereira, 2019; Kimura, 2022; Catsoulis, 2022; Fahey & Wieczorek, 2022; Kettunen & Alvstam, 2023)

❖ and negotiations with the United States (Transatlantic Trade and Investment Partnership, or TTIP, and later the Trade and Technology Council) (Duina, 2022; Bendiek & Stürzer, 2022; Smith, 2022; Jaursch, 2023).

– *Customs Union and Single Market*: The EU's customs union and single market are key elements of its economic diplomacy. They promote the free movement of goods, services, capital, and labor among EU member states, creating a unified economic space (Eisl & Rubio, 2022; Usherwood, 2023).

– *Financial Regulation and Supervision*: The EU plays a significant role in global financial regulation and supervision through bodies like the European Banking Authority (EBA), the European Securities and Markets Authority (ESMA), and the European Insurance and Occupational Pensions Authority (EIOPA). Diplomatic efforts involve negotiations with international partners and organizations to harmonize financial regulations and enhance global financial stability (Donnelly, 2023; Moloney, 2023).

– *Eurozone and Monetary Diplomacy*: Economic diplomacy within the Eurozone involves coordination of monetary policies, fiscal rules, and financial stability mechanisms. The European Central Bank (ECB) and the Eurogroup play pivotal roles. European diplomatic efforts focus on maintaining the stability of the euro and promoting the euro as an international reserve currency (Bulmer, 2022; De Grauwe & Ji, 2022; Justinek, 2022; Manfredi-Sánchez & Smith, 2023).

– *Development Cooperation*: The EU is a major provider of development assistance and humanitarian aid to countries around the world. Development diplomacy aims to promote sustainable development, alleviate poverty, and address global challenges such as climate change and health crises (Culpepper, 2019; Keijzer et al.).

– *Investment Promotion and Protection*: European economic diplomacy involves attracting foreign direct investment (FDI) into the EU and protecting the interests of European investors abroad. Bilateral investment treaties (BITs) and investment promotion efforts are part of this strategy.

– *Global Economic Governance*: European diplomatic efforts are aimed at shaping global economic governance. The EU participates in international organizations such as the G7, G20, World Trade Organization (WTO), and International Monetary Fund (IMF) to advocate for its economic priorities (Martin, 2022; Liu et al., 2022; Buti & Fabbrini, 2023).

– *Energy Diplomacy*: Energy security and sustainability are important aspects of European economic diplomacy. Diplomats engage in negotiations related to energy supply, infrastructure, and climate change agreements to ensure a stable and sustainable energy future (Bocse, 2019; Pastukhova et al., 2020; Petri, 2020; Năstase, 2022).

- *Digital Economy*: European economic diplomacy addresses digital transformation and the regulation of digital markets. The EU has introduced the Digital Services Act (DSA) and the Digital Markets Act (DMA) (Markopoulou et al., 2019; Cabral, 2021; Veale & Zuiderveen Borgesius, 2021; Tirole, 2023) to regulate digital platforms and services.

- *Climate Diplomacy*: Climate diplomacy is a growing focus of European economic diplomacy. The EU is committed to climate action, and diplomats engage in international negotiations to promote climate agreements and support the transition to a green economy (Biedenkopf & Petri, 2019, 2021; Earsom & Delreux, 2021; Dennison & Engström, 2023).

- *Economic Sanctions and Trade Disputes*: Economic diplomacy also encompasses negotiations related to economic sanctions (Li & Li, 2022; van Bergeijk, 2022a, 2022b; Cardwell & Moret, 2023; Morgan et al., 2023) and trade disputes (Garcia, 2022; Ridley et al., 2022; Akhtar, 2023; Bongardt, 2023). The EU uses diplomatic channels to resolve trade conflicts and address issues related to sanctions and restrictions on economic activities.

- *Bilateral and Regional Diplomacy*: European countries, as well as the EU as a whole, engage in bilateral and regional economic diplomacy with various partners and regions, including the United States, China, Africa, and the Middle East.

European economic diplomacy in the 21st century is multifaceted, covering trade, finance, development, energy, and other economic domains. The EU and its member states work together to promote their economic interests, foster cooperation with global partners, and address global challenges in a rapidly changing economic landscape.

2. How Safe Are We? Shaping European Economy by Geopolitical Shocks

Economic Development Has No Secrets...

All international trade theories, from Mercantilism in the 16th century, and the theory of absolute advantage of Adam Smith and comparative advantage of David Ricardo in the 19th century, to Heckscher-Ohlin Model and the New Trade Theory of Paul Krugman in the 20th century, as well as to the recent Theory of Global Value Chains (GVC) in the 21st century, have agreed on the contribution of international trade to economic development, and in many ways:

1. *Market Expansion*: International trade allows countries to access larger markets beyond their domestic borders. This increased market size can lead to economies of scale, greater specialization, and increased production, ultimately boosting economic growth (Bhagwati, 1958; Gereffi et al., 2005; Siamagka & Brouthers, 2020)

2. *Resource Allocation*: Trade allows countries to specialize in the production of goods and services in which they have a comparative advantage. This means they can focus on what they are most efficient at producing, leading to increased productivity and efficiency (Woodland, 1982; Yu, 2012; Jaud et al., 2018).

3. *Increased Product Variety*: Trade exposes consumers to a wider variety of products at competitive prices. This variety can improve living standards by providing access to goods and services that may not be available or affordable domestically (Funke & Ruhwedel, 2001; Feenstra & Kee, 2004; Feenstra, 2010; Gustafsson & Segerstrom, 2010; Gustafsson & Segerstrom, 2011).

4. *Foreign Investment*: International trade often attracts foreign direct investment (FDI). FDI can bring in new technologies, management practices, and capital, leading to increased production efficiency and job creation (Kojima, 1975; Baldwin, 1979; Grossman, 1983, Jones & Dei, 1983; Roberts et al., 2019; Zamani & Tayebi, 2022).

5. *Export-Led Growth*: Many developing countries have achieved significant economic growth by adopting export-led growth strategies. By focusing on producing goods and services for export markets, they can earn foreign exchange, generate revenue, and stimulate economic development (Singh, 2010).

6. *Innovation & Technology Transfer*: Engaging in international trade can foster innovation and technology transfer. When countries interact with each other economically, they may adopt and adapt new technologies and practices, leading to improved productivity and competitiveness (Melitz & Redding, 2021).

7. *Income Generation & Employment*: Export-oriented industries can create jobs and generate income for workers, helping to reduce poverty and raise living standards (McMillan & Verduzco, 1986; Van Ha & Tran, 2017; Keller & Utar, 2023).

8. *Economic Stability*: International trade can provide a buffer against economic shocks. When one sector of the economy faces a downturn, a diverse range of export industries can help stabilize a country's economic health (Acharyya & Kar, 2014).

9. *Foreign Exchange Reserves*: Export earnings contribute to a country's foreign exchange reserves, which are important for maintaining the stability of the national currency and facilitating international transactions (Krušković & Maričić, 2015).

10. *Competition & Efficiency*: Competition from international trade can encourage domestic industries to become more efficient, reducing waste and driving innovation (Montagna, 2001; Scherer, 2002; Chen et al., 2009).

11. *Infrastructure Development*: The need for efficient transportation, logistics, and communication networks to support international trade can lead to infrastructure development that benefits the entire economy (Hochman et al., 2013; Osuna, 2013; Donaubauer et al., 2018; Lorz, 2020).

12. *Access to Resources*: Countries lacking certain natural resources can obtain them through trade, allowing them to access crucial inputs for production (Jinji, 2006; Ruta & Venables, 2012; Lenzen et al., 2013).

From this point of view, the importance of economic and trade counsellors' offices at embassies abroad can be instrumental in advancing a nation's economic interests on the global stage. These offices play a key role in promoting exports, attracting foreign investment, and fostering international economic cooperation (Martin, 2003; Naray, 2008; Yakop & Van Bergeijk, 2009; Naray, 2011; Naray & Bezençon, 2017; Chatterjee, 2020):

a. *Promotion of Exports*: Economic and trade counsellors work to identify export opportunities for their country's businesses and industries. They assist local companies in entering foreign markets, provide market intelligence, facilitate trade missions and exhibitions, and help address trade barriers.

b. *Market Access & Trade Negotiations*: These offices are often involved in trade negotiations and agreements, working to secure favorable terms for their country's exports. They engage in dialogues with foreign governments to address trade-related issues and ensure market access for their country's goods and services (Naray, 2008, 2011; Naray & Bezençon, 2017).

c. *Investment Promotion*: Economic and trade counsellors promote their country as an attractive destination for foreign direct investment (FDI). They identify potential investors, provide information on investment opportunities, and assist foreign businesses in navigating regulatory and investment climate issues (Moons & van Bergeijk, 2017; Thrall, 2023).

d. *Information & Research*: These offices gather economic and market information, conduct research on trade and investment trends, and provide data and analysis to their home government and local businesses. This information helps inform economic policy decisions.

e. *Advocacy* constitutes a wide range of activities conducted to influence decision-makers at different levels (Morariu & Brennan, 2009). Economic and trade counsellors advocate for their country's economic interests abroad, engaging with host governments, international organizations, business associations, and civil society organizations (CSOs, although studies argue that close linkages between government and CSOs are problematic, see Brinkerhoff & Brinkerhoff, 2004; Van Wessel et al., 2020) to address issues that affect their country's economic relations, such as tariffs, regulations, and intellectual property protection (Pacheco & Matos, 2022).

f. They build and maintain a *network* of contacts with local government officials, business leaders, chambers of commerce, and industry associations. These relationships help facilitate business-to-business connections and promote economic cooperation (Metzl, 2001; Sikkink, 2009; Fisher, 2010).

g. *Support for Small & Medium Enterprises* (SMEs): Economic and trade counsellors often provide specific support to SMEs, which may face unique challenges when expanding into international markets. This support can include market entry strategies, export financing guidance, and matchmaking with potential foreign partners (Ellis & Pecotich, 2001; Chitakornkijsil, 2009; Gupta et al., 2023).

h. *Crisis Management*: In times of economic crises or trade disputes, these offices play a role in crisis management and coordination with relevant authorities, both at home and abroad, to protect their country's economic interests.

i. *Promotion of Economic Diplomacy*: Economic and trade counsellors engage in economic diplomacy by fostering goodwill, cooperation, and economic partnerships between their country and host nations. They aim to build positive economic relations that benefit both parties (Moons & van Bergeijk, 2017; Chatterjee, 2020).

j. *Policy Advocacy*: These offices may advocate for specific economic policies and reforms that promote trade, investment, and economic growth in both their host country and their home country. One of the most successful examples is that of the Netherlands: between 2016 and 2020 the Netherlands Ministry of Foreign Affairs are working together with civil society organizations to implement a new policy programme for international cooperation: "Dialogue and Dissent: Strategic Partnerships for Lobby and Advocacy" (Van Wessel et al., 2017).

Economic and trade counsellors' offices at embassies abroad serve as vital bridges between their country's government and the international business community. They work to advance economic growth by promoting exports, attracting foreign investment, and facilitating economic cooperation, ultimately contributing to the overall prosperity of their nation.

Relations Create Risks…

Geopolitical risks refer to the various political, economic, and security challenges that arise from a country's interactions with other nations, often driven by factors such as territorial disputes, competition for resources, ideological differences, and regional power dynamics. These risks can have a profound impact on how a nation's government conducts its foreign affairs (Cheng & Chiu, 2018; Caldara & Iacoviello, 2022; Papastamou, 2023a):

a. Governments regularly assess geopolitical risks to identify *potential threats* to their national security and interests. These assessments inform foreign policy decisions, including the allocation of resources for defense, intelligence, and diplomacy.
b. Geopolitical risks influence the formation of *strategic alliances and partnerships*. Countries may seek alliances with other nations to mitigate risks, enhance their security, and bolster their influence in international affairs (Aras & Ozbay, 2008; Lachininskii & Xiaoling, 2021; Therme, 2021; Nygaard, 2023):
c. Geopolitical risks related to *regional conflicts* or disputes often drive diplomatic efforts to prevent or resolve conflicts. Foreign policy may involve mediation, negotiation, or participation in international peacekeeping missions (Der Derian, 1987; Bercovitch, 1996; Fey & Ramsay, 2010; Hoffman, 2011; Aggestam, 2016; Young et al., 2022).

d. *Access* to critical *resources*, such as energy, minerals, and water, can be a source of geopolitical risk. Foreign policy may focus on securing reliable sources of these resources through trade agreements, partnerships, or diplomatic initiatives (Antonakakis et al., 2017; Bouoiyour et al., 2019).

e. Geopolitical risks can affect a country's *economic interests*, including its ability to engage in international trade and investment. Foreign policy decisions may prioritize economic stability and market access (Cao et al., 2023).

f. Geopolitical risks related to *humanitarian crises*, *global health threats*, and *environmental issues* can shape foreign policy responses. Governments may engage in humanitarian assistance, disaster relief, and collaborative efforts to address global challenges (Falk, 1995; Braem, 2007; Novelli, 2010; O'Reilly, 2019; Saez, 2022).

g. *The power dynamics* within a *region* can create geopolitical risks and opportunities. Foreign policy may aim to balance relations with regional powers, deter aggression, or influence regional stability (Therme, 2021).

h. Geopolitical risks associated with the spread of *nuclear weapons* and other *weapons* of mass destruction can lead to foreign policy efforts to promote arms control agreements and non-proliferation initiatives (Dalby, 2014a, 2014b).

i. Geopolitical risks influence a country's *diplomatic posture and engagement* with international organizations. Nations may seek to build coalitions, exert influence, or advance their interests through multilateral diplomacy. At the military level, this policy was the norm during the Cold War period, but also later on (McSherry, 2015). Recently, the crisis in Ukraine has brought the problem back to the forefront. The attitude of Italy is a typical case in point: in spite of the fact that Italy beneath its Prime Serve, Mario Draghi, not as it were reacted to but viably driven European procedure towards Ukraine amid the emergency – counting supporting Ukraine's enrollment offered – on the inside front the nation was polarized, unwilling to thrust for assist discipline of Russia in see of its financial resonations, but moreover addressing military inclusion within the war in Ukraine. After a fizzled endeavor to accommodate outside desires and residential inclinations, centred around Italy's sponsorship of a "peace plan" for Ukraine, the pressure between the two sets of impacts escalates to the point of accelerating the conclusion of the Draghi government in July 2022, with Italy's reaction to the Ukrainian emergency invoked as one of the most causes of the government's drop. In spite of the fact that the right-wing organization together of political parties that won the resulting common decisions campaigned on a populist and patriot, "Italy first", stage, the country's pose towards the war in Ukraine has not truly changed – beneath its current Prime Serve, Giorgia Meloni, Italy has kept on adjust with the multilateral desires set by the EU and the US. The contrasts in remote arrangement viewpoint inside the current administering fusion, in any case, are not immaterial, and open supposition continues to be separated. This proposes that the pressure fundamental Italy's outside approach within the Ukraine emergency has not been settled – in fact, it may still possibly weaken the country's discretionary pose, as well as the government's claim solidness, within the months to come (Brighi & Giusti, 2023).

j. In response to geopolitical risks, governments may increase *intelligence* gathering and *surveillance* activities to monitor potential threats and inform foreign policy decisions (Hinšt, 2021; Peterson & Hoffman, 2022).

k. Geopolitical risks can escalate into *crises* that require immediate foreign policy responses. These responses may include diplomacy, crisis mediation, sanctions, or military action. That is why the measurement of geopolitical risk is of increasing concern, not only to governments but to all stakeholders: the geopolitical risk (GPR) index spikes around the two world wars, at the beginning of the Korean War, during the Cuban Missile Crisis, and after 9/11. Higher geopolitical risk foreshadows lower investment and employment and is associated with higher disaster probability and larger downside risks. The adverse consequences of the GPR index are driven by both the threat and the realization of adverse geopolitical events. Investment drops more in industries that are exposed to aggregate geopolitical risk. Higher firm-level geopolitical risk is associated with lower firm-level investment (Caldara & Iacoviello, 2022).

l. Geopolitical risks can also shape a nation's foreign policy based on its *values* and *national identity*. Countries may choose to align with like-minded nations or advocate for specific principles on the global stage (Tuathail, 1999; Dijink, 2002; Dalby, 2003; Jaspal et al., 2014; Lubinski & Wadhwani, 2020).

An Era of Major Geopolitical Shocks

Global Interconnectedness often referred to as globalization, is a phenomenon characterized by the growing interdependence and interconnected nature of countries, societies, economies, and cultures around the world. It has been accelerated by advances in technology, communication, transportation, and the liberalization of trade and finance (Hamdaoui & Maktouf, 2019; Kusen & Rudolf, 2019; Aven & Zio, 2021). Global interconnectedness is prominently visible in the realm of international trade and economic integration (Raddant & Kenett, 2021). Countries are deeply connected through the exchange of goods, services, and investments. Global supply chains and the movement of capital have made it possible for products to be manufactured with components sourced from multiple countries: One of the increasingly dominant theories – not without reason, as international statistics unfortunately confirm it – is the theory of deglobalization: the global economy is facing face the possibility of decoupling many trade connections, and this trend favors long-standing processes of deglobalization. favored by populism, nationalism and economic protectionism. It appears that global supply, production and value chains, although economically viable, are no longer safe under national protectionist policies and, therefore, the offshoring of production processes mainly due to increased income levels and wages. developing countries as destinations and reduce the benefits of offshoring (Vargas-Hernández, 2023). Advances in technology, especially the internet and mobile communications, have revolutionized the way people and businesses interact. The instantaneous flow of information, the rise of social media, and digital platforms have connected individuals and organizations across borders (Li et al., 2019). Global interconnectedness is evident in financial markets, where capital flows freely across national borders. Events in one part of the world can have immediate and far-reaching impacts on financial markets worldwide (Hamdaoui & Maktouf, 2019). This was particularly evident during the global financial crisis of 2008. Cultural interconnectedness is facilitated by the exchange of ideas, art, literature, music, and media. Cultural globalization has led to the spread of popular culture and the blending of cultural influences from different parts of the world. There are at slightest three basic reasons why any endeavor to survey the degree of globalization ought to take under consideration social components: To begin with, as the late Richard Weaver expressed, and as scholars such as Lawrence Harrison and Samuel Huntington contend, "ideas have consequences." The values, thoughts, convictions, and belief systems that are encoded into social items, such as media like motion pictures, tv appears, and prevalent music, both express values and offer assistance to transmit values. Diminish Berger's profitable work on globalization in reality contends that the "four faces of globalization" are truly mindsets, or indeed worldviews, that are shared by huge numbers of individuals around the world, unbound by national beginning or citizenship. Mindsets, be that as it may, are troublesome to degree. An alternate route is regularly through the prime transmitter of values and convictions, which is the prevalent media. Sociologists and clinicians have long contended that in spite of the fact that it is outlandish to totally evaluate the effect of media on awareness, it is obvious that individuals do learn around much of the exterior world, and in some cases discover unused thoughts or values that they at that point grasp as their claim. Ho Chi Minh, for case, contended that the American statement of freedom formed his possess sees on patriotism. Since our thoughts and our values do direct our behavior, the way in which these thoughts and values are transmitted and changed over social boundaries have noteworthy results. They may lead us to participation or to struggle. The transmission of cultural capital over societies encompasses a noteworthy effect on the financial, political, and social improvement of countries. For illustration, the development of Buddhism among American celebrities such as Steven Seagal or Richard Gere eventually helps within the advancement of certain political states of mind towards China's relationship with Tibet. Moreover, the spread of individualistic or consumeristic states of mind among Chinese youth has noteworthy suggestions for long term of Chinese legislative issues and social organization. Second, utilization of outside social items infers receptivity. This, maybe more than any other measurement of the globalization record, captures not fair the financial objectives of globalization, but the want to get non-domestic thoughts, values, and aesthetics. The volume of information/entertainment presented from overseas, as compared to domestic generation, could be a vigorous sign of how much the nationals are informed about, responsive to, and affected by other societies in their existence . Hence, as financial pointers of globalization tend to point to financial goals and imply a constrained number of citizens taking part in worldwide financial or commerce action, the receptivity of social items could be a superior brief hand marker of the states of mind towards globalization of a larger segment of society. For illustration, the consequence of a huge number (in number of titles and issues dispersed) of way of life, news, or commerce magazines could be a distant way better pointer of the changing values and states of mind of a populace than financial information, which might degree exclusively one viewpoint of a nation's economy. Third, a number of commentators have argued that globalization has led to the emergence of a "global culture." If this global culture is indeed emerging, it is likely to take on different meanings in every nation in which it occurs, and it is localized and transformed by local responses. Regardless, it is perhaps the best guard against "civilizational fault lines" and the consciousness that shapes identity, which in turn, shapes national responses to other nations and cultures. Moreover, the emergence of common attitudes towards global brands, consumeristic orientations, and a whole host of associated attitudes has real, economic consequences in the globalized world. Finally, social globalization does in fact have statistic measurements, in terms of urbanization, family estimate, instruction, and investing. As social values alter in connection to these issues, countries are changed inside, in numerous ways driving them to more noteworthy participation with their neighbors, or at other times to genuine and enduring struggle in case their modern values bring them into struggle with their more traditionally-minded neighbors. In this way, the globalization of culture has genuine and enduring importance, in social organization, financial conveyance, and geopolitical pressures (Kluver & Fu, 2004).

Increased mobility and *migration* have resulted in diverse and multicultural societies in many countries. People move across borders for work, education, family reunification, and humanitarian reasons, contributing to a global diaspora. Discernments of the impacts of human relocation are major drivers of nation demeanors, approaches, and programs. Progressively complex worldwide interconnecting has modified connections among sending, accepting, and travel nations. The Worldwide North, with its maturing and declining populaces, requires a solid and youthful workforce; the Worldwide South, with restricted assets, a tall birthrate, and an in general young populace, can fill the holes of the previous, but with a few suggestions for accepting and sending countries (Segal, 2019). *Environmental challenges* such as climate change, air pollution, and biodiversity loss are global in nature. Actions in one part of the world can have environmental consequences that affect regions and ecosystems far away (Dalby, 2014a, 2014b; Anser et al., 2021; Bashir et al., 2023). International organizations, treaties, and agreements reflect the need for global governance to address interconnected challenges. Organizations like the United Nations, World Trade Organization (WTO), and World Health Organization (WHO) seek to promote cooperation among nations. The problem lies in design: the largest of the international organisations are often designed by the most powerful states to promote their interests, which is normal in terms of power, but with implications for the distribution of power. On the other hand, there is room for self-determination by the member states of international organisations, with obvious positive effects not only for the future of these states, but also for the "democratization" of international organisations, an issue of great concern to the international community (Barnett & Duvall, 2023). The COVID-19 pandemic underscored the extent of global interconnectedness. The rapid spread of the virus across borders highlighted the importance of international cooperation in managing public health crises. Recent studies showed that:

- COVID-19 outbreak has a greater effect on the US geopolitical risk and economic uncertainty than on the US stock market,
- oil is leading the US market at low and high frequencies throughout the observation period,
- while oil markets may recover through OPEC+ negotiations, the COVID-19 uncertainty remains the main concern of US policymakers (Sharif & Yarovaya, 2020; Sharif et al., 2020),

– the geopolitical disputes in developing nations might deflect public focus from the government's inadequate handling of the COVID-19 pandemic, or it could be the nation's exploitation of neighboring countries' health crises or waning power to its advantage. There is a strong causal relationship between geopolitical risks and both measures of the COVID-19 pandemic's spread. This data suggests that the COVID-19 pandemic's spread may cause serious problems with geopolitical risks in emerging economies. Emerging economies may benefit from lockdowns or other measures to stop the COVID-19 virus from spreading too quickly (Wang et al., 2020).

Security threats, including terrorism and cyberattacks, transcend national borders. The genesis of the risks of terrorism to the homeland can be traced to the unfavorable socioeconomic conditions in less-privileged and developing countries, where civil and religious freedoms are close to nonexistent, and sanitary conditions, health and education, and critical infrastructures of essential utilities are almost at the same level that existed in the United States almost a century ago. It seems interconnected: if we could make progress at improving the quality of life of the billions of people in the developing countries and become more sensitive to their needs, cultures, and heritage, possibly the terrorism would recede. The stakes for developed countries are high: what other measures can they take to reduce terrorism, without compromising their basic cultural and democratic principles or their cultural and social heritage? (Wulf et al., 2003; Wernick, 2006). International cooperation is essential to address these threats effectively.

Human rights and social justice issues are increasingly recognized as global concerns. There are notable differences in the politicization of human rights issues. States have a greater tendency to penalize their geopolitical allies for specific transgressions, and certain norms are more politicized than others. Recent studies presented theories of politicized enforcement in which states penalize human rights breaches differently depending on how "sensitive" the target state is thought to be: states tend to criticize their enemies on delicate matters that threaten the authority and credibility of the target regime, while conversing with friends about more secure subjects (Terman & Byun, 2022). Activists and organizations work to raise awareness and advocate for human rights on a global scale (Randall, 2010; Papastamou, 2023b).

Shifts in Power and Influence with emerging powers like China and regional players gaining influence, can lead to increased competition for resources, influence, and territory, and geopolitical tensions, as established powers seek to maintain their position and emerging powers assert their interests (Akram, 2020; Ioannides, 2022). Managing these tensions and promoting stability often requires skilled diplomacy, international cooperation, and efforts to address the underlying causes of rivalry and competition. As emerging powers like China and India have grown economically, they have increasingly sought access to key resources such as energy, minerals, and agricultural products. This can lead to competition with established powers like the United States and Russia, resulting in geopolitical tensions over resource-rich regions. Shifts in power can revive or exacerbate long-standing territorial disputes. Rising powers may become more assertive in claiming territories they perceive as historically or strategically important, leading to conflicts with neighboring states and regional instability (Fang & Li, 2020; Altman & Lee, 2022). Other countries often react to shifts in power by forming alliances or balancing against the rising power. This can lead to the creation of rival blocs or coalitions, increasing the potential for conflicts or tensions as countries seek to counterbalance the influence of the rising power (Li et al., 2019). Economic power is closely tied to geopolitical influence. When an emerging power becomes a major economic player, it can challenge the economic dominance of established powers, leading to trade disputes, currency wars, and protectionist measures that contribute to geopolitical tensions (Fung, 2023). Shifts in power can prompt countries to invest in their military capabilities to protect their interests and project power. This can lead to arms races, the deployment of military assets in disputed regions, and the potential for accidental conflicts or miscalculations (Demczuk, 2023). Emerging powers may have different ideologies, political systems, or cultural values than established powers, leading to clashes of values and interests. These differences can fuel geopolitical tensions, especially when combined with competition for influence (Rehmann, 2013; Stuenkel, 2017). Geopolitical tensions can be exacerbated by cyberattacks, disinformation campaigns, and information warfare, as countries seek to undermine each other's influence and disrupt their adversaries' institutions and systems (Whyte & Mazanec, 2023). Major powers may support proxy conflicts in other regions as a means of exerting influence without direct confrontation. These conflicts can escalate tensions and complicate efforts to resolve regional disputes peacefully. As power dynamics change, there can be disagreements over the rules and institutions that govern international relations. Established powers may resist efforts to reform global governance structures to accommodate rising powers, leading to friction and geopolitical rivalries (Roger & Rowan, 2023). Rising nationalism and populism in various countries can make it more difficult to manage international relations diplomatically, as leaders may adopt more confrontational or assertive stances to appeal to domestic audiences (Piattoeva et al., 2023).

Resource Scarcity is a significant driver of geopolitical conflicts and tensions. As the world's population continues to grow, and as economic development increases, the demand for essential resources such as water, energy, minerals, food, and arable land has intensified. When these resources become scarce or are unequally distributed, it can lead to various forms of conflict and instability (Hussain, 2022). Access to freshwater is critical for agriculture, industry, and human survival. Competition for freshwater resources, exacerbated by factors like climate change and overuse, has led to conflicts and disputes over shared rivers, lakes, and aquifers (Falkenmark, 1989; Haddadin, 2001; Unfried et al., 2022). For example, the Nile River has been a source of tension between Egypt and Ethiopia due to the construction of the Grand Ethiopian Renaissance Dam (Wiebe, 2001; Swain, 2008, 2011). Oil, natural gas, and other energy resources are vital for economic development and national security. Geopolitical tensions can arise when countries with abundant energy reserves seek to control or monopolize these resources, or when transit routes for energy transportation become contested (Furfari, 2012; Vakulchuk et al., 2020). Valuable minerals, including rare earth elements and metals like lithium and cobalt, are essential for modern technologies, including electronics and renewable energy systems. Competition for access to these resources can lead to geopolitical rivalries and conflicts, especially when they are concentrated in specific countries or regions (Kamenopoulos & Agioutantis, 2020; Hallgren & Hansson, 2021; Pan et al., 2023; Shiquan et al., 2023). As the global population grows, the demand for food increases. Land scarcity and soil degradation can limit agricultural production, contributing to food insecurity. Countries may compete for arable land, which can lead to land disputes and even military conflicts (Hall, 2013; Sommerville et al., 2014; Kurecic, 2015; Scheffran, 2020; Mehrabi et al., 2022). Overfishing and illegal fishing in international waters have depleted fish stocks, leading to conflicts over fishing rights and regulations (Vogel et al., 2023). Territorial disputes in the South China Sea, for example, are intertwined with competition for fishing resources (Guan, 2000; Storey, 2020; Dolven et al., 2021; Macaraig & Fenton, 2021). Climate change can exacerbate resource scarcity by altering weather patterns, causing more frequent and severe natural disasters, and impacting ecosystems. This can lead to displacement of populations, competition for habitable land, and conflicts over dwindling resources (Libiszewski, 1991; Dalby, 2014a, 2014b; Anser et al., 2021; Bashir et al., 2023). Resource scarcity, coupled with environmental degradation and conflict, can lead to forced migration and refugee crises. These movements of people can strain neighboring countries and regions, leading to political and security tensions (Wood, 1994; Metcalfe-Hough, 2015). Certain regions contain critical chokepoints for resource transportation, such as the Strait of Hormuz for oil shipments or the South China Sea for global trade. Competition for control of these chokepoints can escalate into geopolitical conflicts (Peele, 1997; Rodrigue, 2004; Avram, 2012; Mohapatra, 2021). Resource-rich countries may experience corruption, resource mismanagement, and conflict related to the capture of resource wealth by a small elite. This can lead to internal instability and contribute to regional tensions (Demidov et al., 2021). Disruptions in the supply of critical resources due to conflicts or disputes can affect global trade and economic stability, leading to tensions between countries (Johnson & Haug, 2021). Addressing resource scarcity and its associated geopolitical challenges often requires international cooperation, diplomatic negotiations, sustainable resource management practices, and efforts to reduce resource consumption and waste. Failure to address resource-related conflicts can lead to prolonged instability, human suffering, and regional or even global security threats.

The *digital age* has indeed introduced new forms of geopolitical risks and challenges, reshaping the way countries interact with one another and adding complexity to the global geopolitical landscape (Saeed et al., 2023; Sebastian, 2023). The interconnectedness of digital systems has created vulnerabilities that can be exploited by state and non-state actors for various purposes, including espionage, sabotage, and cyberattacks on critical infrastructure. These attacks can disrupt economies, compromise national security, and strain international relations (Saeed et al., 2023; Sebastian, 2023). The digital age has enabled governments and corporations to collect vast amounts of data on individuals and organizations. Concerns about mass surveillance, data breaches, and the misuse of personal information have led to debates about privacy rights and data protection on both domestic and international levels (Barnard-Wills, 2013; Zalnieriute, 2015; Bekkers & Góes, 2022; Irion et al., 2023). State and non-state actors use social media and online platforms to spread disinformation and influence public opinion in other countries. The transatlantic institutions and the global democratic alliance already face policy challenges as a result of the growing geopolitical risks linked to disinformation. The misinformation originates from the establishments of worldwide authoritarian powers, particularly China and Russia, who employ their foreign policies to erode liberal democracies such as the US, the EU, and NATO. Disinformation poses serious risks to the economy, security, and society by undermining fact- and evidence-based policymaking and impacting numerous policy processes. Artificial intelligence is expected to take over many societies in the near future, primarily as a result of misinformation. However, human intelligence will continue to grow and maintain its competitive advantage in critical thinking, civic virtues, argument-based rational public discourse, fact-based and data-driven public policy processes, and more. Fundamental civic competencies are the foundation of the liberal democratic system and can greatly assist individuals, communities, markets, and governments in fending off misinformation and demonstrating democratic resilience. As a result, social scientists, including political scientists, are crucial in developing interdisciplinary strategies to bolster democracy's resistance to misinformation (Hinšt, 2021). Digital technology has made it easier for nations to engage in espionage and intellectual property theft, leading to economic and technological competition and disputes between countries. This can affect industries such as technology, pharmaceuticals, and defense (Alperovitch, 2022). Thus, a major factor influencing the strategic ramifications of digital espionage is the victim state's reaction. The selected response will be shaped by the particular context of bilateral relations between the spying state and the victim state, as was first suggested. As with non-cyber issues, victim states' perceptions of their options are limited by power imbalances. Leader-to-leader relationships and the status of larger diplomatic ties are important, but so is the presence of a successful channel for bilateral intelligence diplomacy. This is a crucial component in the endeavor to preserve balance and prevent the escalation of situations across domains. Sustaining multilateral efforts to promote responsible state behavior in cyberspace requires effective digital intelligence diplomacy to operate alongside traditional cyber diplomacy. Cybersecurity is a topic that both diplomats and secrecy officials should discuss. There may be room for inventive third parties to use convening power to help (re-)establish channels of communication where the current status of bilateral relations prohibits such exchanges. In this sense, Biden's appointment of seasoned cyber officials to senior national security positions is encouraging – other states should take note of this – and it shows how cyber is becoming more widely accepted as a major national security concern (Devanny et al., 2021). Countries with differing views on internet governance, censorship, and content control are often at odds. Disagreements over these issues can lead to diplomatic tensions and affect global internet access and freedoms. The development and adoption of emerging technologies like artificial intelligence (AI), quantum computing, and biotechnology have geopolitical implications. Countries that lead in these fields may gain a competitive edge, while those that fall behind can face security and economic risks. The digital age has led to complex global supply chains for technology products and components. Supply chain disruptions, whether due to geopolitical conflicts or other factors, can have far-reaching economic and security consequences (Shishodia et al., 2023). Trade tensions in the digital age often revolve around issues such as tariffs on digital goods and services, intellectual property protection, and market access for tech companies. These disputes can escalate into broader economic conflicts. The convergence of space and cyberspace presents new challenges. Satellites, which are crucial for communication, navigation, and surveillance, are vulnerable to cyberattacks, potentially leading to security threats and international disputes (Li et al., 2022; Wibowo, 2022; Van Camp & Peeters, 2022; Lee & Falco, 2023). Social media platforms wield significant influence in shaping public discourse and facilitating global communication. Decisions by tech companies about content moderation and access can impact international relations and domestic politics. As data becomes a valuable resource, debates about data governance, data localization, and cross-border data flows have emerged. These issues can lead to trade tensions and affect the ability of companies to operate internationally (Marcucci et al., 2023; Sohrbeck et al., 2023). In response to these new forms of geopolitical risks, countries are developing strategies to protect their interests and adapt to the digital age. International efforts are also underway to establish norms and rules for behavior in cyberspace, but achieving consensus on these issues remains challenging. As the digital landscape continues to evolve, managing and mitigating these risks will be an ongoing priority for policymakers and global leaders.

Climate change, natural disasters, and *environmental degradation* can exacerbate geopolitical tensions, trigger displacement of populations, and lead to resource conflicts (Nazir, 2023). Climate change can exacerbate resource scarcity by affecting the availability of water, arable land, and food. As resources become scarcer, competition for them can lead to conflicts between nations, particularly in regions already experiencing resource stress. Rising sea levels, extreme weather events, and prolonged droughts can displace communities and trigger mass migrations. This can lead to tensions between host countries and displaced populations, as well as conflicts over access to resources in migration-affected regions. Climate change can alter rainfall patterns and reduce the availability of freshwater resources. Competition for access to freshwater can lead to conflicts between upstream and downstream countries that share rivers and aquifers. Although the dynamic relationships between climate change and armed conflict have been extensively discussed, there have been few studies that incorporate aspects of climate adaptation into those processes. The study of Regan and Kim (2020) empirically investigated the effects of climatic and non-climatic conditions on the likelihood of armed conflict in Africa by utilizing geospatial grids for climate change and armed conflict, as well as country-level climate vulnerability measures of sensitivity and adaptive capacity. The findings imply that armed conflict and climate drivers are closely related. Importantly, more adaptive capacities result in a decreased likelihood of armed conflict. From a policy standpoint, their findings imply that improving adaptive capacity under climate pressure will lessen the likelihood of people turning to violence in response to water scarcity (Regan & Kim, 2020). Sea-level rise can lead to the loss of territory for some low-lying coastal nations. This loss can raise sovereignty issues and lead to disputes over maritime boundaries and exclusive economic zones. Climate change can disrupt agricultural production, leading to food shortages and price spikes. Countries heavily reliant on food imports may face increased vulnerability, potentially leading to conflicts or disputes over food trade and distribution. Climate-related disruptions, such as extreme weather events or shifts in energy demand, can affect the reliability and availability of energy resources. This can lead to conflicts over energy access and supply routes. Climate change can threaten critical infrastructure, including transportation networks, power grids, and coastal defenses. Attacks on vulnerable infrastructure can have security implications and potentially lead to conflicts. Forcible population displacement is one of the extensive effects of climate change. Migration caused by the climate is a very complicated topic. According to the New York Declaration for Refugees and Migrants, there are many different reasons people migrate, including natural disasters, terrorism, armed conflict, poverty, food insecurity, persecution, and violations of human rights. It took more than 20 years for climate negotiators to include displacement in climate documents, even though it was acknowledged in the very first IPCC report in 1990 that human migration may have the biggest single impact of climate change (Atapattu, 2020). Climate-induced displacement can strain the capacity of host countries to absorb refugees and asylum-seekers. This can lead to diplomatic tensions and conflicts over border controls and humanitarian aid. The changing climate can alter the strategic significance of certain regions. As the Arctic ice melts, for example, new shipping routes and access to resources become available, leading to increased geopolitical competition in the Arctic region. Geopolitical considerations and limitations have shaped the competing narratives and discussions surrounding Arctic governance. The Arctic's potential has been limited for the majority of the past 30 years by early geopolitical red lines drawn by the US and Russia as well as climate realities. Yet, within that permissible bound, weaker Arctic states and non-state actors have dominated narrative discussions about Arctic governance. In recent times, China has joined the United States and Russia in a contest between their respective governance visions, with the less powerful Arctic states caught in the middle. The major powers of today seem to be following a unilateral, competitive narrative. It is still unclear whether the European Arctic states' combined geopolitical might can be combined with an engaging multilateral story, or if the region will instead imitate the recent unilateralism of great powers (Berkman & Vylegzhanin, 2012; Auerswald, 2020). Some nations may adopt security-focused responses to climate-related challenges, including border fortifications and military deployments. These measures can raise the risk of conflicts if not managed diplomatically. NATO is a case in point. The founding of Committee on the Challenges of Modern Society (CCMS) made NATO – an organisation which was established mainly for territorial defence– deal with the issue of environmental protection. Thus, NATO received, for the first time, a task that was global in its nature and unrelated to its primary traditional concern: the security of its member states. Earlier research has emphasized opposition to the US proposal to establish the committee, which was mounted by the other organization's members. Détente is often portrayed as a time when the issues of military confrontation and arms race between two superpowers, the US and the USSR, became less salient, and competition between the two socioeconomic systems became more peaceful. Détente was also a unique period in the Cold War when NATO was the most permissive to largescale change in order to adapt to new realities of international affairs. At the same time, environmental protection had to essentially be redefined and rebranded in order for NATO to consider it a subject worthy and applicable to its own mission. The architects of CCMS narrowed the concept of environmental security to encompass only the environmental concerns of developed countries, which stemmed from their high levels of technological and industrial development; they drew a line between these issues and the ecological problems of the rest of the world. The formation of CCMS was also an element of the broader process of the development of political consultations in NATO. The understanding of the organisation's mission and tasks in détente limited the amount of change in NATO brought about by introducing the discourse of environmental security (Boguslavskaya, 2016; Al-Marashi & Causevic, 2020). Climate change requires global cooperation to mitigate its effects and adapt to its consequences. Disputes over climate agreements, commitments, and financial contributions can strain international relations. Efforts to address climate-induced geopolitical tensions often require multilateral cooperation, conflict prevention measures, and the development of strategies for adaptation and resilience. As climate change continues to impact the planet, managing its geopolitical consequences will remain a critical global challenge.

Ongoing conflicts, civil wars, and the presence of *fragile* and *failed states* are often associated with regional instability due to a variety of factors and conditions that can spill over into neighboring countries and regions (Robinson, 2023; Väyrynen, 2023). Fragile and failed states may become safe havens for terrorist organizations, criminal networks, and armed militias. These groups can launch attacks not only within the failed state itself but also across borders, destabilizing neighboring countries (Liu et al., 2022; Hammi et al., 2023; Maulana & Fajar, 2023). Political, economic, and security crises in fragile and failed states can lead to large-scale displacement and refugee flows. Neighboring countries often bear the brunt of hosting refugees, straining their resources and potentially causing social and political tensions (Atar et al., 2023; Lee et al., 2023; Stivas, 2023). Instability in a neighboring failed state can lead to the proliferation of weapons and arms trafficking, which can pose a security threat to surrounding regions (Blank, 2023). Economic instability in fragile or failed states can have negative economic consequences for neighboring countries. This can include reduced trade, disruptions to supply chains, and economic shocks that impact regional economies. Critical gaps in the global risk framework are created by communities in fragile states frequently lacking local health governance and the ability to identify, report, and respond to infectious outbreaks. It will be necessary to address the high rates of avoidable mortality that are typical in these environments and to use context-specific messaging when engaging such communities (Forum on Microbial Threats, 2016). Fragile states create a broad range of negative externalities: conflicts within them often have ethnic, religious, or sectarian dimensions. The collapse of central authority, or its failure to take root, can generate the conditions for human rights catastrophes. The absence of state institutions can allow a territory to be exploited by international terrorist organizations or proliferators of WMD. Even though states that remedy these problems provide an international public good, the international legal system continues to protect national sovereignty and place strict limits on the use of force. These tensions can spill over into neighboring countries, exacerbating pre-existing divides and contributing to instability (Yoo, 2011). Competition for limited resources, such as water, arable land, and minerals, can exacerbate tensions between neighboring states and contribute to conflicts over resource access and control. Regional and global powers may become involved in conflicts within fragile or failed states, either directly or by supporting various factions. These proxy conflicts can escalate tensions in the broader region. Failed states may have unresolved border disputes that spill over into neighboring countries, leading to territorial conflicts and tensions (Rotberg, 2003). Indeed, boundary disputes are among the most explosive international flashpoints: they frequently correlate with militarized interstate disputes and are more likely to lead to high intensity conflict than other kinds of frictions. Although analysts have been turning increasing attention to the topic of boundary tensions, significant knowledge gaps remain. We still do not know exactly what factors cause some border controversies to emerge or spur others to intensify to the point of war.

One reason is that the existing literature has paid insufficient attention to the socially-constructed nature of boundaries. Another reason is that researchers have not adequately accounted for the causal import of domestic politics. In his study, Jean-Marc Blanchard offered a novel, two variable explanation, which he termed institutional-statist theory, to explain when border disputes will result in war. His theory stresses the functional value of the contested boundary as well as the disputants' level of stateness. He tested the usefulness of his theory through a case study of the Indo-Pakistani boundary conflict between 1947 and 1965, illuminating why war occurred in 1947/1948 and 1965, and why peace was obtained between the wars. In contrast, competing approaches have difficulty explaining the wars, their timing, or the peace between 1948 and 1965 (Blanchard, 2005). The inability of a failed state to control its territory and enforce its sovereignty can lead to border incursions and territorial disputes with neighboring states. Efforts to address regional instability caused by fragile and failed states often involve diplomacy, humanitarian assistance, peacekeeping missions, and conflict resolution initiatives. Regional organizations and international actors may play a crucial role in managing and mitigating the consequences of state fragility and failure to promote stability and security in affected areas.

Challenges like terrorism, organized crime, pandemics, and mass migration are *transnational* in nature and pose complex geopolitical risks that have far-reaching implications for international relations and global security. These challenges are interconnected and can exacerbate one another, making them particularly challenging to address. Terrorism often operates across national borders, making it a transnational issue. Terrorist organizations can establish safe havens in failed or ungoverned regions, creating security threats for multiple countries. Countries around the world are affected by terrorism and often cooperate in intelligence sharing, law enforcement, and military efforts to counter terrorist activities. However, differing national interests and approaches can lead to tensions and complex alliances. Terrorism can influence a country's foreign policy decisions, including military interventions and counterterrorism efforts, which can have geopolitical repercussions (Esmailzadeh, 2023; Gaibulloev & Sandler, 2023; Godefroidt, 2023; James et al., 2023). Organized Crime groups often operate across borders, engaging in activities such as drug trafficking, human smuggling, and cybercrime. Their activities can undermine national security and regional stability. Organized crime can foster corruption within governments and law enforcement agencies, weakening state institutions and contributing to political instability. The economic impact of organized crime can affect regional and global economies, creating incentives for countries to cooperate on law enforcement and anti-money laundering efforts (Armao, 2004; Di

Nicola, 2022). The spread of infectious diseases, as seen with COVID-19, poses a global health security risk. Responses to pandemics can strain international relations, as countries implement travel restrictions, export bans, and vaccine distribution policies. Pandemics can lead to economic disruptions, including supply chain interruptions and recessionary pressures, with implications for global trade and cooperation. Vaccine distribution efforts have geopolitical implications, as countries seek to gain influence by providing vaccines to other nations or using vaccines as a diplomatic tool. (Ferreira et al., 2021). Conflicts, economic hardships, and environmental factors can lead to mass migrations and refugee crises. These movements of people can strain host countries, trigger security concerns, and lead to political tensions. Mass migration can lead to disputes over border control, asylum policies, and humanitarian assistance, affecting relations between countries. Migration issues can have domestic political implications, including debates over immigration policies and nationalism, which can in turn influence a country's foreign policy and alliances. Addressing these complex geopolitical risks often requires international cooperation, diplomacy, and the development of comprehensive strategies. Regional and international organizations, such as the United Nations, World Health Organization, and Interpol, play crucial roles in facilitating collaboration among countries to mitigate the consequences of these challenges and promote global stability and security.

Geopolitical risks can arise from *diplomatic disputes* and standoffs, as countries pursue competing interests and struggle to find common ground. A diplomatic stalemate occurs when negotiations or diplomatic efforts between two or more parties reach an impasse, often due to a failure to find common ground or resolve key issues. When diplomatic efforts fail to resolve disputes, there is a risk of the conflict escalating. Parties may resort to alternative means of pursuing their objectives, such as military action or economic sanctions, leading to a further deterioration of relations. Failed negotiations or a prolonged diplomatic stalemate can erode trust and confidence between nations. Suspicion and mistrust can make it more challenging to find future diplomatic solutions and can contribute to a cycle of tensions. Diplomatic failures can trigger nationalist sentiments and public backlash in affected countries. Politicians and leaders may feel pressure to take a tougher stance, making it harder to reach compromises or peaceful resolutions. Diplomatic stalemates in one region can have ripple effects, affecting neighboring countries and creating regional instability. In a globalized world, the consequences of regional tensions can also impact international stability. Geopolitical tensions resulting from diplomatic stalemates can disrupt trade, investment, and economic cooperation. This can have adverse effects on the global economy and contribute to economic tensions between nations.

Insecurity stemming from diplomatic failures can lead to arms races as countries seek to bolster their military capabilities. These competitions can escalate tensions and increase the risk of conflict. Stalemates in diplomatic efforts to address humanitarian crises can exacerbate suffering and displacement, leading to increased human rights abuses and international pressure. Diplomatic stalemates can prevent the negotiation and implementation of international agreements, including arms control treaties and environmental accords, which can have far-reaching consequences for global security and cooperation. Diplomatic deadlocks can affect not only bilateral relations but also multilateral organizations and negotiations. Frustration with the inability to make progress in international forums can lead to tensions between states. Prolonged diplomatic stalemates can hinder efforts to mediate and resolve conflicts through peaceful means, making the resolution of long-standing disputes more challenging. Efforts to prevent or mitigate the negative consequences of diplomatic stalemates often require creative diplomacy, increased diplomatic engagement, and the involvement of neutral third-party mediators or international organizations. Diplomatic initiatives may need to address underlying issues, build trust, and create incentives for parties to return to the negotiating table. Additionally, diplomatic solutions may be more successful when backed by a combination of incentives and consequences, including economic incentives and the credible threat of sanctions or international intervention.

The rise of *nationalist and populist movements* in various countries can lead to shifts in foreign policy priorities and create friction in international relations, having significant implications for global diplomacy and cooperation. Nationalist and populist leaders often advocate for protectionist trade policies and economic nationalism. This can lead to trade disputes, tariffs, and barriers to international commerce, causing economic tensions and disruptions in global supply chains. Nationalist and populist movements may be skeptical of international organizations and agreements, such as the United Nations, the World Trade Organization (WTO), and climate accords. They may question the value of multilateralism, which can hinder global cooperation on pressing issues. Nationalist and populist leaders may take a hardline stance on immigration and border security. This can lead to disputes with neighboring countries over immigration policies and border controls, potentially straining relations. Populist leaders may prioritize domestic political interests over international human rights and democratic norms. This can lead to tensions with countries and organizations that advocate for human rights and democratic governance. Nationalist movements often emphasize national sovereignty and may resist international interventions or agreements they perceive as infringing on their sovereignty. This can lead to disputes over issues like international law and military interventions. Populist leaders may question the value of existing security alliances, such as NATO, and demand that other countries contribute more to collective defense efforts. This can create uncertainty and strains within security alliances, and may resist international efforts to combat climate change, potentially impeding progress on global environmental issues. Populist leaders may use confrontational or inflammatory rhetoric in international relations, contributing to diplomatic tensions and adversarial relations with other countries (McDonnell, 2016; Pappas, 2016; Funke et al., 2020; Safitri & Hotimah, 2022; Jones, 2023). Nationalist movements may promote policies aimed at keeping jobs and industries within their own countries, potentially leading to economic conflicts and disputes with trading partners. The reluctance of nationalist or populist governments to engage in international cooperation can hinder collective responses to global challenges such as pandemics, terrorism, and humanitarian crises. Efforts to address the friction caused by nationalist and populist movements often require skilled diplomacy, patience, and a commitment to finding common ground. Multilateral institutions and diplomatic channels can play a crucial role in facilitating dialogue and negotiation. International actors must navigate the complex landscape of domestic politics while seeking to uphold international norms and agreements. Building trust and fostering a sense of shared responsibility for global challenges remain essential for promoting stability and cooperation in the face of rising nationalist and populist sentiments (Winter, 2015).

Trade disputes, protectionist policies, and economic rivalries can generate significant geopolitical risks, disrupting international relations and impacting global stability as countries use economic leverage to pursue their political goals. Trade disputes, including tariffs and trade barriers, can strain economic relations between countries. These tensions can lead to a cycle of retaliation, causing economic disruptions and harming industries on both sides (Selmi et al., 2022; Khan et al., 2023). Protectionist policies, driven by economic nationalism, can prioritize domestic industries and workers but can also lead to trade imbalances and provoke countermeasures from trading partners, creating economic frictions (Gupta et al., 2019; Khan et al., 2023). Disruptions in global supply chains, whether due to trade disputes or protectionist measures, can affect industries that rely on international inputs. This can have broader economic implications and raise security concerns (Kotcharin & Maneenop, 2020; Free & Hecimovic, 2021; Qin et al., 2023). Trade disputes often involve disagreements over market access for goods and services. Such disputes can lead to legal battles and have implications for industries like agriculture, technology, and pharmaceuticals. Trade tensions can be intertwined with broader geopolitical rivalries between countries. Economic disputes can spill over into security issues, exacerbating international tensions. At the same they affect regional economic integration efforts. Regional organizations and trading blocs may face challenges when member countries adopt protectionist policies. Economic conflicts between major economies, such as the United States and China, can have a significant impact on the global economy, affecting not only the countries directly involved but also international financial markets and trade patterns. Trade tensions can lead to currency manipulation and competitive devaluations, creating instability in international currency markets and affecting exchange rates (Evans, 2019; Adler et al., 2021; Blanchard, 2021; Chortane & Pandey, 2022). Countries involved in trade disputes may seek new geopolitical alliances and partnerships, potentially altering the geopolitical landscape and reshaping regional and global dynamics. The effectiveness of international trade rules and dispute resolution mechanisms is challenging, potentially eroding trust in the international trading system. Uncertainty for businesses and investors affects foreign direct investment decisions and global capital flows (Al Mamun et al., 2020; Demir & Danisman, 2021; Le & Tran, 2021). Efforts to address the geopolitical risks arising from trade disputes and protectionist policies often involve diplomatic negotiations, dispute resolution mechanisms like the World Trade Organization (WTO), and efforts to promote international cooperation and adherence to trade rules. Countries may also seek to diversify their trading partners and develop resilience in their economies to mitigate the impacts of trade tensions. However, finding solutions to these complex issues often requires time, negotiation, and a commitment to preserving global economic stability and cooperation.

Ongoing *regional conflicts* and territorial disputes can escalate into wider geopolitical crises and draw in international actors (Tanchum, 2020; Wang et al., 2021; Shen & Hong, 2023). Regional conflicts often attract the attention and involvement of external powers that support various factions or sides. These external actors may provide military assistance, financial support, or diplomatic backing, effectively internationalizing the conflict, depending, of course, on the balance of interests of third countries. Until 2010, scientific research implicitly assumed that the intervention of third countries depends on their ties with the countries where the conflict has occurred. In 2011, Jacob Kathman's work demonstrated that third-party interventions are clearly linked to the cause of the conflict, regardless of geographical proximity, since the risk of spillover also threatens the regional interests of third countries, regardless of their proximity (Kathman, 2011). Regional conflicts can spill over into neighboring countries, leading to cross-border violence, refugee flows, and security threats. These spillover effects can draw additional countries into the conflict, since countries involved in regional conflicts may have security alliances or commitments with other nations. These alliances can compel other countries to become involved in the conflict to fulfill their treaty obligations. Territorial disputes often have economic and resource implications. Countries may seek to assert control over disputed territories for access to resources like energy, minerals, or fisheries, which can trigger international competition and conflict. Ethnic or cultural ties between populations in neighboring countries and those involved in regional conflicts can create pressure for intervention. Countries may feel a responsibility to protect or support their ethnic or cultural kin. Humanitarian crises resulting from regional conflicts, including mass displacement and human rights abuses, can lead to international pressure for intervention or assistance. Major global powers may compete for influence in regions experiencing conflicts. These rivalries can exacerbate tensions and contribute to the internationalization of conflicts. International norms and principles, such as the Responsibility to Protect (R2P), may lead to calls for international intervention in situations of severe human rights abuses or conflict-related crises. Media coverage of regional conflicts can mobilize public opinion and lead to pressure on governments to take action. Public sentiment can influence a country's foreign policy decisions. Neighboring countries may perceive regional conflicts as security threats and take preemptive or defensive measures to protect their interests. These measures can contribute to the escalation of conflicts. Efforts to prevent regional conflicts from escalating into wider geopolitical crises often require diplomatic negotiations, conflict resolution mechanisms, and international mediation. International organizations, such as the United Nations, may play a role in facilitating peaceful resolutions. Crisis management, humanitarian assistance, and the use of preventive diplomacy can help mitigate the impact of regional conflicts on international peace and security. However, addressing these complex challenges often requires coordinated efforts among countries and a commitment to conflict prevention and resolution.

The spread of *misinformation* and disinformation, particularly through digital media platforms, has become a significant driver of geopolitical tensions and international conflicts. Misinformation refers to false or misleading information shared without harmful intent, while disinformation involves the deliberate dissemination of false or misleading information with the intent to deceive or manipulate (Whyte, 2023). Disinformation campaigns can undermine trust between countries and erode diplomatic relations. False or misleading information can lead to misunderstandings, misperceptions, and a breakdown in communication between governments. Disinformation can be used to advance a particular agenda or narrative, including in the context of territorial disputes or geopolitical rivalries. False claims about historical events or territorial boundaries can escalate conflicts and tensions. State-sponsored disinformation campaigns, such as election interference, can influence the outcomes of elections in other countries. Accusations of foreign interference can strain bilateral relations and lead to geopolitical tensions (Hanson et al., 2019; Berzina & Soula, 2020; Ohlin, 2020; O'Connor et al., 2020). Disinformation is often weaponized in information warfare, where state and non-state actors engage in campaigns to manipulate public opinion, destabilize governments, and foment unrest in other countries. It could exacerbate ethnic or religious divisions within countries or regions, contributing to domestic conflicts and potentially spilling over into international disputes. Distorting the image and actions of international actors, leads to false perceptions and hostile reactions. This can complicate diplomatic efforts and negotiations. Cleary, disinformation campaigns can be used in conjunction with cyberattacks to target critical infrastructure, organizations, and governments. These attacks can disrupt operations and lead to accusations and tensions between nations (Buchanan, 2020; Trad, 2022),while the manipulation of media narratives and public discourse, leads to biased reporting and the amplification of divisive rhetoric (Tuathail, 2000; Dempsey & McDowell, 2019; Douzet et al., 2020; Pilgun, 2022). Efforts to mitigate the geopolitical risks posed by misinformation and disinformation require a multifaceted approach. This includes strengthening media literacy, promoting fact-checking and responsible journalism, enhancing digital media regulations, and developing international norms and agreements on cyber behavior. Diplomatic efforts to engage with other countries on disinformation issues, as well as cooperation between governments, tech companies, and civil society, are also crucial in addressing the challenges posed by digital misinformation and disinformation campaigns.

Geopolitical Risks and Financial Markets

Geopolitical tensions can have significant impacts on financial markets, leading to increased volatility, uncertainty, and risk. These tensions can arise from conflicts, trade disputes, sanctions, political instability, or other geopolitical events.

- *Market Volatility*: Geopolitical events often create uncertainty and unpredictability in financial markets. Traders and investors may react to news and developments by buying or selling assets, leading to increased price volatility (Lee et al., 2021; Kamal et al., 2022; Salisu et al., 2022).

- *Risk Aversion*: Heightened geopolitical tensions can make investors more risk-averse. They may seek safe-haven assets like gold, U.S. Treasuries, or the Swiss Franc, causing their prices to rise (Habib & Stracca, 2015).
- *Currency Fluctuations*: Geopolitical events can impact exchange rates. Currencies of countries directly involved in conflicts or facing sanctions may weaken, while those of safe-haven countries may strengthen.
- *Commodity Prices*: Geopolitical tensions can influence commodity markets. For example, oil prices can be affected by disruptions in key oil-producing regions due to conflicts or sanctions.
- *Supply Chain Disruptions*: Trade disputes and geopolitical tensions can disrupt global supply chains, affecting industries that rely on international inputs. Companies may face higher costs and supply chain uncertainties.
- *Investor Sentiment*: Geopolitical events can influence investor sentiment. Negative news can lead to pessimism and lower confidence in financial markets, affecting investment decisions.
- *Flight to Quality*: During geopolitical crises, investors may move their assets from riskier investments to safer options, impacting the performance of stocks, bonds, and other assets.
- *Economic Impact*: Geopolitical tensions can have economic consequences, including reduced trade, business uncertainty, and lower consumer confidence. These factors can affect economic growth and corporate earnings, which in turn influence stock market performance.
- *Emerging Market Vulnerability*: Emerging markets are often more susceptible to geopolitical risks due to their relative political and economic instability. Investors may withdraw capital from these markets during times of heightened tension.
- *Sectoral Impacts*: Specific industries and sectors can be more vulnerable to geopolitical risks. For example, defense stocks may benefit from increased military spending, while tourism and aviation industries can suffer due to travel restrictions and security concerns.
- *Long-Term Investment Decisions*: Geopolitical risks can impact long-term investment decisions, particularly in regions directly affected by conflicts or political instability. These decisions can affect capital flows and economic development.
- *Central Bank Responses*: Central banks may adjust monetary policy in response to geopolitical tensions. They may cut interest rates to stimulate economic growth or raise rates to stabilize currencies and control inflation.

The impact of geopolitical tensions on financial markets can be complex and multifaceted. Market reactions may vary depending on the nature and severity of the geopolitical event, the geographical region involved, and the overall economic and financial conditions at the time. Investors and financial institutions often closely monitor geopolitical developments and incorporate risk management strategies into their portfolios to mitigate potential losses during periods of heightened geopolitical uncertainty. Additionally, governments and central banks may take measures to stabilize markets and promote financial stability during geopolitical crises.

a. *Twenty years of studies*

Unsurprisingly, early work on the role of geopolitical risk in financial markets focused on specific events: terrorist attacks and military mobilizations (Graham & Ramiah, 2012; Chesney et al., 2011; Nikkinen et al., 2000). It took about ten years until (Salisu et al., 2022a) created a predictive model, using of course the GPR Index proposed by Caldara and Iacoviello (2022). The findings of the studies confirmed the effects of geopolitical shocks on stock markets, not only in crisis regions (which is quite natural, as Elsayed & Helmi (2021) demonstrated for MENA countries) but also in developed economies, and with an important finding: not only was the effect of actual geopolitical shocks significant, but also of potential threats, thus demonstrating the sensitivity of the financial market to anything that deviates from normality:

- geopolitical risks increase economic policy uncertainty, as Agoraki et al. (2022) showed in their study of 22 countries: for instance, a recent development is the more than 2 % decline in stock prices following the Russian invasion of Ukraine in February 2022 (Będowska-Sójka et al., 2022),
- the study by Bouras at al. (2019) on 18 emerging countries showed that geopolitical risks increase stock volatility: it is definitely negative (Caldara & Iacoviello, 2022; Das & Kannadhasan, 2019), with statistical confirmation clearly in the suffering regions: the Middle East & North Africa (MENA) countries (Zeremba et al., 2022; Elsayed & Helmi, 2021; Das & Kannadhasan, 2019) and BRICS emerging markets (Balcilar et al., 2019), but also for developed economies (Salisu et al., 2022),
- the recent study by Smales (2021) showed that geopolitical shocks have a negative effect on equities, but a positive effect on the oil market!
- in the same spirit as Smales' study, the study by Abdel-Latif and El-Gamal (2020) had earlier also moved in the same direction but highlighting the domino effect of oil price volatility: low oil prices fuel geopolitical shocks

and these in turn boost the oil price. The lack of liquidity in the financial market also plays an important role, making it difficult to adjust quickly,

- the study by Iwanicz-Drozdowska et al. (2021), which concludes that geopolitical risk is a factor in shaping investment portfolios, since geopolitical risks cause cross-market spillover dynamics (Smales, 2021; Elsayed & Helmi, 2021; Iwanicz-Drozdowska et al., 2021) without clear evidence useful for reshaping both policy and investment decisions (Hedström et al., 2020),

- and the study by Zaremba et al. (2022) also came to an unexpected finding: geopolitical risks have a positive effect on future stock returns! Where does this come from? Probably an overreaction of investors to exogenous events, a reaction that is reversed in the next normalization period.

b. *How do geopolitical risks impact?*

This question continues to occupy scientific research. It is also known that, in 2022, Dario Caldara and Matteo Iacoviello constructed a measure of adverse geopolitical events and associated risks based on counting newspaper articles covering geopolitical tensions, and examining its evolution and economic impact since 1900 (Caldara & Iacoviello, 2022) the Geopolitical Risk Index (GPR): The use of statistical data from 2000 until today (2023) can help to integrate the Index into the "arsenal" of economic policy, but also into investors' decisions, leading them to choose stock market investments that are either unaffected by geopolitical risks or compensate for their impact. We can study the effects of geopolitical risks at two levels:

- in stock markets, through the assessment of volatility spillover dynamics, using the GARCH statistical modeling technique, a useful method to assess risk and expected returns for assets that exhibit clustered periods of volatility in returns. Particular attention should be paid to the study of the different degree of market reaction (both temporal and geographical) and its relationship with market efficiency and the incurring overreactions in the stock markets,

- to investors, by calculating the potential losses to investors from the impact of geopolitical risks on stock markets, using Var (Value at risk) (a method widely used by investment banks), using three methods: the historical, variance-covariance, and Monte Carlo methods.

With this in mind, we propose, given the negative impact of geopolitical risks on financial markets, strategies to hedge geopolitical risk: a useful "tool" both for foreign policy formulation and for investors' portfolios. In other words, are there financial assets whose inclusion in investors' portfolios can offset the negative impact of geopolitical risks? (Będowska-Sójka et al., 2022).

c. *What is the transmission mechanism of crises, and what is it that turns geopolitical shocks into stock market fluctuations?* The study by Wang et al. (2022) focuses on the recent War in Ukraine and concludes that commodities and precious metals "transmit" geopolitical shocks to the financial market!

d. *What could be the appropriate policy to compensate for these negative impacts?*

- the results of the Baur and Smales (2020) study can be exploited by economic diplomats and, of course, by investors: precious metals can be used as a hedge against geopolitical risk,
- and the study by Li et al. (2022) focusing on the relationship between geopolitical risks and oil prices and the stock market in China, concludes that gold and silver can be used as a hedge against geopolitical risks.

Case Study

- Hypothesis development

What is the impact of geopolitical risk on the stock market? How is it possible to mitigate the risk of mitigating investment activities? The following research hypotheses are formulating:

➤ *Hypothesis-1*: Geopolitical shocks negatively affect stock markets, as investors, in an effort to protect themselves from exogenous shocks, seek more stable stocks, causing stock prices to fall (Ang & Chen, 2002; Black, 1976).

➤ *Hypothesis-2*: The above hypothesis translates into a diffusion of effects at the international level, due to the increased degree of globalization of markets. This means that, regardless of the geographical proximity to the geopolitical shock area, clearly stock markets in developed countries will be affected. Uncertainty exacerbates stock market linkages, i.e., in a state of uncertainty, bad news is more easily transmitted (Forbes & Rigobon, 2002; Iwanicz-Drozdowska et al., 2021).

➤ *Hypothesis-3*: Investors, thinking rationally, try to mitigate the impact of geopolitical risks by selling "risky" securities to buy safer ones: precious metals, bonds and works of art.

– Econometric methodology

➤ The starting point of our methodology is the estimation of unexpected changes – which cannot be explained by economic activity. GPRSHOCK[1] explains shocks in the GPR index. To assess geopolitical risk in the stock market, we estimate VAR specification for each country to identify the unanticipated and exogenous changes in the stock market returns. An alternative estimation of the above could be based on the GIR-GARCH model proposed by Glosten et al. (1993), due, among other things, to the advantage that this model considers the leverage effect of the shocks: which shock enhances volatility more? The negative or the positive shocks? The answer can contribute substantially to the formulation of economic diplomacy, and also to investors' portfolio management decisions.

➤ We then focus on the assessment of possible spillover effects within the groups of countries: VAR specification with N=35 number of countries pooled into specific groups such as Developed, Emerging, MENA and SAHEL. GPRSHOCK is inserted as an exogenous variable, while MSCI index, VIX, Economic Uncertainty Index are considered endogenous variables.

➤ And finally, we experiment with alternative investment opportunities based on their possible procyclicality and countercyclicality to geopolitical risk events:

– Sovereign Bonds, since they have a reputation as safe havens during financial and economic crises,

– Gold, like Sovereign Bonds, are a haven for investors in difficult times,

– Copper, and related commodities reflect the expected level of production and the increasing demand for products.

– and Artwork (Modern Art, Paintings, Old Masters and Post War art crafts, because we have statistical data, whereas, unfortunately, for other categories, we do not have sufficient statistical information): the average price of artwork is expected to rise following a negative shock in the stock market.

– Data & sample selection

---

1   $GPRSHOCK_t$ is the residual of the first-order autoregressive process $GPR\_STD_t = \varphi GPR\_STD_{t-1} + v_t$ where GPR_STD_t is the standardized GPR index.

The selection of countries was based on their relevance to geopolitical risks:

- G7: arguably the most important group of countries, in terms of political & economic power, with little likelihood of direct geopolitical risks, but with a strong diffusion of exogenous risks through their stock markets, whose operation incorporates highly sensitive information through the price mechanism,
- BRICS: the second category of countries with considerable economic and political power, but with a higher probability of geopolitical risks compared to the G7 group. As the functioning of their financial markets improves, so does the diffusion of exogenous geopolitical risks, as in the G7 group,
- MENA group of countries: increased likelihood of geopolitical risks. However, to simplify our analysis, we select the following countries: Israel, Saudi Arabia, Egypt, UAE, Jordan, Bahrain, Kuwait, Lebanon, IRAQ, Morocco, Oman, Qatar, and Tunisia, out of the 21 countries belonging to the MENA category, based on the World Bank's ranking,
- SAHEL: group of countries with high political and economic uncertainty, especially after the Arab Spring and the increase in terrorist attacks in the region, this category is also of particular importance for our analysis, but with statistical shortcomings,
- finally, Australia, Turkey, and South Korea are also included in our analysis.

We also calculated nine (9) economic indicators, based on data on a monthly frequency, for 32 years (January 1990–June 2022): Global Industrial Production (OECD IP):[2]

1. Industrial Production Index,[3]
2. Consumer Price Index,
3. central bank interest rates,
4. 10-year sovereign bond yields,

---

2   Industrial production refers to the output of industrial establishments and covers sectors such as mining, manufacturing, electricity, gas and steam and air-conditioning. This indicator is measured in an index based on a reference period that expresses change in the volume of production output.
3   The industrial production index (IPI) is a monthly economic indicator measuring real output in the manufacturing, mining, electric, and gas industries, relative to a base year. In the US, it is published in the middle of every month by the Federal Reserve Board (FRB) and reported on by the Conference Board, a member-driven economic think tank. The FRB also releases revisions to previous estimates at the end of every March.

5. Morgan Stanley Capital International indices for global stocks and emerging markets stocks,
6. Brent oil price,[4]
7. Economic Uncertainty Indicator,
8. and Cboe Global Markets VIC index[5]

As geopolitical risks become more frequent and complex, governments and international organizations face the challenge of managing and mitigating these risks effectively. Diplomacy, conflict resolution, cooperation, and multilateral approaches remain essential tools in addressing these challenges and maintaining global stability. These tools are most effective when used in a coordinated and strategic manner. They help reduce the risk of conflicts, promote peaceful solutions to disputes, and build a foundation of trust and cooperation among nations. In an increasingly interconnected world, diplomatic efforts and multilateral cooperation remain indispensable for addressing complex geopolitical tensions and challenges. Additionally, forward-looking strategies that consider emerging risks and trends are increasingly important in the realm of international relations.

Our results confirm the relationship between geopolitical risk and stock market returns: a 1 % increase in geopolitical risk negatively affects stock market returns by 0.5–0.7 %, given the asymmetric volatility that characterizes stock market fluctuations. In order to hedge geopolitical risk, experience confirms that investors resort to alternative, even illiquid assets such as commodities, government bonds, gold, copper and artworks (Papastamou, 2023a, 2023b).

---

4   MSCI is perhaps best known for its benchmark indexes – including the MSCI Emerging Market Index and MSCI Frontier Markets Index – which are managed by MSCI Barra. The company continues to launch new indexes each year.

5   The VIX Index is a calculation designed to produce a measure of constant, 30-day expected volatility of the U.S. stock market, derived from real-time, mid-quote prices of S&P 500® Index (SPX℠) call and put options. On a global basis, it is one of the most recognized measures of volatility – widely reported by financial media and closely followed by a variety of market participants as a daily market indicator.

3. European Economy and Institutional Liberalism: Post-War Reconstruction of Ukraine

> *But what experience and history teach is this, that peoples and governments have never learned anything from history and acted according to lessons that could have been drawn from it.*
>
> Hegel

Institutional liberalism, also known as liberal institutionalism, is a political and international relations theory that emphasizes the importance of international institutions and organizations in promoting cooperation, maintaining stability, and fostering peace among states. This theory is often associated with the broader framework of liberal international relations theory based on four pillars:

1. *Cooperation & Interdependence*: This is a fundamental premise of the institutional liberal perspective in international relations. Institutional liberals argue that cooperation among states is not only possible but also desirable, and they emphasize the role of international institutions in facilitating and enhancing such cooperation. Economic interdependence, the spread of information, and the global nature of many contemporary issues (e.g., climate change, terrorism, trade) make cooperation through international institutions not only increasingly necessary, but also preferable alternative to conflict and competition among states. They argue that by cooperating, states can address common challenges, pursue shared interests, and avoid the costs and risks associated with hostility or zero-sum competition. For example, trade agreements can lead to increased economic prosperity for all participating countries.

2. *International Institutions*: Institutional liberals argue that international organizations and institutions, such as the United Nations, World Trade Organization (WTO), International Monetary Fund (IMF), and others, play a crucial role in shaping the behavior of states in the international system. They provide formal structures, rules, and mechanisms for states to negotiate, make agreements, and coordinate their actions. These rules can help reduce uncertainty and conflict by providing a framework for states to interact with one another. Liberal institutionalists argue that adherence to these

rules is essential for maintaining international order, since they reduce the transaction costs of cooperation: the time, effort, and resources required for states to negotiate and enforce agreements. Institutions can streamline these processes, making cooperation more efficient. Finally, cooperation through international institutions can build trust among states. When states consistently honor their commitments within the framework of these institutions, it fosters confidence in future cooperative efforts.

3. *Democracy & Human Rights*: Liberal institutionalists often advocate for the promotion of democracy and the protection of human rights as key goals of international institutions. Democratic governance is not only desirable within individual states but also contributes to international stability and cooperation. Democratic states are more likely to cooperate peacefully with one another and are less prone to engage in conflict. As a result, they support efforts to promote democracy worldwide through diplomatic means, election monitoring, and support for democratic institutions. The protection of human rights is a fundamental principle of international relations. International institutions play a vital role in upholding human rights standards and holding states accountable for violations. Human rights issues, such as freedom of speech, freedom of assembly, and protection from torture, are viewed as universal values that should be safeguarded globally. International institutions, including the United Nations, regional organizations, and international courts, are seen as important guardians of democracy and human rights. These organizations:

- set standards for behavior and encourage states to adopt democratic practices and respect human rights as part of their international obligations,
- and provide platforms for addressing human rights abuses, conducting investigations, and imposing sanctions when necessary.

Liberal institutionalists contend that the promotion of democracy and human rights contributes to global peace and stability. They argue that states that respect these principles are more likely to engage in peaceful relations, reduce conflicts, and work together to address common challenges.

4. *Soft power*, the concept popularized by political scientist Joseph Nye, is related to institutional liberalism. Soft power refers to a state's ability to influence others through attraction and persuasion rather than coercion. Institutional liberals believe that participating in international institutions can enhance a state's soft power.

Institutional liberalism stands in contrast to other theories of international relations, such as realism, which emphasize the role of power, self-interest, and the balance of power in shaping international outcomes. While realists are skeptical of the effectiveness of international institutions, institutional liberals argue that these institutions can help mitigate the security dilemmas and conflicts that arise in the international system.

It's important to note that institutional liberalism is a theoretical perspective used to analyze and explain international relations and does not represent a single, unified set of policy prescriptions. Different scholars and policymakers may interpret and apply institutional liberal principles in various ways to address specific international challenges.

Institutional liberalism, despite the strong criticisms it has received, has emerged as an important hermeneutic theory, especially in the periods of Post-War Reconstruction, because the global community recognized the need for a new approach to international relations that emphasized cooperation, diplomacy, and the role of international institutions in preventing conflict and promoting stability in the aftermath of the devastating World War II. This approach was seen as a way to address the shortcomings of traditional power politics and create a more peaceful and orderly world order:

1. *Lessons from World War II*: The devastation caused by World War II led to a recognition that traditional power politics and the balance of power system had failed to prevent global conflict. The scale of destruction and loss of life motivated policymakers and scholars to seek alternative approaches to maintaining peace and stability in the post-war world.

2. *Desire for Cooperation*: In the aftermath of the war, there was a strong desire among many nations to avoid another global conflict. Cooperation and collaboration among states became a central goal. International institutions were seen as a means to facilitate cooperation and reduce the likelihood of armed conflict.

3. *The United Nations* was established in 1945 as a key component of the post-war international order. It was designed to be a forum for international cooperation and a mechanism for addressing global issues peacefully. The UN embodied the principles of institutional liberalism by promoting diplomacy, multilateralism, and collective security.

4. *Promoting Economic Interdependence*: The architects of the post-war international order, such as the Bretton Woods Conference in 1944, established institutions like the International Monetary Fund (IMF) and the World Bank to promote economic stability and growth through cooperation and

integration of national economies. These institutions aimed to prevent the economic conditions that had contributed to the Great Depression and, subsequently, to World War II.

5. *Democratization & Human Rights*: The post-war period witnessed a growing emphasis on democracy and human rights as fundamental values to be promoted at the international level. Liberal democracies played a central role in shaping the post-war order, and international institutions were seen as vehicles for advancing these principles.

6. *Reducing Anarchy & Conflict*: Institutional liberalism, in contrast to realist theories that emphasize the anarchic nature of the international system, promotes the idea that international institutions can help mitigate anarchy and promote order by providing mechanisms for states to resolve disputes peacefully.

7. *Norms & Rules*: Post-war reconstruction saw the development and proliferation of international norms and rules that guided state behavior. Institutions, like the United Nations and the World Trade Organization (WTO), played key roles in establishing and enforcing these rules, which contributed to a more stable and predictable international system.

The intense activity of the World Bank, the IMF, the EBRD, the UNDP, the European Investment Bank, the BSIC, but also of individual states, Britain, Italy, Poland, and others, in direct cooperation and coordination with international and European organizations for the reconstruction of Ukraine, confirms the explanatory value of institutional liberalism, since the policies of international and European organizations strengthen future expectations, build partnerships and useful connections between actors, and create incentives for further actions. Against the realist version of international relations, where states behave arbitrarily, the logic of post-war reconstruction comes to affirm the social utility of institutional liberalism, with hope for a society of reconciliation and cooperation. European economic integration, a historical product of a long process of cooperation and development, offers, once again, the model of post-war reconstruction.

Interpretive Traditions in the Theatre of War

The Russian military intervention in Ukraine in February 2022 and the multidimensional crisis that followed and continues to shake the country, with multiple consequences for neighboring countries (migration, energy crisis, lack of basic raw materials and food, pollution of the natural environment: Fedorenko & Fedorenko, 2022; Liadze et al., 2023) and at the level of international law and democracy (killings, human rights violations, repression of minorities, disregard for the rule of law, destruction of democracy: Trautman & McFarlin, 2023) once again brings the two major interpretive paradigms into conflict: the realist view, in which violence becomes a key instrument of state power in a world devoid of international principles and rules, and liberal institutionalism, or institutional liberalism, in which state violence is abandoned as immoral and ineffective in favor of international cooperation that benefits not only the states that embrace it but also the non-state actors that are chronically marginalized by modernist theory (Keohane & Nye, 1977: 24).

Historically, institutionalism, which focuses on the role of international organisations, has shaken international relations theory with the formulation of principles and norms for the Responsibility to Protect (R2P) (Thakur & Weiss, 2009) and humanitarian intervention (Evans, 2008: 52). Institutional liberalism does not deny political power but treats it as a product of legitimate choice in a democratic society (Ruggie, 1982: 382) and justifies the use of power in building institutions based on this notion of "social purpose" (Keohane, 2012: 126) within a framework of principles and rules in which institutions contribute to transnational cooperation aimed at improving social welfare, maintaining security, and, of course, protecting freedom. This theoretical development acquired enormous practical value during the post-war reconstruction, tentatively from the end of the 19th century and boldly after the two world wars of the 20th century, with the emergence of the role of international organizations in international relations. Since the 1990s, despite the strong criticism (Grieco, 1988; Mearsheimer, 1994; Hoffman, 1999, Von Stein, 2005), the legal protection of international organizations, combined with the emergence of the political society, strengthened the role of institutional realism (Abbott et al., 2000). We recall the famous quote by Stanley Hoffman: "international affairs have been the nemesis of liberalism" (Hoffman, 1999: 162) under the weight of the "ineffective" (sic) policies of the United Nations and the World Bank to address the great challenges of our time: nuclear proliferation, poverty, and the destruction of the natural environment.

Nevertheless, rapid technological progress and unbridled globalization have fostered interconnectedness and network formation. Institutional liberalism has resurfaced, projecting the undeniable benefits of cooperation, while ongoing regional wars have accelerated the momentum of this trend: Alongside domestic politics, international organizations and global movements have claimed a leading role in post-war reconstruction (Donahue & Nye, 2000).

When Everyone Was Agreed

The wise always plan for the next day! This was also the case during the World War II, when the President of the United States Franklin D. Roosevelt and Prime Minister Winston S. Churchill, representing His Majesty's Government in the United Kingdom, accompanied by officials of their two governments, including senior military, naval, and air force officers, met at sea (HMS Prince of Wales, Placentia Bay, Newfoundland) on August 14, 1941, and agreed on the following joint declaration (Brinkley & Facey-Crowther, 1994):

1. Prohibition of territorial and all types of claims by states.
2. Possible territorial claims must be reconciled with the expressed will of the peoples concerned.
3. Respect for the right of peoples to choose the form of government they desire, but also the restoration of sovereign rights and self-government to those who have been forcibly deprived of their rights.
4. Equal access for all states (small and large, victors and vanquished) to the raw materials and trade relations necessary for their economic prosperity.
5. Economic cooperation among all states for social and labor security and economic development.
6. Restoration of peace, without fear and poverty.
7. Freedom of navigation for all people on all seas.
8. Renunciation of the use of force and disarmament of those states which show aggressive intentions. (U.S. State Department, 1941). The fourth clause (international trade) stressed that all (winners, and losers) would have access to the market "on equal terms"! Until then, the losers were punished even more with the conditions of peace (see WWI, Paris Economy Pact).

At the meeting of the Inter-Allied Council in London on September 24, 1941, the governments-in-exile of Belgium, Czechoslovakia, Greece, Luxembourg, the Netherlands, Norway, Poland, and Yugoslavia, as well as the Soviet Union and the representatives of the Free French Forces, decided unanimously to endorse the common principles established by Great Britain and the United States. The position of the Soviet Government was stated by its Ambassador Ivan Maisky as follows: "The Soviet Union defends the right of every nation to the independence and territorial integrity of its country and its right to establish such social order and choose such form of government as it deems expedient and necessary for the better promotion of its economic and cultural prosperity". He added that the Soviet Union supported the need for collective action against aggressors and that "the Soviet Government proclaims its agreement with the basic principles of the declaration of Mr. Roosevelt and Mr. Churchill" (U.S. State Department Bulletin, 1941).

In practice, the distrustful Stalin treated the Marshall Plan as a Trojan horse for Soviet influence after the war and took two steps: he condemned the Marshall Plan and created a similar financial program against the anti-Soviet bloc: the Molotov Plan (Parrish & Narinsky, 1994).

In both cases, postwar reconstruction was entrusted to international organizations, confirming the theory of institutional liberalism:

- two organizations implemented the program, the U.S.-led Economic Cooperation Administration (ECA) and the European-led Organization for European Economic Cooperation (OEEC, April 16, 1948), which brought together 18 countries to develop policies to promote trade and increase production,
- on the other hand, the implementation of the Molotov Plan required the creation of a system of bilateral trade agreements, which led to the establishment of COMECON to create an economic alliance of socialist countries.

Winners and losers confirmed the role of the international society not only in international relations to maintain peace and security, but also within states to promote economic development and social welfare. As Hedley Bull aptly put it, "An international society exists when, according to Hedley Bull (1932–1985), "a group of states, conscious of certain common interests and values, form a society in the sense that they feel bound by common rules in their relations with one another and participate in the work of common institutions"" (Bull, 1977: 13). The post-war world was shaped with the idea of cooperation between states for common goals and interests, as there is not only the danger of arbitrary behavior of states, but also multiple benefits from their harmonious coexistence and cooperation, ceding part of their sovereignty to create "integrated communities" that promote economic growth and respond to regional and international security issues (Lamt, 2005: 213).

An Unpleasant Deviation

Although the Brezhnev Doctrine was the official decision to change course in 1968, it was preceded by two decisive military interventions with the Soviet intervention in Czechoslovakia (Ouimet, 2003):

- the Soviet Union's involvement in the Korean War (1950–53), where it provided war materiel and services (training and information) as well as Soviet pilots and aircraft, primarily MiG-15 fighter jets, to support North Korean and Chinese forces against United Nations forces,

– and the military invasion of Budapest and other regions of Hungary in 1956 (UN General Assembly Special Committee on the Problem of Hungary (1957). Chapter IV. E): about 200,000 Hungarians fled Hungary, about 26,000 Hungarians were tried by the new Soviet-appointed government of János Kádár, and 13,000 of them were imprisoned.

From 1968, the Brezhnev Doctrine officially defined the foreign policy of USSR, with the sole aim of identifying any kind of threat to "socialist rule." In other words, it asserted the right of the Soviet Union to intervene in the affairs of other socialist or communist countries if it believed that the socialist system or the dominance of the Communist Party was under threat (Glazer, 1971). The key elements of the Brezhnev Doctrine included:

i. *Non-interference in socialism*: The doctrine claimed that the socialist countries of Eastern Europe were fraternal allies, and the Soviet Union had a responsibility to protect the gains of socialism in those countries. It implied that any threat to socialism in these nations would not be tolerated.

ii. *Justification for military intervention*: The Brezhnev Doctrine was used to justify the invasion of Czechoslovakia in 1968 when the Prague Spring, a period of political liberalization and reform, was seen as a challenge to the established communist order. The Soviet-led Warsaw Pact countries sent troops to suppress the reforms and restore orthodoxy to Czechoslovakia.

iii. *Maintenance of the status quo*: The doctrine aimed to maintain the political and ideological status quo in Eastern Europe and prevent any deviation from the Soviet model of communism or from strict control by the Communist Party.

iv. *Soviet leadership*: It reaffirmed the central role of the Soviet Union in guiding the socialist camp and implied that the USSR had the authority to make decisions on behalf of the socialist states in Eastern Europe.

The Brezhnev Doctrine was used not only to justify the intervention in Czechoslovakia but also to influence the political climate and actions in other Eastern Bloc countries, ensuring that they remained firmly aligned with the Soviet Union and did not drift towards political pluralism or independence. This Doctrine represented a significant aspect of the Cold War competition, as it underscored the Soviet Union's commitment to maintaining its sphere of influence in Eastern Europe and its willingness to use force to do so. It remained a central tenet of Soviet foreign policy until the late 1980s when Mikhail Gorbachev's policy of perestroika and glasnost signaled a shift in the Soviet approach to Eastern Europe, eventually leading to the end of the Cold War and the dissolution of the Eastern Bloc.

As history shows, the doctrine was effective: no state succeeded in seceding from the Eastern bloc, at least until Brezhnev's death in 1982. His successor, Mikhail Gorbachev, recognizing the fundamentally changed conditions both within the Soviet Union and internationally, abandoned the Brezhnev Doctrine in 1985, ushering in a period of political and economic reform in Russia. Nevertheless, Soviet military interventions continued throughout the world driven by geopolitical considerations, ideological alignment, and a desire to counter Western influence during the Cold War:

i. **Afghanistan (1979–1989)**: One of the most significant Soviet military interventions was the invasion of Afghanistan in December 1979. The Soviet Union sent troops to support the Afghan communist government against anti-communist mujahideen forces. This conflict lasted for nearly a decade and had far-reaching consequences, both for the Soviet Union and the region:

- *Soviet Union's Quagmire*: The Soviet Union's invasion of Afghanistan turned into a protracted and costly conflict. It strained the Soviet economy, military, and morale. The war was unpopular in the Soviet Union and contributed to a perception of overextension.
- *Strengthening of the Mujahideen*: The war fueled the Afghan resistance, known as the mujahideen, who received support from a range of countries, including the United States, Pakistan, and Saudi Arabia. This support helped to intensify the resistance and contributed to the Soviet Union's difficulties.
- *Growing Influence of Radical Islam*: The Afghan War attracted jihadists from various parts of the Muslim world to join the fight against the Soviets. Some of these fighters later formed the core of radical Islamist movements, including Al-Qaeda.
- *Soviet Military Defeat*: The Soviet Union ultimately withdrew its troops in 1989 without achieving its objectives. This withdrawal was seen as a significant military and political defeat for the Soviet Union.
- *Destabilization of Afghanistan*: The withdrawal of Soviet forces left Afghanistan in a state of chaos. Various mujahideen factions turned on each other, leading to a brutal civil war. This conflict set the stage for the rise of the Taliban in the 1990s.
- *Impact on Central Asia*: The war had repercussions on the neighboring Central Asian Soviet republics. It brought concerns about Islamist militancy and instability, which the Soviet Union sought to suppress.
- *Impact on US-Soviet Relations*: The war exacerbated tensions between the United States and the Soviet Union during the Cold War. The United States provided support to the mujahideen, contributing to the broader Cold War rivalry.

- *Resurgence of Islamic Militancy*: The Afghan War contributed to the spread of Islamist militancy and provided a training ground for future jihadists. This had implications for regional and global security.
- *Afghanistan's Ongoing Instability*: The consequences of the Soviet-Afghan War continue to be felt in Afghanistan. The war set the stage for decades of instability, conflict, and political fragmentation in the country.
- *End of Détente*: The Soviet-Afghan War played a role in undermining the détente period in US-Soviet relations, as it led to a renewal of Cold War hostilities.

The Soviet-Afghan War, sometimes referred to as the "Soviet Union's Vietnam," had a profound impact on the course of history in the late 20th century, shaping geopolitics, the spread of radical Islamism, and the fate of Afghanistan. Its legacy continues to influence the region and global politics to this day (Hughes, 2008).

ii. **Angola (1975–1991)**: The Soviet Union supported the communist government of the People's Republic of Angola during its civil war against anti-communist rebel groups, including UNITA and the National Union for the Total Independence of Angola (UNITA). Soviet military and financial aid played a significant role in this conflict having significant and far-reaching consequences for Angola, the region, and the broader Cold War dynamics. This intervention was part of the larger struggle for influence in Africa during the Cold War era, with major implications:

- prolonged the Angolan Civil War,
- had spill-over effects on neighboring countries, particularly Namibia and South Africa. These countries became embroiled in the fighting and provided support to various factions. This regional destabilization contributed to a prolonged period of conflict and insecurity,
- alongside the Soviet Union, Cuba played a significant role in supporting the MPLA government in Angola. Cuban troops were sent to fight alongside Angolan government forces, adding a new dimension to the conflict. This intervention by Cuban forces was crucial in bolstering the MPLA's position and countering the influence of South Africa and the United States.

The prolonged conflict and the heavy foreign involvement exacted a significant economic toll on Angola. The country's resources were diverted to the war effort, leading to economic stagnation and hardship for the population.

The conflict had a devastating impact on the civilian population. Thousands of Angolans were killed, and many more were displaced, leading to a severe humanitarian crisis.

The Angolan Civil War officially ended in 2002, and Angola has since experienced some stability and economic growth. However, the legacy of the Cold War conflict and foreign intervention continues to influence politics and society in Angola to some extent (James, 2020).

iii. **Ethiopia (1977–1991)**: The Soviet Union provided military and economic aid to the Ethiopian government, led by Mengistu Haile Mariam and the Derg, a Marxist-Leninist junta. This support helped the Ethiopian government consolidate power and maintain its grip on the country. The government's brutal tactics and widespread human rights abuses, as well as the conflict with various rebel groups, including the Tigray People's Liberation Front (TPLF) and Eritrean People's Liberation Front (EPLF), contributed to a protracted and devastating conflict. The Civil War, coupled with drought and famine in the region, led to a severe humanitarian crisis. The 1983–1985 famine in Ethiopia, particularly in the northern regions of Tigray and Eritrea, attracted international attention and resulted in widespread suffering and death.

1. *Disintegration of Ethiopia*: The Soviet-backed Ethiopian government's inability to quell regional rebellions and economic challenges ultimately contributed to the disintegration of Ethiopia. Eritrea gained independence in 1993, and the TPLF-led Ethiopian People's Revolutionary Democratic Front (EPRDF) took control in Addis Ababa in 1991, effectively ending the Derg regime.

2. *Regional Impact*: The Ethiopian Civil War and Soviet involvement had a significant impact on the Horn of Africa region. Eritrea's independence led to tensions between the two countries, resulting in the Eritrean-Ethiopian War of 1998–2000. The conflict also affected neighboring countries, such as Sudan and Somalia.

3. *Shift in Alliances*: The Soviet Union's involvement in Ethiopia further entrenched the country as an ally in the broader Cold War context. However, as the Derg regime's stability waned, the Soviet Union began to distance itself from Ethiopia and withdraw its support, signaling a shift in alliances.

4. *Legacy of Conflict*: The legacy of the Ethiopian Civil War and Soviet intervention continues to affect Ethiopia's politics, security, and socio-economic development. The TPLF, which played a significant role in

toppling the Derg regime, later became a dominant force in Ethiopian politics.

5. *Economic Consequences:* The Soviet-backed policies of the Derg, including nationalization and collectivization, had a detrimental effect on Ethiopia's economy. The transition to a more market-oriented economy post-1991 was challenging and required significant reforms (Remnek, 1992).

iv. **Nicaragua (late 1970s–1990):** The Sandinista National Liberation Front (FSLN), a leftist revolutionary group, overthrew the authoritarian regime of Anastasio Somoza in 1979. This revolution marked the beginning of the Sandinista government's rule in Nicaragua. The Sandinistas sought support from the Soviet Union and received both military and economic aid. The Soviet Union and other Eastern Bloc countries supplied arms, equipment, and training to the Sandinista government. The United States, during the Reagan administration, opposed the Sandinista government, viewing it as a pro-communist regime and a threat to U.S. interests in the region. The U.S. supported anti-Sandinista rebel groups known as the Contras. Nicaragua became a battleground for the Cold War, with the United States and the Soviet Union providing indirect support to opposing sides. The conflict in Nicaragua was part of a broader struggle in Central America, with the U.S. supporting anti-Sandinista forces in several countries. In 1990, after years of conflict and economic hardship, Nicaragua held elections, and the Sandinistas were defeated by Violeta Chamorro, who represented a coalition of anti-Sandinista forces. This marked the end of the Sandinista government's rule in Nicaragua. With the end of the Sandinista government, Soviet support for Nicaragua waned, as the political landscape in the country shifted away from socialism and toward a more market-oriented system (Watier, 2017).

v. **Vietnam (1979–1989):** The Vietnam War, which lasted from the mid-1950s until 1975, saw the Soviet Union providing support to North Vietnam, while the United States supported South Vietnam. This support included military aid, economic assistance, and diplomatic backing. The war ended in 1975 with the reunification of North and South Vietnam under communist control. After the end of the Vietnam War in 1975, Vietnam faced the challenge of post-war reconstruction and consolidation of power. The Soviet Union continued to support the newly reunified Vietnam, particularly in economic and military aspects. Vietnam was considered a close ally of the Soviet Union during the Cold War. In February 1979, China launched a brief invasion of Vietnam in response to perceived provocations and territorial disputes. The Soviet Union condemned China's actions but did not directly intervene in the conflict. Instead, the Soviet Union increased its support to Vietnam in response to the Chinese invasion. During the 1980s, Vietnam continued to receive military and economic assistance from the Soviet Union, which helped in rebuilding the war-torn country and strengthening its military capabilities. The Soviet Union's support for Vietnam continued until the late 1980s when the Soviet Union itself was facing internal and economic challenges. As a result, the level of support decreased, and by the end of the 1980s, the Soviet Union started to withdraw its military and economic assistance to Vietnam (Kimball, 1997).

vi. **Other conflicts**: The Soviet Union also provided support to communist or leftist movements in various conflicts in Africa, Asia, and Latin America during this period, often in alignment with its ideology and Cold War interests.

The dissolution of USSR as a sovereign state led to the republics gaining full independence on December 26, 1991.

Russia's military interventions changed international perceptions that had emerged after 1991 and gave the international community unpleasant surprises, most recently the invasion of Ukraine (Charap et al., 2021). Despite Russia's relatively low economic importance (Russia ranks 11th with a GDP of $1.48 trillion in 2022, while the United States, China, Japan, Germany, the United Kingdom, India, France, Italy, Canada, and South Korea rank in the top ten". (World Bank, 2023), Russia has conducted more interventions since the end of the Cold War than any other competitor to the United States. In its report Russia's Military Interventions. Patterns, Drivers, and Signposts, Samuel Charap, Edward Geist, Bryan Frederick, John J. Drennan, Nathan Chandler & Jennifer Kavanagh examined when, where, and why Russia conducts military interventions by analyzing the 25 interventions Russia has undertaken since 1991, including detailed case studies of the 2008 Russia-Georgia War and Moscow's involvement in the ongoing Syrian civil war (Charap et al., 2021).

Russian Invasion of Ukraine: Destruction and Costs

In December 2021, Russia deploys troops to the Ukrainian/Russian border. Russian President Vladimir Putin publishes an article claiming Russians and Ukrainians are "one people," and on February 24, 2022, Russia invades to annex the "breakaway" regions of Ukraine (Donbass). The invasion is approved by the UN General Assembly (UN General Assembly, 2022: GA /12407) and was immediately condemned worldwide, including in Russia (the first demonstration took place on 24 February 2022 and since then protests of all kinds have proliferated, with an uncertain outcome, and caused the largest refugee crisis in Europe since World War II. More than 8 million refugees from Ukraine have been registered across Europe, 6.5 million have been displaced within Ukraine, and 12 million people are trapped in a war zone". (UNCHR, 2023).

What is the cost of the disaster to Russia, which caused it? Russian journalist Boris Grozovski told Newsweek that the total military cost of the Russian invasion in 2002 was $346 billion, including $46.1 billion in direct military spending and $36.9 billion in police and security spending. Sean Spoonts, editor-in-chief of the Special Operations Forces Report (SOFREP), told Newsweek that Grozovski's figures were probably too optimistic: By the third month of the invasion, Spoonts estimated that it cost Russia as much as $900 million a day to maintain its military effort. It depends on how the numbers are calculated, he added. "If Russia spends $1 million to build a missile and then fires it, we think it has spent $2 million: $1 million to build it and another million to replace the missile," Spoonts said. "I think that's a very good estimate. I think most estimates only consider the initial cost. If you have a $50,000 car that burns up in a fire, you are out the $50,000 plus everything you spend to replace it because you need a car" (Mordowanec, 2023). Russia is estimated to have lost more than half of its tanks in Ukraine – a total of 1,769 vehicles – according to Oryx, a website that monitors military losses in the war-torn country. Ukraine's Defense Ministry reported in early February that Russia has lost nearly 130,000 troops, more than 6,300 armored combat vehicles and nearly 300 military jets since Feb. 24, 2022. Sergei Aleksashenko, Russia's former deputy finance minister, wrote on Al-Jazeera in December that the 2022 budget item "General national affairs" had increased by 50% to 2.629 trillion rubles ($42 billion). This spending generally comes from the administrative activities of all branches of the government, he said. "Assuming that the surplus funds in this item are related to the war, that's an additional 869 billion rubles ($13.8 billion) in defense spending," Aleksashenko said. The budget deficit of 3 trillion rubles that Russia is expected to have from 2022 to 2024 is equivalent to about 2% of GDP, he noted. For Putin, however, this is not a cause for concern, as state-owned banks will continue to buy government bonds. The scheme will slightly increase inflation but maintain funding for the war. The cost of the sacrifice has been incalculable in terms of human lives and enormous in terms of severe damage to Ukraine's infrastructure and most productive industries. Recent estimates by the Kyiv School of Economics put the value of the damage caused by the invasion now at $138 billion (Kyiv School of Economics, 2023), and President Zelensky has announced that rebuilding the country could cost over $1 trillion (Siang, 2023).

Institutional Liberalism in Practice

The truth is that Ukraine had been facing significant challenges and had not yet fully recovered from the conflict in eastern Ukraine, which began in 2014. The conflict resulted in extensive damage to infrastructure, displacement of people, and economic difficulties. Since then, several developments may have occurred in Ukraine's post-war reconstruction efforts:

i. *Conflict Resolution*: Institutional liberalism emphasizes the role of international institutions in facilitating peaceful conflict resolution. Efforts by organizations like the Organization for Security and Cooperation in Europe (OSCE) to mediate and monitor the ceasefire in eastern Ukraine are consistent with this perspective. These institutions provide a forum for dialogue and negotiation.

ii. *Soft Power & Diplomacy*: Institutional liberalism recognizes the value of soft power and diplomacy in international relations. Ukraine's engagement with international organizations and adherence to international norms can enhance its global standing and diplomatic efforts, potentially leading to greater support for its reconstruction efforts.

iii. *Infrastructure Rebuilding*: Reconstructing damaged infrastructure, including roads, bridges, schools, hospitals, and utilities, is a crucial step in post-war reconstruction. These efforts aim to restore normalcy and improve living conditions for the affected population.

iv. *Humanitarian Aid*: Providing humanitarian assistance to internally displaced persons (IDPs) and vulnerable populations is essential. This includes food, shelter, medical care, and psychosocial support.

v. *Housing and Shelter*: Rebuilding homes and providing shelter solutions for those who lost their residences during the conflict is a significant challenge. Housing reconstruction programs are often central to post-war recovery.

vi. *Economic Recovery*: Stimulating economic recovery and job creation is vital for rebuilding the affected regions. This can involve supporting local businesses, offering microloans, and attracting investments. International financial institutions, such as the International Monetary Fund (IMF) and the World Bank, can play a vital role in providing financial support and technical expertise for economic reconstruction efforts in Ukraine. This support can help stabilize the economy, promote investment, and rebuild infrastructure.

vii. *Security and Demining*: Ensuring the security of the population is crucial. Efforts to clear landmines and unexploded ordnance are essential to prevent further casualties and enable safe return and resettlement of IDPs.

viii. *Reconciliation & Social Cohesion*: Promoting social cohesion and reconciliation among different ethnic and religious groups is vital for long-term stability. This may involve initiatives to foster dialogue and understanding.

ix. *Governance & Rule of Law*: Strengthening governance structures and the rule of law helps restore public confidence and ensure accountability in post-conflict areas. International institutions can help establish and reinforce norms and rules related to conflict resolution, human rights, and governance. In Ukraine's case, international organizations and agreements can provide a framework for addressing issues like the rights of internally displaced persons (IDPs), the protection of minority rights, and the peaceful resolution of disputes with Russia.

x. *Democratic Governance and Human Rights*: Institutional liberals often advocate for the promotion of democratic governance and the protection of human rights. International institutions can encourage Ukraine to uphold democratic principles, strengthen the rule of law, and protect the rights of all its citizens, including those in conflict-affected areas.

xi. *International Assistance*: International organizations, governments, and NGOs often play a critical role in supporting post-war reconstruction efforts through financial aid, technical expertise, and resources. Institutional liberals emphasize the importance of international institutions and organizations in providing humanitarian aid and financial support to countries in need. Ukraine has received assistance from various international actors, including the United Nations, the European Union, and the World Bank, to help address the humanitarian and economic challenges resulting from the conflict.

xii. *International Coordination*: International institutions can facilitate coordination among donor countries, humanitarian agencies, and NGOs involved in Ukraine's reconstruction. This coordination helps ensure that aid is effectively delivered and that resources are used efficiently.

xiii. *Education and Healthcare*: Rebuilding the education and healthcare systems is essential for the long-term well-being of the population. Schools, universities, and healthcare facilities need to be restored or rebuilt.

xiv. *Psychological Support*: Many individuals who have experienced conflict may suffer from trauma and other mental health issues. Providing psychological support and counseling services is essential for their recovery.

WTO: The Russian Federation has been a member of the WTO since August 22, 2012. The five permanent members have the right to veto the original resolution.

The five permanent members are China, France, Russia, the United Kingdom, and the United States. The war in Ukraine is causing immeasurable human suffering. At the same time, it poses another major challenge to the global economy (WTOa, 2023). The war has reduced trade growth, but to a much lesser extent than we originally feared. In October 2021, the WTO projected that trade in goods would grow by 4.7% in 2022 (WTOb, 2023). the worst-case scenarios predicted for food prices and security at the outset of the war have not yet materialized. Instead, the initial impacts have been contained, thanks in part to the openness of the multilateral trading system and the transparency and commitments it requires of its members. This demonstrates that resilience is ultimately best ensured by promoting deeper and more diverse international markets based on open and predictable trade rules (WTOa, 2023).

World Bank: According to the World Bank, Ukraine's GDP shrank by 35 % in 2022, and it is projected that by October 2023, the share of the population with income below the national poverty line will rise to nearly 60 %. To date, the World Bank has mobilized over $23 billion in emergency assistance to Ukraine, of which $20 billion has been disbursed. This includes grants, guarantees, and related parallel financing from the United States, the United Kingdom, European countries, and Japan. According to recent World Bank estimates, the cost of reconstruction and recovery in Ukraine has now grown to $411 billion, more than twice the size of Ukraine's prewar economy in 2021 (The World Bank, 2023).

IMF: On Tuesday, February 21, 2023, IMF Managing Director Kristalina Georgieva said after her visit to Kyiv, "I saw an economy that works, despite enormous challenges." (IMF, 2023). On March 31, 2023, the IMF Executive Board approved $15.6 billion under a new Extended Fund Facility (EFF) for Ukraine as part of an overall $115 billion support package. Ukraine's program, supported by EFF, aims to anchor policies that maintain fiscal, external, price, and financial stability and support economic recovery, while improving governance and strengthening institutions to promote long-term growth related to post-war reconstruction and Ukraine's path to EU accession. Approval of the EFF is expected to mobilize substantial concessional financing from international donors and Ukraine's partners to help resolve Ukraine's balance of payments problem, achieve medium-term external sustainability, and restore debt sustainability on a forward-looking basis in both a baseline and downside scenario (IMF, 2023).

UNDP: In April 2022, UNDP Ukraine and the Restart Ukraine consortium launched a joint initiative to collect and analyze innovative solutions for post-war reconstruction:

- analyzing different local housing solutions
- cooperation with the rubble management
- documenting intangible impacts
- exploring forward-looking approaches to community development
- joint planning programs for planning
- mapping and assessment of tangible and intangible damage
- temporary infrastructure for the displaced
- removal, recycling, and reuse of debris
- provision of improved living conditions in towns and villages,
- cooperation on the tangible and intangible heritage of the pre- and post-war period,
- rethinking urban and rural planning of destroyed settlements to make them more resilient and, above all, to put people first,
- funding by building on existing mechanisms and creating new ones,
- involving all stakeholders and civil society to ensure a people-centered approach in all phases of post-war reconstruction.

EBRD: According to recent EBRD estimates, Ukraine's recovery will require an additional $50 billion per year from abroad, mainly foreign private investment (EBRD, 2023; Bennett, 2023). Historical experience confirms this: At least 7 out of 10 war-torn countries needed to be at peace for at least 25 years after the war to achieve long-term growth, and only 3 out of 10 countries achieved satisfactory growth rates (i.e., at least as much as before the war) within 5 years of post-war recovery (Mac Sweeney, 2009; Mills & Fan, 2006; Peschka, 2011). The EBRD report is clear: to achieve Ukraine's recovery target within five years of the ceasefire, a growth rate of more than 14 % would be required, i.e., an average GDP of about $225 billion (in constant prices), starting from $150 billion in 2022. Private investment would certainly be the most important source. Before the war, investment was essentially financed by savings, and in 2010–21 capital inflows amounted to 3 % of GDP. One of the first things the war hits is credibility, i.e., foreign direct investment. Experience shows that Central and Eastern European countries, which suffered from investment weakness in the early 2000s, were boosted by FDI. However, the question is how to absorb higher levels of investment without the necessary governance structures that translate into efficiency, speed, transparency, and control of procedures. Only foreign financing can narrow the gap between needed investment and weak domestic savings, estimated at 20 % of GDP or $50 billion per year (EBRD, 2023; Kappner et al., 2022). Moreover, the private sector provides not only the inflow of capital, but also expertise, know-how, and cost efficiencies, in all areas of infrastructure: from the primary sector (agricultural machinery) and energy to transport, energy, and municipal infrastructure. One thing is the sine qua non: the shielding of political and economic institutions, because bureaucracy and corruption thrive in an institutional vacuum. As it turns out, the EBRD's pledge of more than EUR 3 billion in additional investment in Ukraine over the 2022–2024 period is just the beginning (Chupkin & Kóczán, 2022; Gorodnichenko et al., 2022; Kappner et al., 2022, World Bank, the Government of Ukraine, the EU and the UN, 2023).

European Commission: The European Commission's actions are supported by various national and international stakeholders (European Commission, 2023). A call for proposals for three projects has already been announced: two for the reconstruction of Ukraine and one for skills development in sustainable construction. The calls for Reconstruction of Ukraine are part of the "Phoenix" initiative announced in February by Commissioner Virginijus Sinkevičius and are funded by the LIFE programme. The aim of ^{3}cPhoenix^{3}d is to tap into and make available to Ukrainian cities the cutting-edge expertise of the New European Building Community (NEB) in the field of affordable and sustainable reconstruction. The initiative also brings Ukrainian cities together with like-minded cities in the EU to share experiences on their path to carbon neutrality and greater energy efficiency. Two LIFE projects will support cities in identifying and implementing a holistic, sustainable city planning approach, including innovative effective solutions and support for the rapid reconstruction of destroyed or damaged infrastructures and facilities. They will focus on sustainable and circular (re)construction including waste management, the reuse of debris resulting from damage and destruction, or the management of hazardous waste. They will also cover water treatments, including decontamination. They will build on mappings and strategies previously financed by European funds.

In parallel, another LIFE project will contribute to the NEB Academy, which aims to develop, foster, and increase skills for sustainable construction. The project will contribute to mapping skilling initiatives on sustainability in the construction ecosystem, with a focus on bio-based materials and circularity, test pilot projects on using sustainable materials for construction (focusing on wood and other biomaterials), and promote skill-sharing initiatives. This call was particularly relevant in the context of the European Year of Skills. It will help develop the NEB Academy and develop training on sustainable construction, circularity, and bio-based materials to accelerate the transformation of the construction sector.

At the same time, there is a call by the New European Bauhaus to map already existing learning materials and possible contributions to the NEB Academy. This call was opened until 25 April. The New European Bauhaus (NEB) is an environmental, economic, and cultural project launched by President von der Leyen in the State of the Union in 2020. NEB focuses on community building and bottom-up approaches to implement the European Green Deal by promoting beautiful, sustainable, and inclusive places, products, and services. Only two years after its launch, the NEB has grown into a movement with an active and growing community of more than 1,000 members from a wide variety of sectors (e.g., education, construction, and fashion) operating across all EU Member States and beyond (Bason et al., 2020; Rosado-García et al., 2021).

Since the start of the Russian war of aggression against Ukraine, the NEB community has shown readiness to support Ukrainians, always with the approach of combining, as much as possible, emergency actions with longer-term needs in the country. A total funding of €3 million is available for the projects announced today, in addition to €8 million under existing LIFE funding for the NEB, for which similar proposals could also be eligible.

European Investment Bank (EIB): According to Gelsomina Vigliotti, Vice President of the European Investment Bank (EIB), $14 billion is needed as Ukraine's most urgent priority in 2023, and we need to focus on investments that cannot wait until the end of the war. We must address these needs and support the economy to avoid further damage. So far, the EIB has lent €2 billion to utilities and infrastructure projects, such as hospitals and educational facilities, and is ready to support Italian partners looking to invest in reconstruction. There will be roads and railways to be reopened, actions for drinking water, sanitation systems, and resources to ensure private-sector development. We need to ensure a continuous flow through Ukraine' (European Investment Bank, 2023).

Black Sea Economic Cooperation (BSEC): A similar assessment by the Black Sea Economic Cooperation (BSEC): The Ukrainian grain crisis changed everything, and the Russian blockade of Ukrainian grain exports highlighted the importance of the region in the agricultural (food) sector. In the field of trade, Turkish trade with Russia and Ukraine alone is estimated to exceed 40 billion dollars per year. For the BSEC, Ukrainian reconstruction is not a limited focus of economic strategy, but a pole of expanded economic cooperation, which in turn will boost economic growth and reduce conflict. Strong economic cooperation refers to the stability, security, and strength of institutions, that is, society, involving not only the countries of the region, but also the European Union and the United States (Aligica, 2023; Józwiak et al., 2023).

International Ukraine Recovery Conference: On 21–22 June 2023, the international Ukraine Recovery Conference -one of the most important initiatives, which had set, from its very first session, the Lugano Principles for the reconstruction of Ukraine in four key areas of reforms–economy, environment and energy, society, and governance–will address the issue.

According to the Lugano Principles, the recovery process must have seven characteristics to sustain and enhance the mobilization of the private and public sectors (URC, 2022):

i. should be based on cooperation of the Government of Ukraine with international organizations and states, based on needs and priorities assessment, rational planning, accountability for financial flows, and effective coordination (partnership),

ii. should focus on faster and deeper reforms in a broader context (reform focus),

iii. be characterized by transparency and accountability to Ukraine's society, with strengthening of the rule of law (fair & transparent funding),

iv. should be a product of collective effort with democratic participation of society (democracy),

v. should encourage the participation of all stakeholders: private sector, public sector, local government, academia & local government,

vi. should encourage the participation of both genders, respecting human rights and aiming at reducing all kinds of discrimination (inclusive & gender equal process)

vii. and should be sustainable, as defined by the UN principles.

J.P. Morgan: On February 9, the Prime Minister of Ukraine Denys Shmyhal and representatives of the Ministry of Economy of Ukraine met with partners from the United States banking holding J.P.. Morgan. The main topic of the meeting was to discuss the most prospective investments in Ukraine. Results of the meeting between the Ministry of Economy and J.P. Morgan was signing a Memorandum of Understanding (Ukraine Invest, 2023). During the meeting, Denys Shmyhal noted that Ukraine needed investment for reconstruction and post-war growth, and the government did everything possible to create a favorable investment environment. 'The Cabinet of Ministers of Ukraine has a special office "UkraineInvest," which is currently supporting eight major projects for USD 1.35 billion to the following areas: the agricultural sector, digital technologies, energy, natural resources, and of course, infrastructure reconstruction' (Izzeldin et al., 2023).

Italy-Ukraine Bilateral Conference: According to Italian Prime Minister Georgia Meloni, investing in the reconstruction of Ukraine is not a foolhardy investment but one of the most prudent and far-sighted investments that can be made at this time. Italy will play a leading role as it takes over the rotating presidency of the G7. Reaffirming her commitment to Ukraine, Meloni also proposed that Italy host the Ukraine Recovery Conference in 2025. "Italy has played a key role in supporting Ukraine's accession to the EU. We will remember this", said Denis Shmyhal, Prime Minister of Ukraine, while Foreign Minister Dmytro Kuleba stressed that contacts between the Italian and Ukrainian governments are "more dynamic than ever". On the Italian side, Foreign Minister and Deputy Prime Minister Antonio Tajani said that "Italy wants to be at the forefront, to lay the foundations for reconstruction." Approximately 600 Italian companies were present at the event to share their expertise with their Ukrainian counterparts. The idea of the Italian government involved as many companies as possible in the preliminary phase. Of course, Kyiv must continue with REFORMS to ensure its legality and transparency. Economy Minister Giancarlo Giorgetti announced Italy's contribution of €100 million to the EIB's EU for Ukraine guarantee fund.

2nd International exhibition & conference ReBuild Ukraine: On 14–15 November 2023, the 2nd International exhibition & conference ReBuild Ukraine took place for funding recovery projects, materials, technologies, equipment, and investments required to rebuild Ukraine's war-torn economy, with an emphasis on infrastructure, industry, energy, and housing. The general trend remained to provide housing and reconstruction solutions quickly to meet the immediate and urgent needs of the population. At the same time, there is also a need to fully engage all stakeholders in the recovery process to make it more sustainable, and to ensure that all material and immaterial dimensions of recovery are included, such as those related to trauma, people's hope for their future homes, as well as environmental aspects (e.g., green recovery, zero waste cities). Failure to fully integrate could lead to "temporary" unsustainable solutions and the opportunity for people-centered reconstruction could be missed!

Epilogue

In the case of the Post-War Reconstruction of Ukraine, all four characteristics (as described by Keohane & Nye in the 1970s) that differentiate institutionalism from realism apply to Post-War Reconstruction:

i. complex linkages that create channels of interconnection between actors and non-state actors, as in any development activity of international and European institutions,

ii. there is no hierarchical preference for issues under negotiation on the basis of state interests (contrary to what realism advocates), since all issues are equally important for Post-War Reconstruction, as is confirmed by the UNDP's categorization of projects under funding,

iii. there is no distinction between high and low politics, contrary to what realism advocates with its emphasis on security issues,

iv. the limitation of military force is the means by which a policy is determined.

Using logic from historical institutionalism, John Ikenberry argues that institutions may be highly durable, in particular to rebuild order after wars, for at least five reasons:

a. They strengthen their expectations of future behavior.

b. They build coalitions, routines, and connections between actors, creating incentives for continuity.

c. They lead to spillovers, as other forms of cooperation are built around existing institutions.

d. High start-up costs prevent actors from setting up challenging institutions.

e. Learning effects create incentives for actors to stick with existing institutions (Ikenberry, 2001: 23). In this sense, the functioning of the institutions is "the sum of available best practice. It awards societies the opportunity to have integrated peacebuilding that connects the ending of violence with wider social, political, and economic developments. Moreover, it offers ideas (democracy, pluralism, and liberalism) that should guard against conflict recidivism" (Mac Ginty & Richmond, 2007: 497).

"Nothing great in the world has ever been accomplished without passion." The reconstruction of Ukraine is based on the passion of people of many nationalities, which is why it will succeed, largely with the help of international and European organisations.

4. Trade, Development Aid & Democracy

The EU Approach

There is no effective economic diplomacy without democratic values, and this in the EU is at the core of european political and economic integration itself: political stability and trust, democratic governance, civil society engagement, accountability, and transparency, form the pillars of effective EU development aid (Haas, 1978; Vogelgesang, 1979; Snow, 2020; Papastamou, 2022). Even where the EU engages with non-democratic countries, this is to facilitate humanitarian assistance in times of crisis and to strengthen democratic reforms. This assistance can include food, shelter, medical care, and support for vulnerable populations.

The EU also provides development assistance to support economic and social development in non-democratic countries. This aid can be directed towards projects aimed at reducing poverty, improving healthcare, education, and infrastructure, and promoting sustainable development (Luong & Weinthal, 1999; Rose & Mishler, 2002). Vietnam is a one-party state, but it has received development assistance from the EU to support its economic and social development efforts, including poverty reduction and education (Sicurelli, 2017). The EU has supported various development projects in Tajikistan, a country with a semi-authoritarian political system, to address issues like education, water resource management, and infrastructure (Fumagalli, 2007; Boonstra & Shapovalova, 2012).

The EU engages with non-democratic countries through diplomacy to address various issues, including regional stability, conflict resolution, and the promotion of human rights and democratic values. Diplomatic efforts can involve negotiations, dialogue, and mediation. The EU has provided development assistance to Belarus to support civil society, promote human rights, and enhance economic opportunities (Bosse, 2012).

Economic interests often play a significant role in the EU's engagement with non-democratic countries: trade agreements and economic cooperation can be used to promote economic growth, investment, and job creation. The EU has provided development assistance to Uzbekistan in areas such as education, healthcare, and governance reforms (Hall, 2007; Ismailov & Jarabik, 2009; Tsereteli, 2018).

The EU may engage with non-democratic countries to address security challenges, such as counterterrorism efforts and the prevention of the proliferation of weapons of mass destruction. For example, China is a one-party state, and the EU has engaged with China on security matters, including discussions on regional stability, arms control, and counterterrorism cooperation (Pavlićević, 2022). Also, the EU has been involved in diplomatic efforts to address security concerns related to North Korea's nuclear program and regional stability (Frank, 2002; Lee, 2005; Pardo, 2017). The EU, along with other international partners, has engaged with Iran to address security challenges related to Iran's nuclear program and regional conflicts in the Middle East (Batmanghelidj & Hellman, 2018). Several countries in Central Asia have non-democratic political systems. The EU engages with these countries on various security issues, such as counterterrorism, border security, and regional stability (Luong & Weinthal, 1999; Fumagalli, 2007; Boonstra & Shapovalova, 2012; Tsereteli, 2018).

Climate change and environmental issues are global challenges that require international cooperation. The EU may work with non-democratic countries to address climate change, reduce greenhouse gas emissions, and promote environmental sustainability. The EU has provided development assistance to Cuba, focusing on areas such as agriculture, renewable energy, and sustainable development (Tvevad, 2017).

The EU often engages with non-democratic countries to manage migration flows and address refugee and asylum-related issues, particularly if the countries are sources of migration or transit routes. The EU's approach to migration management often includes a combination of measures, such as financial support, capacity building, and diplomatic dialogue. These efforts aim to reduce irregular migration, improve border control, and address the humanitarian aspects of migration, while also promoting cooperation and addressing the root causes of migration. The specifics of engagement with each country can vary depending on the country's role in the migration route and the nature of the challenges involved:

i. *Turkey:* The EU has a migration deal with Turkey, which plays a crucial role in controlling the flow of migrants and refugees into the EU. This agreement involves financial support to Turkey, among other measures, in exchange for its cooperation in managing migration.

ii. *Libya:* Libya is a key transit country for migrants attempting to reach Europe. The EU has been involved in efforts to support Libya in improving border control and addressing the humanitarian and security aspects of migration.

iii. *Niger:* Niger is a transit country for migrants traveling through the Sahel region. The EU has engaged with Niger to strengthen border management and combat human trafficking along migration routes.

iv. *Morocco:* The EU collaborates with Morocco on migration issues, including border control, and has provided financial support to address the challenges posed by migration in the region.

v. *Algeria:* Algeria is involved in efforts to manage migration flows in the Mediterranean region, and the EU has engaged with Algeria on issues related to border security and combating irregular migration.

vi. *Egypt:* Egypt has been involved in efforts to address migration challenges, especially in the context of the Mediterranean route, and the EU has worked with Egypt on border control and humanitarian assistance.

vii. *Tunisia:* The EU has engaged with Tunisia on migration issues, supporting the country in managing its borders and addressing the economic and social aspects of migration.

viii. *Western Balkan Countries:* Several countries in the Western Balkans have been important transit points for migrants heading to the EU. The EU has worked with these countries to enhance border security and manage migration flows.

Also, the EU may collaborate with non-democratic countries on public health issues, especially in the context of global health crises like pandemics. The specific objectives and methods of engagement can vary depending on the situation and the country in question. The EU has provided development assistance to Myanmar (Burma) with a focus on improving healthcare, education, and promoting peace and reconciliation (Marchi, 2014).

While humanitarian assistance is a key aspect of the EU's engagement with non-democratic countries, it is just one part of a broader range of interactions and policy goals aimed at addressing various challenges and promoting the EU's interests and values. The application of clear criteria for assessing human rights in the exercise of economic diplomacy, with the help of political experience and technology, is the great stake of EU integration (Youngs, 2012; Von Soest & Grauvogel, 2015; Börzel, 2017; Sicurelli, 2017; Zimmer & Obuch, 2022).

Background of a Difficult Policy Triptych

The promotion of democracy, development assistance, and economic diplomacy in Europe have all evolved into interrelated facets of the EU's foreign policy. The EU, a significant player on the international stage, is aware of the significance of using its economic might to advance democratic ideals and aid in recipient nations' sustainable development.

European Economic Diplomacy is the term used to describe the EU's diplomatic efforts to advance and defend its economic interests abroad. In order to increase its competitiveness, support its member states, and influence global economic governance, the EU uses trade, investment, and other economic tools in its economic diplomacy. The establishment of the European External Action Service (EEAS), which includes EU delegations, and "the new EU competence for foreign direct investment under the Treaty of Lisbon have provided the Union with the instruments to establish a distinct self in economic diplomacy" (Bouyala Imbert, 2017).

a. *The European External Action Service* (EEAS) was officially established in December 2009 as a result of the Treaty of Lisbon. Its creation aimed to streamline the EU's external relations, improve coordination among member states, and enhance the EU's ability to act as a unified actor in international affairs. In its initial years (2010s) the EEAS faced several challenges, including establishing itself as a coherent and effective institution. It had to strike a balance between representing EU interests and respecting the sovereignty of member states in foreign policy matters. The EEAS played a significant role in managing various international crises, including the Ukraine crisis, the Arab Spring, and the conflict in Syria. It coordinated the EU's response, including sanctions, diplomatic efforts, and humanitarian aid. The EEAS expanded the EU's diplomatic network with the opening of new EU Delegations worldwide. This increased the EU's presence and influence in various regions. The EEAS has developed several strategic frameworks and initiatives, such as the Global Strategy for the European Union's Foreign and Security Policy in 2016, which aimed to provide a common vision for EU foreign policy. The EEAS will need:

➢ to adapt to emerging global challenges, including cybersecurity threats (to adapt to the use of digital tools and social media in diplomacy and public outreach), climate change, migration issues, and the changing global balance of power,

➢ to gain its strategic autonomy in foreign and security policy since the EU has already expressed the desire to enhance its role. This involves a more assertive role for the EEAS in shaping the EU's independent foreign policy and security initiatives,

➢ to play a pivotal role in coordinating efforts to deepen integration in various areas, including defense and security, such as the Permanent Structured Cooperation (PESCO) in defense,

➢ to continue to foster and strengthen partnerships with other countries and regional organizations. This includes working closely with the United Nations, NATO, the African Union, and other international entities,

➢ to remain central in managing international crises, whether they involve conflicts, humanitarian emergencies, or public health crises like pandemics,

➢ to continue to play a role in the EU's enlargement process and the European Neighborhood Policy, working to stabilize and strengthen relations with neighboring countries.

The EEAS has evolved since its establishment and is likely to continue adapting to the changing global landscape. Its role in shaping the EU's foreign policy, managing crises, and building partnerships remains crucial, and it will likely face new challenges and opportunities in the years ahead as the EU seeks to assert itself as a global actor (Van Vooren, 2011; Spence, 2012; Duke, 2013; Vanhoonacker & Pomorska, 2013; Dür & Gastinger, 2023; Keukeleire & Delreux, 2022).

b. *The new EU competence for foreign direct investment* covers the conclusion of international investment agreements (IIAs), which typically aim to protect and/or liberalize foreign direct investment. Since then, the EU has ratified protection IIAs (or provisions in trade agreements) with Canada, Singapore and Vietnam. Early on, concerns were raised as to the specific EU competence. Opinions requested from the Court of Justice of the EU (CJEU) established that the EU had neither exclusive competence in portfolio international investments (which, unlike direct investments, provide limited control over a firm) nor in the investor-state dispute settlement (ISDS) mechanism – two domains covered by EU protection IIAs. EU Member State approval on these provisions was therefore needed. Moreover, to tackle stakeholders' general misgivings about the ISDS system – currently based on arbitral tribunals and perceived by some as insufficiently transparent and predictable – the EU is actively contributing to the multilateral talks to reform the current system, the objective being to establish a fully-fledged "multilateral investment court" with an appeal tribunal and its own judges. Furthermore, EU Member States have protection IIAs with other Member States in place (intra-EU IIAs), which envisage arbitral ISDS mechanisms. However, the CJEU ruled in 2018 that arbitral decisions between Member States are incompatible with EU law, and most Member States have agreed to terminate their intra-EU IIAs, raising major stakeholder concerns; the European Commission has launched an initiative to address these with a proposal for a regulation. Finally, the EU implemented Regulation (EU) 2019/452, which became fully operational on October 11, 2020. This regulation sets up a mechanism for the screening of FDI that could affect the security or public order of EU member states. While it didn't grant the EU full competence over FDI, it did enable closer coordination and information sharing among member states. The FDI screening regulation encouraged EU member states to cooperate and exchange information about foreign investments. Member states could review and potentially block foreign investments on grounds of security or public order, and they were encouraged to notify each other and the European Commission about these decisions. The European Commission plays a facilitating role in the investment screening process. It can issue opinions on FDI cases that may affect security or public order in multiple EU member states. While the Commission's opinions are non-binding, they can influence member state decisions. It was anticipated that the EU might continue to expand its competence in the field of FDI. Discussions on a common EU approach to FDI were ongoing, and the EU could potentially develop more comprehensive policies in the future.

Economic diplomacy has evolved over time to encompass the promotion of the EU's ideals and tenets, including democracy, human rights, and sustainable development (Petitville, 2003).

c. *Promoting democracy* has been a major goal of the EU's foreign policies: fostering democratic governance is a key objective that leads to peace, stability, and development (EPRS, 2018, 2019; Gómez et al., 2016). The promotion of democracy includes a variety of initiatives, such as backing free and fair elections, fortifying institutions, empowering civil society, and advancing the rule of law.

   i. *Democratic Conditionality*: The EU often links its cooperation, trade agreements, and financial assistance to democratic conditionality. It means that countries seeking closer ties or financial support from the EU are expected to uphold democratic principles, including holding free and fair elections, respecting human rights, and ensuring the independence of the judiciary.

   ii. *European Neighbourhood Policy*: The EU's European Neighbourhood Policy (ENP) focuses on promoting stability and democracy in neighboring countries. It aims to create a ring of well-governed countries that share common values with the EU. The ENP involves various tools and initiatives to support political and economic reforms in partner countries (Smith, 2005; Barbé & Johansson-Nogués, 2008; Browning & Joenniemi, 2008; Haukkala, 2008; European Commission, 2015).

iii. *Democracy Support Instruments*: The EU provides financial and technical assistance to civil society organizations, election monitoring missions, and programs aimed at strengthening democratic institutions. This support helps to build and sustain democratic processes in partner countries.

iv. *Rule of Law and Human Rights*: The EU places a strong emphasis on the rule of law and human rights in its foreign policy. It conducts regular dialogues with countries to address human rights abuses and advocates for the protection of fundamental freedoms worldwide.

v. *Election Observation Missions*: The EU frequently deploys election observation missions to monitor and report on the conduct of elections in various countries. These missions help ensure transparency, fairness, and the integrity of electoral processes.

vi. *Conflict Prevention*: The EU's promotion of democracy is closely linked to conflict prevention efforts. By supporting democratic governance and inclusive political systems, the EU aims to reduce the risk of conflicts and instability.

vii. *Support for Civil Society*: The EU recognizes the vital role of civil society organizations in promoting democracy. It provides funding and support to these organizations, enabling them to advocate for democratic reforms, human rights, and social justice.

viii. *Multilateral Engagement*: The EU collaborates with international organizations, such as the United Nations and the Organization for Security and Cooperation in Europe (OSCE), to advance democracy and strengthen global governance.

ix. *Sanctions and Diplomacy*: In cases where democracy is under threat or violated, the EU may resort to diplomatic pressure, sanctions, and other measures to encourage democratic transitions and protect democratic values. The EU often combines sanctions with diplomatic efforts, political dialogue, and engagement in an attempt to achieve its policy objectives, which may include promoting human rights, resolving conflicts, and upholding international law:

- Russia: The EU has imposed sanctions on Russia in response to its actions in Ukraine, including the annexation of Crimea and ongoing conflict in eastern Ukraine. Sanctions have also been applied in relation to issues such as the poisoning of Russian opposition figures.
- Belarus: The EU has imposed sanctions on Belarus in response to its contested presidential election in 2020 and the subsequent crackdown on opposition figures, journalists, and protesters.

- Iran: Sanctions have been used against Iran in the past in response to its nuclear program. However, the EU, along with other world powers, has also engaged in diplomatic efforts, such as the Joint Comprehensive Plan of Action (JCPOA), to address concerns about Iran's nuclear activities.
- North Korea (Democratic People's Republic of Korea): The EU has implemented sanctions in line with United Nations Security Council resolutions aimed at countering North Korea's nuclear and missile programs.
- Syria: The EU has imposed sanctions on the Syrian government and individuals associated with it in response to human rights abuses and the ongoing conflict.
- Venezuela: The EU has used sanctions in response to political and human rights crises in Venezuela.
- Myanmar (Burma): Sanctions and other measures have been applied in response to the military coup in Myanmar and subsequent human rights abuses.
- China: The EU has adopted measures related to human rights concerns, particularly in relation to the situation in Xinjiang and Hong Kong. These measures have included sanctions and diplomatic pressure.
- Turkey: The EU has used diplomatic pressure and sanctions in response to issues such as human rights concerns and disputes over territorial waters in the Eastern Mediterranean.

d. According to the European Commission's European Development Policy, *development aid* is a vital part of the EU's foreign policy and is crucial in tackling global issues, decreasing poverty, and fostering sustainable development. The EU is one of the world's largest providers of development assistance, and it has a comprehensive approach to addressing global development challenges.

   i. *Humanitarian Assistance*: The EU provides humanitarian aid to countries facing crises, including natural disasters, armed conflicts, and public health emergencies. This aid helps save lives, alleviate suffering, and provide essential services to affected populations.
   ii. *Poverty Reduction*: A primary goal of the EU's development aid is poverty reduction. Through various programs and initiatives, the EU works to improve living conditions, access to education, healthcare, and economic opportunities for vulnerable populations in developing countries.
   iii. *Sustainable Development*: The EU aligns its development aid with the United Nations Sustainable Development Goals (SDGs). It supports projects and policies aimed at addressing climate change, protecting the

environment, and promoting sustainable economic growth in partner countries.

iv. *Gender Equality*: The EU emphasizes gender equality and women's empowerment in its development efforts, funding programs that promote women's rights, access to education, and economic opportunities for women and girls.

v. *Good Governance*: Development aid often comes with requirements for partner countries to strengthen governance, promote the rule of law, combat corruption, and improve public administration. These efforts contribute to political stability and better development outcomes.

vi. *Support for Civil Society*: The EU provides funding and support to civil society organizations in partner countries. These organizations play a crucial role in advocating for human rights, democratic values, and social justice.

vii. *Trade and Economic Integration*: The EU promotes trade and economic integration with developing countries through preferential trade agreements and development-focused trade initiatives. These efforts aim to boost economic growth and job creation in partner countries.

viii. *Health and Education*: The EU invests in healthcare and education projects to improve access to quality healthcare services and education in partner countries. This includes initiatives to combat diseases like HIV/AIDS, malaria, and COVID-19.

ix. *Infrastructure Development*: The EU supports infrastructure projects, including transportation, energy, and water supply, to enhance the economic development and connectivity of partner countries.

x. *Global Partnerships*: The EU collaborates with international organizations, donor countries, and non-governmental organizations to maximize the impact of its development aid. It participates in joint initiatives to address global challenges, such as humanitarian crises and climate change.

xi. *Multilateral Engagement*: The EU is a significant contributor to multilateral development organizations, including the United Nations Development Programme (UNDP) and the World Bank. It plays an active role in shaping global development policies.

The EU's development aid reflects its commitment to global solidarity, poverty reduction, and the promotion of human rights and sustainable development. It is an essential tool for advancing the EU's foreign policy objectives and contributing to global stability and prosperity.

Evolution of the Nexus

Over time, a connection has developed between European economic diplomacy, democracy, and development assistance. Initially, democracy and development assistance were considered as independent policy realms, and the majority of the EU's economic diplomacy was concentrated on trade and investment problems (Bouyala Imbert, 2017). However, the EU has progressively incorporated these elements into its foreign policies as it has come to understand the interdependencies and synergies between economic, democratic, and development goals.

Further emphasizing the EU's dedication to coherence in its exterior actions, particularly economic diplomacy and development cooperation, the Treaty of Lisbon, which came into effect in 2009, was important. As guiding principles for EU foreign policy, the Treaty recognized the promotion of democracy, the rule of law, and human rights. The EU's approach to development aid has changed as a result of the fusion of economic diplomacy and democratic principles, resulting in a more thorough and strategic engagement with partner nations. In order to be a global actor that blends economic interests with values-driven policies, the EU is committed to using its economic influence to promote democratic principles and sustainable development (European Union Global Strategy, 2016).

Since the creation of the EU's "Trade for All" trade plan in 2015, the EU has led the way in global economic interactions by emphasizing principles like openness, sustainable development, and human rights. The EU is paying more attention to difficult issues, providing more internal market access, establishing international standards and norms, and creating political alliances through trade agreements (Titievskaia, 2023). While the European Parliament is increasing its political influence on trade and foreign investment problems, unified external commercial strategy defines FDI as an EU competence.

The entire picture, though, shows a contradiction:

– On the one hand, the EU changed its border controls from standard tariffs to "defensive" tariffs, which are permitted by the WTO in the event that others apply banned measures, and this is standard practice at the international level: According to Moens and Aarup (2023), "as geopolitics and U.S.-China competition elbow their way into the picture," the European Commission "is preparing to ditch its long-held free-market ideals." Brussels' new thinking is exemplified by France's pushback against China's advantages in export sectors such as electric cars. The "European Commission is discussing whether to launch an investigation which would allow Brussels to impose additional levies, known as anti-dumping and anti-subsidy tariffs, on Chinese electric cars, in addition to other anti-China offensives. Despite risk of a Chinese backlash, conviction is growing that Brussels shouldn't just grumble about unfair trading practices, but also take practical action against them" (Moens & Aarup, 2023).

- The European Union, on the other hand, is more welcoming to investment and offers greater incentives to draw capital, most recently the European Commission's proposal on June 19 to "change the way investors pay withholding tax in the European Union, to attract more cross-border trade in securities and help develop the bloc's capital market" (Strupczewski, 2023). Since only a small number of agreements have been able to be approved with Asian nations thus far, the main challenge is identifying strong allies on the international economic chessboard. China, Japan, and the Republic of Korea (South Korea) are the only three Asian nations among the EU's ten strategic allies (Carleton University & Canada-Europe Transatlantic Dialogue, 2015).

Sadly, "to date, we have seen a lack of leadership and coherence in the 'external component' of European Economic Diplomacy, resulting in confusion and inefficiency" (Rudloff & Laurer, 2016).

Six significant obstacles face European economic diplomacy, whose resolution will influence the direction of the EU's major programs among other things:

1. Increasing agreement complexity
2. The gimmick of bilateralism and new protectionism
3. Participation and openness among a new generation of
4. Trade Accords
6. Emerging Powers
6. Avoiding collapse and new protectionism

Therefore, there is a pressing need for a shared, unambiguous, and complete vision with regard to the expansion of the European business community's global footprint, which will help to boost market share for European businesses and, in turn, growth and employment at home.

European Econoomic Diplomacy and Development Aid

According to the European Commission (2018), the EU has become a major contributor to international efforts to fight poverty and advance sustainable development. It is dedicated to achieve the Sustainable Development Goals (SDGs) of the United Nations and actively participates in international development cooperation, all while upholding democracy, human rights, good governance, and environmental sustainability. Key ideals and principles support European economic diplomacy in development assistance, including the advancement of democracy, human rights, the rule of law, social inclusion, gender equality, and environmental sustainability.

In order to ensure the relevance and efficacy of assistance measures, the EU strongly emphasizes the ownership and partnership approach and works closely with recipient nations (Góra et al., 2020). The EU uses a range of economic diplomacy tools, including trade-related assistance, technical cooperation, capacity building, financial assistance, and policy discussion, to support development aid.

In order to encourage inclusive economic growth, increase trade and investment, and advance sustainable development in partner nations, the EU makes use of its economic clout and influence (European Union External Action, 2021). In the context of development aid, trade and investment are essential elements of European economic diplomacy. The EU promotes trade as a catalyst for economic growth and the eradication of poverty by giving developing nations preferential access to its markets. It also assists partner nations in strengthening their trade capacities, addressing trade barriers, and improving trade infrastructure.

In its economic diplomacy regarding development aid, the EU places a strong emphasis on policy coherence for development (PCD) (European Commission, 2019). By ensuring that all EU policies, including those pertaining to trade, agriculture, the environment, and migration, are consistent with the overarching goal of reducing poverty and promoting sustainable development, PCD works to ensure that the EU as a whole. PCD seeks to maximize synergies for beneficial development results while minimizing any potential negative effects of EU policies on developing nations.

The EU's commitment to promote democratic principles, sustainable development, and poverty reduction is reflected in economic diplomacy via development aid. The EU works to provide a comprehensive and cogent approach to development cooperation by integrating economic, political, and social factors. The EU strives to promote inclusive growth, support democratic governance, and advance sustainable development in partner countries through its economic diplomacy instruments and focus on trade and investment (Marková, 2019; Justinek, 2023).

The Case for Democracy

The promotion of democratic norms and principles is a key component of European economic diplomacy (Killian, 2021). Democracy is viewed by the EU as a core virtue that supports both its internal governance and external relations.

The Treaty on European Union, which highlights the promotion of democracy, human rights, and the rule of law as essential objectives of the EU's external activities, is one of the legal frameworks that upholds the EU's commitment to democracy.

European economic diplomacy often incorporates conditionality measures, which link economic cooperation, trade, and financial assistance to the adherence to democratic principles (Bergeijk et al., 2011). The EU uses conditionality to encourage recipient countries to uphold democratic norms, respect human rights, and implement governance reforms. Conditionality mechanisms aim to incentivize democratic practices and hold governments accountable for their commitments,

Through the negotiation and implementation of association agreements with adjacent countries and the accession procedures for candidate nations, European economic diplomacy: – helps the promotion of democracy. These agreements and procedures offer a framework for expanding political and economic cooperation, as well as for enacting democratic reforms, bolstering institutions, and adhering to EU norms and standards. They also actively support democratic institutions, civil society organizations, and government agencies. The EU supports groups in the civil society sector that fight to advance democracy, human rights, and good governance with financial support, capacity building, and technical support. The EU also supports the growth and reinforcement of democratic institutions, electoral systems, and the rule of law, and invests in institutional capacity building.

European economic diplomacy engages in negotiations and political discussion with partner nations to advance democratic governance. With the goal of addressing democratic difficulties, exchanging best practices, and promoting political reforms, the EU participates in dialogue with governments, civil society, and other stakeholders. The EU uses diplomatic channels to promote democratic principles, voice concerns about human rights abuses, and assist democratic transitions. This includes a variety of programs designed to strengthen democracy and improve democratic governance and civic engagement. In order to support democratic changes, electoral processes, independent media, and the empowerment of underprivileged communities, these programs offer financial resources, technical skills, and forums for knowledge sharing. Such initiatives support inclusive democratic behaviors and the building of democratic institutions.

Focusing on advancing democracy through economic diplomacy shows how committed the EU is to democratic values as crucial elements of its external relations. The EU works to promote democratic reforms, improve democratic governance, and assist democratic transitions in partner countries by utilizing economic means and applying a variety of approaches. The EU's integrated strategy for advancing democratic ideals both inside and outside of its borders is highlighted by the merger of economic diplomacy and democracy promotion.

Policy Recommendations

1. To maintain consistency with the goals of development assistance and democracy promotion, strengthen Policy Coherence for Development (PCD) across all EU programs: a complex and multifaceted task that involves ensuring that all EU policies and initiatives contribute to the overarching goals of poverty reduction and sustainable development in partner countries (Picciotto, 2005; Barry et al., 2010; Carbone, 2013; Forster & Stokke, 2013; Carbone & Keijzer, 2016; Siitonen, 2016; Sianes, 2017). How to enhance PCD within the European Union?

   - *Political Commitment and Leadership*: High-level political commitment is crucial. EU leaders and decision-makers should champion the cause of PCD, emphasizing its importance in achieving the EU's development objectives.
   - *Legal and Institutional Frameworks*: Develop and enforce legal and institutional frameworks that require all EU policies and programs to undergo a PCD assessment. Ensure that PCD becomes an integral part of EU policymaking.
   - *Impact Assessment and Ex-ante Analysis*: Conduct thorough PCD impact assessments for all proposed EU policies, including trade, agriculture, environment, and security, before implementation. Identify potential positive or negative effects on development goals.
   - *Mainstreaming* PCD: Integrate PCD considerations into the design and implementation of all EU policies, rather than treating it as a separate and optional process.
   - *Inter-Institutional Cooperation*: Foster cooperation and coordination between different EU institutions, including the European Commission, European Parliament, and Council of the EU, to ensure PCD is consistently applied.
   - *Capacity Building and Training*: Provide training and capacity-building programs for EU officials and policymakers on PCD principles and methods to help them understand and apply PCD in their respective areas.

- *Monitoring and Accountability*: Establish mechanisms to track and evaluate the impact of EU policies and programs on development goals. Hold EU institutions accountable for delivering on PCD commitments.
- *Stakeholder Engagement*: Involve civil society organizations, development partners, and experts in the PCD process to provide diverse perspectives and expertise.
- *Data and Research*: Invest in research and data collection to better understand the impact of EU policies on development and to inform PCD assessments.
- *Policy Coherence Dialogues*: Conduct regular dialogues and consultations with partner countries to align EU policies with their development priorities. Engage in policy coherence dialogues at both bilateral and multilateral levels.
- *Policy Flexibility*: Be open to adapting policies when necessary to align with development goals, particularly in rapidly changing global contexts.
- *Communication* and Awareness: Raise awareness about PCD among EU citizens, policymakers, and stakeholders to build public support for coherent development policies.
- *Consistency with International Commitments*: Ensure that EU policies and actions are consistent with international agreements and commitments related to development, such as the Sustainable Development Goals (SDGs) and the Paris Agreement on climate change.
- *Learning and Best Practices Sharing*: Encourage knowledge-sharing and exchange of best practices within the EU and with other international actors that are working on PCD.
- *Flexibility for Least Developed Countries* (LDCs): Provide flexibility and tailored approaches for the Least Developed Countries to ensure that EU policies do not hinder their development progress.

Achieving policy coherence for development across all EU programs is an ongoing and evolving process that requires dedication, political will, continuous monitoring and adaptation, and collaboration among various stakeholders within and outside the EU to ensure that development remains a central focus of EU policymaking.

2. Strengthening democratic conditionality in aid for development initiatives is essential to ensure that development assistance supports democratic governance, human rights, and the rule of law in recipient countries (Stokke, 1995;

Smith, 1998; Zanger, 2000; Montinola, 2010; Koch, 2015; Bodenstein & Faust, 2017; Hackenesch, 2019).

- *Clear and Transparent Criteria*: Develop clear and transparent criteria for democratic conditionality in EU aid programs. These criteria should include benchmarks related to free and fair elections, respect for human rights, freedom of the press, and the independence of the judiciary.
- *Regular Assessments*: Conduct regular assessments of the political and human rights situation in recipient countries to determine their eligibility for EU aid. These assessments should be based on objective and credible information, and they should involve input from civil society organizations and local stakeholders.
- *Consultation with Civil Society*: Engage with civil society organizations, including local NGOs and human rights defenders, to gather information and perspectives on the state of democracy and human rights in recipient countries. Civil society can play a crucial role in monitoring and advocating for democratic reforms.
- *Gradual Approach*: Consider adopting a gradual approach to democratic conditionality. This means that countries with better democratic records receive more aid, while countries with poor records face reductions or suspensions of aid until they make improvements.
- *Technical Assistance*: Provide technical assistance and capacity-building support to strengthen democratic institutions in recipient countries. This can include support for electoral commissions, parliaments, civil society, and the media to ensure they can fulfill their roles effectively.
- *Dialogue and Diplomacy*: Engage in diplomatic dialogue with recipient countries to discuss concerns related to democratic backsliding or human rights violations. Use diplomatic leverage and incentives to encourage democratic reforms.
- *Conditionalities in Agreements*: Embed democratic conditionality clauses in aid agreements, trade agreements, and partnership agreements with recipient countries. Clearly specify the consequences of non-compliance with democratic standards.
- *Sanctions and Incentives*: Consider using targeted sanctions, such as travel bans or asset freezes, against individuals or entities responsible for undermining democracy or committing human rights abuses. Conversely, provide positive incentives for countries that make progress in democratic reforms.

- *Support for Independent Media*: Support independent media and journalism in recipient countries to ensure that citizens have access to reliable information and diverse viewpoints.
- *Civil Society Strengthening*: Allocate funding to strengthen the capacity and resilience of civil society organizations working on democracy and human rights. This includes supporting organizations that monitor elections, promote civic education, and advocate for political reforms.
- *Coordination with International Partners*: Coordinate efforts with other international donors and organizations to maximize the impact of democratic conditionality. Collaborative action can exert more significant pressure for positive change.
- *Public Awareness and Engagement*: Educate the public in EU member states about the importance of democratic conditionality in development aid. Building public support for these principles can help sustain political commitment.
- *Regular Review and Adaptation*: Periodically review and adapt democratic conditionality measures to respond to evolving political situations and challenges in recipient countries.

Strengthening democratic conditionality in EU aid for development initiatives requires a holistic and flexible approach that considers the specific context of each recipient country. It aims to incentivize and support democratic reforms while ensuring that development aid aligns with democratic values and principles.

3. Assist democratic institutions and civil society groups in their efforts to advance democracy, human rights, and civic engagement. These efforts contribute to promoting good governance, strengthening the rule of law, and ensuring respect for human rights in partner countries (Raik, 2006; Lane, 2010; Fagan, 2011; Kurki, 2011; Sanchez Salgado, 2014; Fiedlschuster, 2016):

- *Financial Assistance*: The EU can allocate funding to support democratic institutions, such as electoral commissions, parliaments, and judiciaries, as well as civil society organizations working on democracy and human rights. These funds can be used for capacity-building, training, and operational expenses.
- *Technical Assistance*: Provide technical expertise and know-how to help democratic institutions operate effectively and transparently. This includes assistance in conducting free and fair elections, improving legislative processes, and enhancing the independence of the judiciary.

- *Civic Education*: Support programs that promote civic education and political literacy among citizens. These programs help people understand their rights, participate in the democratic process, and engage with government institutions.
- *Election Monitoring*: Support local and international election monitoring missions to ensure the integrity of electoral processes. These missions help detect irregularities and ensure that elections are conducted fairly.
- *Media Freedom*: Advocate for and support media freedom and pluralism. Assist in the development of independent and professional media outlets, journalism training programs, and initiatives to combat disinformation and promote media literacy.
- *Civil Society Capacity-Building*: Strengthen the capacity of civil society organizations (CSOs) to operate effectively, advocate for policy change, and engage with government institutions. This includes providing training on advocacy, fundraising, and project management.
- *Networking and Collaboration*: Facilitate networking and collaboration among civil society groups, enabling them to share experiences, strategies, and best practices for advancing democracy and human rights.
- *Legal Reforms*: Support legal reforms that enhance the protection of human rights, freedom of expression, and the rights of civil society. Advocate for legal frameworks that enable CSOs to operate without undue restrictions.
- *Advocacy and Lobbying*: Encourage and support CSOs in their advocacy efforts to hold governments accountable, promote transparency, and advocate for democratic reforms.
- *Access to Information*: Advocate for and support the adoption of laws and mechanisms that provide citizens with access to government information, fostering transparency and accountability.
- *Gender Equality*: Promote gender equality and the participation of women and marginalized groups in the political process. Support programs that empower women to engage in politics and decision-making.
- *Conflict Prevention*: Invest in conflict prevention and resolution efforts to address political tensions and disputes peacefully, thereby preserving democratic institutions and processes.
- *Dialogue and Consultation*: Foster dialogue and consultation between governments, civil society, and other stakeholders to address political challenges and promote national reconciliation when necessary.
- *Protection of Human Rights Defenders*: Advocate for the protection of human rights defenders and provide support for their safety and well-being.

– *Monitoring and Evaluation*: Establish mechanisms to monitor and evaluate the impact of support programs on democracy, human rights, and civic engagement to ensure effectiveness and accountability.

By assisting democratic institutions and civil society groups in their efforts, the EU can contribute to building resilient democracies, upholding human rights, and promoting civic engagement in partner countries. These efforts align with the EU's commitment to democracy, peace, and stability both within and beyond its borders.

4. Encourage inclusive and participatory governance approaches that incorporate minority communities, women, youth, and underrepresented groups in decision-making (Armstrong, 2006; Skelcher & Torfing, 2010; Cortright et al., 2017; Bekemans, 2018). These activities increase openness, responsibility, and public participation in decision-making, promote a setting that upholds democratic ideals and encourage sustainable growth:

– *Transparency*: The EU promotes transparency by making a wide range of information accessible to the public. This includes publishing legislative proposals, meeting agendas, and minutes of meetings held by EU institutions. The EU also maintains a public register of lobbyists to ensure that decision-makers are accountable for their interactions with interest groups.

– *Citizen Engagement*: The EU encourages public participation through initiatives like the European Citizens' Initiative (ECI). The ECI allows citizens to propose legislative changes and gather support from across the EU. When an ECI collects a sufficient number of signatures, it triggers a formal response from the European Commission.

– *Consultation and Feedback*: EU institutions regularly consult with stakeholders, including civil society organizations, businesses, and citizens, to gather input on policy decisions. They seek feedback during the policy-making process to ensure that a broad range of perspectives is considered.

– *Open Data*: The EU promotes the use of open data, making various datasets available to the public. This supports transparency and enables citizens, businesses, and researchers to access and utilize valuable information for various purposes, including innovation and accountability.

– *Access to Justice*: The EU ensures that citizens and organizations have access to justice when they believe their rights have been violated. This includes the right to appeal decisions made by EU institutions and the ability to bring cases before the European Court of Justice.

- *Environmental and Sustainability Initiatives*: The EU places a strong emphasis on sustainability and environmental protection. It has established policies and regulations aimed at addressing climate change, protecting biodiversity, and promoting sustainable development. These policies often involve public consultations and stakeholder engagement.
- *Economic Governance*: The EU promotes responsible economic governance through mechanisms like the European Semester. This process involves coordination of economic and budgetary policies among member states and includes a public consultation phase to gather input on country-specific recommendations.
- Civil Society Support: The EU provides financial support to civil society organizations that work to promote democracy, human rights, and civic engagement. Funding programs like the European Instrument for Democracy and Human Rights (EIDHR) aim to strengthen the role of civil society in decision-making processes.
- *Rule of Law Mechanism*: The EU has established a mechanism to monitor and address threats to the rule of law in member states. This mechanism reinforces the importance of upholding democratic values and the independence of the judiciary.
- *Education and Awareness*: The EU supports educational programs and campaigns to raise awareness about democratic principles, European values, and civic participation. Initiatives like the European Year of Citizens aim to foster a sense of belonging and active citizenship among EU citizens.

5. Developing Mainstream Democracy: Make ensuring that democratic government, human rights, and social inclusion are prioritized in development programs and humanitarian operations. Include technical help and capacity building to improve democratic institutions, elections, and the rule of law (Santiso, 2002; Perlin, 2003; Börzel & Risse, 2004; Schimmelfennig, 2007; Baracani, 2008):

- *Funding & Grants*: The EU can allocate funds and provide grants to support democratic reforms and capacity-building initiatives. This financial assistance can be channeled to government agencies, civil society organizations, and other relevant stakeholders to strengthen institutions and electoral processes.
- *Training & Workshops*: The EU can organize training programs, workshops, and seminars for government officials, election administrators, judges, and civil society actors. These sessions can focus on topics such as election management, human rights, and rule of law principles. The

EU's capacity building initiatives are often carried out through various financial instruments, including the European Development Fund (EDF), the European Neighbourhood Instrument (ENI), and the Development Cooperation Instrument (DCI). The specific countries and programs supported can change over time based on evolving development priorities and objectives, as well as the needs of partner countries:

➢ *African, Caribbean, and Pacific* (ACP) *Countries*: The EU provides capacity building support to ACP countries through the European Development Fund (EDF) and other development programs. This assistance often includes areas such as governance, institutional strengthening, education, healthcare, and economic development.

➢ *Eastern Partnership Countries*: The EU supports capacity building efforts in the Eastern Partnership countries (Armenia, Azerbaijan, Belarus, Georgia, Moldova, and Ukraine) to enhance governance, the rule of law, and economic development.

➢ *Western Balkans*: The EU offers capacity building assistance to the countries in the Western Balkans to support their progress towards European integration. This includes areas such as public administration reform, justice, and security sector reform.

➢ *Sub-Saharan Africa*: The EU provides capacity building support to various countries in sub-Saharan Africa, including initiatives focused on education, health, agriculture, and sustainable development.

➢ *Middle East & North Africa*: The EU supports capacity building efforts in the Middle East and North Africa region to address a range of issues, including governance, civil society development, and economic reforms.

➢ *Asia and the Pacific*: The EU engages in capacity building programs in countries across Asia and the Pacific, with a focus on areas such as education, environmental sustainability, and trade capacity building.

➢ Latin America & the Caribbean: The EU provides capacity building assistance to countries in Latin America and the Caribbean to promote inclusive and sustainable development, including areas like climate change resilience and social cohesion.

– *Technical Expertise*: The EU can deploy technical experts and advisors to partner countries to provide on-the-ground support and expertise. These experts can help design and implement reforms, improve electoral systems, and strengthen the legal framework.

- *Exchange Programs*: Facilitating exchange programs between officials and experts from different countries can be valuable for sharing best practices and experiences. The EU can organize study visits and peer-to-peer learning opportunities.
- *Legal & Constitutional Reforms*: The EU can assist in reviewing and revising legal and constitutional frameworks to ensure they adhere to democratic principles and the rule of law. This may involve helping countries draft or amend constitutions and legislation.
- *Civil Society Strengthening*: Supporting civil society organizations that work to promote democracy, human rights, and the rule of law is crucial. The EU can provide financial support, technical assistance, and capacity-building programs to empower civil society actors.
- *Election Observation Missions*: The EU can deploy election observation missions to assess the fairness and transparency of elections in partner countries. The findings and recommendations of these missions can be used to guide electoral reforms.
- *Media Development*: A free and independent media is essential for a functioning democracy. The EU can support media development initiatives, including training journalists, promoting media ethics, and ensuring media pluralism.
- *Judicial Independence*: The EU can work to enhance the independence and efficiency of the judiciary by providing training and technical assistance to judges and legal professionals. This helps ensure that the rule of law is upheld.
- *Anti-Corruption Efforts*: Corruption undermines democratic institutions and the rule of law. The EU can support anti-corruption initiatives, including the establishment of anti-corruption agencies, whistleblower protection mechanisms, and transparent procurement processes.
- *Monitoring & Evaluation*: Implementing robust monitoring and evaluation mechanisms is crucial to assessing the impact of capacity-building efforts. The EU can support partner countries in developing and implementing effective monitoring systems to measure progress.
- *Dialogue & Diplomacy*: Engaging in diplomatic efforts and dialogue with partner countries is essential to encourage democratic reforms. The EU can use diplomatic channels to advocate for democratic principles, rule of law, and respect for human rights.
- *Conditional Assistance*: The EU can link financial and technical assistance to specific benchmarks related to democratic reforms and the rule of law. This incentivizes partner countries to make meaningful changes.

- *Long-Term Engagement*: Sustainable improvements in democratic institutions and the rule of law often require long-term engagement. The EU can commit to providing continuous support and adapting its strategies as needed.

6. Trade and investment policies should be in line with democratic principles and should promote sustainable growth. Encourage ethical economic conduct, adherence to social and environmental norms, and observance of human rights in trade and investment agreements. Encourage commerce that promotes inclusive growth, job creation, and the eradication of poverty while upholding labor rights and the sustainability of the environment:

- *Trade Agreements with Social and Environmental Clauses*: The EU can negotiate trade agreements that include clauses on labor rights and environmental protection. These clauses ensure that trade partners adhere to certain labor standards and environmental regulations, promoting fairness and sustainability (Bartels, 2013; Cuyvers, 2014; Van den Putte, 2015; Gammage, 2018; Perulli, 2018; Vatta, 2018).
- *Promoting Sustainable Practices*: The EU can encourage businesses to adopt sustainable practices through certification programs, incentives, and public awareness campaigns. This can include certifications like Fair Trade or promoting sustainable supply chain management.
- *Development Assistance*: The EU can provide development assistance to support economic development and poverty eradication in less developed regions. These programs can focus on job creation, infrastructure development, and capacity building.
- *Investment in Research and Innovation*: Encouraging innovation in sustainable technologies and industries can lead to job creation and inclusive growth. The EU can fund research and innovation projects that address environmental challenges while creating economic opportunities.
- *Support for Small and Medium-sized Enterprises* (SMEs): SMEs are often significant drivers of job creation. The EU can provide financial support, access to financing, and business development services to help SMEs grow and thrive.
- *Social Entrepreneurship*: Encouraging social entrepreneurship can be a means to achieve social and environmental goals while promoting commerce. The EU can provide support for social enterprises that prioritize inclusive growth and environmental sustainability.
- *Labor Market Policies*: The EU can implement labor market policies that protect workers' rights, such as minimum wage regulations, workplace

safety standards, and fair working conditions. These policies ensure that economic growth benefits all citizens.

- *Environmental Regulation*: Strict environmental regulations and standards can promote sustainability in commerce. The EU can continue to enforce and strengthen such regulations to ensure that economic activities minimize negative environmental impacts.
- *Corporate Social Responsibility* (CSR): Encouraging businesses to engage in CSR activities that align with the EU's objectives can promote inclusive growth and environmental sustainability. The EU can provide guidance and incentives for companies to adopt responsible business practices.
- *Circular Economy*: Promoting a circular economy can reduce waste and environmental damage while creating new business opportunities. The EU can support initiatives that encourage recycling, reusing, and reducing waste in commerce.
- *Financial Instruments*: The EU can establish financial instruments and incentives that support sustainable commerce. This may include green financing, tax incentives for eco-friendly businesses, and subsidies for renewable energy projects.
- Consumer Education: Educating consumers about the importance of sustainable and ethical consumption can drive demand for responsible products and services. The EU can run campaigns to raise awareness about sustainable choices.
- *Monitoring and Reporting*: The EU can require businesses to report on their social and environmental impact, promoting transparency and accountability.
- *International Cooperation*: The EU can collaborate with international organizations and other countries to promote sustainable commerce on a global scale. This can involve sharing best practices, coordinating efforts, and advocating for sustainability in international fora.

7. Funding for development aid should be increased, especially for initiatives that support equitable development and democracy. Make sure that budgetary allocations reflect the EU's dedication to democratic principles and sustainable development goals. Utilize cutting-edge finance techniques and collaborations with other donors to mobilize more resources:

- *Innovative Financing Instruments* (Zaharioaie, 2012; Vasilescu, 2014; Migliorelli & Dessertine, 2018; Liubkina et al., 2019; Bertoldi et al., 2021):

➢ Green Bonds: Issue green bonds to finance environmentally friendly projects. These bonds attract investors interested in sustainable investments and can fund projects related to climate change, renewable energy, and environmental conservation.

➢ Social Impact Bonds: Utilize social impact bonds to fund projects that address social issues. Investors provide upfront capital, and returns are tied to the achievement of specific social outcomes, such as reducing poverty or improving educational outcomes.

➢ Blended Finance: Combine public and private sector funding to finance development projects. The EU can partner with private investors, development banks, and philanthropic organizations to pool resources and share risks.

➢ Venture Capital & Startup Funding: Foster innovation and economic growth by investing in startups and technology companies through venture capital funds. This can stimulate entrepreneurship and create jobs while attracting private capital.

➢ Blockchain & Cryptocurrency: Explore the use of blockchain technology and cryptocurrencies for fundraising and financial transactions. These technologies can enhance transparency, reduce transaction costs, and attract a new generation of investors.

– *Strategic Partnerships and Collaborations*:

➢ Multilateral Institutions: Collaborate with international organizations such as the United Nations, World Bank, and International Monetary Fund to coordinate resources and maximize impact on global issues like poverty eradication and climate change.

➢ Public-Private Partnerships (PPPs): Develop partnerships with private sector companies to jointly invest in infrastructure projects, innovation, and sustainable development initiatives.

➢ Development Banks: Work closely with regional and national development banks to co-finance projects and leverage their expertise in financing development activities.

➢ Philanthropic Foundations: Partner with philanthropic foundations that share similar goals to pool resources and expertise for projects related to healthcare, education, poverty alleviation, and environmental conservation.

➢ Local and Regional Governments: Collaborate with subnational governments to support decentralized development initiatives and share the financial burden of large-scale projects.

- *Technical Assistance and Capacity Building*:
  ➤ Provide technical assistance to help countries and organizations access and effectively utilize financial resources. This can involve capacity building in project design, proposal writing, and financial management.
  ➤ Offer training programs for financial institutions and organizations to improve their ability to structure and manage complex financing arrangements.

- *Impact Measurement and Reporting*:
  ➤ Develop rigorous impact measurement and reporting frameworks to demonstrate the effectiveness of EU-funded initiatives. This can attract more investors and donors who are interested in evidence-based outcomes.
  ➤ Utilize technology, data analytics, and artificial intelligence to assess and report on the impact of projects in real-time.

- *Policy Advocacy and Diplomacy*:
  ➤ Advocate for favorable global and national policies that support innovative financing and resource mobilization efforts and promote regulatory environments that encourage private sector investment and philanthropy.
  ➤ Engage in diplomatic efforts to secure commitments from other countries and regions to support shared development goals.

- *Knowledge Sharing and Best Practices*:
  ➤ Share knowledge and best practices with other donors and organizations to promote the adoption of innovative financing techniques and collaboration models.
  ➤ Establish platforms for dialogue and knowledge exchange to foster a community of practice in resource mobilization.

8. Create effective monitoring & evaluation systems to determine how European economic diplomacy affects the provision of aid for development and the advancement of democracy (Crawford, 2004; Kusek & Rist, 2004; Segone, 2008; Boehmer & Zaytsev, 2019). Evaluate frequently how well policies, programs, and conditionality measures are working to promote democracy and sustainable development. Make use of evaluation results to enhance upcoming programs and policies:

- *Clear Evaluation Framework*: Develop a clear and comprehensive evaluation framework for each program or policy from the outset. This should include well-defined objectives, key performance indicators (KPIs), and measurable outcomes.

- *Independent Evaluation*: Conduct evaluations independently or with the involvement of external evaluators to ensure objectivity and impartiality. Independent evaluations can provide more reliable and credible results.
- *Regular and Ongoing Evaluation*: Implement a culture of ongoing evaluation rather than just post-implementation assessments. Regular monitoring and formative evaluations can provide timely feedback for program adjustments.
- *Utilize Mixed Methods*: Employ a mix of qualitative and quantitative evaluation methods to capture both quantitative data and the nuanced context and experiences of program beneficiaries and stakeholders.
- *Engage Stakeholders*: Involve stakeholders, including policymakers, program implementers, beneficiaries, and civil society organizations, in the evaluation process. Their input can provide valuable perspectives and insights.
- *Timely Reporting and Dissemination*: Ensure that evaluation results are reported in a timely manner. Transparency in sharing findings is essential for accountability and learning.
- *Adaptive Management*: Embrace adaptive management principles, which involve making mid-course corrections based on evaluation findings. Adjust policies and programs as needed to improve effectiveness and achieve desired outcomes.
- *Cross-Program Learning*: Encourage cross-program learning by sharing evaluation results and best practices across different EU programs and policies. This can help identify successful strategies that can be applied elsewhere.
- *Capacity Building*: Invest in the capacity of EU institutions and member states to conduct evaluations effectively. Ensure that staff have the necessary skills and resources to carry out high-quality evaluations.
- *Feedback Mechanisms*: Establish feedback mechanisms for program beneficiaries and stakeholders to provide input on evaluation findings and recommendations. This can help ensure that the evaluation process is inclusive and responsive.
- *Learning Networks*: Foster learning networks and communities of practice within the EU and among member states. These networks can facilitate the exchange of evaluation experiences and knowledge.
- *Strategic Use of Evaluation Results*: Develop a strategy for how evaluation results will be used to inform policy decisions and program design. Ensure

that there is a clear link between evaluation findings and subsequent actions.

– *Continuous Improvement*: Emphasize a commitment to continuous improvement. Use evaluation results not only to fix problems but also to identify opportunities for innovation and excellence.

– *Accountability Mechanisms*: Establish accountability mechanisms to ensure that action is taken based on evaluation recommendations. Hold relevant actors responsible for implementing changes.

– *Evaluation of the Evaluation Process*: Regularly evaluate the effectiveness of the EU's own evaluation processes and mechanisms. This includes assessing the quality of evaluations, the relevance of their scope, and the timeliness of their implementation.

9. To advance democracy and development aid, foster global cooperation with international organizations, regional organizations, and other donors (Mehtap, 2014; Derlukiewicz et al., 2020). To maximize the impact of democratic governance projects and ensure complementarity, combine efforts, exchange best practices, and pool resources.

– *Strategic Planning & Coordination*:
   i. Establish Clear Objectives: Clearly define the objectives of democratic governance projects to ensure alignment with the EU's broader policy goals.
   ii. Coordinate Across Institutions: Promote coordination among different EU institutions, including the European Commission, European Parliament, and the Council of the EU, to avoid duplication of efforts and ensure coherence in policy and project design.

– *Stakeholder Engagement*:
   i. Engage Civil Society: Involve civil society organizations, including non-governmental organizations (NGOs) and community-based groups, in the planning and implementation of projects. They often have valuable grassroots knowledge and can mobilize local support.
   ii. Consult Member States: Collaborate closely with EU member states to ensure that national-level initiatives complement EU projects and vice versa. Member states can provide insight into local contexts and help bridge the gap between EU policies and local implementation.

– *Pooling Resources*:
   i. Multi-Funding Mechanisms: Create multi-funding mechanisms that allow different EU institutions, member states, and external partners

to contribute to a common fund for democratic governance projects. This pooling of financial resources can increase the scale and impact of initiatives.

ii. Leverage External Partnerships: Collaborate with external partners, including international organizations and donor countries, to share the financial burden and maximize the available resources for democratic governance projects.

– *Knowledge Sharing & Best Practices*:
  i. Establish Learning Networks: Create networks and platforms for the exchange of best practices, lessons learned, and expertise among EU institutions, member states, and implementing partners.
  ii. Knowledge Repository: Develop a centralized repository for storing and sharing project documentation, research, and reports. This can facilitate access to valuable information and experiences.

– *Capacity Building*:
  i. Train Project Teams: Provide training and capacity-building programs for project teams, civil servants, and local partners involved in democratic governance projects. This ensures that they have the necessary skills to implement initiatives effectively.
  ii. Support Local Capacity: Invest in building the capacity of local organizations and institutions in partner countries to ensure that they can take ownership of democratic governance projects in the long term.

– *Monitoring & Evaluation*:
  i. Standardized Metrics: Develop standardized monitoring and evaluation frameworks with clear indicators to assess the impact of democratic governance projects. This allows for consistent assessment and comparison of outcomes.
  ii. Regular Reporting: Require regular reporting from implementing partners to track progress and identify areas for improvement. Make evaluation results publicly accessible to promote transparency.

– *Flexibility & Adaptation*:
  i. Adaptive Management: Embrace adaptive management principles, allowing for adjustments in project design and implementation based on ongoing monitoring and evaluation results.
  ii. Responsive to Local Needs: Ensure that projects are responsive to the specific needs and priorities of the target countries and populations. Flexibility in design can enhance relevance and impact.

- *Advocacy & Diplomacy*:
  i. Advocate for Democratic Values: Use diplomatic channels and advocacy efforts to promote democratic values and practices in partner countries. Work diplomatically to address challenges to democratic governance.

- *Long-Term Commitment*:
  i. Sustained Engagement: Recognize that promoting democratic governance is a long-term endeavor. Commit to sustained engagement and support, beyond the duration of individual projects, to consolidate democratic gains.

- *Public Awareness & Communication*:
  i. Communication Strategy: Develop a communication strategy to raise awareness among EU citizens about the importance of democratic governance projects and the impact they have on global stability and prosperity.

These policy suggestions can help European economic diplomacy efficiently advance development assistance while upholding democratic ideals. This all-encompassing strategy will support democratic governance, enable inclusive growth, and foster social progress while also helping to meet sustainable development goals.

5. Organizing Competitive Postgraduate Programs on Economic Diplomacy

The Discipline

International relations studies as an academic discipline began to take shape in the early 20th century. The field emerged in response to the changing global political landscape and the need to understand and analyze international issues.

1. *The Treaty of Westphalia (1648)*: While not the formal beginning of international relations as a field of study, the Treaty of Westphalia is often cited as a foundational event in the development of modern state-centric international relations. The treaty played a crucial role in shaping the principles of state sovereignty and non-interference in the domestic affairs of other states, which are fundamental concepts in the study of international relations. It ended the Thirty Years' War in Europe and the Eighty Years' War between Spain and the Dutch Republic. It consisted of a series of agreements, including the Peace of Westphalia and the Peace of Osnabrück, which were signed in the Westphalian cities of Münster and Osnabrück. These agreements helped establish a new European order and contributed to the emergence of the modern state system, where states were recognized as sovereign entities with the authority to govern their own territories without interference from external powers. While the formal academic discipline of international relations emerged much later, the concepts and principles associated with the Treaty of Westphalia have had a lasting impact on the study of international relations and the organization of the global political order. Perhaps the greatest scholar of international relations at that time was Hugo Grotius (1583–1645). Though his most significant work, "The Law of War and Peace," dates back to the 17th century, Grotius's contributions to international law and the theory of just war continued to be influential in the study of international relations before World War II (Bull et al., 1990).

2. *Woodrow Wilson & the League of Nations (1919)*: As the academic field of international relations began to take shape, a few universities, primarily in the United States and Europe, started offering courses in diplomatic history and international law. These early courses laid the groundwork for the formal study of international relations. The aftermath of World War I and the establishment of the League of Nations marked a significant turning point in international relations. This period stimulated academic interest in understanding

the causes of war and the possibilities for international cooperation (Lieber, 2007; Knutsen, 2008).

3. *Interwar Period*: This era saw the emergence of international relations as a formal academic discipline, particularly in the United States and the United Kingdom. Many universities began to establish programs and departments dedicated to the study of international relations.

  i. *Oxford University* offered courses in "International Law" as part of its legal curriculum. These courses covered the principles and practices of international law, including topics like the law of nations and the legal rules governing state interactions.

  ii. *Cambridge University* had a long-standing tradition of teaching international law. Courses often covered subjects such as the laws of war, state sovereignty, and the legal aspects of diplomacy.

  iii. *The University of Paris* offered courses in diplomatic history, often focusing on the history of European diplomacy and the treaties and agreements between states. It also offered instruction in international law, examining the legal aspects of state interactions and conflicts.

  iv. *Harvard University* offered courses in "Diplomatic History" and "International Law." These courses explored the history of international relations and the legal framework governing states' interactions, respectively.

  v. *Humboldt University of Berlin* (*Humboldt-Universität zu Berlin*, Germany) offered courses in "Völkerrecht" (international law) and "Diplomatische Geschichte" (diplomatic history). These courses delved into the legal principles of international relations and the historical development of diplomacy.

  vi. The *University of Vienna* (*Universität Wien*) with its rich history in international relations studies, offered courses in "Völkerrecht" (international law) and "Diplomatische Geschichte" (diplomatic history), which explored the legal and historical aspects of international relations.

  vii. St. Petersburg State University (Санкт-Петербургский государственный университет, Russia): Russian universities like St. Petersburg State University offered courses on diplomatic history and international law, with a focus on the Russian perspective and its interactions with other European states.

Before the outbreak of World War II, several notable scholars and thinkers made significant contributions to the field of international relations. While the formal academic discipline of international relations as we know it today was still emerging during this period, these individuals laid the groundwork for the study of international politics and diplomacy. Some famous scholars and thinkers of international relations before World War II include:

i. **Hans Morgenthau** (1904–1980): A German-American political scientist, Morgenthau is often considered one of the founders of the realist school of international relations. His work, "Politics Among Nations: The Struggle for Power and Peace," is a classic in the field and emphasized the importance of power and state interests in international relations.

ii. **E.H. Carr** (1892–1982): An influential British scholar, Carr is known for his book "The Twenty Years' Crisis," in which he critiqued the prevailing idealist views of international relations and argued for a more realist understanding of power and national interest.

iii. **Alfred Zimmern** (1879–1957): Zimmern, a British scholar, made significant contributions to international relations theory, emphasizing the role of ethics and morality in international politics. His work helped shape discussions on the ethical dimensions of foreign policy.

iv. **Sir Norman Angell** (1872–1967): An English author and lecturer, Angell gained prominence for his book "The Great Illusion," in which he argued that modern economic interdependence made war among major powers irrational. His work contributed to the debate on the causes of war and the role of economic factors in international relations.

v. **Woodrow Wilson** (1856–1924): While primarily known as the 28th President of the United States, Wilson played a pivotal role in the development of international relations through his advocacy for the League of Nations and the promotion of the idea of self-determination and collective security.

vi. **Ivy Lee** (1877–1934): Lee is considered one of the pioneers of public relations and communication in international affairs. He advised both governments and corporations on how to manage their public image and communicate with foreign audiences.

These scholars and thinkers, among others, helped shape the early intellectual foundations of the study of international relations. Their works and ideas continue to be influential and relevant in contemporary discussions about global politics, diplomacy, and international cooperation.

4. *Formation of the United Nations (1945)*: The end of World War II and the establishment of the United Nations further solidified the importance of international relations as a field of study. It also highlighted the need for

research and analysis to support international diplomacy and cooperation. Many universities adapted their programs to address the needs of a world order that required expertise in international diplomacy, global politics, and international organizations.

5. *Cold War Era (1947–1991):* The Cold War between the United States and the Soviet Union, along with the complex web of international alliances and conflicts that characterized this period, provided rich material for the study of international relations. It also led to significant growth in academic programs and research in the field. Universities around the world developed specialized courses and research programs on topics such as nuclear deterrence, regional conflicts, and superpower diplomacy.

6. *Post-Cold War Era* (1991 onward): The end of the Cold War opened new avenues for research and inquiry in international relations. It marked the beginning of a more complex and multipolar international system, with new challenges and opportunities for scholars to explore. Universities incorporated topics like transnational actors, economic globalization, human rights, and environmental issues into their programs. In the latter half of the 20th century, there was a growing trend toward an interdisciplinary approach to international relations education. Many universities integrated insights from political science, economics, sociology, and other disciplines into their international relations programs.

Numerous scholars made significant contributions to the discipline during this time. Here are some famous scholars of international relations from that era:

i. **Hans J. Morgenthau** (1904–1980): Although Morgenthau was mentioned earlier in the context of pre-World War II scholars, his work remained influential in the post-war period. He continued to advocate for realist perspectives and authored important works such as "Scientific Man vs. Power Politics."

ii. **Kenneth Waltz** (1924–2013): Waltz is widely regarded as one of the most influential international relations scholars of the 20th century. His book "Theory of International Politics" introduced neorealism, which focused on the structural aspects of the international system and the balance of power among states.

iii. **Joseph Nye** (1937–present): Nye is known for his concept of "soft power" and his work on the changing nature of power in international relations. His book "Soft Power: The Means to Success in World Politics" is a seminal work in the field.

iv. **Robert Keohane** (1941–present): Keohane is a prominent scholar in the field of international relations, particularly known for his work on neoliberalism and the idea that international institutions can influence state behavior. He co-authored the influential book "Power and Interdependence" with Joseph Nye.

v. **Hedley Bull** (1932–1985): Bull was a key figure in the development of international relations theory, particularly with his contributions to the English School of international relations. His work on the anarchical international society and the nature of international order had a lasting impact.

vi. **Robert O. Keohane** & **Joseph Nye** (1977): Together, Keohane and Nye co-authored the widely cited article "Power and Interdependence: World Politics in Transition." Their ideas on complex interdependence and regime theory have had a significant influence on the field.

vii. **Kenneth N. Waltz** (1979): In "Theory of International Politics," Waltz introduced structural realism, which argued that the international system's structure, rather than state behavior, was the primary determinant of international outcomes.

viii. **Francis Fukuyama** (1952–present): Fukuyama's book "The End of History and the Last Man" generated significant debate by proposing that liberal democracy may represent the endpoint of mankind's ideological evolution.

ix. **Samuel P. Huntington** (1927–2008): Huntington's "The Clash of Civilizations and the Remaking of World Order" argued that post-Cold War conflicts would be characterized by cultural and civilizational differences.

x. **Susan Strange** (1923–1998): Strange made significant contributions to the field of international political economy. Her work explored the role of transnational corporations, financial markets, and the power dynamics in the global economy.

7. Today, international relations is a well-established academic discipline taught at universities worldwide. As technology played an increasingly important role in international affairs, universities began offering courses on cybersecurity, digital diplomacy, and the impact of the internet on international relations. The development of online education and massive open online courses (MOOCs) has made international relations education more accessible to a global audience, allowing students from various backgrounds and locations to study the field. Many universities incorporated practical elements into their international relations programs, offering students opportunities for internships, simulations, and experiential learning to better prepare them for

careers in diplomacy, international organizations, and other related fields. It encompasses a wide range of topics, including international diplomacy, conflict resolution, international organizations, international law, global politics, and more. The teaching of international relations continues to evolve in response to new challenges and developments in the international system. It remains a dynamic and critical field of study in universities around the world. The 21st century has seen the emergence of several influential scholars who have made significant contributions to the discipline:

i. **John Mearsheimer** (1947–present): Mearsheimer is a prominent realist scholar known for his theory of offensive realism. His work explores great power politics, security competition, and the impact of power on international relations.

ii. **Anne-Marie Slaughter** (1958–present): Slaughter has contributed to the study of international law, international organizations, and global governance. She served as the Director of Policy Planning at the U.S. Department of State and is known for her work on the concept of "networked power."

iii. **Joseph S. Nye Jr.** (1937–present): Nye, previously mentioned in the context of the late 20th century, continues to be a leading voice in international relations. He has made significant contributions to the understanding of power, soft power, and the concept of "smart power."

iv. **Robert Pape** (1960–present): Pape is known for his research on the strategic logic of suicide terrorism and the causes of conflict. His work has helped shape discussions on the motivations of non-state actors in international relations.

v. **G. John Ikenberry** (1954–present): Ikenberry has explored the liberal international order, multilateralism, and the role of international institutions. His work contributes to debates on the nature of global governance.

vi. **Martha Finnemore** (1962–present): Finnemore is a leading scholar in the field of international relations, known for her work on international norms, the social construction of international reality, and the role of non-state actors.

vii. **Barry Buzan** (1946–present): Buzan is a key figure in the development of the English School of international relations and has made significant contributions to the understanding of regional security complexes.

viii. **Robert M. Cutler** (1956–present): Cutler is an expert in the field of energy and international relations, and his work explores the geopolitics of energy, particularly in the Eurasian region.

ix. **Andrew Hurrell** (1957–present): Hurrell has contributed to the study of international relations theory, focusing on the role of great powers, global governance, and the changing dynamics of the international system.

x. **Kishore Mahbubani** (1948–present): Mahbubani is known for his work on Asian perspectives in international relations and the rise of Asia in global politics. He has explored issues of global governance and power shifts.

These scholars have made significant impacts on the study of international relations in the 21st century. Their research and ideas continue to shape discussions on global politics, international cooperation, and the evolving dynamics of the international system, and of course to inspire and guide the teaching of international relations in universities (Booth & Erskine, 2016).

Economic diplomacy, the practice of using economic tools and negotiations to achieve diplomatic goals, has been an important aspect of international relations for centuries. However, the formal academic study of economic diplomacy likely began to gain prominence in the latter half of the 20th century (Phlipot & Bartholomees, 2012; Charles & Emrouznejad, 2022; McCarthy, 2018). The exact date when economic diplomacy started being taught in universities can vary depending on the institution and country. As globalization and the interdependence of economies increased in the post-World War II era, universities and academic institutions began to recognize the need for specialized education in international economic relations and diplomacy. The establishment of academic programs and courses specifically focused on economic diplomacy might have gained traction in the 1970s and 1980s, as the world saw significant developments in international trade, finance, and negotiations. This period saw the growth of international organizations like the World Trade Organization (WTO), the increasing use of economic sanctions, and the negotiation of trade agreements. Since then, the study of economic diplomacy has likely expanded and evolved to reflect the changing landscape of global economic relations. Today, many universities around the world offer courses, programs, and degrees in international relations, economics, and diplomacy that may include elements of economic diplomacy within their curriculum.

"No need to choose between diplomacy or international business if you don't want to! The Postgraduate Flagship Programme in Economic Diplomacy and International Business is a comprehensive and highly specialised programme which prepares students for careers in both diplomacy and international

business"[6] mentioned on the website of Vrije Universiteit Brussel, Belgium, thus confirming the general trend of strengthening educational programmes combining diplomacy and business. Krems University, Austria, offers an International Business and Economic Diplomacy master's degree programme, *"giving students managerial skills that will enable them to confidently hold their own in a competitive and constantly changing environment"*[7] as mentioned on its website. Similar trend in the US, with the School of Global Policy and Strategy, UC San Diego, to offer a Graduate Program in Economic Diplomacy *"focusing on how technological changes, governance, politics and social and environmental issues all converge to form the dynamic playing field of nations and their economies."*[8]

In our days, the academic field of diplomacy focuses on a variety of topics and different approaches to conflict resolution. Students learn about cultural diplomacy; communication strategy; political, economic and psychological strategies; direction; and intelligence and counterintelligence. By 2023, in Europe, 33 master's programs in diplomacy are offered. Overall, economic diplomacy is at the top of the training list.[9]

Multidisciplinary Curriculum

Economic diplomacy is a multidisciplinary field that draws from various academic disciplines to understand and address the complex interactions between economics and international relations (van Bergeijk et al., 2018; Bokhan & Zalizniuk, 2022; van Bergeijk et al., 2011). At least eight disciplines contribute to shaping economic diplomacy:

1. **Economics**: As Susan Strange wrote: "the economics taught by the economists and the politics or international relations (and come to that the philosophy) have less and less relevance to one another, rather than more and more. Nor is any very serious attempt made from either side to relate the courses to one another. The economists do not even try to deal with the political aspects

6   https://www.vub.be/en/studying-vub/all-study-programmes-vub/bachelors-and-masters-programmes-vub/flagship-programme-economic-diplomacy-international-business

7   https://www.fh-krems.ac.at/en/study/master/part-time/international-business-and-economic-diplomacy/

8   https://gps.ucsd.edu/executive-education/economic-diplomacy/graduate-summer-program.html

9   https://www.masterstudies.com/masters-degree/diplomacy/europe

of international economic relations and international economic problems; and few political scientists even try to explore the economic dimension of international politics or diplomacy" (Strange, 1970: 313). But still, economic theory and analysis provide the foundation for understanding how economic policies, trade, investment, and financial systems influence international relations. Economists study the impact of trade agreements, economic sanctions, foreign investment, and other economic interactions on the global stage. Economics is an essential tool for diplomats engaged in economic diplomacy because it equips them with the knowledge and analytical skills needed to navigate the complex web of international economic relations, promote their country's economic interests, and contribute to global economic stability and development (Van Bergeijk et al., 2011; Gribincea & Gribincea, 2014).

i. *Fundamental Understanding*: Economics provides students with a fundamental understanding of how economies function, including the principles of supply and demand, market behavior, and economic systems. This knowledge is crucial for diplomats when engaging with other countries on economic matters.

ii. *Policy Formulation*: Economic diplomacy often involves crafting and implementing economic policies to advance a country's interests. A solid understanding of economics enables diplomats to analyze economic data, assess the impact of policies, and make informed decisions.

iii. *Trade Negotiations*: Trade agreements and negotiations are a significant component of economic diplomacy. Economics helps diplomats comprehend trade-related concepts such as tariffs, quotas, and trade balances, allowing them to negotiate effectively.

iv. *Economic Development*: Economic diplomacy frequently aims to foster economic development, both domestically and internationally. Understanding economic theories and development strategies is essential for diplomats to promote economic growth and reduce poverty in their home countries and partner nations.

v. *Financial Stability*: Diplomats must be aware of the economic challenges and vulnerabilities that can impact a nation's financial stability. Economic knowledge helps them address issues like inflation, exchange rate fluctuations, and fiscal policies.

vi. *Global Economic Trends*: Economic diplomacy involves staying abreast of global economic trends and understanding their implications. This knowledge allows diplomats to anticipate and respond to economic shifts that may affect their country's interests.

vii. *International Finance and Institutions*: Diplomats may engage with international financial institutions like the IMF, World Bank, and WTO. A background in economics is beneficial when navigating the complexities of these organizations and participating in discussions about global economic governance.

viii. *Cross-Border Investments*: Economic diplomacy often deals with foreign investments, mergers, and acquisitions. Knowledge of economics aids diplomats in assessing the potential benefits and risks associated with such activities.

ix. *Economic Soft Power*: A country's economic strength can be a source of soft power and influence on the global stage. A strong economy can enhance a nation's credibility and leverage in diplomatic negotiations.

x. *Conflict Resolution*: Economic disputes can escalate into diplomatic conflicts. Understanding economic principles can help diplomats mediate and resolve such disputes peacefully.

In the 21st century, international trade has continued to be a subject of significant research and debate. Many scholars have made important contributions to the field, advancing our understanding of the complexities of global trade, the effects of trade policies, and the impact of globalization on economies and societies. Their research, influencing, inter alia, the formation of university studies in economic diplomacy:

i. **Marc Melitz** is known for his work on international trade and the "Melitz model." His research focuses on the effects of firm heterogeneity on international trade patterns, which has had a significant impact on the field.

ii. **Giovanni Maggi** has contributed to trade theory, particularly in the areas of preferential trade agreements and the political economy of trade policy.

iii. **Pablo Fajgelbaum's** research addresses international trade, geography, and the distributional effects of trade. He has studied how trade affects the spatial distribution of economic activity.

iv. **Pol Antràs** is known for his work on the organization of firms in international trade, as well as research on the impact of globalization and offshoring on economies.

v. **Nina Pavcnik** has conducted research on the effects of trade on labor markets and poverty in developing countries, contributing to our understanding of the impact of trade on economic development.

vi. **Amit K. Khandelwal's** research focuses on topics such as international trade, firm dynamics, and the effects of trade liberalization on firms and workers.

vii. **Céline Carrère** has conducted research on trade, trade policy, and trade costs, with a particular focus on the impact of trade openness on income distribution.

viii. **Caroline Freund** has researched topics related to trade, globalization, and development. Her work addresses issues such as trade policy, economic geography, and the effects of trade on poverty and inequality.

ix. **Chad Bown** is known for his work on trade policy and trade disputes. He has contributed to our understanding of trade agreements and their effects on international trade.

x. **David Weinstein's** research spans international trade, macroeconomics, and economic geography. His work includes analyzing the role of transportation costs in shaping international trade patterns.

International finance is a dynamic field that has seen significant developments and contributions from scholars in the 21st century, equally affecting the study of economic diplomacy:

i. **Maurice Obstfeld** is a prominent economist known for his work on international finance, monetary policy, and exchange rates. He has served as the Chief Economist at the International Monetary Fund (IMF) and has made substantial contributions to the understanding of global financial markets.

ii. **Carmen Reinhart** is an economist renowned for her research on financial crises, sovereign debt, and the history of international financial markets. Her work has been influential in understanding the patterns and consequences of financial crises.

iii. **Kenneth Rogoff** is an economist and co-author with Carmen Reinhart of the influential book "This Time Is Different," which analyzes the history of financial crises. He has also made contributions to research on exchange rates and monetary policy.

iv. Nobel laureate **Eugene Fama** is known for his work on efficient markets and asset pricing. His research has implications for international finance and the pricing of assets in global markets.

v. Nobel laureate **Robert Shiller** is a leading expert on behavioral finance and asset bubbles. His research has had implications for understanding international financial markets and their inherent psychology.

vi. **Raghuram Rajan**, the former Governor of the Reserve Bank of India, has conducted research on financial crises, banking, and international finance. His work has informed discussions on the stability of the global financial system.

vii. **Atif Mian** is an economist who has researched the relationship between finance, real estate, and the macroeconomy. His work has implications for understanding financial crises and housing markets in an international context.

viii. **Mervyn King**, the former Governor of the Bank of England, has made significant contributions to the field of international finance, especially during the global financial crisis. His work on financial regulation and central banking is notable.

ix. **Olivier Blanchard**, former Chief Economist at the IMF, has conducted research on a wide range of topics in international finance, including fiscal policy, exchange rates, and international macroeconomics.

x. **Barry Eichengreen** is known for his research on international monetary systems, currency crises, and financial globalization. His work has contributed to the understanding of the international financial architecture.

2. **International Relations**: International relations provide the framework for understanding how countries interact with each other in the political and diplomatic arena. Teaching international relations to students of economic diplomacy is essential because it provides the theoretical and practical foundations needed to navigate the complex and interconnected world of diplomacy, where economic interests are just one part of a larger diplomatic landscape. Understanding the broader context of international relations enhances the effectiveness of economic diplomats in advancing their countries' economic objectives on the global stage:

i. *Contextual Understanding*: International relations provide the broader context in which economic diplomacy operates. Students learn about the political, social, and cultural factors that influence diplomatic interactions, which is crucial for crafting effective economic strategies.

ii. *Interconnectedness*: Economic diplomacy often intersects with various other international issues, such as security, human rights, and environmental concerns. A solid understanding of international relations helps students appreciate these connections and address multidimensional challenges.

iii. *Diplomatic Strategy*: Students of economic diplomacy must develop diplomatic strategies that align with a country's overall foreign policy goals. International relations education equips them with the knowledge and tools to integrate economic objectives into a broader diplomatic framework.

iv. *Negotiation Skills*: Diplomacy involves negotiation, and international relations courses typically include instruction on negotiation techniques, conflict resolution, and diplomatic communication, all of which are directly applicable to economic diplomacy.

v. *Global Governance*: Economic diplomacy often involves engagement with international organizations and institutions like the United Nations, World Trade Organization (WTO), and World Bank. International relations education helps students understand these organizations' structures, roles, and how they influence economic policies.

vi. *Understanding Geopolitical Dynamics*: Economic diplomacy frequently occurs in the context of geopolitical rivalries and alliances. International relations courses help students grasp the dynamics of power, cooperation, and competition among nations, which can inform economic decision-making.

vii. *Trade and Security*: There is often a close connection between economic interests and security concerns. Understanding international relations helps students assess the security implications of economic decisions and vice versa.

viii. *Crisis Management*: Economic crises can have diplomatic repercussions, and vice versa. International relations education equips students with crisis management skills and helps them analyze how economic crises may impact a country's diplomatic relationships.

ix. *Cultural Sensitivity*: Economic diplomats often work with individuals from diverse cultural backgrounds. International relations training fosters cultural sensitivity and cross-cultural communication skills, essential for effective diplomacy.

x. *Soft Power and Influence*: Economic diplomacy is a tool for exercising a country's soft power on the global stage. International relations knowledge enables students to appreciate how diplomacy contributes to a nation's soft power and influence.

xi. *Global Perspective*: Economic diplomacy involves dealing with a range of international actors, from developed to developing countries. A solid grounding in international relations helps students appreciate different global perspectives and interests.

3. **Political Science**: Political science contributes by examining the role of governments, political institutions, and decision-making processes in shaping economic policies and negotiations. teaching political science to students of economic diplomacy is important because it provides the theoretical and

practical knowledge necessary to navigate the complex political dimensions of economic diplomacy. A strong foundation in political science equips economic diplomats with the skills and insights needed to formulate effective strategies, assess political risks, and engage with political actors in pursuit of their country's economic interests on the global stage (Smith, 2011):

i. *Political Context*: Economic diplomacy operates within a political context. Students of economic diplomacy must understand the political systems, structures, and processes of their own country and the countries with which they interact. Political science provides the knowledge needed to navigate these political landscapes effectively.

ii. *Policy Formulation*: Economic diplomacy often involves crafting and implementing economic policies to advance a nation's interests. Political science education equips students with the tools to analyze policy options, assess their political feasibility, and understand how policies are formulated and implemented within a political system.

iii. *Political Risk Assessment*: Economic diplomats need to assess the political risks associated with economic decisions and investments. A background in political science helps students evaluate factors such as political stability, government policies, and the impact of elections on economic stability.

iv. *International Relations*: Political science is closely linked to international relations, which is a crucial component of economic diplomacy. Students learn about the dynamics of international politics, the role of international organizations, and the impact of geopolitics on economic relations.

v. *Negotiation and Diplomacy*: Political science courses often include instruction on negotiation techniques, diplomacy, and conflict resolution, which are highly relevant to economic diplomacy. These skills are essential for effective negotiation of economic agreements and resolving diplomatic disputes related to economic issues.

vi. *Understanding Political Actors*: Economic diplomats interact with a variety of political actors, including government officials, legislators, and political interest groups. Political science education helps students understand the motivations, interests, and roles of these actors in shaping economic policy.

vii. *Lobbying and Advocacy*: Economic diplomacy often involves lobbying and advocacy efforts to promote a country's economic interests. Political science provides insights into how lobbying and advocacy work within political systems and how to influence decision-makers effectively.

viii. *Public Opinion and Public Policy*: Economic diplomacy can be influenced by public opinion and public policy preferences. Political science education helps students understand how public opinion is formed and how it can impact economic diplomacy.

ix. *Global Governance*: Economic diplomacy often requires engagement with international institutions and governance structures. Political science courses introduce students to the workings of these organizations and the role they play in shaping global economic policies.

x. *Crisis Management*: Political science education includes the study of crisis management, which is valuable for economic diplomats who may need to respond to political or economic crises that affect their country's interests.

xi. *Geopolitical Analysis*: Economic diplomacy is often influenced by geopolitical factors. Political science provides tools for analyzing the geopolitical landscape and understanding how it affects economic relations and decision-making.

4. **Law**: International law and trade law play a crucial role in economic diplomacy. Teaching law to students of economic diplomacy is important because it provides the legal expertise and knowledge necessary to navigate the intricate legal aspects of economic diplomacy. Economic diplomats must understand international and domestic legal frameworks, trade and investment laws, dispute resolution mechanisms, and other legal aspects to protect their country's economic interests and ensure compliance with applicable laws and regulations (Grewe, 1999; Bolewski, 2007):

i. *Legal Frameworks*: Economic diplomacy often involves negotiations and agreements related to trade, investment, and economic cooperation. Understanding international and domestic legal frameworks is crucial for diplomats to ensure that these agreements are compliant with national and international laws.

ii. *Trade Law*: Trade is a central component of economic diplomacy. Students need a solid grasp of international trade law, including principles established by organizations like the World Trade Organization (WTO), to effectively negotiate trade agreements, resolve trade disputes, and ensure compliance with trade regulations.

iii. *Investment Law*: Economic diplomats frequently engage in discussions about foreign direct investment (FDI) and investment protection. Knowledge of international investment law and bilateral investment treaties (BITs) helps students navigate these complex issues and protect their country's economic interests.

iv. *Intellectual Property Rights*: Understanding intellectual property rights and international agreements like the Agreement on Trade-Related Aspects of Intellectual Property Rights (TRIPS) is essential for addressing intellectual property concerns in economic diplomacy, especially in industries like technology, pharmaceuticals, and entertainment.

v. *Dispute Resolution*: Economic disputes can arise in various forms, including trade disputes, investment disputes, and contractual disagreements. Knowledge of international dispute resolution mechanisms, such as arbitration and the International Court of Justice, is valuable for resolving these conflicts.

vi. *Sanctions and Export Control*: Economic diplomats must be aware of international sanctions regimes and export control laws. Compliance with these regulations is critical to avoid legal issues and maintain good diplomatic relations.

vii. *Bilateral and Multilateral Agreements*: Economic diplomacy often involves negotiating and implementing bilateral and multilateral agreements. Legal expertise is essential for drafting, interpreting, and ensuring compliance with these agreements.

viii. *Customary International Law*: Understanding customary international law is crucial for diplomats to navigate diplomatic customs, norms, and traditions that can affect economic relations.

ix. *Legal Advocacy*: Diplomats may need to advocate for their country's legal positions in international forums, such as international courts or dispute resolution panels. Legal training helps them effectively present and defend their country's legal arguments.

x. *Regulatory Compliance*: Economic diplomats need to ensure that their country's economic activities, such as exports and imports, comply with international and domestic regulations. Legal knowledge helps in navigating regulatory requirements.

xi. *Negotiation Skills*: Legal education often includes negotiation and conflict resolution techniques that are valuable in diplomatic negotiations, including those related to economic issues.

xii. *Contractual Expertise*: Economic diplomacy often involves negotiating complex contracts and agreements. Legal training equips students with the skills to draft, review, and enforce these agreements effectively.

5. **Public Policy**: Teaching public policy to students of economic diplomacy is important because it provides a holistic and practical understanding of the

policymaking process and equips diplomats with the skills and knowledge needed to formulate, evaluate, and advocate for policies that promote their country's economic interests in a complex and dynamic global environment (Melissen, 2005; Gregory, 2008; Snow, 2020):

i. *Policy Formulation*: Economic diplomacy often involves crafting and implementing policies related to trade, investment, and economic cooperation. Public policy education equips students with the tools to analyze policy options, assess their impact, and understand how policies are formulated and implemented within a government context.

ii. *Policy Evaluation*: Students learn how to evaluate the effectiveness of economic policies, trade agreements, and investment strategies, which is essential for diplomats to make informed decisions and assess the outcomes of their diplomatic efforts.

iii. *Interdisciplinary Approach*: Public policy education often incorporates elements of economics, political science, law, and other disciplines. This interdisciplinary approach is valuable for understanding the multifaceted nature of economic diplomacy.

iv. *Stakeholder Engagement*: Economic diplomacy involves engaging with a wide range of stakeholders, including government agencies, businesses, advocacy groups, and international organizations. Public policy education helps students navigate these complex stakeholder relationships effectively.

v. *Problem-Solving Skills*: Diplomats often encounter complex economic challenges that require innovative solutions. Public policy training fosters problem-solving skills and encourages students to think critically about how to address economic issues.

vi. *Analytical Tools*: Public policy courses teach students to use data and analytical tools to assess economic trends, evaluate policy options, and make evidence-based decisions, skills that are highly relevant in economic diplomacy.

vii. *Global Policy Issues*: Public policy education can cover a wide range of global policy issues, including those related to trade, development, sustainability, and technology. This broader perspective helps students understand the global context in which economic diplomacy operates.

viii. *Regulatory Understanding*: Economic diplomats need to understand regulatory environments in various countries and regions. Public policy education provides insights into regulatory frameworks and their impact on economic activities.

    ix. *Crisis Management*: Economic diplomats must be prepared to respond to economic crises and emergencies. Public policy training includes crisis management techniques and helps students analyze the implications of economic crises.

    x. *Ethical Considerations*: Public policy education often includes discussions of ethical considerations in decision-making. This knowledge is valuable for diplomats facing ethical dilemmas related to economic diplomacy.

    xi. *Communication Skills*: Diplomats must communicate effectively with various stakeholders and convey policy positions clearly. Public policy courses emphasize communication skills, which are essential in diplomatic negotiations and advocacy.

    xii. *Understanding Public Opinion*: Public policy education often examines how public opinion and public perceptions can shape policy decisions. Economic diplomats need to be aware of public sentiment in both their home country and abroad.

6. **Geography**: Geography can also play a role in economic diplomacy, as the location and physical attributes of countries can influence their economic interactions and trade patterns. Teaching geography to students of economic diplomacy is important because it provides the spatial context and insights needed to assess economic opportunities and challenges on a global scale. A solid understanding of geography allows economic diplomats to make informed decisions, optimize economic strategies, and navigate the geographical complexities that underlie economic diplomacy efforts (Henrikson, 2004; Da Vinha, 2018).

    i. *Spatial Understanding*: Geography provides students with a spatial understanding of the world, including the locations of countries, regions, and key economic hubs. This knowledge is essential for diplomats when assessing the geographic distribution of economic resources and opportunities.

    ii. *Resource Geography*: Economic diplomacy often revolves around the access and management of natural resources, such as minerals, energy, and water. Geography helps students understand the distribution of these resources and their economic significance.

    iii. *Trade Routes and Transportation*: Understanding geography is crucial for identifying and optimizing trade routes and transportation networks. Economic diplomats need to consider the geographical factors that influence trade, including proximity to markets, transportation infrastructure, and logistical challenges.

iv. *Regional Economic Blocs*: Geography plays a pivotal role in defining regional economic blocs and trade agreements. Students need to grasp the geographical boundaries and economic dynamics of regional organizations like the European Union, ASEAN, and Mercosur.

v. *Environmental* Geography: Geography encompasses environmental factors like climate, topography, and ecosystems. Economic diplomats must consider these factors when addressing environmental and sustainability issues in economic diplomacy.

vi. *Cultural Geography*: Geography is intertwined with culture and ethnicity. Understanding cultural geography helps diplomats appreciate the cultural nuances and sensitivities that can impact economic negotiations and relationships.

vii. *Border Disputes*: Geography often intersects with border disputes and territorial claims. Economic diplomats must navigate these sensitive issues when engaging in economic diplomacy, especially in regions with historical conflicts.

viii. *Global Value Chains*: Geography influences global value chains and production networks. Students need to comprehend the spatial distribution of supply chains to promote economic cooperation and investment.

ix. *Market Access*: Economic diplomats need to identify and analyze potential markets for their country's products and services. Geography helps in identifying target markets, assessing their accessibility, and understanding their economic conditions.

x. *Geopolitical Considerations*: Geography plays a critical role in geopolitics, affecting alliances, rivalries, and regional dynamics. Economic diplomats must understand these geopolitical factors that can influence economic relationships and trade agreements.

xi. *Resource Scarcity*: Geography informs diplomats about regions facing resource scarcity, which can impact trade negotiations and resource management agreements.

xii. *Infrastructure Investment*: Geography helps diplomats identify infrastructure investment opportunities, such as ports, highways, and railways, that can enhance economic connectivity and trade.

7. **Sociology & Anthropology**: Understanding cultural norms, societal values, and human behavior is essential for effective negotiations and cooperation. Teaching sociology and anthropology to students of economic diplomacy is

important because it equips diplomats with the knowledge and skills needed to navigate the complex social and cultural dimensions of international economic relations. This understanding fosters effective communication, promotes cultural sensitivity, and allows diplomats to address social issues and inequalities, ultimately enhancing the success of economic diplomacy efforts (Jazbec, 2013; Vienne & Nahum-Claudel, 2020):

   i. *Cultural Understanding*: Sociology and anthropology provide students with a deep understanding of cultures, societies, and human behavior. This knowledge is invaluable for diplomats when engaging with individuals and communities in foreign countries, as cultural sensitivity is critical in economic diplomacy.

   ii. *Social Dynamics*: Sociology and anthropology shed light on social dynamics, including issues related to class, gender, ethnicity, and social hierarchies. Diplomats need to be aware of these dynamics when addressing economic disparities and inequalities in diplomatic negotiations.

   iii. *Human Behavior*: Economic diplomacy often involves negotiations and interactions with people from various backgrounds. Understanding human behavior and social norms helps diplomats build rapport, resolve conflicts, and foster positive relationships.

   iv. *Social Impact of Economic Policies*: Diplomats must consider the social implications of economic policies and trade agreements. Sociology and anthropology help students analyze how economic decisions can affect different segments of society and address potential social consequences.

   v. *Cross-Cultural Communication*: Effective communication is a cornerstone of diplomacy. Sociology and anthropology education promote cross-cultural communication skills, enabling diplomats to convey their messages and understand the perspectives of others in culturally sensitive ways.

   vi. *Conflict Resolution*: Diplomats frequently engage in conflict resolution efforts, and sociology and anthropology provide valuable insights into the root causes of conflicts, including social, cultural, and economic factors.

   vii. *Development and Poverty Reduction*: Economic diplomacy often aims to promote economic development and alleviate poverty. Sociology and anthropology help students understand the complexities of development and how to design policies that benefit marginalized communities.

   viii. *Human Rights*: Economic diplomacy intersects with human rights issues, such as labor rights and social justice. Sociology and anthropology equip students with the knowledge to address these rights-based concerns in economic negotiations.

ix. *Social Networks*: Building and maintaining networks is essential in diplomacy. Sociology and anthropology provide tools for understanding social networks, which can be leveraged to advance economic interests.

x. *Social Impact Assessments*: Understanding the social implications of economic projects and investments is vital. Students with a background in sociology and anthropology can conduct social impact assessments to ensure that economic activities align with societal values and norms.

xi. *Cultural Diplomacy*: Diplomacy often involves promoting a country's culture and values. Sociology and anthropology provide insights into cultural diplomacy, which can enhance economic diplomacy efforts.

xii. *Local Engagement*: Economic diplomacy often involves working at the local level, whether through trade with indigenous communities or foreign direct investment in specific regions. Sociology and anthropology help diplomats engage with local communities effectively.

8. **History:** Historical context is crucial for understanding the evolution of economic relationships between countries. Teaching history to students of economic diplomacy is important because it provides the historical context, lessons, and insights necessary for diplomats to navigate the complexities of international economic relations. Understanding the historical roots of economic issues and diplomatic relationships allows diplomats to make informed decisions, learn from past experiences, and adapt strategies to the evolving global economic landscape (Schweizer & Schumann, 2008; Weisbrode, 2013; Aksoy & Çiçek, 2018).

i. *Historical Context*: History provides students with a deep understanding of the historical context in which economic diplomacy operates. Past events, conflicts, and agreements shape the present economic landscape and can influence diplomatic decisions.

ii. *Lessons from the Past*: Historical analysis allows students to learn from past successes and failures in economic diplomacy. Studying historical examples of trade agreements, economic alliances, and diplomatic negotiations can inform contemporary economic strategies.

iii. *Historical Trade Routes*: Historical knowledge helps students understand the development of trade routes, such as the Silk Road, and their impact on the global economy. This understanding is valuable for assessing the potential of emerging trade corridors.

iv. *Colonial Legacies*: Many countries have colonial histories that continue to influence economic relations. Knowledge of colonial legacies and post-colonial dynamics is crucial for understanding economic disparities and trade imbalances.

v. *Diplomatic Milestones*: History is replete with diplomatic milestones, including the signing of significant trade agreements and the establishment of international organizations like the United Nations and the World Trade Organization. Understanding these historical events is essential for diplomats.

vi. *Conflict Resolution*: Historical conflicts often have economic underpinnings. Studying the history of conflicts and their resolutions can provide insights into the economic dimensions of diplomacy and how to address them effectively.

vii. *Geopolitical Shifts*: History illustrates geopolitical shifts and the rise and fall of global powers. Economic diplomats must be aware of these historical shifts to navigate the current global economic order.

viii. *Economic Revolutions*: Historical economic revolutions, such as the Industrial Revolution and the Digital Revolution, have had profound effects on international trade and economic diplomacy. Understanding these revolutions helps diplomats anticipate economic changes.

ix. *Economic Crises*: Historical economic crises, such as the Great Depression and the 2008 financial crisis, have shaped economic policies and international relations. Knowledge of how past crises were managed informs economic diplomacy strategies during economic downturns.

x. *Bilateral and Multilateral Agreements*: Historical treaties and agreements, both bilateral and multilateral, provide lessons in diplomacy. Economic diplomats often engage in negotiations that build upon or amend these historical agreements.

xi. *Trade Patterns*: Historical trade patterns and the evolution of globalization offer insights into how trade has expanded and transformed over time. This understanding is crucial for shaping contemporary trade policies.

xii. *Cultural and Social History*: Socio-cultural history provides insight into how cultural factors and social norms have influenced economic relations and diplomatic negotiations throughout history.

Given the complexity of economic diplomacy and its intersection with various aspects of international relations, it's important for practitioners and scholars to draw insights from these diverse disciplines to formulate effective strategies and policies.

Scholars emphasize the importance of a multidisciplinary curriculum that integrates these fields to provide students with a comprehensive understanding of the intricate interactions between economics and diplomacy (Mesot, 2022; Narlikar & Watson, 2014). Such curricula ensure that graduates possess a nuanced perspective on the economic dimensions of international relations and can navigate intricate policy discussions.

Practical Skill Development

Effective economic diplomats need a combination of theoretical knowledge and practical skills to navigate the complexities of international economic relations: balancing theoretical knowledge with practical skills ensures that economic diplomats can navigate the real-world challenges of international economic relations while advancing their country's economic interests and promoting global cooperation

At least 14 key practical skills are crucial for economic diplomats:

1. **Negotiation Skills**: Diplomats must be skilled negotiators who can effectively represent their country's interests in international economic negotiations. This involves understanding the nuances of diplomatic language, cultural sensitivities, and negotiation strategies (Faizullaev, 2022). Negotiation skills are essential for promoting economic prosperity and maintaining peaceful relations in the global arena:

   i. *Achieving Diplomatic Objectives*: Economic diplomats represent their countries' interests in international economic and trade negotiations. To effectively advance their nation's goals, they must possess strong negotiation skills. These skills enable them to navigate complex negotiations and reach favorable agreements that benefit their country.

   ii. *Complexity of Economic Issues*: Economic negotiations often involve intricate issues such as trade policies, investment agreements, and economic cooperation. Negotiators need the skills to understand, analyze, and communicate these complex economic matters effectively during negotiations.

   iii. *Balancing Interests*: Economic diplomats must strike a delicate balance between protecting their country's interests and fostering international cooperation. Negotiation skills help them find common ground, build trust, and develop relationships with counterparts from other nations.

iv. *Conflict Resolution*: Disputes can arise during economic negotiations, and effective negotiation skills are essential for resolving conflicts peacefully. Skilled diplomats can find mutually acceptable solutions, preventing disputes from escalating into more significant conflicts.

v. *Maximizing Economic Benefits*: The ability to negotiate favorable trade agreements, investment terms, and economic partnerships can have a significant impact on a nation's economic well-being. Economic diplomats with strong negotiation skills are better positioned to secure advantageous deals that benefit their country's economy.

vi. *Adaptation to Changing Circumstances*: Economic conditions and global dynamics are constantly evolving. Diplomats need negotiation skills to adapt to changing circumstances and respond effectively to emerging economic challenges and opportunities.

vii. *Communication and Persuasion*: Effective negotiation is not just about making demands; it also involves persuasive communication. Economic diplomats must be able to articulate their country's position persuasively, convincing other nations to agree to terms that align with their own objectives.

viii. *Building Trust and Relationships*: Successful economic diplomacy often requires building trust and long-term relationships with foreign counterparts. Strong negotiation skills can help diplomats establish rapport and maintain productive relationships with their international counterparts.

ix. *International Norms and Protocols*: Economic diplomats need to be well-versed in international norms, protocols, and best practices related to negotiations. These skills ensure that negotiations are conducted in a manner consistent with international standards.

x. *Conflict Prevention*: Effective negotiation skills can help prevent economic disputes from escalating into larger geopolitical conflicts. By resolving economic issues through diplomacy, economic diplomats contribute to regional and global stability.

2. **Communication Skills** are a cornerstone of economic diplomacy, enabling diplomats to represent their countries effectively, build relationships, navigate negotiations, manage crises, and advocate for their nation's economic interests. These skills are indispensable for promoting economic cooperation and safeguarding national interests in the complex world of international economics and trade:

i. *Effective Representation*: Economic diplomats serve as ambassadors for their countries in international economic and trade relations. Effective communication is crucial for representing their nation's interests persuasively, accurately, and diplomatically.

ii. *Building Rapport*: Establishing and maintaining positive relationships with foreign counterparts is vital in diplomacy. Strong communication skills help economic diplomats build rapport, trust, and goodwill with their international counterparts, facilitating productive negotiations and cooperation.

iii. *Negotiation Success*: Negotiation is a core aspect of economic diplomacy. Effective communication skills, including active listening, clear articulation, and persuasive speaking, enhance the likelihood of achieving favorable outcomes in negotiations.

iv. *Crisis Management*: Economic diplomats may encounter crises or disputes during their diplomatic missions. Effective communication is essential for managing and de-escalating these situations, preventing them from spiraling into larger conflicts.

v. *Cross-Cultural Understanding*: Economic diplomacy involves interacting with individuals from diverse cultural backgrounds. Communication skills enable diplomats to bridge cultural gaps, avoid misunderstandings, and show respect for different customs and norms.

vi. *Public Diplomacy*: Economic diplomats often engage with the public, including through media interviews, public speeches, and outreach events. Effective communication skills help them convey their nation's economic policies and achievements to domestic and international audiences.

vii. *Conflict Resolution*: Economic diplomats may be involved in resolving economic disputes between nations. Strong communication skills are essential for facilitating discussions, understanding the root causes of conflicts, and finding mutually acceptable solutions.

viii. *Advocating for Policies*: Diplomats are responsible for advocating their country's economic policies and positions. Effective communication allows them to convey the benefits and rationale of these policies to foreign governments and organizations.

ix. *Information Gathering*: Economic diplomats need to gather information and intelligence related to economic and trade matters. Effective communication skills help them elicit valuable information from their contacts and sources.

x. *Diplomatic Notes and Correspondence*: Diplomatic communication often involves the exchange of official letters and notes. Precise and clear writing skills are necessary to draft diplomatic correspondence that adheres to diplomatic protocols and conveys messages accurately.

xi. *Conflict Prevention*: Diplomats can play a role in preventing economic disputes from escalating into larger geopolitical conflicts. Effective communication helps in early detection of potential issues and facilitates diplomatic interventions to prevent escalation.

xii. *Global Advocacy*: Economic diplomats may need to advocate for their country's economic policies and initiatives on the global stage. Effective communication skills enable them to engage with international organizations, forums, and conferences to promote their nation's economic agenda.

3. **Analytical Skills** are essential for economic diplomats to navigate the complexities of international economics, make informed decisions, advocate for their country's economic interests, and contribute to the formulation of effective economic policies. These skills are instrumental in promoting economic prosperity and safeguarding national interests in the global arena:

i. *Understanding Complex Economic Issues*: Economic diplomacy often involves intricate economic and trade matters. Economic diplomats need analytical skills to comprehend and dissect complex economic data, policies, and trends, allowing them to make informed decisions and recommendations.

ii. *Policy Formulation*: Diplomats play a role in shaping their country's economic policies and strategies. Analytical skills enable them to assess the potential impact of different policy options, evaluate risks, and provide evidence-based recommendations to policymakers.

iii. *Identifying Opportunities and Threats*: Economic diplomats must identify economic opportunities for their country, such as potential markets for exports or investment opportunities. Analytical skills help them assess market conditions, competitive landscapes, and potential risks, enabling informed decision-making.

iv. *Assessing Trade Agreements*: Economic diplomats are often involved in negotiating trade agreements. Analytical skills are essential for assessing the economic implications of trade deals, including their potential benefits and drawbacks, and ensuring they align with their country's interests.

v. *Economic Intelligence*: Diplomats need to gather economic intelligence and stay informed about global economic developments. Analytical skills assist them in interpreting economic data, reports, and intelligence to identify trends and emerging issues that may impact their country's economic interests.

vi. *Risk Assessment*: Economic diplomacy can involve financial, market, and geopolitical risks. Analytical skills allow diplomats to assess these risks and develop strategies to mitigate them, safeguarding their country's economic interests.

vii. *Conflict Resolution*: In cases of economic disputes, diplomats must analyze the root causes and assess the potential solutions. Analytical skills help in understanding the complexities of conflicts and devising strategies for resolution.

viii. *Monitoring Economic Performance*: Diplomats are often tasked with monitoring the economic performance of their host countries or regions. Analytical skills enable them to track economic indicators, evaluate economic policies, and provide timely updates to their governments.

ix. *Data-Driven Decision-Making*: In the era of big data and analytics, economic diplomats must be able to make data-driven decisions. Analytical skills are essential for interpreting economic data and using it to inform policy recommendations and negotiations.

x. *Policy Coordination*: Economic diplomacy often involves coordination with various government departments and agencies. Analytical skills aid diplomats in understanding and aligning the economic policies of different stakeholders to ensure a coherent and effective approach.

xi. *Adaptation to Changing Circumstances*: The global economic landscape is constantly evolving. Economic diplomats with strong analytical skills are better equipped to adapt to changing circumstances, seize opportunities, and address new challenges effectively.

xii. *Strategic Planning*: Analytical skills are crucial for long-term strategic planning in economic diplomacy. Diplomats need to assess the economic implications of different scenarios and develop strategies to achieve their country's economic goals over time.

4. **Crisis Management** is a vital skill set for economic diplomats, as it enables them to protect their country's economic interests, respond effectively to unexpected challenges, maintain public confidence, and contribute to diplomatic solutions during economic crises:

i. *Unexpected Economic Shocks*: Economic diplomats may encounter unexpected economic crises or shocks during their assignments, such as financial market turmoil, currency crises, or economic downturns. Being trained in crisis management equips them to respond effectively to such situations.

ii. *Protection of Economic Interests*: During a crisis, the protection of a country's economic interests becomes paramount. Economic diplomats need crisis management skills to assess the impact of the crisis on their country's economy and develop strategies to mitigate potential damage.

iii. *Swift Response*: Economic crises often require immediate responses to prevent further escalation and damage. Diplomats trained in crisis management can act swiftly and decisively to address emerging economic challenges and provide timely recommendations to their governments.

iv. *Communication during Crises*: Effective communication is crucial during a crisis. Diplomats must be able to communicate the situation, potential solutions, and any necessary actions to their government, international counterparts, and the public in a clear and reassuring manner.

v. *Coordination with Stakeholders*: Crisis management often involves coordination with various stakeholders, including government agencies, financial institutions, and international organizations. Diplomats need to collaborate with these entities to develop coordinated responses to economic crises.

vi. *Negotiation under Pressure*: Economic diplomats may find themselves negotiating under intense pressure during a crisis, such as debt restructuring or emergency financial assistance agreements. Crisis management skills help them remain calm and focused while making strategic decisions in high-stress situations.

vii. *Risk Assessment and Scenario Planning*: Diplomats need to assess the potential risks associated with various crisis scenarios and develop contingency plans. Crisis management training helps them evaluate the likely consequences of different actions and make informed choices.

viii. *Conflict Prevention*: Effective crisis management can help prevent economic disputes or crises from escalating into larger geopolitical conflicts. Diplomats trained in crisis management can work to defuse tensions and find diplomatic solutions to economic disputes.

ix. *Resource Allocation*: During a crisis, resource allocation is critical. Diplomats must prioritize their efforts and allocate resources effectively to address the most pressing economic issues and protect their country's interests.

x. *Public Confidence*: Maintaining public confidence is essential during an economic crisis. Economic diplomats with crisis management skills can communicate effectively with the public, provide reassurance, and offer a sense of stability and direction.

xi. *Long-Term Recovery Planning*: After a crisis has passed, economic diplomats play a role in long-term recovery planning. Crisis management training helps them assess the economic damage and formulate strategies for rebuilding and restoring economic stability.

xii. *Geopolitical Implications*: Economic crises can have geopolitical implications. Diplomats must understand the broader geopolitical context and consider how the crisis may affect their country's international relations and alliances.

5. **Cross-Cultural Competence**: Economic diplomats interact with representatives from various cultures and backgrounds. Cross-cultural competence is a fundamental skill for economic diplomats, as it enhances their ability to communicate effectively, build relationships, negotiate successfully, and navigate the complexities of international diplomacy in an increasingly interconnected and diverse world:

i. *Effective Communication*: Economic diplomats need to communicate and negotiate with individuals from diverse cultural backgrounds. Cross-cultural competence helps them understand different communication styles, non-verbal cues, and cultural nuances, improving their ability to convey messages accurately and build rapport with international counterparts.

ii. *Respect for Cultural Differences*: Diplomats must demonstrate respect for the cultural norms and values of their host countries and international partners. Cross-cultural competence promotes cultural sensitivity and helps diplomats avoid unintentional cultural misunderstandings or insensitivity.

iii. *Building Trust and Relationships*: Trust is a cornerstone of diplomacy. Diplomats with cross-cultural competence can establish trust more easily by demonstrating an understanding and appreciation of the cultural context in which they are working. Strong relationships are often critical for successful economic diplomacy.

iv. *Adaptation to Local Customs*: Economic diplomats stationed abroad may need to adapt to local customs, protocols, and business practices. Cross-cultural competence enables them to navigate unfamiliar cultural environments, making their diplomatic efforts more effective.

v. *Avoiding Cultural Offenses*: Lack of cross-cultural competence can lead to cultural offenses or misinterpretations that can harm diplomatic relationships. Diplomats need to be aware of potential pitfalls and cultural taboos to prevent misunderstandings.

vi. *Enhancing Negotiations*: Cross-cultural competence can significantly improve negotiation outcomes. Diplomats who understand the cultural preferences and expectations of their counterparts can tailor their negotiation strategies to be more effective in cross-cultural contexts.

vii. *Conflict Resolution*: In cases of disputes or conflicts, cross-cultural competence is essential for finding mutually acceptable solutions. Diplomats with this skill set can mediate effectively, bridging cultural gaps and facilitating compromise.

viii. *Cultural Intelligence*: Cross-cultural competence enhances a diplomat's cultural intelligence, which is the ability to adapt to different cultural settings and interact effectively with people from diverse backgrounds. This adaptability is valuable in a constantly changing global diplomatic landscape.

ix. *Public Diplomacy*: Economic diplomats often engage with the local population and media in their host countries. Cross-cultural competence helps them communicate their country's economic policies and achievements in a way that resonates with the local audience and fosters positive public perceptions.

x. *Promoting International Cooperation*: Economic diplomacy often involves cooperation on economic issues with other nations. Cross-cultural competence is essential for building alliances and partnerships, as it fosters trust and mutual understanding among diplomats from different cultures.

xi. *Conflict Prevention*: Understanding cultural dynamics can help diplomats identify potential sources of conflict and take proactive steps to prevent misunderstandings or disputes from arising in the first place.

xii. *Diversity and Inclusion*: As diplomats represent their countries on the global stage, they should embody principles of diversity and inclusion. Cross-cultural competence promotes inclusive diplomacy by recognizing and respecting the diversity of cultures and perspectives worldwide.

6. **Trade Knowledge**: A deep understanding of international trade policies, regulations, and agreements is essential. Economic diplomats need to promote their country's trade interests and address any trade-related issues:

i. *Core Responsibility*: Economic diplomats are primarily responsible for promoting their country's economic interests in international trade. A deep understanding of trade principles and practices is essential for fulfilling this core responsibility effectively.

ii. *Negotiating Trade Agreements*: Economic diplomats are often involved in negotiating trade agreements and treaties. Trade knowledge is crucial for understanding the intricacies of these agreements, ensuring that they align with their country's trade objectives and comply with international trade rules.

iii. *Market Access and Barriers*: Economic diplomats must be knowledgeable about international markets, including trade barriers, tariffs, quotas, and non-tariff measures. This knowledge helps them identify opportunities for market access and address trade barriers that may hinder their country's exports.

iv. *Promoting Exports*: Encouraging and facilitating exports is a key objective of economic diplomacy. Trade knowledge enables diplomats to identify export opportunities, promote their country's products and services, and assist domestic businesses in accessing foreign markets.

v. *Supporting Domestic Industries*: Diplomats need to stay informed about the needs and concerns of domestic industries. Trade knowledge helps them advocate for policies and measures that support these industries and ensure their competitiveness in the global market.

vi. *Navigating Trade Disputes*: In the event of trade disputes, economic diplomats must understand trade rules and dispute settlement mechanisms, such as those within the World Trade Organization (WTO). This knowledge allows them to represent their country effectively and protect its trade interests.

vii. *Monitoring Trade Trends*: Staying up-to-date with global trade trends and developments is essential for diplomats. Trade knowledge helps them assess the potential impact of these trends on their country's economy and make informed policy recommendations.

viii. *Trade Policy Formulation*: Diplomats play a role in formulating their country's trade policies. Trade knowledge is indispensable for evaluating the consequences of various policy options and developing strategies that align with the nation's trade goals.

ix. *International Trade Organizations*: Economic diplomats often engage with international trade organizations and forums. A solid understanding of trade principles and regulations is vital for participating effectively in these organizations and advocating for their country's interests.

x. *Trade Promotion*: Economic diplomats may organize trade missions, exhibitions, and promotional events to showcase their country's products and services. Trade knowledge helps them plan and execute these initiatives successfully.

xi. *Trade-related Legal Frameworks*: Trade diplomats must be familiar with trade-related legal frameworks and agreements, including regional trade blocs and bilateral trade agreements. This knowledge ensures they can navigate legal complexities and maximize trade opportunities.

xii. *Economic Impact Assessment*: Economic diplomats often need to assess the economic impact of trade policies, agreements, or disputes. Trade knowledge enables them to conduct economic impact assessments and provide data-driven recommendations to their governments.

7. **Business Acumen**: Understanding the private sector's perspective is vital, as economic diplomats often work with businesses to promote investments, exports, and economic partnerships. It is the fundamental skill that enables economic diplomats to bridge the gap between government policies and the needs of the business community. Diplomats with this skill set are better equipped to promote investment, facilitate trade, support domestic industries, and foster economic growth in an ever-evolving global economy:

i. *Understanding Business Needs*: Diplomats often interact with businesses and industries in their host countries and must understand their needs, challenges, and objectives. Business acumen helps diplomats grasp the economic concerns and priorities of domestic industries.

ii. *Promoting Investment*: Economic diplomats play a key role in attracting foreign investment to their country. Business acumen allows them to identify potential investors, understand their investment criteria, and present compelling investment opportunities that align with their country's economic goals.

iii. *Facilitating Trade*: Diplomats are responsible for facilitating international trade. A strong understanding of business practices, supply chains, and logistics enables them to assist businesses in navigating export-import procedures and expanding their global reach.

iv. *Supporting SMEs*: Small and medium-sized enterprises (SMEs) often face unique challenges in international trade. Diplomats with business acumen can provide tailored support to SMEs, helping them overcome barriers and access foreign markets.

v. *Economic Intelligence*: Business acumen helps diplomats interpret economic data, market research, and industry reports effectively. This skill is crucial for gathering economic intelligence and identifying trends that can inform economic policies and diplomatic strategies.

vi. *Economic Impact Assessment*: Economic diplomats must assess the potential impact of economic policies, trade agreements, or investment projects. Business acumen allows them to conduct thorough economic impact assessments, considering factors such as job creation, economic growth, and industry competitiveness.

   vii. *Supporting Export Promotion*: Promoting exports is a key diplomatic objective. Diplomats with business acumen can assist local businesses in developing export strategies, accessing export financing, and navigating international markets.

   viii. *Private Sector Partnerships*: Economic diplomacy often involves partnering with the private sector to achieve economic objectives. Business acumen helps diplomats build effective partnerships with businesses and industry associations to advance mutual interests.

   ix. *Trade Negotiations*: Understanding the priorities and concerns of businesses is crucial during trade negotiations. Diplomats can advocate for trade agreements that benefit domestic industries and address their specific needs when they possess business acumen.

   x. *Risk Assessment*: Business acumen aids diplomats in assessing the economic risks associated with various trade or investment decisions. This includes evaluating financial risks, market volatility, and potential regulatory challenges.

   xi. *Crisis Management*: During economic crises or disruptions, diplomats with business acumen can collaborate with businesses to develop crisis management strategies that protect economic interests and mitigate damage.

   xii. *Public-Private Dialogue*: Diplomats often facilitate public-private dialogues to address economic issues. Business acumen enhances their ability to engage in meaningful discussions with business leaders and industry representatives.

   xiii. *Innovation and Technology*: Understanding business trends in innovation and technology is increasingly important. Economic diplomats with business acumen can identify opportunities for technology transfer, research collaboration, and innovation partnerships.

8. **Technical Knowledge**: a strong grasp of economic theories, international finance, trade theories, and global economic institutions is essential for economic diplomats:

   i. *Informed Decision-Making*: Economic diplomats need a solid understanding of economic theories to make informed decisions and recommendations. This knowledge allows them to assess the potential consequences of various economic policies and diplomatic actions.

   ii. *Negotiation Advantage*: In trade negotiations and economic diplomacy, diplomats who are well-versed in trade theories and economic principles have a distinct advantage. They can strategically position their country's interests and navigate complex negotiations effectively.

iii. *Trade Policy Development*: Economic diplomats often contribute to the development of their country's trade policies. A deep understanding of trade theories helps them design policies that align with their nation's economic goals and global trade trends.

iv. *International Finance*: Knowledge of international finance is crucial for economic diplomats, as it enables them to evaluate financial markets, exchange rates, and capital flows. This understanding is vital for monitoring economic stability and making informed decisions during financial crises.

v. *Market Access*: Understanding global economic institutions and trade agreements is essential for assessing market access opportunities. Economic diplomats can use this knowledge to identify barriers to entry, negotiate favorable terms, and promote their country's exports.

vi. *Diplomatic Strategy*: A strong foundation in international finance and economic theories allows diplomats to develop strategic approaches to economic diplomacy. They can anticipate economic trends, assess the impact of policy decisions, and adapt their diplomatic strategies accordingly.

vii. *Economic Intelligence*: Economic diplomats need to gather and interpret economic data and intelligence. A solid grasp of economic theories helps them analyze economic indicators, assess market conditions, and identify opportunities or risks.

viii. *Crisis Management*: During economic crises, diplomats with knowledge of economic theories and global economic institutions can respond effectively. They understand the underlying economic dynamics and can engage in crisis management and negotiations to protect their country's interests.

ix. *Global Economic Institutions*: Economic diplomats often engage with international organizations like the World Trade Organization (WTO), International Monetary Fund (IMF), and World Bank. Familiarity with these institutions and their operations is essential for effective diplomacy and advocacy on behalf of their country.

x. *Economic Diplomacy in a Global Context*: Economic diplomacy takes place in a global context, and diplomats must be aware of global economic trends and challenges. A strong foundation in economic theories and international finance enables them to contribute to the resolution of global economic issues.

xi. *Trade Policy Compliance*: Economic diplomats must ensure that their country's trade policies and practices comply with international trade agreements and norms. Knowledge of trade theories and global economic institutions helps them navigate the intricacies of international trade law.

9. **Networking**: Building and maintaining relationships with foreign diplomats, international organizations, business leaders, and experts is important for effective economic diplomacy. Networking helps economic diplomats establish relationships, access information, identify opportunities, and navigate the complexities of economic diplomacy:

   i. *Building Relationships*: Networking is essential for building and nurturing relationships with foreign counterparts, government officials, business leaders, and other diplomats. These relationships are the foundation of effective economic diplomacy.

   ii. *Access to Information*: Networking provides access to valuable information and insights about economic trends, market conditions, and political developments. Diplomats can use this information to make informed decisions and recommendations.

   iii. *Business Opportunities*: Diplomats who network effectively can identify business opportunities, potential investors, and trading partners for their country's businesses. This can lead to increased trade, investment, and economic growth.

   iv. *Crisis Management*: During economic crises, a strong network can be a valuable resource for gathering information, mobilizing support, and coordinating responses. Networking helps diplomats access the expertise and resources needed to manage crises effectively.

   v. *Negotiation Support*: Building rapport and trust through networking can facilitate more productive negotiations. Diplomats who have established relationships with their counterparts may find it easier to reach mutually beneficial agreements.

   vi. *Diverse Perspectives*: Networking exposes diplomats to diverse perspectives and viewpoints. This broadens their understanding of economic issues and allows them to consider a wider range of options and solutions.

   vii. *Public Diplomacy*: Diplomats often engage with the public, media, and civil society organizations. Networking helps them connect with key stakeholders, convey their country's economic messages, and build support for their economic initiatives.

   viii. *International Organizations*: Networking within international organizations, such as the United Nations or World Trade Organization, is critical for influencing global economic policies and agreements. Diplomats can leverage their connections to advocate for their country's interests.

ix. *Access to Decision-Makers*: Effective networking can provide diplomats with access to decision-makers in foreign governments and international institutions. This access can be crucial for advancing economic objectives and resolving disputes.

x. *Cultural Understanding*: Networking often involves interacting with people from diverse cultural backgrounds. This experience enhances diplomats' cross-cultural competence and their ability to navigate cultural differences effectively.

xi. *Peer Learning*: Diplomats can learn from their peers in other countries through networking. Exchanging ideas and best practices with colleagues from different diplomatic missions can lead to innovative approaches to economic diplomacy.

xii. *Promoting Economic Diplomacy*: Building a strong network of allies who understand and support economic diplomacy is essential for promoting the practice within the diplomatic community and among policymakers.

xiii. *Fostering Diplomatic Cooperation*: Networking enables diplomats to collaborate with their counterparts on shared economic goals. It can lead to joint initiatives, partnerships, and coordinated efforts to address regional or global economic challenges.

10. **Problem-Solving Skills**: Economic diplomats face complex challenges that require creative problem-solving. This might involve finding innovative solutions to trade disputes, investment barriers, or economic imbalances.

i. *Navigating Complex Issues*: Economic diplomacy often involves dealing with complex economic, trade, and financial issues. These problems can range from negotiating trade agreements to resolving disputes related to intellectual property or market access. Effective problem-solving skills are crucial for diplomats to navigate these intricate issues successfully.

ii. *Conflict Resolution*: Economic diplomats may encounter conflicts and disputes between countries or trade partners. The ability to identify the root causes of these conflicts and work towards resolution is a fundamental aspect of their role. Problem-solving skills help diplomats find mutually beneficial solutions and mitigate potential economic and political tensions.

iii. *Maximizing Economic Opportunities*: Economic diplomats work to promote their country's economic interests abroad. To do this effectively, they must identify and capitalize on opportunities for trade, investment, and economic cooperation. Problem-solving skills enable diplomats to assess market conditions, identify barriers to entry, and strategize ways to promote economic growth.

iv. *Adapting to Changing Environments*: The global economic landscape is constantly evolving. Economic diplomats must be able to adapt to changing economic conditions, emerging technologies, and geopolitical shifts. Problem-solving skills allow them to analyze new situations quickly, develop innovative strategies, and respond effectively to unforeseen challenges.

v. *Building Alliances and Partnerships*: Economic diplomacy often involves building alliances and partnerships with other countries, international organizations, and businesses. Effective problem-solving skills help diplomats identify areas of cooperation and facilitating the formation of productive relationships.

vi. *Risk Management*: Economic diplomats need to assess and manage various types of risks, such as economic, political, and regulatory risks. Problem-solving skills enable them to develop risk mitigation strategies and contingency plans to safeguard their country's economic interests.

vii. *Negotiation*: Negotiation is a core aspect of economic diplomacy. Diplomats negotiate trade agreements, investment treaties, and other economic arrangements. Problem-solving skills are critical in these negotiations, as diplomats must find compromises and win-win solutions that benefit their country while also respecting the interests of their counterparts.

viii. *Effective Communication*: Diplomats must convey their ideas, proposals, and concerns persuasively. They also need to listen actively to understand the perspectives of others, which is crucial for collaborative problem-solving.

ix. *Crisis Management*: Economic diplomats may need to address economic crises, such as financial market turmoil or trade disputes. Strong problem-solving skills are essential in managing and mitigating the impact of these crises and finding solutions to restore economic stability.

11. **Multilateral Diplomacy**: Economic diplomats operate in a globalized world where economic issues transcend borders. Multilateral diplomacy is an essential skill set for them to effectively represent their country's economic interests, navigate complex international systems, and contribute to cooperative efforts to address global economic challenges. By understanding and engaging in multilateral diplomacy, economic diplomats can play a vital role in shaping international economic policies and promoting economic stability and prosperity for their country and the global community:

i. *Global Interconnectedness*: In today's interconnected world, economic issues are rarely confined to bilateral relationships. Multilateral diplomacy is essential because economic challenges often require cooperation and coordination among multiple countries and international organizations. Economic diplomats need to engage in multilateral forums to address global economic issues effectively.

ii. *International Organizations*: Many economic matters, such as trade agreements, economic sanctions, and financial regulations, are governed by international organizations like the United Nations, the World Trade Organization (WTO), the International Monetary Fund (IMF), and the World Bank. Economic diplomats must understand how these organizations function, how to navigate their complex decision-making processes, and how to advocate for their country's interests within these frameworks.

iii. *Trade Negotiations*: Multilateral trade negotiations, such as those under the WTO, involve numerous countries working together to establish common trade rules and resolve trade disputes. Economic diplomats must participate in and contribute to these negotiations to promote their country's trade interests and ensure a level playing field for their exporters.

iv. *International Agreements*: Economic diplomats may need to negotiate and participate in the implementation of international agreements and treaties related to economic matters. Understanding multilateral diplomacy is essential for effectively negotiating, ratifying, and adhering to these agreements.

v. *Crisis Management*: In times of economic crisis or global economic challenges, multilateral diplomacy becomes critical. Economic diplomats must engage with other nations and international organizations to coordinate responses, share information, and collectively address issues such as financial instability, economic recessions, or natural disasters.

vi. *Diversity of Perspectives*: Multilateral diplomacy exposes economic diplomats to a wide range of perspectives and interests from different countries. This experience helps diplomats gain a deeper understanding of the global economic landscape and the diverse viewpoints that shape international economic policies.

vii. *Soft Power and Influence*: Active participation in multilateral diplomacy allows countries to exercise soft power and influence on a global scale. Economic diplomats can promote their country's economic interests, values, and policies through active engagement in international forums and negotiations.

viii. *Conflict Prevention*: Multilateral diplomacy can serve as a platform for preventing economic conflicts and disputes from escalating into larger geopolitical crises. Economic diplomats can work to find peaceful and negotiated solutions to economic disagreements, reducing the risk of conflicts that could harm their country's economic interests.

ix. *Information Sharing*: Multilateral forums provide opportunities for information exchange and networking. Economic diplomats can gather valuable economic intelligence, stay informed about global economic trends, and build relationships with counterparts from other nations, which can be beneficial for their country's economic strategies.

12. **Policy Advocacy**: Economic diplomats need the skills to advocate for their country's economic policies and interests effectively. This involves making persuasive arguments and building coalitions of support:

i. *Representation of National Interests*: Economic diplomats are tasked with representing their country's economic interests abroad. Policy advocacy equips them with the tools to articulate and advocate for their nation's economic policies, priorities, and objectives effectively.

ii. *Influencing Economic Policies*: Economic diplomats play a vital role in influencing the economic policies and decisions of host countries or international organizations. Through strategic policy advocacy, they can shape the regulatory and economic environment to be more favorable to their country's businesses, trade, and investments.

iii. *Building Alliances*: Diplomats often work to build alliances and partnerships with other countries. Policy advocacy skills are essential in these efforts, as diplomats need to persuade other nations to align their economic interests with those of their country, fostering cooperation and collaboration on various economic issues.

    iv. *Negotiating Agreements*: Economic diplomats engage in negotiations to establish trade agreements, investment treaties, and other economic arrangements. Effective policy advocacy helps them convey their country's positions clearly, build consensus, and secure favorable terms in these negotiations.

    v. *Problem Solving*: Policy advocacy is a valuable tool for diplomats when encountering economic challenges and disputes. They can use advocacy techniques to identify common ground, seek compromises, and find mutually beneficial solutions to economic problems.

    vi. *Stakeholder Engagement*: Diplomats often interact with a wide range of stakeholders, including government officials, business leaders, civil society organizations, and academic experts. Policy advocacy skills enable diplomats to engage with these diverse groups, gather input, and build support for their country's economic initiatives.

    vii. *Risk Mitigation*: Economic diplomats must be proactive in identifying and mitigating risks that could impact their country's economic interests. Effective policy advocacy includes developing risk assessment strategies and contingency plans to address potential challenges.

    viii. *Promoting Economic Diplomacy Initiatives*: Diplomats engage in economic diplomacy initiatives, such as trade missions, investment promotion, and business forums. Policy advocacy helps them promote these initiatives to attract foreign investment, expand market access, and strengthen economic ties.

    ix. *Crisis Management*: In times of economic crises or disputes, policy advocacy is essential for managing and resolving these situations. Diplomats can advocate for their country's position and work towards diplomatic solutions to prevent or mitigate economic crises.

    x. *Communication Skills*: Effective policy advocacy involves clear and persuasive communication. Diplomats must convey complex economic policies and positions in a way that resonates with their counterparts and stakeholders, fostering understanding and cooperation.

    xi. *Adapting to Changing Environments*: Economic diplomats must stay informed about evolving economic trends and adapt their advocacy efforts accordingly. Being agile in policy advocacy allows diplomats to respond effectively to emerging economic challenges and opportunities.

13. **Language Proficiency** is a valuable asset for economic diplomats, as it enhances their ability to communicate effectively, build relationships, understand local cultures, and navigate complex diplomatic situations. Proficiency

in foreign languages is an investment that can significantly improve the effectiveness of economic diplomacy and contribute to the achievement of diplomatic objectives in the European and international arena:

i. *Effective Communication*: Economic diplomats need to communicate with their counterparts in host countries, international organizations, and foreign businesses. Language proficiency ensures that diplomats can communicate clearly and directly, reducing the risk of misunderstandings and fostering effective communication.

ii. *Cultural Understanding*: Proficiency in the language of the host country can help economic diplomats understand the local culture, customs, and nuances of communication. This cultural understanding is essential for building relationships, navigating diplomatic protocols, and demonstrating respect for the host country.

iii. *Negotiation and Diplomacy*: Economic negotiations often require detailed discussions and compromises. Language proficiency allows diplomats to engage in nuanced negotiations, where precise wording and subtle expressions can be critical in reaching mutually beneficial agreements.

iv. *Market Research and Analysis*: Economic diplomats frequently engage in market research to assess business opportunities and economic conditions. Proficiency in the local language can aid in gathering accurate information, conducting interviews, and analyzing market data effectively.

v. *Building Relationships*: Language skills can facilitate the development of personal and professional relationships. When diplomats speak the language of the host country, it can foster trust and rapport with local officials, business leaders, and other stakeholders, making it easier to achieve diplomatic goals.

vi. *Access to Information*: In some cases, critical information may only be available in the local language. Proficiency in the language ensures that economic diplomats have access to a broader range of information sources, which is valuable for decision-making and policy advocacy.

vii. *Public Diplomacy*: Economic diplomats often engage with the public, including through media interviews, speeches, and public events. Language proficiency enables them to communicate effectively with local audiences, conveying their country's economic policies and fostering positive public perception.

viii. *Interpretation and Translation*: Economic diplomats may be required to provide interpretation and translation services during diplomatic meetings and negotiations. Proficiency in multiple languages allows diplomats to fulfill these roles accurately and professionally.

ix. *Crisis Management*: In times of economic crises or emergencies, language proficiency is essential for diplomats to communicate swiftly and accurately with local authorities and affected individuals. This can be critical in coordinating responses and aiding with their country's citizens or businesses.

x. *Enhanced Influence*: When diplomats can converse in the local language, they often gain greater influence and credibility. Host-country officials may be more inclined to listen to and collaborate with diplomats who make the effort to speak their language.

xi. *Diplomatic Etiquette*: Understanding the language is essential for adhering to diplomatic etiquette and protocols. Diplomats must be able to engage in formal and diplomatic conversations, exchange pleasantries, and follow local customs.

14. **Experiential learning** in economic diplomacy involves gaining practical knowledge and skills through hands-on, real-world experiences (Cohen, 2019). This approach goes beyond traditional classroom learning and textbooks, providing postgraduate students and practitioners with opportunities to engage directly in economic diplomacy scenarios:

i. *Simulations & Role-Plays*: Simulations recreate diplomatic scenarios, such as trade negotiations or international economic forums. Participants take on roles of diplomats, policymakers, and other stakeholders, making decisions and engaging in negotiations as if in real situations. This helps learners understand the complexities and challenges of economic diplomacy.

ii. *Model United Nations* (MUN) *Conferences*: MUN conferences focus on simulating the workings of the United Nations and other international organizations. Participants represent different countries and engage in debates, negotiations, and drafting of resolutions on economic issues (Krein, 2023).

iii. *Internships & Attachments*: Students and early-career professionals can benefit from internships or attachments with diplomatic missions, international organizations, government agencies, or trade associations. These experiences provide insights into the practical aspects of economic diplomacy.

iv. *Field Trips & Study Tours*: Visits to international organizations, trade hubs, and diplomatic missions offer a first-hand look at how economic diplomacy is practiced. Observing negotiations, meeting diplomats, and experiencing international trade environments can enhance understanding.

v. *Mock Trade Agreements*: Creating mock trade agreements allows students to delve into the complexities of trade negotiations. This can involve researching trade policies, engaging in negotiations, and drafting agreements.

vi. *Business-Government Dialogues*: Organizing dialogues between government officials and business leaders provides a platform for discussing economic policies, trade barriers, and investment opportunities. Students and professionals can participate in or observe these dialogues.

vii. *Policy Analysis Projects*: Assigning projects that involve analyzing real-world economic diplomacy issues helps learners apply theoretical concepts to practical situations. This could include studying the impact of trade agreements or evaluating the effectiveness of economic sanctions.

viii. *Participation in Trade Missions*: Joining trade missions led by government officials or business associations can provide insights into economic diplomacy on an international level. Participants can witness trade promotion efforts and networking in action.

ix. *Diplomatic Workshops & Seminars*: Attending workshops and seminars conducted by experienced diplomats, economists, and international relations experts exposes participants to current trends and challenges in economic diplomacy.

x. *Mock Diplomatic Briefings*: Having students prepare and deliver mock diplomatic briefings on economic issues enhances their research, presentation, and communication skills. This can simulate the type of work economic diplomats do.

xi. *Case Studies*: Analyzing real-world cases of economic diplomacy successes and failures can help learners understand the practical implications of different strategies.

xii. *Participation in Trade Negotiation Teams*: Some educational institutions offer opportunities for students to be part of trade negotiation teams participating in international competitions. This exposes them to real negotiation dynamics.

Faculty Expertise and Practitioner Involvement

The expertise of faculty members is a fundamental factor in the success of postgraduate programs in economic diplomacy. Faculty members play a pivotal role in shaping the curriculum, providing guidance to students, conducting research, and contributing to the overall academic environment.

i. *Curriculum Development*: Experienced faculty members with a deep understanding of economic diplomacy can design a curriculum that covers relevant topics, theories, and practical skills. They can ensure that the program aligns with the evolving needs of the field.

ii. *Teaching Quality*: Faculty expertise translates into high-quality teaching. Professors who have practical experience or research background in economic diplomacy can offer real-world insights, case studies, and examples that enrich the learning experience for students.

iii. *Current Knowledge*: Economic diplomacy is a dynamic field influenced by global events, economic trends, and policy changes. Faculty members who actively engage in research and stay updated on current developments ensure that students are exposed to the latest knowledge and trends.

iv. *Networking*: Professors with strong networks within the diplomatic and economic sectors can facilitate guest lectures, workshops, and internships for students. These connections enhance students' exposure to real-world practitioners and opportunities.

v. *Mentorship*: Faculty members serve as mentors to students, guiding them in their academic pursuits and career aspirations. Their expertise can help students navigate challenges, explore research opportunities, and make informed decisions.

vi. *Research*: Faculty research contributes to the academic advancement of the field. Their research findings can influence policy discussions and provide valuable insights into economic diplomacy practices.

vii. *Engagement with Practitioners*: Experienced faculty can foster collaborations with diplomats, policymakers, and industry experts, bringing real-world perspectives into the classroom through guest lectures and workshops.

viii. *Customized Learning*: Faculty who understand the diverse backgrounds and goals of students can tailor their teaching approaches to accommodate different learning styles and career aspirations.

ix. *Interdisciplinary Insights*: Economic diplomacy draws from various disciplines. Faculty members with expertise in economics, international relations, law, and other relevant fields can offer interdisciplinary insights that enrich students' understanding.

   x. *Ethical Considerations*: Economic diplomacy often involves ethical dilemmas. Faculty members can engage students in discussions about ethical considerations, helping them develop a well-rounded perspective.

  xi. *Thought Leadership*: Professors with a strong reputation in the field can contribute to thought leadership through publications, conferences, and media engagement. This enhances the program's credibility and attracts students seeking renowned faculty.

 xii. *Continuous Improvement*: Faculty members who actively seek feedback from students and industry partners can continuously improve the program, ensuring its relevance and effectiveness.

In essence, faculty expertise brings credibility, practicality, and depth to postgraduate programs in economic diplomacy. Students benefit from learning directly from professionals who have navigated the complexities of economic diplomacy and can provide insights that go beyond textbooks. Scholars emphasize the significance of recruiting faculty members with diverse backgrounds, including academia and practice, to provide students with a well-rounded education (Trachtman, 2019). Involvement of practitioners, such as diplomats and trade negotiators, as guest lecturers and mentors enhance the program's practical relevance and exposes students to real-world perspectives (Cantwell & Krug, 2017).

International Collaboration and Cultural Sensitivity

Economic diplomacy often involves negotiations across cultures and borders. International collaboration among universities and fostering cultural sensitivity among students are indeed crucial elements for postgraduate programs focusing on economic diplomacy.

   i. *Diverse Perspectives*: Economic diplomacy involves navigating complex international relationships, trade agreements, and negotiations. Bringing together students from various countries, backgrounds, and cultures enriches the classroom experience. Diverse perspectives foster creative problem-solving, provide a well-rounded understanding of global economic dynamics, and expose students to different diplomatic traditions and perspectives (Makinda & Higgott, 2002).

  ii. *Cross-Cultural Communication*: Economic diplomacy requires effective communication across cultures. Students who are attuned to cultural nuances can navigate sensitive issues more skillfully. Learning to respect, understand, and adapt to different cultural norms is a valuable skill for future diplomats and negotiators. Such collaborations enhance cross-cultural understanding and prepare graduates to navigate diverse international environments with cultural sensitivity (Gilboa, 2001).

iii. *Networking Opportunities*: Collaborative postgraduate programs that involve multiple universities provide students with a broader network. Networking opportunities span across borders, allowing students to build relationships with peers, professors, and professionals from around the world. These connections can be invaluable in their future careers.

iv. *Real-World Exposure*: Collaboration among universities often entails joint research projects, internships, or fieldwork in different countries. This exposure provides students with hands-on experience and insights into economic diplomacy in diverse contexts, preparing them for the challenges they may face in their careers.

v. *Cultural Intelligence*: Economic diplomacy involves more than just understanding economic policies; it's about grasping the historical, social, and cultural contexts that influence international relations. Cultural sensitivity helps students make informed decisions and negotiate effectively, avoiding unintended misunderstandings.

vi. *Conflict Resolution Skills*: Economic diplomacy can involve delicate negotiations and conflict resolution. Cross-cultural understanding aids in defusing tensions and finding common ground, contributing to successful outcomes in negotiations.

vii. *Global Citizenship*: Postgraduate programs focusing on economic diplomacy aren't just about professional development; they also contribute to creating global citizens who are well-informed about international issues and are equipped to make positive contributions on the global stage.

viii. *Soft Skills*: Collaborative international programs often emphasize soft skills like adaptability, empathy, and open-mindedness. These skills are invaluable in economic diplomacy, where building trust and rapport with counterparts from different cultures is key.

To ensure the effectiveness of such programs, universities should incorporate these elements intentionally into their curriculum and program design. This might include cultural immersion experiences, intercultural communication workshops, guest lectures from experienced diplomats, and opportunities for students to engage in real-world economic diplomacy scenarios.

By emphasizing international collaboration and cultural sensitivity, postgraduate programs on economic diplomacy can produce graduates who are not only knowledgeable in economic matters but also adept at building relationships and navigating the intricate landscape of global economic relations.

Technological Integration

The integration of technology in economic diplomacy is rapidly evolving. Research emphasizes the necessity of incorporating training in digital tools and methodologies, such as data analysis and digital communication platforms, to equip graduates with the skills needed to analyze complex economic data and communicate effectively in a digital age (Cooper, 2020). This integration ensures that economic diplomats remain relevant and effective in an increasingly digitized world.

i. *Global Communication*: Digital tools enable instant communication across borders, allowing diplomats and negotiators to engage with counterparts from different countries in real-time. Platforms like video conferencing, email, and instant messaging facilitate efficient and timely communication.

ii. *Data Analysis*: Economic diplomacy often requires understanding complex data sets related to trade, investment, and economic indicators. Proficiency in data analysis tools equips diplomats with the ability to interpret and leverage data for evidence-based decision-making.

iii. *Digital Diplomacy*: Diplomacy is increasingly being extended into the digital realm, with nations engaging in diplomatic efforts through social media, websites, and online platforms. Teaching students how to use these platforms effectively and ethically is essential (Manor, 2023).

iv. *Virtual Meetings & Conferences*: With the rise of remote work and virtual events, diplomats and negotiators need to be adept at participating in and leading virtual meetings, conferences, and negotiations.

v. *Cybersecurity Awareness*: In an era of cyber threats and digital espionage, diplomats must be aware of cybersecurity risks and best practices to protect sensitive information (Pawar & Singh, 2023).

vi. *Digital Trade & E-Commerce*: The growth of digital trade and e-commerce has introduced new economic dimensions. Understanding digital trade agreements and e-commerce regulations is vital for economic diplomats.

vii. *Geospatial Analysis*: Geographic information systems (GIS) and geospatial analysis tools can provide valuable insights into trade routes, transportation networks, and economic zones. Proficiency in these tools can enhance economic diplomacy strategies (Cederman, 2023).

viii. *Simulations & Modeling*: Digital simulations and economic modeling tools can help students understand the potential impact of different diplomatic decisions on economic outcomes.

ix. *Crisis Management*: Digital tools are essential for crisis communication and management. Students can learn how to leverage social media and other platforms to disseminate accurate information during economic or diplomatic crises.

x. *Blockchain & Digital Identity*: Understanding emerging technologies like blockchain and their implications for economic transactions and diplomatic processes can be valuable for future diplomats (Cirnu & Vasile, 2022).

To effectively incorporate digital training, programs should offer courses dedicated to digital diplomacy, data analytics, cybersecurity, and emerging technologies. Additionally, practical workshops, case studies, and projects that involve the application of digital tools in real-world economic scenarios can provide students with hands-on experience.

As the landscape of economic diplomacy continues to evolve, diplomats and negotiators who are well-versed in digital tools and methodologies will be better equipped to navigate the complexities of global economic relations and drive effective diplomatic outcomes.

Ethical Dimensions

The ethical considerations of economic diplomacy cannot be overlooked. Scholars stress the importance of addressing ethical dilemmas in postgraduate programs, using case studies to engage students in discussions about integrity, transparency, and the responsible use of economic leverage (Vucetic, 2013). Developing ethical reasoning skills prepares graduates to navigate ethically complex situations while upholding national and international norms:

i. *Balancing Interests*: Economic diplomats must balance national interests with global ethical standards. Ethical reasoning equips them to make decisions that promote their country's interests while adhering to principles of fairness, justice, and human rights.

ii. *Cultural Sensitivity*: Ethical norms vary across cultures and countries. Graduates with strong ethical reasoning skills can navigate cultural nuances sensitively and avoid inadvertently causing offense or misunderstanding (Chaban, 2023).

iii. *Conflicts of Interest*: Economic diplomacy may involve negotiations that touch on personal interests or relationships. Ethical reasoning helps diplomats identify and manage conflicts of interest, ensuring transparency and integrity in their actions.

iv. *Complex Negotiations*: Negotiations often involve trade-offs and compromises. Ethical reasoning allows diplomats to assess the moral implications of these compromises and make decisions that align with their country's values.

v. *Human Rights & Labor Standards*: Economic decisions can impact human rights and labor conditions. Diplomats need to consider the ethical implications of trade agreements and economic policies on issues like child labor, workers' rights, and environmental sustainability.

vi. *Transparency & Accountability*: Ethical diplomats prioritize transparency and accountability in their interactions. They seek to uphold the trust of their citizens by acting in ways that are consistent with ethical principles (Hofius, 2022).

vii. *Managing International Agreements*: Ethical reasoning helps diplomats navigate the negotiation and implementation of international agreements, ensuring that commitments are honored in good faith.

viii. *Crisis Management*: In times of economic or diplomatic crises, ethical reasoning guides diplomats in responding ethically and responsibly to minimize harm and resolve conflicts.

ix. *Promoting Global Cooperation*: Ethical diplomats understand the importance of building and maintaining trust among nations. Ethical decision-making contributes to an environment of cooperation and collaboration.

To integrate ethical reasoning into postgraduate programs on economic diplomacy:

➤ *Ethics Courses*: Offer dedicated courses on ethics in international relations and economic diplomacy, covering real-world case studies and ethical dilemmas.

➤ *Debates and Discussions*: Organize debates, seminars, and discussions that encourage students to engage in ethical debates surrounding economic diplomacy.

➤ *Ethical Simulation Exercises*: Design simulation exercises presenting students with ethically challenging scenarios, allowing them to practice making ethical decisions in a controlled environment.

➤ *Guest Speakers*: Invite experienced diplomats, ethicists, and experts to share their insights on ethical decision-making in economic diplomacy.

➤ *Research Projects*: Assign research projects that require students to analyze the ethical dimensions of specific economic policies or negotiations.

By equipping graduates with strong ethical reasoning skills, postgraduate programs ensure that future economic diplomats can navigate complex situations with integrity, contribute positively to international relations, and uphold both national and global ethical standards.

Continuous Adaptation

Economic diplomacy is influenced by geopolitical shifts, economic trends, and technological advancements. Scholars argue that postgraduate programs must remain adaptable and regularly update their curriculum to address emerging issues (Fels & Weiss, 2001). This adaptability ensures that graduates are well-prepared to address new challenges and opportunities in the field.

i. *Dynamic Global Environment*: Economic diplomacy is influenced by shifting geopolitical, economic, and technological trends. Graduates need to be equipped with the most up-to-date knowledge to navigate these changes effectively.

ii. *Emerging Issues*: New economic challenges and opportunities constantly arise, such as the rise of digital trade, sustainability concerns, and the impact of global crises. Programs should address these emerging issues to produce relevant and skilled diplomats.

iii. *Technological Advancements*: Technology plays a significant role in economic diplomacy. Programs should integrate training in digital tools, artificial intelligence, data analytics, and other emerging technologies to prepare graduates for modern diplomatic practices.

iv. *Changing Trade Relations*: Trade dynamics, agreements, and alliances shift over time. Programs need to ensure that graduates understand the latest trade policies, agreements, and trade relations between nations.

v. *Sustainability & Environmental Concerns*: Economic diplomacy now often includes negotiations related to environmental protection and sustainable development. Integrating these issues into the curriculum reflects the changing priorities of the global community.

vi. *Crisis Management*: Global crises like pandemics, economic downturns, and geopolitical tensions can significantly impact economic diplomacy.

Programs should teach crisis management strategies and the role of economic diplomats during such situations (Constantinou, 2015).

vii. *Global Governance & Regulation*: As international regulations and governance frameworks evolve, diplomats need to be aware of the changing landscape to advocate for their country's interests effectively.

viii. *Cultural & Social Dynamics*: Societal shifts and cultural changes influence economic diplomacy. Graduates should be attuned to these dynamics to facilitate effective cross-cultural negotiations.

To ensure adaptability and curriculum relevance:

❖ *Regular Review*: Conduct regular reviews of the curriculum to identify areas that need updating or new topics that should be introduced.

❖ *Advisory Boards*: Establish advisory boards comprising experienced diplomats, industry experts, and academics to provide insights into current trends and needs (Blechman et al., 2009).

❖ *Flexibility in Course Structure*: Design the curriculum with flexibility, allowing for the integration of new courses or modules as emerging issues arise.

❖ *Professional Development*: Offer continuous professional development opportunities for faculty to stay current with trends and bring the latest insights to the classroom.

❖ *Industry Collaboration*: Collaborate with industry partners and diplomatic missions to understand their needs and align curriculum accordingly.

❖ *Research and Innovation*: Encourage students and faculty to engage in research and innovation related to economic diplomacy, fostering a culture of exploration and adaptation.

By remaining adaptable and responsive to emerging issues, postgraduate programs on economic diplomacy can produce graduates who are equipped to tackle the challenges and opportunities of a rapidly changing global economic landscape. After all, it is always a two-way street: well-informed diplomats mean upgrading international relations (Knight, 2022).

Professional Development and Networking

Beyond academic knowledge, economic diplomats require a range of professional skills, including negotiation techniques, public speaking, and policy advocacy. Researchers highlight the value of incorporating workshops and networking opportunities to enhance graduates' ability to represent their countries effectively on the global stage (Sinkovics & Sinkovics, 2009).

i. *Practical Skill Refinement*: Workshops provide a platform for graduates to practice and refine essential diplomatic skills such as negotiation, conflict resolution, diplomatic protocol, and effective communication in a supportive and controlled environment.

ii. *Real-World Application*: Through workshops, graduates can apply theoretical knowledge to practical scenarios, gaining insight into the challenges and complexities of economic diplomacy they might encounter in their careers (Paquette et al., 2019).

iii. *Experiential Learning*: Hands-on workshops allow students to experience the dynamics of diplomatic interactions firsthand, enabling them to understand the nuances of cross-cultural communication and negotiation (Doole et al., 2022).

iv. *Crisis Management Preparation*: Workshops centered around crisis simulations help graduates develop the skills needed to navigate high-pressure situations, equipping them to handle unexpected challenges with composure and tact.

v. *Cultural Sensitivity*: Networking events and workshops involving diverse participants encourage cultural awareness and sensitivity, which are vital in economic diplomacy where understanding cultural nuances is crucial.

vi. *Networking Opportunities*: These events facilitate connections with experienced diplomats, international business professionals, academics, and policymakers. Such connections can lead to mentorship, collaborations, and potential career opportunities (Niklasson, 2020).

vii. *Global Perspective*: Interacting with peers and professionals from various backgrounds broadens graduates' perspectives on international relations, economic dynamics, and different diplomatic approaches.

viii. *Confidence Building*: Networking events and workshops enhance graduates' self-assurance in social settings, empowering them to engage confidently with high-ranking officials, business leaders, and fellow diplomats.

ix. *Industry Insights*: Engaging with experts and practitioners exposes graduates to real-world insights and current trends in economic diplomacy, ensuring their knowledge is relevant and up to date.

x. *Enhanced Soft Skills*: Networking opportunities foster skills such as active listening, relationship-building, and effective communication – all of which are essential for successful diplomatic interactions (Kamin, 2013).

xi. *Professional Development*: Many workshops offer certificates or recognized credentials, adding to graduates' qualifications and boosting their career prospects.

xii. *Global Network*: Graduates can build an international network of contacts that can provide valuable information, support, and collaborative opportunities throughout their careers.

To maximize the benefits, programs should collaborate with experienced diplomats, diplomatic missions, international organizations, and industry partners to design workshops and networking events that reflect the realities of modern economic diplomacy. This integration ensures that graduates are well-prepared to navigate the intricate landscape of global economic relations and contribute effectively as representatives of their countries.

Therefore, organizing competitive postgraduate studies on economic diplomacy requires a holistic approach that integrates multidisciplinary education, experiential learning, faculty expertise, and international collaboration. By fostering a generation of adept economic diplomats with a strong theoretical foundation and practical skills, these programs contribute to effective global economic engagement and the advancement of national interests. As the world continues to evolve, these programs will play a pivotal role in shaping the future of economic diplomacy.

6. Bridges of Diplomacy & Prosperity: The Dual Role of European Universities

It is said that the oldest university in Europe, is the University of Bologna, Italy, founded in 1088. Not true. The oldest university-like institution in the Byzantine Empire was the "University of Constantinople," also known as the *"Imperial University of Constantinople"* "Pandidacterium" (Greek: "Πανδιδακτήριον τῆς Μαγναύρας", "Magna Aula"). It was founded by the Roman Emperor Theodosius II in 425 AD, during the later period of the Roman Empire and the early period of the Byzantine Empire. The most prestigious educational institution in the Byzantine Empire served as a center of learning and scholarship with 31 chairs for law, philosophy, medicine, arithmetic, geometry, astronomy, music, rhetoric and other subjects. Fifteen chairs were assigned to Latin and 16 to Greek. The university was reorganized by Michael III (842–867) and flourished down to the 14th century. The University of Constantinople was a prominent center of education and culture in the Byzantine world, and it played a significant role in the preservation and transmission of knowledge during a time of great historical change and upheaval. The Pandidakterion was refounded in 1046 by Constantine IX Monomachos who created the Departments of Law (Greek: Διδασκαλεῖον τῶν Νόμων) and Philosophy (Greek: Γυμνάσιον) It should be noted that while it resembled modern universities in some ways, the structure and organization of educational institutions in the Byzantine Empire were different from contemporary universities, reflecting the historical and cultural context of the time (Rosser, 2001; Kazhdan & Wharton, 1985; Markopoulos, 2008; Gavroglu, 2001).

Alongside the Imperial University of Constantinople, several notable institutions of higher learning played a crucial role in the preservation and transmission of knowledge, as well as in the education of Byzantine scholars, theologians, philosophers, and diplomats. They contributed to the cultural and intellectual vibrancy of the Byzantine Empire and had a lasting impact on the development of education and scholarship in the Eastern Roman Empire:

- The School of Athens, founded by Emperor Justinian I in the 6th century, was a philosophical and legal institution that was part of the Church of the Holy Apostles complex in Constantinople. It was known for its emphasis on the study of Roman law (Watts, 2004).
- The School of Alexandria was an important center of learning in a major city of the Byzantine Empire. It was renowned for its contributions to mathematics, science, and medicine (Oliver, 2015).

- The School of Antioch focused on theological studies. It had a distinct theological tradition and was known for its emphasis on literal interpretation of scripture. (Schor, 2007).
- The School of Nisibis (modern-day Nusaybin, Turkey) was known for its emphasis on Syriac language and literature. It played a crucial role in preserving Syriac Christian texts and contributed to the development of early Christian theology (Becker, 2006).
- The School of Edessa (modern-day Urfa, Turkey) was known for its contributions to Syriac Christianity. It was a center of learning and theological scholarship (Drijvers, 1995).
- Monasteries in the Byzantine Empire often had their own schools where monks received education in theology, philosophy, and various academic disciplines. The most famous of these monastic schools was the Stoudios Monastery in Constantinople (Browning, 1978; Empire, 2020).

The Byzantine Empire had its share of famous diplomats who played significant roles in the diplomacy of the Eastern Roman Empire, all of them scholars or military men, who were educated at the above schools (Stathakopoulos, 2023):

- Procopius of Caesarea (Greek: Προκόπιος ὁ Καισαρεύς, 500–565), prominent historian, lawyer (rhetor, ῥήτωρ) and diplomat, was accompanying the Roman general Belisarius in Emperor Justinian's wars (during the Vandal War of 533–534, the war with the Ostrogoths, from 535, and the campaigns against the Persians) and became the principal Roman historian of the 6th century, writing the *History of the Wars*, the *Buildings*, and the *Secret History*, the only work of its kind in all Byzantine historiography, written in deep secrecy, it reveals with complete honesty, and, in many cases, exaggeration, the vices of the empire and its rulers (Kaldellis, 2012; Turquois & Turquois, 2013; Lillington-Martin, 2017; Kruse, 2018).
- Belisarius (c. 505–565), a prominent general, was involved in diplomatic missions on behalf of Emperor Justinian I. His military campaigns in the West and East often required diplomatic negotiations with local rulers and adversaries (Mathisen, 1986; Lillington-Martin, 2009).
- Narses (Greek: Ναρσῆς, c. 478–573), also a general, was responsible for leading the Byzantine forces against the Ostrogoths in Italy under the command of Belisarius, and a year earlier he appears as duke of Thebaid in Egypt, when by order of Justinian he suppressed the pagan religion on the southern border of Egypt (Osborne, 1999; Rance, 2005; Sarantis, 2009).
- Theophilus of Edessa (Greek: Θεόφιλος Εδεσσηνός, 695–785), astrologer and scholar, was served as an envoy to the caliph of the Abbasid Caliphate

and played a significant role in fostering diplomatic relations between the Byzantines and the Islamic world (Woods, 2012).

- Saint Methodius (c. 815–885), monk, theologian, and diplomat, one of the two brothers (the other being Cyril) who created the Glagolitic alphabet and the Cyrillic script. Their work was instrumental in spreading Christianity and Byzantine culture among the Slavic peoples of Eastern Europe (Laleva, 2019).
- John Kourkouas (c. 895–946) a Byzantine general and diplomat who led successful military campaigns against the Arab and Bulgarian forces. His diplomatic skills were evident in his negotiations with the Bulgarian Tsar Peter I.
- Nikephoros Phokas (912–969) a prominent general and later emperor, was involved in diplomacy during his campaigns in the East. His negotiations with the Hamdanid Emirate of Aleppo were instrumental in securing a truce (Shepard & Franklin, 1992; Sullivan, 2012; Fattori, 2013).
- Leo of Tripoli (c. 860–912) an acclaimed admiral and diplomat, who played a key role in the diplomatic efforts against the Arabs in the 9th century. He was known for his diplomacy during the Arab-Byzantine Wars (Panayiotou, 2019).
- Demetrios Palaiologos Kantakouzenos (Greek: Δημήτριος Παλαιολόγος Καντακουζηνός; fl. 1420–1453) was the *mesazon* (chief minister) of the Emperors John VIII Palaiologos and his brother, Constantine XI. His colleague in the office as *mesazon* was Loukas Notaras (Nicol, 1968).
- Manuel Komnenos (Greek: Manuel Komnenos, 1145–1185;), the eldest son of the Byzantine emperor Andronikos I Komnenos and ancestor of the Great Komnenos dynasty of the Empire of Trebizond, was served his uncle, Manuel I Komnenos, as a diplomatic envoy to the Russian principalities and the Kingdom of Jerusalem (Magdalino, 1978, 2002).

In summary, institutions of higher education, such as the various schools and academies, in the Byzantine period, played a significant role in shaping and supporting diplomatic efforts. Byzantine institutions of higher education, such as the University of Constantinople, played a central role in the training of the imperial elite, including diplomats and foreign ambassadors. These institutions provided education in fields like rhetoric, philosophy, law, and theology, which were essential for individuals involved in diplomacy. After all, the as today, diplomacy often required proficiency in multiple languages. Byzantine scholars and educational institutions promoted the study of Greek and Latin languages, making it easier for diplomats to communicate effectively with their counterparts from other cultures and regions. Byzantine diplomats received formal training in the art of diplomacy, which included negotiation, protocol, and understanding of foreign customs and traditions. Institutions of higher learning played a role in providing this training. The Byzantine Empire was a stronghold of Christianity, and religious matters were often intertwined with diplomacy. Theological debates and negotiations, such as those related to the Councils of Nicaea and Chalcedon, were important diplomatic events in which religious scholars and theologians played a crucial role. This was the aspect of religious diplomacy, equally strong in the Byzantine Empire. Finally, we should not ignore the role of cultural diplomacy: Byzantine scholars and educators were responsible for preserving and transmitting the knowledge of the ancient world, a valuable tool in diplomacy, as it allowed Byzantine diplomats to engage with foreign powers on a cultural and intellectual level. The Byzantine Empire served as a bridge between the East and the West, facilitating cultural exchange and diplomacy between various civilizations.

It should be noted that Byzantine diplomacy is considered an example of successful diplomacy since it succeeded in maintaining the Empire for more than a thousand years, even in the face of many enemies and given Byzantium's limited military power. From the tradition of the kingdoms of Mesopotamia, Egypt, Ancient Greece and the Roman Empire, Byzantine diplomacy borrowed important models. From the diplomacy of ancient Near East (Mesopotamia, Egypt, Persia): elaborate protocol and ceremonies, dynastic marriage to cement an alliance, trade diplomacy by merchant ambassadors. From Ancient Greek diplomacy: the use of rhetoric as a tool of public diplomacy (although Byzantine envoys relied far less on oratory than those dispatched by the Greek city-states). From the Roman Empire: divide and conquer tactics, using civil-engineering projects to impress foreigners. However, it created a unique tradition, with innovations that today form the building blocks of a modern foreign policy:

i. Through its "Office of Barbarian Affairs" (Greek: Σκρίνιον των Βαρβάρων, Latin: scrinium barbarorum), the Byzantine Empire's diplomacy transitioned from ad hoc to organized government operations. Since all foreigners were referred to as "barbarians," the position may be known as the "office of foreign affairs." In addition to housing a large number of interpreters and translators, the office performed functions akin to those of a contemporary ministry of foreign affairs, including organizing foreign dignitaries' visits to Constantinople, preparing international treaties, and preparing Byzantine envoys for missions outside. Archives were maintained by the office as a means of maintaining institutional memory. Byzantine diplomacy lacked permanent diplomatic missions, in contrast to modern diplomacy. Even though it took years to resolve some difficulties, envoys were dispatched to other countries to handle particular matters (Herbst, 2019).

ii. Early on, the Byzantines realized how crucial it was to win over their neighbors' hearts and minds. The empire converted its neighbors from probable adversaries to allies and friends wherever it could. The converting of nomadic tribes (particularly Slavs) to Christianity, using festivities to impress foreign guests, and training future neighboring rulers in Constantinople's institutions of higher learning were all part of their public diplomacy toolkit. Several of these methods of public diplomacy are still in use today. The location and civil engineering of Constantinople (such as the Hagia Sophia and the Hippodrome of Constantinople) remain stunning even today, demonstrating the empire's exceptional proficiency in the use of procedure and ceremonies to impress foreign dignitaries. The golden lions and tweeting birds surrounding the mechanized gilded throne of the Byzantine emperor, who hosted foreign guests in the Magnaura. Visitors were left with a lasting impression when the throne was raised to the ceiling using a unique hydraulic mechanism. Constantine VII (945–959) wrote the *Book of Ceremonies*, which outlines court customs, seating arrangements, and other procedural information (Khapaev & Glushich, 2020).

iii. Written diplomatic reports were to be returned to Constantinople by envoys. The reports were kept on file at the Barbarian Affairs Office. The diplomatic reports and cables released by WikiLeaks showed that the content of the reports was not all that unlike that of reports from the present day. They discussed issues such as power struggles, leader personalities, and local political events.

iv. The Empire established the first intelligence service, which was made up of a network of dispatched overseas official and unofficial operatives, including missionaries, merchants, and military men, in order to gather the necessary information. They improved the Caesar cipher encryption method even more to guarantee safe connection (Haldon, 2020).

v. Traveling merchants, priests, and other people were employed by the Byzantine Empire. As Byzantine diplomats, they were all obligated to report back to Constantinople on their trips. Byzantine diplomacy was able to accomplish the challenging goal of upholding a vast empire with relatively little financial and military might in this way (Lazzarini, 2022).

vi. Since the Emperor claimed to be the world's ruler, the Byzantines negotiated international treaties with neighboring tribes, although they were actually framed as unilateral decrees. Over time, the empire gained by establishing stable and lawful relationships with the hitherto lawless tribes residing within its boundaries. It looked for legal excuses, such as the idea of "just war" (recovering lost territory or defending the empire), even when it had to go to war. The development of more civilized relations in Europe and the Mediterranean was significantly influenced by the introduction of a legal component to interactions with foreigners. Legality often limited the ability for maneuvering for the usually extremely pragmatist Byzantines, yet even in these circumstances, they never broke the law. They were experts in interpretation and constructive ambiguities because they used a very complicated reading of the signed accords to support their conduct.

Byzantium acted as a protective barrier between Europe from countries in Central Asia and the Middle East. By fending off invasions and assiduously assimilating foreign populations, the Byzantine Empire allowed Europe to heal from wars and epidemics. Even in the 21st century, Byzantine diplomacy still has many essential components. Through the Italian city-states, particularly Venice, they were transmitted until the modern age. The first permanent embassies were founded by city-states in Italy. The diplomatic model that originated in Italy spread to newly formed European nations. In the 17th century, France established the first official ministry of foreign affairs, and other European nations soon after. When we strip away the modern distractions, we see that many of the Byzantine diplomatic instruments are still in use today.

Medieval Universities and Diplomacy: Shaping the Diplomatic Landscape

Many European universities have centuries-old traditions, dating back to the Middle Ages, from roughly the 5th century AD to the late 15th century AD. These institutions played a pivotal role in the development of higher education and the advancement of knowledge in various fields (Verger, 1973; Hilde de Ridder-Symoens, 1992; De la Croix et al., 2020):

– In Italy:[10]

    i. The University of Bologna, Italy, founded in 1088, is often considered the world's oldest university. It has a rich history of academic achievement and has made significant contributions to various fields of study.

---

10 During the Middle Ages, the Italian Peninsula was divided into various city-states, kingdoms, and regions, each with its own rulers and governments: the Kingdom of Sicily and Naples, the Papal States, the Republic of Venice, the Republic of Florence, the Kingdom of Sardinia, the Duchy of Milan, the Kingdom of Naples, the Republic

ii. The University of Padua (Università di Padova), established in 1222, is one of the oldest universities in Italy and Europe. It is known for its strong emphasis on research and innovation.

iii. The University of Naples Federico II (Università degli Studi di Napoli Federico II), founded in 1224, it is one of Italy's oldest universities and is named after Holy Roman Emperor Frederick II.

iv. The University of Siena (Università degli Studi di Siena), established in 1240, has a long history of academic excellence and is known for its contributions to the arts and sciences.

v. The University of Salerno (Università degli Studi di Salerno), although it dates back to the 9th century as a medical school, it received formal recognition as a university in the 12th century.

vi. The University of Pisa (Università di Pisa), founded in 1343, has a strong tradition in mathematics and the sciences.

- In the UK:

i. The University of Oxford, United Kingdom, established around 1096, is one of the most famous and prestigious universities in the world. It has a strong tradition of academic excellence and is known for its collegiate system.

ii. The University of Cambridge, United Kingdom, founded in 1209, is another prestigious institution known for its rigorous academic programs and rich history of scholarship.

iii. The University of Glasgow, established in 1451, is one of Scotland's ancient universities and has made significant contributions to education and research.

iv. The University of Aberdeen, founded in 1495, is one of the oldest universities in Scotland and the UK. It has a strong tradition in various academic disciplines.

- In France:[11]

i. The University of Paris (Université de Paris) often referred to as La Sorbonne, is one of the oldest universities in Europe. It has its roots in the 12th century and was officially founded in 1150. It was a leading

---

of Genoa, the Republic of Pisa, the Kingdom of Sardinia, the Kingdom of the Two Sicilies, the Duchy of Savoy and the Duchy of Modena and Reggio.

11   During the Middle Ages, what is now present-day France was divided into various regions, territories, and states, each with its own rulers, governance systems, and often distinct cultures. The core and most influential state during this period, the Kingdom

institution of higher learning in the Middle Ages and played a significant role in the development of Western intellectual thought.

ii. The University of Montpellier (Université de Montpellier), established in 1289, is one of the oldest universities in France. It has a strong tradition in the fields of medicine and law.

iii. The University of Toulouse (Université de Toulouse) was founded in 1229, and it is known for its historical contributions to legal studies and theology.

iv. The University of Orleans (Université d'Orléans), founded in 1306, has a long history of academic excellence, particularly in the fields of law and the humanities.

v. The University of Poitiers (Université de Poitiers), established in 1431, is known for its strong focus on the arts and humanities.

- In Spain:[12]

  i. The University of Salamanca (Universidad de Salamanca), established in 1134, is one of the oldest universities in Spain and one of the oldest in

---

of France, with Paris as its center, gradually expanded its control over other regions and territories, playing a pivotal role in the formation of the modern French nation. Located in the northwestern part of present-day France, the Duchy of Normandy was a powerful and semi-independent duchy that had a significant impact on the history of England as well through the Norman Conquest in 1066. The County of Flanders in the northern part of modern France and parts of modern-day Belgium, was a prosperous county known for its cloth industry and trade. In the south of France, the County of Toulouse was a wealthy and culturally diverse region with a history of interaction between Christian and Cathar communities. Located in the southwest of France, the Duchy of Aquitaine was often under the control of the King of England during the Angevin Empire. In the southeastern part of France, Provence was known for its distinct culture and troubadour poetry during the Middle Ages. The County of Champagne, situated in northeastern France, was an important center for trade and culture, known for its fairs and markets. The County of Burgundy was located in the eastern part of modern France and was a significant political entity during the Middle Ages. The Duchy of Brittany, in the northwest of France, maintained a degree of autonomy and a unique Breton culture. The Duchy of Lorraine in the northeastern part of present-day France, was a region with a complex history of political and territorial changes.

12　The Kingdom of Castile, located in the north and central parts of the Iberian Peninsula, Castile, was one of the most powerful and influential medieval kingdoms in what is now Spain. The Kingdom of Aragon, situated in the northeastern part of the Iberian Peninsula, along with its union with the County of Barcelona, played a

Europe. It is known for its contributions to the study of humanities and sciences.

ii. The University of Valladolid (Universidad de Valladolid), founded in 1241, is one of the oldest universities in Spain and has a strong tradition in various academic disciplines.

iii. The University of Barcelona (Universitat de Barcelona), founded in 1450, is one of the oldest universities in Spain. It is known for its contributions to research and education.

iv. The University of Valencia (Universitat de València), established in 1499, is one of the oldest universities in Spain and has a rich history of academic excellence.

v. The University of Alcalá (Universidad de Alcalá), founded in 1499, is known for its historical significance in Spanish literature and the arts.

In Portugal:[13]

i. The University of Coimbra (Universidade de Coimbra), founded in 1290, is one of the oldest universities in Europe. It has a rich history and was

---

significant role in the formation of modern Spain. The Kingdom of Navarre, located in the northern part of the Iberian Peninsula, had its own distinct history and identity. The marriage of Ferdinand of Aragon and Isabella of Castile in 1469 led to the union of the Crown of Castile and the Crown of Aragon, which marked a significant step toward the unification of Spain. The Kingdom of León, situated to the northwest of the Iberian Peninsula, was a medieval kingdom with its own history and heritage. The Kingdom of Galicia in the northwest of Spain, was another distinct medieval kingdom with its own cultural and historical characteristics. Part of the Crown of Aragon, the Kingdom of Valencia was an important region in the east of the Iberian Peninsula. Also part of the Crown of Aragon, the Kingdom of Majorca included the Balearic Islands. In the southern part of the Iberian Peninsula, the Kingdom of Granada was the last Muslim state in Spain.

13 The County of Portugal, with its center in the northern region, was a significant precursor to the Kingdom of Portugal. Henry of Burgundy, known as Henry the Navigator, was a notable count during this period. Located in the central part of Portugal, the County of Coimbra was another important entity that contributed to the formation of the Portuguese state. The County of Portucale, also located in the north, played a central role in the emergence of Portugal as a distinct entity. The neighboring Kingdom of León, situated to the east and north, had influence over the region and played a role in early Portuguese history. The County of Galicia, in the northwest of the Iberian Peninsula, had connections with the northern parts of what is now Portugal.

originally located in Lisbon before being moved to Coimbra in 1537. It is known for its contributions to various academic fields.

ii. The University of Lisbon (Universidade de Lisboa) was established in 1290. The modern University of Lisbon is a result of mergers and reorganizations of several higher education institutions in the city.

In Germany:[14]

i. The University of Heidelberg (Ruprecht-Karls-Universität Heidelberg), established in 1386, is one of the oldest universities in Germany and has a strong tradition in various academic disciplines.

ii. The University of Leipzig (Universität Leipzig), founded in 1409, is one of the oldest universities in Germany and is known for its contributions to philosophy, theology, and the sciences.

iii. The University of Rostock (Universität Rostock), established in 1419, is one of the oldest universities in Germany and the Baltic Sea region. It has a long history of academic achievement.

iv. The University of Greifswald (Universität Greifswald), founded in 1456, is one of the oldest universities in Germany and is known for its contributions to research and education.

v. The University of Freiburg (Albert-Ludwigs-Universität Freiburg), established in 1457, is one of the oldest universities in Germany and has a strong tradition in the humanities and sciences.

---

14 During the Middle Ages, the area that is now present-day Germany was not a unified nation-state, but a collection of numerous independent and semi-autonomous states: the Holy Roman Empire was the nominal head of the empire. The East Frankish Kingdom became the Kingdom of Germany. The Duchy of Bavaria was one of the largest and most influential duchies in the Holy Roman Empire. The Duchy of Swabia was located in the southwestern part of the Holy Roman Empire. The Duchy of Saxony was a prominent region in the northern part of the Holy Roman Empire. The Duchy of Franconia was located in the northern and central parts of the empire and was known for its cultural and historical significance. The Duchy of Lorraine, in the western part of the Holy Roman Empire, had a complex history and was often disputed between different powers. The Margraviate of Brandenburg, situated in the northeastern part of the empire, was a key territory that later played a role in the formation of Prussia and modern Germany. While not part of present-day Germany, the County of Flanders had important trade and cultural connections with the Holy Roman Empire.

- In Austria, the University of Vienna (Universität Wien), founded in 1365, is one of the oldest universities in Austria and one of the oldest in the German-speaking world. It has a rich history of academic excellence and is known for its contributions to various academic fields.
- In Central Europe:

   i. Charles University, Prague, Czech Republic, founded in 1348, is one of the oldest universities in Central Europe and is named after Emperor Charles IV. It has a strong reputation for academic excellence.

   ii. The University of Pécs (Pécsi Tudományegyetem), founded in 1367, is one of the oldest universities in Hungary and in Central Europe. It has a strong tradition of academic excellence.

   iii. The Jagiellonian University, Krakow, Poland: Established in 1364, Jagiellonian University is one of the oldest universities in Poland and Central Europe. It has a rich history of scholarship and cultural contributions.

These universities, along with many others across Europe, have deep-rooted traditions, historic buildings, and a legacy of academic excellence that continues to influence education and research today. Universities in the Middle Ages were pivotal in shaping the education, skills, and cultural context of diplomats. They provided the knowledge and intellectual foundation necessary for diplomatic endeavors and contributed to the effectiveness of diplomatic interactions in a diverse and complex medieval world. They provided education and training for individuals who aspired to become diplomats. Diplomats needed a range of skills, including knowledge of languages, history, law, and rhetoric, which could be acquired through university education. Universities offered courses in law and diplomacy, which were valuable for individuals interested in diplomatic careers. Understanding legal frameworks and diplomatic protocols was crucial for successful diplomatic negotiations. At the same time, they were essential in teaching languages, including Latin, which was widely used in diplomatic correspondence during the Middle Ages. Professors and scholars from universities sometimes accompanied diplomatic missions to serve as advisors or intermediaries. Their expertise in various fields, including theology and philosophy, could be valuable in negotiations and intellectual exchanges. Universities sometimes served as venues for negotiations or mediations, particularly in disputes involving the Church. The University of Paris played a significant role in theological disputes and negotiations within the Church. The university's scholars and theologians often engaged in discussions and resolutions related to religious controversies. The University of Bologna sometimes served as a venue for mediating disputes related to canon law and church governance during the Middle Ages. The University of Oxford was involved in intellectual and theological debates during the Middle Ages. It contributed to discussions surrounding church matters. The University of Salamanca occasionally played a role in mediating theological disputes. The University of Heidelberg was involved in theological and religious debates, particularly during the Reformation era. The University of Padua was occasionally involved in discussions and negotiations regarding church matters. The University of Toulouse participated in debates related to religious doctrine and church governance. The University of Coimbra (Portugal) sometimes served as a platform for mediating theological disputes. These universities were not only centers of learning but also forums for intellectual and theological debates. They often hosted gatherings, colloquia, and debates in which scholars and theologians engaged in discussions about religious and church-related matters. In some cases, these discussions led to resolutions or played a role in mediating disputes within the Church, reflecting the close connection between academia and ecclesiastical affairs during the Middle Ages.

Renaissance Universities: Forging Diplomacy and Cultural Renaissance

Several universities were founded during the Renaissance in Europe. These institutions contributed to the flourishing of learning, arts, and sciences during this period.

– In Germany:[15]

  i. The *University of Würzburg* was founded in 1402, and it was one of the first universities established in the Holy Roman Empire during the early Renaissance (Vollmuth & Keil, 2003).

---

15 During the Renaissance, the territories that make up modern-day Germany were part of the Holy Roman Empire which included various territories and regions that correspond to modern Germany, as well as parts of other modern European countries: seven electorates, which were influential territories responsible for electing the Holy Roman Emperor. These electorates included the Electorate of Brandenburg, the Electorate of Saxony, and the Electorate of the Palatinate. Various kingdoms and duchies, such as the Duchy of Bavaria, the Duchy of Württemberg, and the Margraviate of Baden, were also part of the Holy Roman Empire. There were numerous free imperial

- In Austria:[16]
  i. The *University of Graz* (Universität Graz) was established in 1585 and supported by the Jesuit order. The University of Graz's curriculum initially consisted of basic humanistic studies and further studies in philosophy and theology.
  ii. Considered to be the third oldest university in Austria, the *University of Innsbruck* was founded in 1669, with roots dating back even earlier, to 1562 when a Jesuit college was established.

- In Central Europe:

  i. *Eötvös Loránd University* (Eötvös Loránd Tudományegyetem), Budapest although it officially dates its establishment to 1635, it has rooted that trace back to the Jesuit University of Trnava in the 17th century.
  ii. *Palacký University Olomouc* is the second oldest university in the Czech Republic. Its tradition reaches back to 1573, when the former Jesuit College

---

cities, such as Nuremberg, Augsburg, and Frankfurt, which were self-governing and enjoyed a degree of independence. Many small principalities, bishoprics, and smaller territories existed within the Holy Roman Empire, each with its own ruler. The Hanseatic League was a confederation of merchant cities and towns in northern Germany and other parts of Europe, which played a significant role in trade and commerce during the Renaissance. Parts of what is now Switzerland were also part of the Holy Roman Empire during the Renaissance.

16 During the Renaissance, the territories that make up modern-day Austria were part of the Habsburg Monarchy that included various territories that are now part of modern-day Austria, as well as parts of other modern European countries: Archduchy of Austria was the core territory of the Habsburg Monarchy and included regions that are now part of modern-day Austria, such as Lower Austria (Niederösterreich) and Upper Austria (Oberösterreich). Styria, located in the southeast of present-day Austria, was part of the Habsburg Monarchy during the Renaissance. Carinthia, a region in the southern part of modern Austria, was also part of the Habsburg Monarchy. Carniola situated to the southwest of modern Slovenia, was part of the Habsburg Monarchy during this period. The Tyrol region in the western part of modern Austria was under Habsburg control. Further Austria (Vorderösterreich) included parts of present-day southwestern Germany and northern Switzerland and was part of the Habsburg Monarchy. The Habsburg Monarchy also included the territories that make up modern-day Belgium and Luxembourg. The Kingdom of Bohemia, with its capital in Prague (in what is now the Czech Republic), was part of the Habsburg Monarchy. Parts of the Kingdom of Hungary were also under Habsburg rule, including present-day western Hungary and parts of Slovakia.

gained privileges equal to those of other European universities, granted by Maximilian II, Holy Roman Emperor. The university consisted of two faculties at the dawn of its history, providing education in Liberal Arts and Theology. University education itself started three years after the foundation of the university, in 1576, when the Englishman George Warr started to lecture on Philosophy. That same year, the first students were officially enrolled in the university's registry. The university gained recognition outside the Czech Lands, and its sphere of influence extended from Moravia and Silesia, over to Poland, Hungary, and the Austrian lands, to Germany, Scandinavia, and Eastern Europe. However, during the Bohemian Estates Revolt (1618–1620) the Jesuit Order was driven out of Moravia and the university temporarily ceased operations. It was again restored in 1621 after the revolt was crushed.

– In the Netherlands:[17]

i. *Leiden University* was the first university to be established in the Netherlands. William of Orange gave Leiden Academia Lugduno Batava in 1575, it is said in recognition of the city's courageous resistance against the seige by the Spanish invaders.

ii. Although the Dies Natalis of *Utrecht University* is 26 March 1636, the city of Utrecht already suggested the founding of a university in 1470 when the city of Utrecht proposes that a university be established in Utrecht. In 1580, the city of Utrecht was converted to Protestantism, and the libraries

---

17   During the Renaissance, the territories that make up modern-day Netherlands were part of a larger region known as the Low Countries consisted of a number of separate territories and regions, some of which are now part of the modern Netherlands, Belgium, and Luxembourg. The County of Holland roughly corresponds to the modern province of South Holland in the Netherlands, which includes cities like The Hague and Rotterdam. The County of Zeeland is another province in the southwestern part of the modern Netherlands. The County of Flanders covered parts of present-day Belgium, including cities like Ghent, Bruges, and Antwerp, as well as areas of northern France. The Duchy of Brabant encompassed modern-day Belgian and Dutch Brabant, including cities like Brussels and Leuven. The County of Hainaut included parts of modern Belgium and France. The County of Namur is located in modern Belgium. The Duchy of Limburg was divided into several parts, including a Dutch and a Belgian province, as well as a part in Germany. Overijssel and Gelderland are in the eastern part of the modern Netherlands. The city and province of Utrecht in the central Netherlands were also part of the Low Countries. The Grand Duchy of Luxembourg was also a part of the historical Low Countries during the Renaissance.

of Catholic monasteries and convents were confiscated. A city library was founded. In 1634, Humanism and the Protestant Reformation formed the Utrecht foundation – paid for by the city – for the founding of an Illustrious School. The Illustrious School was using the "Groot Kapittelhuis", the Auditorium of the current Utrecht University Hall for its classes.

iii. The *Groningen University* (Rijksuniversiteit Groningen) was stablished in 1614, is considered one of the oldest universities in the Netherlands and is renowned for its research and academic programs.

- In Switzerland:[18]

i. The University of *Basel* was stablished in 1460 and played a significant role in humanism and the study of Greek and Latin classics.

- In Denmark:[19]

i. The University of *Copenhagen* was founded in 1479 and became a center for Renaissance humanism in Northern Europe.

While universities during the Renaissance were not "platforms of diplomacy" in the modern sense, they did play a supporting role in the education and development of individuals who would later become diplomats and foreign policy experts (Dooley, 1989; Gavroglu, 2001; Grendler, 2002, 2003, 2004, 2022; Rothman, 2021).

---

18 During the Renaissance, the territories that make up modern-day Switzerland consisted of a patchwork of regions, cities, and cantons, each with its own degree of autonomy and often subject to the influence of neighboring powers. The Swiss Confederation was formed through a series of alliances and agreements between different cantons. Some of the original cantons included Uri, Schwyz, and Unterwalden, which formed the core of the Swiss Confederation. The city and cantons of Zürich, Bern, Basel, Geneva, Appenzell, Valais, Graubünden were important economic, religious and cultural hubs during the Renaissance.

19 During the Renaissance, the territories that make up modern-day Denmark were part of the Kingdom of Denmark that included not only the Danish peninsula but also several other territories, including parts of what is now modern Sweden and Norway. The Danish Peninsula includes the Jutland Peninsula, the main part of modern-day Denmark, as well as the islands of Funen, Zealand, and many smaller islands. Norway was in a personal union with Denmark during this period, with the Danish monarch also ruling over Norway. Skåne, Halland, and Blekinge located in the southern part of modern Sweden, were under Danish rule during the Renaissance, although they were sometimes contested with Sweden. Dithmarschen was a semi-independent region that was part of the Holy Roman Empire but had close ties to Denmark.

Additionally, the emphasis on language, culture, and the exchange of knowledge contributed to the diplomatic activities of the time. European universities offered a humanist education, which included the study of languages, history, rhetoric, and other subjects relevant to diplomacy. Scholars and philosophers associated with universities often provided intellectual and diplomatic advice to rulers and statesmen. They played a role in shaping diplomatic strategies and foreign policy decisions. Niccolò Machiavelli (1469–1527), diplomat, and philosopher, served as an ambassador for the Republic of Florence. He is best known for his work *The Prince*, which explores political strategy and leadership. Sir Thomas More (1478–1535), lawyer, statesman, and humanist, served as an ambassador for King Henry VIII of England. He is also known for his work *Utopia*, a satirical commentary on the political and social issues of his time. Baldassare Castiglione (1478–1529), courtier and diplomat, served as an ambassador to the courts of various Italian city-states. He wrote *The Book of the Courtier*, a famous guide on courtly etiquette and behavior. Ermolao Barbaro (1454–1493), humanist and diplomat, served as the Venetian ambassador to the Papal States. He was a proponent of classical education and philosophy. Desiderius Erasmus (1466–1536), humanist and theologian, traveled extensively throughout Europe and acted as an informal ambassador for the promotion of humanism and the reform of the Catholic Church. Albrecht Dürer (1471–1528), artist, and printmaker, served as an ambassador for Emperor Maximilian I. He used his diplomatic missions to learn about the artistic developments in other European regions. Alfonso de Valdés (c. 1490–1532), Spanish diplomat, served as the secretary and ambassador to Emperor Charles V. He played a significant role in diplomacy during the early 16th century. Francesco Guicciardini (1483–1540), historian, diplomat, and statesman, served as an ambassador for the Republic of Florence and the Papal States. His writings provide valuable insights into the political events of his time. Renaissance universities emphasized the study of classical languages, such as Latin and Greek, which were essential for diplomatic correspondence and communication during that era. Renaissance universities, cosmopolitan in nature, attracted students and scholars from various regions. This diversity contributed to cultural exchange and a broader understanding of different nations and their customs. Some universities, such as the *University of Siena* in Italy, offered courses in *diplomatics* (the study of historical documents) and the art of diplomacy. These courses provided practical training for individuals entering the diplomatic service.

Enlightened Academia: European Universities' Diplomatic Influence in the Enlightenment Era

During the Enlightenment (which roughly spanned from the late 17th to the 18th century, was characterized by a shift toward rationalism, humanism, and a focus on reason, science, and individual rights) European universities continued to play a role in the education of individuals who would later become diplomats and foreign policy experts. However, the Enlightenment was primarily a period of intellectual and philosophical development, with universities focusing on the advancement of knowledge and the spread of Enlightenment ideals rather than serving as explicit "platforms of diplomacy." European universities continued to educate individuals who pursued careers in diplomacy. Students received a broad education in various subjects, including history, languages, politics, and law, which were relevant to diplomatic service. Notable personalities who were educated during the Enlightenment and went on to become influential diplomats, often contributing to the spread of Enlightenment ideas and the shaping of international relations during the 18th century. Charles-Maurice Talleyrand-Perigord (1754–1838) who served under various French governments, including during the French Revolution and the Napoleonic era, was studied theology at the Sorbonne until the age of 21. He later represented France as an ambassador in several European capitals, including London and Vienna, became minister of foreign affairs and prime minister (1830-'34, appointed by Louis Philippe I). Joseph de Maistre (1753–1821), a Savoyard philosopher, writer, lawyer, and diplomat served as the ambassador of the Kingdom of Sardinia to Russia. He was educated by the Jesuits (Herbermann, 1913), and completed his training in the law at the University of Turin in 1774. De Maistre advocated social hierarchy and monarchy in the period immediately following the French Revolution. He is known for his conservative and counter-Enlightenment ideas, claiming, inter alia, that the crimes of the Reign of Terror were the consequence of Enlightenment thought (Lebrun, 1967). After the defeat of Napoleon and the restoration of the House of Savoy's dominion over Piedmont and Savoy under the terms of the Congress of Vienna, he returned in 1817 to Turin and served as magistrate and minister of state until his death in 1821. Count Axel von Fersen (1755–1810) who played a key role in Swedish diplomacy during the late 18th century (he was associated with the French royal family, particularly Marie Antoinette), was studied at military academies in Brunswick, Turin, Strasbourg and Lüneburg. Marquis de Lafayette (1757–1834), a French aristocrat, military officer, and statesman, who served as a diplomat in the United States during the American Revolution, was studied at the prestigious Académie de Versailles.

He became a prominent advocate of Enlightenment principles and a symbol of Franco-American friendship (Auricchio, 2014; Vowell, 2015). Johann Wolfgang von Goethe (1749–1832), the famous German writer and poet, was studied law at Leipzig University from 1765 to 1768. Later, he attended the University of Strasbourg. His time at these universities exposed him to Enlightenment ideas, literature, and philosophy, which greatly influenced his intellectual develop-ment. In 1776, Goethe was appointed as a Privy Counsellor and head of the War Commission in the Duchy of Saxe-Weimar-Eisenach. In this role, he was respon-sible for the administration of the university in Weimar. He held this position for many years and played a crucial role in the development of the University of Jena, which was closely associated with Weimar's intellectual and cultural circles. In addition to his literary works, Goethe made contributions to the field of natural sciences. He wrote extensively on botany, geology, and color theory, and he was involved in scientific discussions with leading scientists and scholars of his era. Goethe received honorary degrees and recognitions from various universities, including the University of Oxford and the University of Berlin (Jaeck, 1917).

During the Enlightenment era, many universities hosted public lectures, debates, and discussions on political topics that contributed to the intellectual and diplomatic discourse of the time:

- The *University of Edinburgh*, particularly in the 18th century, was a hub for Enlightenment thinking. Professors like Adam Smith and David Hume, who were associated with the university, contributed to the intellectual and politi-cal discussions of the time through their writings and lectures (Allan, 2015).
- The University of Glasgow, like its counterpart in Edinburgh, played a signif-icant role in the Enlightenment. Adam Smith, often regarded as the father of modern economics, held the Chair of Moral Philosophy at the university and delivered lectures on political economy. At a time when the Glasgow economy was booming in the strength of its trade with America, notable Glasgow men of science and learning were making major contributions to the European world of philosophy, law, political economy, natural philosophy, medicine, and religious toleration (Hook & Sher, 2001).
- The *University of Cambridge* and the *University of Oxford* played a role in shaping Enlightenment thinking through the works of scholars like John Locke and Edmund Burke (Gascoigne, 2002; Aston, 2023).
- The *University of Paris*, with its long history, was an influential center of intel-lectual and political discourse during the Enlightenment. Enlightenment

thinkers like Voltaire and Rousseau frequented the city's salons and academic circles (Comsa et al., 2016).

- The *University of Göttingen* (Georg-August-Universität Göttingen founded in 1734 by George II, King of Great Britain and Elector of Hanover, and starting classes in 1737) became a renowned institution for Enlightenment philosophy and political thought. It attracted scholars like Immanuel Kant and Georg Wilhelm Friedrich Hegel (Biskup; Kunoff, 1972).
- The *University of Halle* was a significant center for Enlightenment philosophy and education in Germany. It hosted debates and discussions on political topics that influenced the development of Enlightenment ideas (Holloran, 2000).
- While Spain had a less prominent role in the Enlightenment compared to other European countries, the *University of Salamanca* was known for its contributions to political thought, particularly in the area of international law (Peset, 2006; Astigarraga, 2015).

Universities and Diplomacy in the Age of Industrial Revolution: Shaping a Changing World

The Industrial Revolution, which began in the late 18th century and continued into the 19th century, was marked by significant advancements in manufacturing, transportation, and technology. During the Industrial Revolution, European universities primarily focused on education, scientific and technological advancement, and the development of industry-related knowledge rather than explicitly serving as "platforms of diplomacy." However, they indirectly played a role in diplomatic efforts by contributing to economic and technological advancement, since they were at the forefront of scientific and technological discoveries that contributed to economic growth and industrial development. These advancements indirectly influenced diplomatic relations by making nations more competitive in the global market. Also, and this is particularly important, the starting point of the industrial revolution's creative contacts with European universities is found in the pioneering idea of establishing laboratories within universities. These research initiatives had economic and industrial implications, influencing national policies and diplomatic relations. Also, universities introduced technical education programs to train a workforce for the emerging industries. These programs produced skilled engineers and scientists who played a key role in technological advancement and economic growth. The Industrial Revolution witnessed the rise of numerous educated individuals who made significant contributions to various fields, including science, technology, industry, and social reform. James Watt (1736–1819) was renowned for his work on improving the steam engine: his inventions were critical in powering the Industrial Revolution and the growth of factories and mechanized industries. George Stephenson (1781–1848), often called the "Father of Railways," played a pivotal role in the development of steam locomotives and the expansion of the railway network. Michael Faraday (1791–1867) made significant contributions to the fields of electromagnetism and electrochemistry, laying the foundation for the development of electrical technology. Sir Richard Arkwright (1732–1792) was known for inventing the spinning frame and water frame, key inventions in the textile industry that revolutionized textile manufacturing. Sir Robert Peel (1788–1850), who served twice as Prime Minister of the United Kingdom (1834–1835, 1841–1846), simultaneously serving as Chancellor of the Exchequer (1834–1835), and twice as Home Secretary (1822–1827, 1828–1830), played a significant role in the political and social reforms of the Industrial Revolution era. He is known for his leadership in creating the Metropolitan Police Force (the "Bobbies") and for the repeal of the Corn Laws. Jeremy Bentham (1748–1832), philosopher, jurist, and social reformer is often regarded as the founder of utilitarianism. His ethical and political ideas had a substantial impact on social and legal reforms during the era. The work of the British chemist and physicist John Dalton (1766–1844) in atomic theory and the development of the modern atomic model, had a lasting impact on the field of chemistry. Italian Alessandro Volta (1745–1827) was credited with the invention of the first electric battery, known as the "Voltaic Pile." His work laid the foundation for the study of electricity and electrochemistry. Scientific inventions of all these gifted people helped shape the industrial revolution, thus influencing the field of international relations at all levels (Pearton, 1984; Morris, 2022).

Notable individuals educated in various European universities and became ambassadors and diplomats during the Industrial Revolution, contributing to the diplomatic and political developments of their respective countries and the broader international landscape during this transformative era. Klemens von Metternich (1773–1859), Austrian diplomat and statesman, played a crucial role in European diplomacy during and after the Napoleonic Wars. He studied at the University of Strasbourg and later served as the Austrian ambassador in various European capitals, including Paris and London. Lord Castlereagh (1769–1822), Irish statesman, studied at St. John's College, Cambridge. He served as the British Foreign Secretary and played a significant role in the Congress of Vienna (1814–1815) and post-Napoleonic diplomacy. Baron vom Stein (Heinrich Friedrich Karl vom und zum Stein, 1757–1831), the Prussian statesman who introduced the Prussian reforms, which paved the way for the unification of Germany, studied at the University of Göttingen. George Canning (1770–1827), the British statesman, was educated at Eton College and Christ Church, Oxford. He served as the British Foreign Secretary and played a role in diplomatic negotiations and policy during the early 19th century. Lord Palmerston (1784–1865), British Foreign Secretary and later Prime Minister, was educated at the University of Edinburgh and St. John's College, Cambridge.

The Industrial Revolution had a profound impact on diplomacy and international relations during the 19th century since it led to increased economic production and the expansion of international trade. Nations sought to secure favorable trade agreements and access to new markets for their manufactured goods and raw materials. Diplomats were often tasked with negotiating trade treaties and resolving trade-related disputes. Yet another aspect of economic diplomacy. After all, the Industrial Revolution had fueled the colonization and imperialism of many European powers. The quest for new colonies and resources to sustain industrial production led to competition, conflicts, and diplomatic negotiations between colonial powers. The "Scramble for Africa" is a prime example of this. The roles and impacts of European universities during the colonial era were complex and multifaceted. While they played a significant role in education, administration, and research, universities were also associated with the spread of European cultural and political influence in colonial territories, which had far-reaching consequences for both the colonized peoples and the colonizers. True to their educational role, european universities provided education and training for individuals who were involved in colonial administration, governance, and the management of overseas territories. This education often included topics related to law, diplomacy, and the administration of colonies (Lugard, 1933; Dimier, 2006). Some european universities, often closely linked to colonial powers, developed academic programs and research focused on colonial studies, which included the study of colonial history, cultures, languages, and societies:

– Oxford's School of Geography and the work of geographers like Halford Mackinder[20] and Sir Ronald Ross[21] contributed to the study of colonial

---

20 One of the founding fathers of geopolitics and geostrategy, he was the first Principal of University Extension College, Reading, which became the University of Reading, from 1892 to 1903, and Director of the London School of Economics from 1903 to 1908. While continuing his academic career part-time, he was also the Member of Parliament from 1910 to 1922.

21 Nobel Prize for Medicine in 1902 for his work on the transmission of malaria.

territories and their geography. Oxford also hosted various colonial institutes and research centers.

- Cambridge established several academic initiatives, including the Centre of South Asian Studies, which focused on the history and politics of South Asian regions and played a crucial role in the study of the British Empire in India.
- School of Oriental and African Studies (SOAS), University of London, specifically founded in 1916 to promote the study of Asia and Africa, reflecting the colonial interests of the British Empire. It has been a leading institution for colonial and post-colonial studies.
- University of Leiden (Netherlands) with a long history of Oriental and colonial studies, became a center for colonial studies, particularly important during the Dutch colonial period, especially in the study of the Dutch East Indies.
- The University of Paris also played a significant role in colonial studies, with scholars who contributed to the understanding of colonialism in Africa.
- Belgium's colonial presence in Africa led to academic research and studies on the Congo, which was a Belgian colony. The University of Brussels and the University of Leuven were involved in the study of colonial administration and the Congo.
- Portugal had a colonial empire in Africa, Asia, and South America, and the University of Lisbon was involved in the study of these colonial possessions. The university's Institute of Tropical Scientific Research (Instituto de Investigação Científica Tropical) conducted research related to Portuguese colonial territories.

Also, many European universities:

- had strong ties to religious institutions, and they played a role in the training of missionaries and religious leaders who traveled to colonial territories to spread Christianity and establish missions,
- facilitated cultural exchange and understanding by hosting students and scholars from colonial territories. This exchange contributed to the transfer of knowledge, ideas, and cultures between Europe and the colonies,
- educated individuals who would later become colonial administrators, civil servants, and diplomats. These individuals played key roles in the governance and management of colonial territories,
- supported research and exploration activities that contributed to the discovery and mapping of new territories. Academic institutions often had geographic and scientific societies that were involved in these endeavors,
- provided language training in colonial languages, which was essential for communication and administration in overseas territories. They also studied the languages of the colonized peoples,

- offered education and training in economics, trade, and commerce, which was relevant to the economic activities of colonial powers in their overseas colonies,
- often organized and supported scientific expeditions to colonial territories. These expeditions collected data on flora, fauna, geology, and anthropology, contributing to scientific knowledge.

The ideas and values disseminated by European universities often influenced colonial societies and contributed to changes in cultural, social, and political norms.

Intellectual Battlegrounds: European Universities and Diplomacy in the First World War

The impact of World War I on European universities varied from one country to another, depending on the extent of the conflict's involvement in each nation. While the war disrupted academic life and, in some cases, led to the suspension of regular activities, universities continued to adapt and fulfill various roles during this tumultuous period (Cardwell & Jones, 1975; Herrmann, 1997; Rüegg, 2004; Irish, 2015; Horne, & Pietsch, 2016; Stöckmann, 2020; Stoilova, 2020; Gottlieb, 2021):

- *Research & Innovation*: European universities conducted research related to various aspects of the war, including weaponry, medical treatment, and communication technology. Scientific and technical advancements were critical during the war.
- *Military Training*: Many European universities contributed to the war effort by providing military training programs for students who became officers in their respective nations' armed forces.
- *War-related Studies*: Universities offered courses and programs related to the war, including military strategy, international relations, and war economics. These programs trained individuals who would go on to work in various war-related capacities.
- *Humanitarian Aid*: Some universities were involved in humanitarian efforts to assist the wounded and refugees. Medical schools and students provided essential support to military hospitals and field hospitals.
- *Intellectual Exchange*: Despite the conflict, European universities continued to be centers of intellectual exchange. Professors and scholars contributed to discussions and debates related to the war, its causes, and its consequences.

- *Post-War Rebuilding*: After the war, universities played a role in the post-war reconstruction and recovery efforts. They educated a new generation of leaders and professionals who would be involved in rebuilding war-torn Europe.
- *Analysis & Reflection*: European universities conducted research and analysis on the causes and consequences of the war. Scholars examined the geopolitical, economic, and social factors that led to the conflict.
- *Memory & Commemoration*: Some universities became sites of memory and commemoration, with monuments and memorials dedicated to those who had served and died in the war.

Academic Diplomacy: European Universities' Post-World War II Global Influence

The role of European universities during World War II was complex and varied, reflecting the diversity of experiences across different countries and institutions. While some universities actively contributed to the war effort, others faced significant challenges and disruptions, and many played important roles in the recovery and reconstruction that followed the war (Lobkowicz, 1987; Cardozier, 1993; Rüegg, 2004):

- *Disruption & Closures*: In countries directly affected by the war, many universities faced disruption and temporary closures. Some universities in occupied territories were forced to halt their activities, while others continued to operate under strict restrictions imposed by occupying forces.
- *Research for the War Effort*: In countries engaged in the war, universities played a crucial role in conducting research related to the conflict. This research included military technology, medical advancements, and other war-related fields.
- *Academic Mobilization*: Students and faculty members were often mobilized for the war effort. Students joined the military or worked in various capacities to support the war, and professors provided their expertise in areas such as strategy, intelligence, and logistics.
- *Resistance & Underground Education*: In occupied countries, some universities played a covert role in resistance movements. Professors and students engaged in underground education and research, often under the threat of discovery by occupying forces.
- *Exile & Displacement*: Many scholars, intellectuals, and students fled from countries occupied by the Axis powers, seeking refuge in neutral or Allied countries. Exiled academics contributed to research, published work, and established educational institutions abroad.

- *Post-War Reconstruction*: After the war, European universities played a critical role in the post-war reconstruction of Europe. They trained professionals, educators, and leaders who would contribute to rebuilding war-torn societies.
- *Memory & Commemoration*: In the post-war era, some universities became sites of memory and commemoration, with monuments and memorials dedicated to those who served and died in the war.
- *Challenges to Academic Freedom*: Universities in occupied territories faced challenges to academic freedom, as they were subject to censorship and ideological control by occupying authorities. This had long-lasting effects on intellectual and academic life.
- *Reorganization & Rebuilding*: Many European universities had to reorganize and rebuild their academic programs, infrastructure, and faculties in the post-war period. The war had caused significant disruption and damage to universities and their facilities.

In our days, European universities have increasingly become platforms of diplomacy, playing a significant role in fostering international relations, intercultural understanding, and collaboration on a global scale:

i. *Cultural Exchange*: European universities host a diverse international student body, creating a rich cultural exchange environment. Students from various countries and backgrounds come together to learn, collaborate, and share their cultures, fostering mutual understanding and respect.

ii. *Academic Partnerships*: European universities establish academic partnerships and exchange programs with institutions around the world. These collaborations facilitate joint research, student and faculty exchanges, and the sharing of knowledge and expertise.

iii. *Diplomatic & International Relations Programs*: Many European universities offer academic programs in diplomacy, international relations, and related fields. These programs produce diplomats, policymakers, and experts in international affairs who contribute to diplomatic efforts.

iv. *Global Research Collaborations*: European universities engage in international research collaborations, addressing global challenges and fostering diplomatic relations through joint research initiatives.

v. *Peacebuilding & Conflict Resolution*: Some European universities have dedicated research centers and programs focused on peacebuilding, conflict resolution, and diplomacy. They contribute to the resolution of conflicts and the promotion of peace.

vi. *Cultural Diplomacy*: European universities often host cultural events, exhibitions, and programs that promote cultural diplomacy. These activities showcase the culture, arts, and traditions of their countries and regions.

vii. *International Conferences & Forums*: European universities frequently host international conferences and forums that bring together experts, policymakers, and diplomats to discuss global issues and solutions.

viii. *Language Learning & Multilingualism*: European universities offer a wide range of language courses, fostering linguistic diversity and promoting multilingualism, which is essential for effective diplomacy.

ix. *Global Networks*: Many European universities are part of international networks and associations that facilitate collaboration and diplomacy, such as the Erasmus+ program, the European University Association (EUA), and more.

x. *Public Diplomacy*: European universities contribute to public diplomacy efforts by engaging with the global public through educational and cultural initiatives, promoting positive perceptions of their countries and regions.

Research and Knowledge Creation

European universities are renowned for their research contributions across various fields, including science, humanities, engineering, and social sciences. They have been at the forefront of groundbreaking discoveries, academic publications, and advancements in knowledge (Greenwood & Levin, 2001; Bonaccorsi & Daraio, 2007; Castiaux, 2007; Carlsson et al., 2009; Di Cagno et al., 2014; Fabrizi et al., 2016; Olcay & Bulu, 2017):

In the UK:

- The University of Oxford is known for research excellence in a wide range of fields, including science, medicine, humanities, and social sciences. It has a strong reputation in areas such as mathematics, physics, literature, and history.
- The University of Cambridge is known for its strengths in science and engineering, as well as the humanities and social sciences.
- Imperial College is known for its expertise in science, engineering, medicine, and business. It is particularly renowned for research in areas like bioengineering, artificial intelligence, and health-related sciences.
- University College London (UCL) is a leading research university with strengths across multiple fields, including the sciences, arts, and social sciences. UCL is known for its research in areas like neuroscience, architecture, and social sciences.
- The University of Edinburgh is highly regarded for its research in various domains, including medicine, science, and the humanities. It has a strong focus on life sciences and informatics.

- The University of Manchester is known for research in materials science, physics, and life sciences. It has a strong emphasis on interdisciplinary research and innovation.
- The London School of Economics and Political Science (LSE) is a world-leading institution in the social sciences, including economics, political science, sociology, and law.
- King's College London is renowned for its research in health and life sciences, as well as the arts and humanities.
- The University of Warwick is known for research in mathematics, business, and social sciences. In Switzerland.

In Germany:

- Max Planck Institutes, Germany: A network of research institutions covering various scientific disciplines and known for their groundbreaking work.
- Ludwig Maximilian University of Munich is one of Germany's most prestigious universities and excels in various fields, including natural sciences, humanities, and social sciences. It is known for its research in physics, chemistry, and medicine.
- Technical University of Munich (TUM) is a leading technical university known for its research in engineering, natural sciences, and technology. It has strong programs in areas such as mechanical engineering, computer science, and robotics.
- Heidelberg University is known for its research in life sciences, including biology and medicine. It also has strengths in the humanities and social sciences.
- The University of Freiburg is renowned for its research in the natural sciences, especially in the fields of physics, chemistry, and mathematics.
- Humboldt University is highly regarded for its research in the humanities and social sciences. It has a strong focus on philosophy, history, and political science.
- Göttingen is known for its strengths in mathematics, physics, and biology. It has a long history of contributions to the natural sciences.
- The University of Stuttgart is recognized for its research in engineering, particularly in automotive engineering, civil engineering, and computer science.
- RWTH Aachen is one of Germany's top technical universities, with a focus on engineering and technology. It is known for research in fields like mechanical engineering and electrical engineering.

- The University of Mannheim is renowned for its research in business and economics. It has a strong business school and a focus on social sciences.
- The University of Tübingen is known for its research in various fields, including medicine, law, and the humanities. It has a strong medical faculty and is known for its research in neurosciences.

In France:

- The University of Paris (Sorbonne University) is known for its research in the humanities, social sciences, and natural sciences. It has a strong reputation in fields such as philosophy, literature, and environmental science.
- École Normale Supérieure (ENS Paris) is one of the most prestigious institutions in France, known for its excellence in the humanities, science, and social sciences. It is renowned for research in mathematics, philosophy, and literature.
- The University of Strasbourg is recognized for its research in life sciences, chemistry, and physics. It has a strong emphasis on medical research and is known for its contributions in various scientific fields.
- Aix-Marseille University is known for research in a wide range of disciplines, including medicine, natural sciences, and social sciences. It is particularly strong in the fields of marine science and neuroscience.
- Paris Sciences et Lettres (PSL) University is a group of institutions, including the Collège de France and the Paris Observatory, known for their excellence in various fields. They have strengths in the arts, social sciences, and natural sciences.
- The University of Lyon is known for its research in engineering, materials science, and technology. It has a strong focus on interdisciplinary research and innovation.
- Pierre and Marie Curie University (UPMC) which is now part of Sorbonne University, was known for its expertise in natural sciences and medicine. It had a strong reputation in fields such as physics, chemistry, and biology.
- Sciences Po Paris is a leading institution in social sciences and political science research. It is known for its contributions in areas like international relations and political theory.
- Toulouse School of Economics is renowned for its research in economics and related fields. It is a hub for economic research in France and Europe.
- The University of Nice is recognized for its research in mathematics, computer science, and climate science. It has a strong focus on environmental and climate-related research.

In Switzerland:

- ETH Zurich (Swiss Federal Institute of Technology) is one of Europe's leading technical universities and excels in various fields, including natural sciences, engineering, and computer science. It is known for research in areas such as robotics, data science, and materials science.
- The University of Zurich is a comprehensive research university with strengths in the natural sciences, medicine, and social sciences. It has a strong reputation in fields such as neuroscience, economics, and veterinary medicine.
- The University of Geneva is renowned for its research in social sciences, international relations, and humanities. It is a hub for research in political science and international diplomacy.
- EPFL (École Polytechnique Fédérale de Lausanne) is known for its expertise in engineering, life sciences, and technology. It has strengths in areas like computer science, biotechnology, and sustainable energy.
- The University of Basel is recognized for its research in life sciences, particularly in the fields of biology and medicine. It is known for its contributions to medical research and pharmaceutical sciences.
- The University of Lausanne is renowned for research in social sciences, sports science, and law. It is a leading institution in the field of sports and exercise science.
- The University of Bern has strengths in natural sciences, medicine, and the humanities. It is known for research in areas like climate science, space research, and history.
- The University of St. Gallen is a leading business school known for its research in management, economics, and law. It is one of Europe's top institutions for business and management research.
- The University of Neuchâtel is known for its research in mathematics, physics, and environmental sciences. It has a strong focus on research related to the environment and sustainability.
- The University of Fribourg is recognized for its research in linguistics, theology, and law. It has a strong tradition in the study of languages and religious studies.

In Sweden:

- Karolinska Institute is one of the world's leading medical universities and is renowned for its research in the life sciences, medicine, and healthcare.

It has a strong reputation in fields such as immunology, molecular biology, and epidemiology.

- Lund University is one of Sweden's top research universities and has strengths in a wide range of disciplines, including natural sciences, social sciences, and humanities. It is known for research in physics, materials science, and environmental studies.
- Uppsala University is one of Europe's oldest universities and has a strong focus on research in the natural sciences, medicine, and the humanities. It is renowned for its contributions in fields such as pharmacy, theology, and archaeology.
- Stockholm University is known for its research in the social sciences, humanities, and natural sciences. It has strengths in areas like environmental science, political science, and economics.
- KTH is Sweden's leading technical university and excels in engineering, technology, and natural sciences. It is known for research in areas such as information technology, sustainable energy, and materials science.
- Chalmers is another top technical university with expertise in engineering and technology. It is renowned for research in areas like automotive engineering, robotics, and nanotechnology.
- Linköping University is known for research in technology, natural sciences, and social sciences. It has strengths in fields such as computer science, medical technology, and cognitive science.
- Umeå University is recognized for its research in the life sciences, social sciences, and the humanities. It is known for its contributions in fields like molecular biology, epidemiology, and archaeology.
- The University of Gothenburg has strengths in social sciences, humanities, and natural sciences. It is renowned for research in marine science, cultural studies, and global studies.
- Luleå University of Technology is known for research in engineering, technology, and natural resources. It has a strong focus on mining and metallurgy, sustainable energy, and civil engineering.

In Italy:

- The University of Bologna is one of Europe's oldest universities and is known for research in various fields, including the humanities, social sciences, and natural sciences. It has a strong reputation in areas such as

- The University of Milan (Università degli Studi di Milano) is recognized for its research in natural sciences, medicine, and the humanities. It has strengths in areas like physics, chemistry, and literature.
- The University of Rome "La Sapienza" (Università di Roma "La Sapienza") is Italy's largest university and is renowned for research in engineering, physical sciences, and life sciences. It is known for contributions in fields such as physics, aerospace engineering, and medicine.
- Politecnico di Milano is one of Italy's top technical universities and excels in engineering, architecture, and design. It is known for research in areas like industrial design, architecture, and mechanical engineering.
- The University of Padua (Università di Padova) is one of Italy's oldest universities and has strengths in natural sciences, humanities, and social sciences. It is renowned for research in astronomy, philosophy, and law.
- The University of Florence (Università degli Studi di Firenze) is known for research in art, humanities, and natural sciences. It has strengths in areas like art history, environmental science, and pharmacology.
- The University of Pisa (Università di Pisa) is recognized for its research in physics, computer science, and engineering. It is known for contributions in fields such as mathematics and information technology.
- The University of Milan-Bicocca (Università degli Studi di Milano-Bicocca) is known for research in the natural and social sciences, including physics, psychology, and economics. It has strengths in areas like particle physics and environmental economics.
- The University of Turin (Università degli Studi di Torino) is renowned for research in economics, law, and medicine. It is known for contributions in fields like legal studies and medical research.
- Scuola Superiore Sant'Anna (Sant'Anna School of Advanced Studies) is a prestigious institution in Italy, known for research in economics, social sciences, and engineering. It has strengths in areas like economics and management.

In Spain:

- The University of Barcelona (Universitat de Barcelona) is known for research in a wide range of fields, including the natural sciences, social sciences, and the humanities. It has strengths in areas such as chemistry, medicine, and linguistics.
- Complutense University of Madrid (Universidad Complutense de Madrid) is one of Spain's most prestigious universities and is recognized for its

research in various disciplines, including the humanities, social sciences, and natural sciences. It has a strong reputation in fields like history, economics, and biology.

- The University of Valencia (Universitat de València) is known for its research in the natural sciences, mathematics, and the humanities. It has strengths in areas like chemistry, physics, and history.
- The Autonomous University of Barcelona (Universitat Autònoma de Barcelona) is renowned for research in various fields, including the social sciences, natural sciences, and engineering. It is known for its contributions in areas like environmental science, computer science, and psychology.
- The Polytechnic University of Valencia (Universitat Politècnica de València) is a leading technical university known for its research in engineering, technology, and architecture. It is recognized for contributions in areas like civil engineering, telecommunications, and robotics.
- The University of Seville (Universidad de Sevilla) is known for research in the humanities, social sciences, and natural sciences. It has strengths in areas like literature, archaeology, and biology.
- The University of Granada (Universidad de Granada) is renowned for its research in the natural sciences, including chemistry, physics, and biology. It is known for its contributions in fields like renewable energy and environmental studies.
- The University of Zaragoza (Universidad de Zaragoza) is recognized for research in various fields, including engineering, mathematics, and the social sciences. It has strengths in areas like water resources, mechanical engineering, and economics.
- Pompeu Fabra University (Universitat Pompeu Fabra) is known for research in social sciences, economics, and communication. It is renowned for contributions in areas like political science and communication studies.
- The University of Santiago de Compostela (Universidade de Santiago de Compostela) is recognized for its research in the humanities, natural sciences, and engineering. It has strengths in areas like geology, medicine, and civil engineering.

In the Netherlands:

- The University of Amsterdam (Universiteit van Amsterdam) is known for research in a wide range of fields, including the humanities, social sciences, and natural sciences. It has strengths in areas such as social psychology, cultural studies, and quantum physics.

- Delft University of Technology (Technische Universiteit Delft) is a leading technical university known for its research in engineering, technology, and applied sciences. It is recognized for contributions in fields like aerospace engineering, civil engineering, and robotics.
- Leiden University (Universiteit Leiden) is known for research in the humanities, social sciences, and natural sciences. It has strengths in areas like international law, archaeology, and astronomy.
- Utrecht University (Universiteit Utrecht) is recognized for its research in various disciplines, including the humanities, social sciences, and natural sciences. It is known for its contributions in fields like environmental science, pharmacology, and history.
- Wageningen University & Research is renowned for research in agriculture, life sciences, and environmental studies. It is a global leader in fields such as food science, agronomy, and environmental management.
- Erasmus University Rotterdam (Erasmus Universiteit Rotterdam) is known for research in economics, business, and social sciences. It has strengths in areas like international business, economics, and public administration.
- Eindhoven University of Technology (Technische Universiteit Eindhoven) is a leading technical university known for research in engineering, technology, and innovation. It is recognized for contributions in fields like electrical engineering, computer science, and industrial design.
- Groningen University (Rijksuniversiteit Groningen) is known for research in the humanities, social sciences, and natural sciences. It has strengths in areas like international relations, energy studies, and astronomy.
- Maastricht University (Universiteit Maastricht) is recognized for its research in health and life sciences, social sciences, and law. It is known for its contributions in fields like health economics, European law, and neuroscience.
- VU University Amsterdam (Vrije Universiteit Amsterdam) is known for research in a variety of fields, including social and behavioral sciences, theology, and natural sciences. It has strengths in areas like communication science, theology, and psychology.

In Austria:

- The University of Vienna (Universität Wien) is known for research in a wide range of fields, including the humanities, social sciences, and natural sciences. It has strengths in areas such as cultural studies, linguistics, and particle physics.

- Vienna University of Technology (Technische Universität Wien) is a leading technical university known for its research in engineering, technology, and natural sciences. It is recognized for contributions in fields like electrical engineering, computer science, and materials science.
- The University of Innsbruck (Universität Innsbruck) is known for research in the humanities, natural sciences, and social sciences. It has strengths in areas such as alpine research, physics, and political science.
- Graz University of Technology (Technische Universität Graz) is another top technical university known for its research in engineering and technology. It is renowned for contributions in fields like civil engineering, computer science, and biomedical engineering.
- The University of Graz (Universität Graz) is known for research in the humanities, social sciences, and natural sciences. It has strengths in areas like psychology, environmental science, and linguistics.
- Vienna University of Economics and Business (Wirtschaftsuniversität Wien) is recognized for research in business, economics, and social sciences. It is known for its contributions in fields like economics, business administration, and international business.
- The Medical University of Vienna (Medizinische Universität Wien) is renowned for research in medicine, health sciences, and life sciences. It is recognized for contributions in fields like medical research, immunology, and molecular biology.
- The University of Salzburg (Universität Salzburg) is known for research in the humanities, social sciences, and natural sciences. It has strengths in areas like musicology, law, and psychology.
- Karl-Franzens University of Graz (Universität Graz) is recognized for research in a wide range of disciplines, including the humanities, social sciences, and natural sciences. It has strengths in areas like archaeology, sociology, and environmental science.
- Linz University (Johannes Kepler Universität Linz) is known for research in the natural sciences, computer science, and engineering. It has strengths in areas like computer science, industrial mathematics, and mechatronics.

In Belgium:

- KU Leuven (Katholieke Universiteit Leuven) is one of Europe's oldest and most prestigious universities, known for research in a wide range of fields, including the humanities, social sciences, and natural sciences. It has strengths in areas such as nanotechnology, theology, and biomedical sciences.

- Ghent University (Universiteit Gent) is recognized for its research in various disciplines, including life sciences, engineering, and social sciences. It is known for its contributions in fields like biotechnology, environmental sciences, and linguistics.
- The University of Brussels (Université libre de Bruxelles – ULB) is known for research in the humanities, social sciences, and natural sciences. It has strengths in areas like law, political science, and physics.
- The University of Antwerp (Universiteit Antwerpen) is renowned for research in a wide range of fields, including social sciences, natural sciences, and business. It is known for its contributions in areas like drug discovery, economics, and history.
- Catholic University of Leuven (Université catholique de Louvain – UCLouvain) is known for research in the humanities, social sciences, and natural sciences. It has strengths in areas like philosophy, economics, and medical sciences.
- Hasselt University (Universiteit Hasselt) is recognized for research in life sciences, environmental sciences, and mobility. It is known for contributions in fields like biomedicine, environmental law, and transportation economics.
- Vrije Universiteit Brussel (VUB) is known for research in the social sciences, humanities, and natural sciences. It has strengths in areas like communication science, political science, and photonics.
- The University of Liège (Université de Liège) is renowned for research in the natural sciences, life sciences, and social sciences. It is known for its contributions in fields like space sciences, veterinary medicine, and law.
- The University of Namur (Université de Namur) is recognized for research in philosophy, law, and engineering. It is known for its contributions in fields like bioinformatics, robotics, and economics.

In Denmark:

- The University of Copenhagen is known for research in various fields, including the humanities, social sciences, and natural sciences. It has strengths in areas such as life sciences, environmental science, and law.
- Aarhus University is recognized for its research in the humanities, social sciences, and natural sciences. It is known for its contributions in fields like psychology, economics, and agricultural science.

In Norway:

- The University of Oslo is known for research in a wide range of disciplines, including the humanities, social sciences, and natural sciences. It has strengths in areas like Viking studies, physics, and political science.
- The University of Bergen is renowned for research in the humanities, natural sciences, and social sciences. It is known for its contributions in fields like marine science, global health, and literature.
- Norwegian University of Science and Technology (NTNU) (Norway) is known for research in technology, engineering, and natural sciences. It is recognized for its contributions in fields like marine technology, energy research, and medicine.

In Finland:

- The University of Helsinki is renowned for research in the humanities, social sciences, and natural sciences. It has strengths in areas like education, genetics, and philosophy.
- Aalto University is recognized for research in technology, design, and business. It is known for its contributions in fields like information technology, industrial design, and economics.

In Iceland, the University of Iceland is known for research in various fields, including the humanities, social sciences, and natural sciences. It has strengths in areas like geology, Viking studies, and environmental science.
In Central Europe:

- Charles University, located in Prague, is known for research in the humanities, natural sciences, and social sciences. It has strengths in areas like mathematics, astronomy, and literature.
- Masaryk University, based in Brno, is known for research in the humanities, natural sciences, and social sciences. It has strengths in areas like genetics, psychology, and law.
- Eötvös Loránd University, based in Budapest, is renowned for research in the humanities, natural sciences, and social sciences. It is known for contributions in fields like mathematics, physics, and psychology.
- The University of Warsaw is known for research in a wide range of disciplines, including the humanities, social sciences, and natural sciences. It has strengths in areas like philosophy, linguistics, and computer science.

- Jagiellonian University, located in Kraków, is recognized for its research in the humanities, social sciences, and natural sciences. It is known for contributions in fields like history, law, and physics.
- The University of Ljubljana is recognized for its research in a wide range of disciplines, including natural sciences, social sciences, and humanities. It is known for contributions in fields like computer science, economics, and theology.
- The University of Zagreb is known for research in the humanities, social sciences, and natural sciences. It has strengths in areas like political science, medicine, and electrical engineering.
- Comenius University in Bratislava (Slovakia) is known for research in the humanities, social sciences, and natural sciences. It has strengths in areas like linguistics, medicine, and geography.

In Portugal, the University of Lisbon is known for research in a wide range of disciplines, including the humanities, social sciences, and natural sciences. It is known for its contributions in fields like literature, economics, and environmental science.

In Cyprus, the University of Cyprus is recognized for its research in the humanities, social sciences, and natural sciences. It has strengths in areas like archaeology, economics, and computer science.

In Malta, the University of Malta is renowned for research in various fields, including the humanities, social sciences, and natural sciences. It has strengths in areas like archaeology, history, and marine biology.

Innovation and Technology Transfer

European universities are important hubs for innovation and technology transfer. They collaborate with industries and startups, fostering research and development that leads to technological advancements, patents, and economic growth (Hagen, 2008; Youtie & Shapira, 2008; Maes et al., 2011; Dornbusch & Brenner, 2013; González-Pernía et al., 2013; Comunian et al., 2014; Brighton, 2015; Schaeffer & Matt, 2016; Gál & Ptáček, 2019):

- *Imperial College London* (UK) has a strong reputation for technology transfer and commercialization of research. It has a dedicated innovation and entrepreneurship ecosystem that supports startups and spin-off companies.
- *The University of Cambridge* (UK) has a long history of innovation and has fostered numerous successful startups, including those in the tech and biotech sectors. The Cambridge Cluster, also known as the "Silicon Fen," is a hub

for technology companies. It is known for breakthroughs in fields such as semiconductors, software development, artificial intelligence, pharmaceuticals, and biotechnology. The cluster benefits from access to venture capital firms and investors who are interested in supporting technology startups and innovative ventures.

- *The Technical University of Munich* (TUM), Germany, has a strong focus on technology transfer and supports spin-off companies through its TUM Entrepreneurship Center. It is known for its contributions to the German startup ecosystem.
- *Eindhoven University of Technology* (TU/e), Netherlands, is recognized for its role in the Brainport Eindhoven region, a technology and innovation hub. It supports technology transfer and collaboration with industry.
- EPFL (*École polytechnique fédérale de Lausanne*), Switzerland, is known for its strong ties with industry and for facilitating technology transfer through its Innovation Park, which hosts numerous startups and tech companies.
- KTH *Royal Institute of Technology*, Sweden, is actively involved in technology transfer and supports the development of innovative ideas and startups through various initiatives.
- *University of Oxford* (UK) has a robust ecosystem for innovation and technology transfer. Its Oxford University Innovation (OUI) is responsible for commercializing research and supporting spin-off companies. OUI manages and protects the intellectual property (IP) generated by University of Oxford researchers (patents, copyrights, and trademarks). They work to ensure that the university's IP is properly protected and can be licensed or commercialized effectively. It identifies opportunities to license university-developed technologies to existing companies or startups. They negotiate licensing agreements that allow external organizations to use and develop Oxford's technology for various applications.
- *Jagiellonian University*, Poland, has been involved in technology transfer and supports startups and innovation in the Krakow region.
- *Politecnico di Milano*, Italy, has a strong focus on technology transfer and entrepreneurship. It collaborates with industry and supports the development of innovative solutions.
- *Aalto University*, Finland, has a reputation for innovation and supports technology transfer through initiatives such as Aalto Ventures Program and A Grid, a startup hub.

Multinational and Multicultural Environment

European universities often attract students and faculty from around the world, creating diverse and multicultural academic environments. This internationalization contributes to a rich exchange of ideas and perspectives (Guo & Jamal, 2007; Banks, 2009; Wang et al., 2012; Fabricius et al., 2017; Killick, 2017). Creating diverse and multicultural academic environments can be a powerful tool for advancing economic diplomacy. Multicultural academic environments foster cultural exchange and understanding. Cross-cultural awareness, tolerance, and empathy are essential qualities for building positive diplomatic relationships and resolving international conflicts. These universities can serve as sources of "soft power" for a country and can positively impact economic and diplomatic relations. Also, multinational and multicultural academic environments create extensive networks of individuals with connections around the world. These networks can be leveraged for economic diplomacy, as individuals often maintain relationships and connections in their home countries and contribute to economic ties. A diverse student body and faculty bring a wide range of skills, knowledge, and perspectives. This diversity can enhance a nation's human capital, making it more competitive in the global economy. Diverse skill sets can be advantageous for diplomatic efforts in areas such as trade negotiations, technology exchanges, and collaborative research. International and diverse academic communities often lead to a broader spectrum of research topics and innovation. This can lead to long-term economic benefits and strengthen diplomatic relationships with students' home countries. Diverse academic environments can facilitate partnerships between institutions in different countries. Collaborative projects, joint degrees, and research collaborations can promote cross-border economic initiatives and trade relationships. Cultural diplomacy, which aims to promote a nation's culture and values, can be advanced through multicultural academic environments. Students and faculty become cultural ambassadors who share their home cultures with their peers and the broader community, enhancing cultural diplomacy efforts. Multicultural academic environments can stimulate economic development in the host country. International students often contribute to the local economy through tuition, living expenses, and part-time employment. Faculty and researchers can bring in funding through research projects and collaborations. Graduates who have studied in diverse academic environments are often well-connected and can serve as bridges to international trade and investment opportunities. They understand the economic landscape of their home countries and can facilitate business relationships.

In the United Kingdom, the *University of Oxford* (UK) has a diverse and international student and faculty body. It welcomes scholars and students from around the world to engage in academic excellence and research. The *University of Cambridge* (UK) the prestigious world-renowned university attracts students and faculty from diverse cultural backgrounds. *Imperial College London* (UK) has a strong global reputation and is known for its diverse academic community. *London School of Economics and Political Science* (LSE) has a diverse student body and faculty from around the world that contribute to a global academic community. Graduates often take on key roles in international organizations, multinational corporations, and government agencies, fostering economic diplomacy.

In Sweden, *Stockholm University*'s commitment to diversity and inclusion helps create a multicultural academic atmosphere. The global reach of its graduates and researchers supports Sweden's economic diplomacy efforts, particularly in innovation and sustainability. Also, *Lund University* is known for its global perspective and is committed to internationalization in research and education.

In Germany, *Free University of Berlin* (Freie Universität Berlin) is known for its global perspective and international research collaborations. As one of Germany's leading technical universities, TUM attracts a diverse student and faculty population. Its research collaborations and connections with industry strengthen Germany's economic diplomacy, particularly in technology and innovation.

The *University of Amsterdam* (Universiteit van Amsterdam or UvA) is a popular destination for international students due to its wide range of programs offered in English. The university offers a diverse selection of English-taught undergraduate and graduate programs in various fields, making it appealing to students from around the world. After all, Amsterdam is an international city with a rich cultural scene, and the Netherlands is known for having a high level of English proficiency among its population, making it easier for international students to navigate daily life. Studying at UvA provides students with the opportunity to experience a diverse and vibrant cultural environment. UvA's diverse student body and faculty offer ample opportunities for international students to build global networks and gain a global perspective.

The *University of Vienna* (Universität Wien) is indeed recognized for its international programs and a multicultural campus. Vienna is known for its multicultural and cosmopolitan atmosphere, attracting people from various backgrounds, contributing to the diversity and international nature of the university. Besides, *Universität Wien* has a long history and a strong reputation for offering a wide range of programs, research opportunities, and a welcoming environment for students from all around the world. The university emphasizes a global perspective in its research and teaching, encouraging students to explore issues from an international standpoint, since partnerships with other universities and institutions worldwide, facilitates academic and research collaborations.

The *University of Copenhagen* (Københavns Universitet) in Denmark is known for actively promoting internationalization and maintaining a welcoming environment for students and scholars from around the world. Copenhagen, the capital city of Denmark, is a cosmopolitan and diverse city known for its international atmosphere. It offers a high quality of life and a welcoming environment for students from abroad.

In Switzerland, *École Polytechnique Fédérale de Lausanne* (EPFL) is known as an international research university that attracts a diverse community of students and researchers from around the world. EPFL offers a range of English-taught Bachelor's, Master's, and Ph.D. programs, making it accessible to non-French-speaking international students. The university is known for its cutting-edge research and is highly regarded in various scientific and technological disciplines. Researchers from different countries are attracted to EPFL for its research opportunities. After all, Lausanne, where EPFL is located, is a city with a strong international presence due to its status as an Olympic capital and home to various international organizations. This adds to the multicultural atmosphere. Swiss Federal Institute of Technology Zurich (ETH Zurich, Eidgenössische Technische Hochschule Zürich) is another internationally recognized institution in Switzerland with a strong reputation for research and education and actively that welcomes scholars and students from various countries. Zurich is a cosmopolitan city known for its international atmosphere and quality of life. It provides a welcoming environment for students from abroad.

Community Engagement

European universities are deeply engaged with their local communities, offering educational opportunities, cultural events, and outreach programs. They contribute to the cultural and social fabric of their cities and regions (Boucher et al., 2003; Chatterton, 2000; Reichert, 2006; Goddard & Puukka, 2008; Compagnucci & Spigarelli, 2020; Bell & Lewis Jr, 2023):

In Austria, the *University of Vienna* is not only one of the oldest universities in Europe but also a major cultural institution in the Austrian capital. It hosts numerous cultural events and lectures, making it a hub for intellectual and artistic activities in Vienna.

In Spain, the *University of Barcelona* is deeply involved in the cultural life of the city. It hosts cultural events, museums, and promotes local arts and heritage. It contributes to the vibrant cultural scene of Bologna through various events and initiatives.

- *Leiden University* has strong ties to the city of Leiden and contributes to the cultural and intellectual life of the region through its museums, libraries, and public lectures.
- *Charles University* contributes to Prague's cultural heritage through its academic and cultural events, historical sites, and partnerships with local cultural institutions.
- As one of the oldest universities in Europe, *Jagiellonian University* plays a vital role in the cultural life of Krakow and supports various cultural activities in Poland.

European universities are hubs of knowledge and expertise. When universities engage with local businesses, industries, and startups, they can transfer valuable knowledge and technologies that enhance local economic development. This, in turn, strengthens the economic ties of the local community with other regions and nations. These universities often play a central role in creating innovation ecosystems that foster entrepreneurship, research, and development, leading to the creation of new products and services, and thus they attract foreign investment and partnerships. A well-educated and skilled local workforce can attract foreign businesses and investments, which can lead to economic growth and enhance international economic relationships. It is a domino effect of positive actions. Outward-looking universities engage in research collaborations with local industries and international partners. Collaborative research projects often involve cross-border partnerships, which can lead to increased trade and economic diplomacy between countries. Undoubtedly, the presence of a university in a community can have a significant economic impact through job creation, student spending, and local purchasing. A key element of their extroversion is the development of fruitful relationships with the business community: many european universities often support entrepreneurship and the creation of startups. These startups can become important contributors to the local economy and can also seek international markets, fostering economic diplomacy through trade and collaboration. University partnerships lead to international education opportunities for students, furthering cultural understanding and diplomatic relations. Scientific research feeds the policy debate. Thus, the university fulfils its basic social role: it becomes the bridge between society and the new generation.

European universities are addressing societal challenges through research and community engagement. They play key roles in areas such as healthcare, environmental sustainability, social justice, and poverty alleviation (Benneworth et al., 2014; Maassen et al., 2019; Assunção & Moreira, 2020; Amiano Bonatxea et al., 2022; Bell & Lewis Jr, 2023).

- *Uppsala University* (Sweden) is committed to sustainability and actively engages with the local community. It works on projects related to climate change, sustainable urban development, and global health. The university has set ambitious goals to reduce its environmental impact, promote sustainable research and education, and engage with the local community in sustainable development efforts. This includes efforts to reduce energy consumption, minimize waste, and promote sustainable transportation options. The campus itself is an example of sustainable urban planning and architecture.
- *Aarhus University* (Denmark) focuses on research and community engagement in areas such as environmental sustainability, health, and social development. It collaborates with local organizations to address societal challenges. It conducts research on a wide range of sustainability-related topics, including climate change, energy efficiency, biodiversity, and social sustainability.
- The *University of Amsterdam* (The Netherlands) is dedicated to addressing societal challenges like climate change, inequality, and urban development through interdisciplinary research, and engages with the local community to find solutions.
- *Lund University* (Sweden) is involved in various sustainability initiatives and has research programs aimed at addressing climate change, environmental conservation, and public health. Lund University presents sustainability awards to individuals and organizations that have made significant contributions to sustainability in the local community and beyond. The university encourages green campus initiatives, has implemented green areas, sustainable landscaping, and biodiversity projects across its campuses, and it encourages the use of sustainable transportation options, such as biking and public transit.
- The *University of Edinburgh* (UK) has research centers and initiatives dedicated to addressing social inequality, health, and sustainability, such as the Centre for Research on Families and Relationships (CRFR), the Institute for Social Policy, Housing, Equalities Research (I-SPHERE), the Global Justice Academy, the Usher Institute, the Centre for Population Health Sciences, the Centre for Cardiovascular Science, Edinburgh Climate Change Institute, the

Global Environment and Society Academy, and the Edinburgh Centre for Carbon Innovation.

- The *University of Zurich* (Switzerland) is known for its interdisciplinary research on global challenges, including climate change, public health, and sustainable development. It collaborates with local and international partners to find solutions.
- *Trinity College Dublin* (Ireland) is committed to addressing societal challenges through research and community engagement. It focuses on areas such as public health (epidemiology, healthcare systems, infectious diseases, and other aspects of public health), sustainability (environmental science, renewable energy, climate change, and sustainable development) and social justice (research on inequality, human rights, and other social issues).
- *Charles University* (Prague, Czech Republic) engages with societal challenges by conducting research on areas like public health, social inequality, and sustainable development, and by collaborating with local organizations.

European Union (EU) Programs in Higher Education

Several European Union (EU) programs have played a significant role in strengthening the European higher education community and promoting cooperation among European universities. These programs aim to enhance mobility, foster collaboration, and promote excellence in higher education (Beerkens & Vossensteyn, 2011; Garben, 2012; Bergan, 2019; Dakowska, 2019; Curaj et al., 2020; Gaston, 2023; Highman et al., 2023; Hill & Vanhoonacker-Kormoss, 2023):

- *Erasmus+ Program*: The Erasmus+ program is one of the most well-known EU initiatives in the field of higher education. It supports student and staff mobility, academic cooperation, and innovation in teaching and learning. Erasmus+ has enabled millions of students, educators, and researchers to study, teach, and conduct research in other European countries, fostering a sense of European identity and collaboration. Student mobility and exchange fosters cultural understanding and the development of a highly skilled workforce that can contribute to economic diplomacy efforts. Graduates who have studied in the EU can be highly sought after by international businesses and organizations, contributing to economic relations between their home countries and the EU.
- *Horizon Europe*: While primarily focused on research and innovation, the Horizon Europe program also supports higher education institutions in conducting cutting-edge research, collaborating across borders, and addressing

global challenges. Graduates and researchers who launch startups and innovative ventures can strengthen economic ties and foster innovation partnerships with other countries.

- *European Research Council* (ERC): Part of the Horizon Europe program, the ERC provides funding for excellent researchers and their teams, supporting innovative and groundbreaking research across various disciplines.
- *Marie Skłodowska-Curie Actions*: Also under the Horizon Europe program, these actions support the training and career development of researchers through international and intersectoral mobility.
- *European University Alliances*: The European University Initiative aims to create networks of European universities that collaborate closely, share resources, and develop joint programs. These alliances promote mobility, research, and innovation, contributing to the development of a European higher education area: efficient networks that can be leveraged for economic diplomacy, trade, and investment opportunities.
- *Bologna Process*: While not an EU program, the Bologna Process is a voluntary intergovernmental initiative that has greatly influenced European higher education. It aims to create a common European Higher Education Area by harmonizing degree structures, quality assurance, and recognition of qualifications, among other aspects.
- *TEMPUS & Capacity Building Projects*: These initiatives, which have evolved into Erasmus+, supported the modernization of higher education systems in neighboring countries and partner regions. They encouraged cooperation between European and non-European institutions and contributed to capacity building in higher education.

It is no coincidence that the European universities often have a strong global reputation. This reputation can be a form of soft power, enhancing the influence of European countries and supporting their diplomatic efforts.

Global Collaboration

European universities are active participants in international research collaborations and partnerships. They work with institutions worldwide to address global challenges and share knowledge (Mattsson et al., 2010; Knobel et al., 2013; Lind et al., 2013; Lebeau & Papatsiba, 2016; Kwiek, 2021; Ursić et al., 2022):

- *Imperial College* (London) has a strong focus on global research collaborations, particularly in science, technology, engineering, and medicine. It partners with institutions and organizations worldwide. During the COVID-19 pandemic, Imperial College played a pivotal role in global research collaborations related to epidemiology, modeling, and public health. The college's COVID-19 Response Team worked with international organizations and governments to analyze the impact of the pandemic and recommend public health interventions. Collaborations with institutions in Africa, India, and other regions focus on issues like infectious diseases, maternal health, and healthcare system strengthening. Imperial College collaborates with international space agencies and institutions on space research and exploration projects. These collaborations include partnerships with NASA, the European Space Agency (ESA), and other space research organizations.

- *Cambridge University* is known for its extensive international research collaborations and partnerships in a wide range of disciplines. Cambridge's research in biomedicine and life sciences includes collaborations with institutions across the globe. These partnerships address genomics, medical research, drug development, and related areas.
- *ETH Zurich* is a global leader in scientific research and has partnerships with institutions and industries worldwide. ETH Zurich collaborates with international climate organizations and research institutions to address climate change. The university's expertise in climate science and modeling contributes to global efforts to understand and mitigate climate change.
- *Copenhagen University* is actively engaged in international research collaborations, particularly in the fields of health, social sciences, and humanities.
- *Heidelberg University* has a strong international profile and collaborates with universities and research institutions worldwide.
- The *University of Edinburgh* actively participates in international research projects and initiatives, particularly in medicine, informatics, and social sciences.
- *Amsterdam University* is involved in numerous international research collaborations and initiatives across various disciplines.
- *Trinity College Dublin* is committed to international research collaborations and has partnerships with institutions and organizations globally.
- The *University of Helsinki* is actively involved in international research collaborations, particularly in natural sciences, social sciences, and humanities.
- *Oslo University* actively collaborates with international partners in various research projects and initiatives.

Entrepreneurship and Startups

European universities incubate entrepreneurial talent and support the development of startups. University-based innovation ecosystems help bridge the gap between academia and industry (Clarysse et al., 2005; Lendner, 2007; Jansen et al., 2015; Dalmarco et al., 2018; Van Weele et al., 2018; Ricci et al., 2019; Ṇikitina et al., 2020):

– *Imperial College* has an Innovation Hub and a Venture Mentoring Service to support entrepreneurs. It also hosts the Imperial White City Innovation District that is underpinned by the London Borough of Hammersmith & Fulham's industrial strategy, Economic Growth for Everyone. Together, they laid the foundations for an ecosystem which has since attracted entrepreneurs and established innovators, all seeking new solutions to the world's greatest challenges.

– The *University of Cambridge* has several entrepreneurship programs, including the Judge Business School's Entrepreneurship Centre and the Cambridge Innovation Center.

– EPFL (*École polytechnique fédérale de Lausanne*) has an Innovation Park and numerous programs to support entrepreneurship and innovation, including Venturelab. Cambridge Enterprise is responsible for the commercialisation of University of Cambridge intellectual property and is a wholly owned subsidiary of the University. Cambridge Enterprise provides access to angel and early-stage capital through the Cambridge Enterprise Seed Funds and Cambridge Enterprise Venture Partners, and offers business planning, mentoring, specialist surgeries and other related programmes.

– *Delft University of Technology* (The Netherlands) has the YES!Delft incubator, which supports tech startups, and it is a part of the European Institute of Innovation & Technology (EIT) network. According to the Dutch government website business.gov.nl, "a start-up is not just any starting business [...] a start-up is a business that translates an innovative idea into a scalable and generic product or service, using new technology." YES!Delft was established in 2005 in collaboration with TU Delft, the Municipality of Delft and TNO and has so far supported more than 200 companies, 90 % of which are still active.

– KTH *Royal Institute of Technology*, Sweden: KTH Innovation supports entrepreneurial initiatives from students, researchers, and alumni, providing guidance and resources for startups.

- *Karlsruhe Institute of Technology* (Germany) has the KIT Innovation Management to support startups and commercialize research results.
- ETH *Zurich* supports startups through its Pioneer Fellowship program and the ETH Entrepreneur Club.
- The *University of Helsinki* has an entrepreneurship program and collaborates with Helsinki Think Company to support student startups.
- *Lund University* (Sweden) actively supports entrepreneurship through its Lund University Innovation System (LUIS).
- *Aalto University* (Finland) has the Aalto Entrepreneurship Society (Aaltoes) and the A Grid, a startup hub supporting early-stage companies.

Cultural Exchange

European universities foster cultural exchange and understanding through academic programs, student exchanges, and research projects that transcend borders and promote global citizenship (De Vita, 2007; Heitor, 2015; De Wit, 2016; Fabricius et al., 2017; Bohm et al., 2019; Čeginskas & Lähdesmäki, 2023; Mäkinen et al., 2023). Cultural exchanges create opportunities for students, faculty, and researchers to build international networks. These connections can lead to collaborations on research projects, joint academic programs, and business ventures. Collaborative research and academic projects resulting from cultural exchanges can lead to knowledge transfer and innovation. This can have practical applications in various industries, contributing to economic development. Exposing students and academics to different educational systems and approaches helps enhance their skills and expertise. This can result in a more skilled and adaptable workforce, which is crucial for economic growth and competitiveness. Moreover, cultural exchanges can stimulate entrepreneurial activities as individuals with diverse backgrounds come together. Exposure to different perspectives and business environments can inspire new business ideas and ventures. Universities are key influencers of a country's soft power. Building a positive reputation through cultural exchanges can enhance a nation's attractiveness, potentially opening doors for economic collaborations and investments. Successful examples of cultural exchanges in European universities are:

- The *University of Geneva* in Switzerland offers numerous international programs and research initiatives. Geneva's international community and diverse student body contribute to a rich cultural exchange environment
- *SOAS University of London* specializes in the study of Asia, Africa, and the Middle East. Its programs and research initiatives promote cross-cultural

understanding and global perspectives. SOAS hosts numerous cultural events, lectures, seminars, and conferences that focus on the regions of Asia, Africa, and the Middle East. These events often feature guest speakers, scholars, and experts who share their insights, fostering a deeper understanding of these cultures.

- The *University of Groningen* (Netherlands) actively supports international students and promotes cultural exchange through its diverse academic programs.
- *Vienna University* (Austria) actively fosters cultural exchange and understanding through its diverse student body and numerous international programs.
- *Stockholm University* (Sweden) encourages cultural exchange and global perspectives through its international master's programs and research collaborations.
- *Sapienza University of Rome* (Italy) promotes cultural exchange and understanding through its global partnerships and a diverse student community.
- *Helsinki University* (Finland) promotes internationalization and cultural exchange through its academic programs, international partnerships, and research collaborations.
- The *University of Edinburgh* (UK) has a strong focus on internationalization and encourages students to engage in cultural exchange and understanding.
- The *University of Barcelona* (Spain) fosters cultural exchange through its numerous international programs, study abroad opportunities, and collaborations with institutions around the world.

The New Frontier: European Universities in the Digital Diplomacy Era

European universities are crucial in preparing the next generation of diplomats and international relations professionals to navigate the complex digital landscape. They also contribute to research, policy development, and diplomatic practice in the digital realm, playing a pivotal role in shaping the future of digital diplomacy in Europe and beyond:

- European universities provide education and training in digital diplomacy, international relations, and related fields. They equip students with the knowledge and skills needed to navigate the digital landscape in diplomatic contexts.
- Academic institutions engage in research related to digital diplomacy, including the impact of technology on international relations, cybersecurity, and the

role of social media in diplomacy. Their research informs diplomatic strategies and policies:

➢ *DiploFoundation* (*University of Malta*): DiploFoundation, affiliated with the University of Malta, is a pioneer in the field of digital diplomacy and international relations. It offers online courses, training, and conducts research on various aspects of digital diplomacy, including cybersecurity and internet governance. Several key conditions and factors have contributed to DiploFoundation's status as a leader in digital diplomacy education:

❖ Early Recognition of Digital Diplomacy: DiploFoundation was among the early institutions to recognize the growing significance of digital technology in diplomacy. Its founders understood the transformative potential of the internet and digital tools for international relations and diplomacy.

❖ Innovative Online Learning: DiploFoundation embraced the internet as a platform for education, offering innovative online courses and training programs. This online approach allowed for flexible and accessible learning, attracting diplomats, government officials, and international affairs professionals from around the world.

❖ Global Accessibility: The online format of DiploFoundation's courses made education in digital diplomacy accessible to a global audience. Diplomats and professionals from various countries and regions could participate without the need for physical attendance, creating a diverse and global student body.

❖ Academic Affiliation: DiploFoundation's affiliation with the University of Malta provided academic recognition and accreditation for its educational programs, enhancing the credibility of its courses and attracting students seeking accredited education.

❖ Multistakeholder Engagement: DiploFoundation actively engaged with multiple stakeholders, including governments, international organizations, academia, and the diplomatic community. This multistakeholder approach created a dynamic and inclusive environment for learning and research.

❖ Capacity Building: DiploFoundation has focused on capacity building for diplomats and international affairs professionals. Its training programs provide specialized education to help individuals understand and effectively use digital tools in their diplomatic roles.

❖ Research and Knowledge Dissemination: DiploFoundation conducts research on various aspects of digital diplomacy, producing valuable insights and publications. This research contributes to the academic and practical discourse on the topic.

❖ Collaboration with International Organizations: DiploFoundation collaborates with international organizations, such as the United Nations, to offer digital diplomacy courses and training to their staff and officials. These partnerships extend its reach and influence.

❖ Community Building: DiploFoundation fosters a global community of practice in digital diplomacy. It provides a platform for diplomats and professionals to exchange ideas, share experiences, and collaborate on common challenges related to digital technology in diplomacy.

❖ Focus on Multilateral Diplomacy: DiploFoundation has a strong emphasis on multilateral diplomacy, recognizing the unique challenges and opportunities that arise in a digital age, particularly in a multilateral context.

➢ *Oxford Internet Institute* (*University of Oxford*, UK): The Oxford Internet Institute conducts research on the societal implications of the internet and digital technologies. It explores topics such as online diplomacy, cybersecurity, and the impact of digital tools on global politics. It is important to stress that, the Oxford Internet Institute was made possible by a major donation from the Shirley Foundation of over £10m, with public funding totaling over £5m from the Higher Education Funding Council for England. The idea originated with Derek Wyatt MP and Andrew Graham, then Master-Elect of Balliol.

➢ *Sciences Po* (*Paris School of International Affairs*, France): Sciences Po conducts research on international relations, including digital diplomacy, cyber governance, and the role of social media in diplomacy. It offers relevant academic programs for students.

➢ *The Hague University of Applied Sciences* (Netherlands): The Centre for Professional Learning at The Hague University specializes in digital diplomacy, offering courses and conducting research on topics like cyber diplomacy, international law, and digital statecraft.

➢ *Leiden University* (Netherlands): Leiden University has a dedicated research group focusing on digital diplomacy, analyzing the use of digital tools in international relations, public diplomacy, and conflict resolution.

➢ *King's College London* (UK): The *Department of War Studies* at King's College London conducts research on digital diplomacy, cybersecurity, and the impact of technology on contemporary conflict and international politics.

> *Swedish Institute of International Affairs* (Sweden): This institute conducts research on international relations, security, and diplomacy, including the role of digital technology in shaping global politics.
> *Norwegian Institute of International Affairs* (NUPI): NUPI conducts research on digital diplomacy, cybersecurity, and the intersection of technology and international relations. It provides insights into the digital aspects of Norwegian foreign policy.
> *University of Tartu* (Estonia): The University of Tartu conducts research on cybersecurity, e-governance, and digital diplomacy, reflecting Estonia's experience as a pioneer in e-governance and digital governance.
> *Danish Institute for International Studies* (DIIS): DIIS conducts research on digital diplomacy, cyber threats, and the impact of technology on international security and conflict resolution.

– Some European universities provide specialized programs, courses, and training in digital diplomacy and related fields, preparing future diplomats and international relations professionals to navigate the digital challenges and opportunities in contemporary diplomacy. The specific programs may vary in their offerings and focus areas, but they collectively contribute to the education of diplomats for the digital age:

> *DiploFoundation* (*University of Malta*): As mentioned, DiploFoundation, affiliated with the University of Malta, offers a range of online courses and training programs in digital diplomacy, including a Master's in Contemporary Diplomacy with a specialization in diplomatic practice and a focus on digital diplomacy.
> *Sciences Po* (*Paris School of International Affairs*, France): Sciences Po offers a Master's in International Public Management with a concentration in digital, new technology, and public policy. This program equips students with the skills needed for modern diplomacy.
> *The Hague University of Applied Sciences* (Netherlands): The Centre for Professional Learning at The Hague University offers courses and training in digital diplomacy and cybersecurity, designed for current and future diplomats and international affairs professionals.
> *Leiden University* (Netherlands): Leiden University offers a Master's program in International Relations and Diplomacy with a specialization in

Digital Politics. This program provides students with insights into digital diplomacy and the impact of technology on international relations.

➢ *King's College London* (UK): King's College London offers a Master's in International Relations with a concentration in Cyber Diplomacy, preparing students for careers in digital diplomacy and the analysis of cyber threats in international relations.

➢ *University of Tartu* (Estonia): The University of Tartu offers a Master's program in International Relations and Regional Studies with a focus on cybersecurity and digital diplomacy, drawing from Estonia's expertise in e-governance.

➢ *University of Oxford* (UK): The University of Oxford offers a Master's in Global Governance and Diplomacy with modules on digital diplomacy, cybersecurity, and the role of technology in contemporary diplomacy.

➢ *Norwegian School of Economics* (NHH): NHH offers a Master's in Economics and Business Administration with a concentration in Digital Diplomacy and Global Governance, focusing on the intersection of economics, technology, and diplomacy.

– Language departments within universities offer courses in foreign languages essential for diplomacy and international communication, enabling effective diplomacy in digital environments.

– Several European universities have extensive networks and partnerships related to digital diplomacy, collaborating with academic institutions, governmental organizations, international agencies, and non-governmental organizations to advance research and education in this field:

➢ *DiploFoundation* (*University of Malta*): As a leader in digital diplomacy education, DiploFoundation collaborates with numerous international organizations, universities, and diplomatic academies to offer online courses, training, and research in digital diplomacy.

➢ *Oxford Internet Institute* (University of Oxford, UK): The Oxford Internet Institute maintains partnerships with academic institutions, research organizations, and international bodies to study the impact of the internet on society, including its role in diplomacy and international relations.

➢ *The Hague University of Applied Sciences* (Netherlands): The Centre for Professional Learning at The Hague University collaborates with various diplomatic academies, government institutions, and international organizations to deliver courses and research on digital diplomacy and cybersecurity.

- ➤ *Leiden University* (Netherlands): Leiden University partners with academic institutions, think tanks, and government agencies to conduct research and organize events on digital diplomacy, exploring the use of technology in international relations.
- ➤ *King's College London* (UK): King's College London collaborates with international partners and government entities on research projects and initiatives related to digital diplomacy, cybersecurity, and technology in international politics.
- ➤ *University of Tartu* (Estonia): The University of Tartu maintains connections with organizations involved in cybersecurity, digital governance, and e-diplomacy, reflecting Estonia's leadership in e-governance.
- ➤ *Norwegian Institute of International Affairs* (NUPI): NUPI collaborates with other research institutions, government bodies, and international organizations to conduct research on digital diplomacy, international security, and cyber governance.
- ➤ *Swedish Institute of International Affairs* (Sweden): The institute partners with academic institutions, think tanks, and government agencies to research the role of digital technology in international relations and diplomacy.
- ➤ *Danish Institute for International Studies* (DIIS): DIIS collaborates with a wide range of national and international partners on research projects related to cybersecurity, digital diplomacy, and international security.

- European universities often host events, seminars, and conferences that promote diplomatic discussions and public diplomacy efforts, engaging both domestic and international audiences through digital platforms.
- Scholars and experts at universities contribute to the development of policies related to digital diplomacy, cyber diplomacy, and international governance of digital technologies.
- Universities foster cross-cultural understanding through international student bodies and exchange programs. They promote cultural exchange and intercultural dialogue in digital diplomacy.
- European universities teach digital skills that are essential for modern diplomacy, including data analysis, social media management, digital security, and digital storytelling.
- Universities provide education and research on cybersecurity, which is critical in safeguarding diplomatic communications and infrastructure in the digital age.

- Universities contribute to the dissemination of knowledge and best practices in digital diplomacy through publications, academic journals, and policy briefs.
- Academic institutions actively engage with digital diplomacy by using social media and digital platforms to share research, insights, and expertise, thus contributing to public discourse and understanding.

Diplomatic Alliances: European Universities and Ministries of Foreign Affairs

Several European foreign ministries have strong connections with universities and academic institutions, and they work closely together on diplomatic and international relations issues. For instance, the UK's Foreign, Commonwealth & Development Office (FCDO) often collaborates with universities, think tanks, and research institutions on various foreign policy and international relations issues. British universities, including King's College London and the University of Oxford, have well-established programs in international relations and diplomacy. These collaborations are part of the UK government's efforts to engage with experts and academic researchers to inform and shape its foreign policy decisions. The FCDO frequently commissions research projects from universities to gain insights into complex international issues. Universities contribute to in-depth studies and analysis that inform foreign policy decisions. Academic experts from universities are often consulted by the FCDO for their expertise on specific regions, issues, or international relations theories. They provide advice and recommendations to shape diplomatic strategies. Some UK universities, such as the University of Oxford and King's College London, offer programs and courses in international relations and diplomacy. These programs can be attended by FCDO staff and diplomats to enhance their skills and knowledge. British universities are involved in cultural and academic exchange programs supported by the FCDO. These programs foster people-to-people ties and enhance the UK's diplomatic and cultural relations with other countries. The FCDO collaborates with think tanks and research centers affiliated with universities to access a wealth of expertise on foreign policy, international law, security, and development issues. British universities often host events, seminars, and conferences related to international relations, diplomacy, and foreign policy. The FCDO frequently participates in or sponsors these events. The FCDO and universities share knowledge and research findings to stay informed about global trends and emerging challenges, ensuring that foreign policy decisions are well-informed.

This collaboration between the FCDO and universities underscores the importance of academic research and expertise in shaping the UK's foreign policy and diplomatic efforts. It also reflects a commitment to fostering partnerships that contribute to informed and effective diplomacy on a global scale.

In France, Ministère de l'Europe et des Affaires étrangères maintains partnerships with academic institutions and research organizations in France and abroad. Sciences Po in Paris, for example, has a long history of involvement in diplomatic education and research. These partnerships are an integral part of France's diplomatic efforts and play a crucial role in informing and shaping the country's foreign policy. The ministry often collaborates with universities, think tanks, and research centers to conduct research on international relations, foreign policy, and global issues. Academic experts provide valuable insights and analysis that inform France's diplomatic strategies. Academic institutions in France offer specialized programs and courses in international relations and diplomacy. These programs are attended by French diplomats and foreign service professionals to enhance their knowledge and skills. Academic experts and scholars are consulted by the ministry for their expertise on specific regions, international conflicts, and global challenges. They provide recommendations and policy advice to guide France's foreign policy decisions. Partnerships with universities often extend to cultural exchange programs, language education, and academic collaborations that promote French culture and values abroad. The ministry supports academic and student exchanges with partner countries, fostering international cooperation and educational opportunities. Collaborations with academic institutions can include organizing events, conferences, and cultural activities that promote France's image and engagement with foreign audiences. The ministry supports the teaching and study of the French language and culture at foreign universities and schools. Academic institutions in France are often involved in hosting and organizing international conferences and symposia on global issues, bringing together diplomats, scholars, and experts. These partnerships with academic institutions reflect France's commitment to academic excellence, research, and intellectual contributions to the field of international relations. By working closely with universities and academic experts, the French Ministry for Europe and Foreign Affairs ensures that its foreign policy decisions are well-informed, forward-thinking, and grounded in deep understanding and analysis of global issues.

The Dutch Ministry of Foreign Affairs (Ministerie van Buitenlandse Zaken) maintains close ties with several universities and academic institutions in the Netherlands and beyond. These partnerships are essential for informing the country's foreign policy, diplomacy, and international engagement. While the specific universities may vary over time, some notable universities and academic institutions with which the Dutch Ministry of Foreign Affairs has close ties include:

- *Leiden University*, with its long history of involvement in diplomacy and international relations, collaborates with the ministry on research, training, and academic programs in diplomatic studies.
- The *University of Amsterdam* conducts research and offers programs related to international relations and diplomacy, with the Dutch Ministry of Foreign Affairs often engaging with its experts.
- *Utrecht University* has a strong focus on international relations and offers academic programs in this field. The Ministry collaborates with the University on research projects and diplomacy-related initiatives.
- The Centre for Professional Learning at the *Hague University* provides training and courses in diplomacy, often in collaboration with the ministry, to prepare diplomats and international affairs professionals.
- While not a university, the *Clingendael Institute* in The Hague is a prominent think tank specializing in international relations and diplomacy. It works closely with the Dutch Ministry of Foreign Affairs on research and policy advice.

The Ministry maintains partnerships with international academic institutions, including universities and think tanks in other countries, to foster global academic collaboration and research on international affairs. The Netherlands and Belgium have a history of close diplomatic and academic collaboration. *KU Leuven*, located in Belgium, is one of the prominent universities in the region and may engage in partnerships with the Dutch Ministry of Foreign Affairs. The *University of Oxford* in the United Kingdom is a renowned institution for international relations and diplomacy. Collaboration with the Dutch ministry may involve research, policy analysis, and academic exchanges. *Sciences Po* in France is a prestigious university with a strong focus on international relations and diplomacy. Collaboration with Sciences Po may include research initiatives and academic programs. *Georgetown University*'s School of Foreign Service is known for its international affairs programs. The Dutch Ministry of Foreign Affairs may engage in partnerships with U.S. universities for research & diplomatic exchanges. The Dutch Ministry of Foreign Affairs may maintain ties with universities in countries with which the Netherlands has diplomatic relations. These partnerships may involve cultural exchange, language programs, and academic collaboration.

The Norwegian Ministry of Foreign Affairs (Utenriksdepartementet) engages with universities on various international issues, and Norwegian universities conduct research on topics related to diplomacy and international relations:

– The *University of Oslo* (Universitetet i Oslo) is a leading academic institution in Norway and has a strong presence in international relations and diplomacy. It collaborates with the ministry on research, policy analysis, and academic programs.
– The *Norwegian Institute of International Affairs* (NUPI – Norsk Utenrikspolitisk Institutt) is a think tank and research institute specializing in international relations and foreign policy. It has a close relationship with the ministry, providing valuable research insights and analysis.
– The Norwegian Ministry of Foreign Affairs maintains close ties with various foreign universities and academic institutions to facilitate international cooperation, diplomacy, research, and cultural exchange. The Norwegian Ministry of Foreign Affairs collaborates with *Harvard Kennedy School*, *Columbia University*, the *University of Oxford*, *Sciences Po* in France, and the *Institut de hautes études internationales et du développement* (IHEID) in Switzerland. Moreover, the Norwegian Ministry of Foreign Affairs often collaborates with universities in countries with which Norway has diplomatic relations. These partnerships may focus on cultural exchange, language programs, and academic collaboration.

Universities as Catalysts for Economic Resilience: Policy Recommendations for Navigating Crises

European universities possess a wealth of expertise across various fields. During economic crises, they actively engage with policymakers, offering evidence-based recommendations and insights to shape economic recovery strategies (European Parliament, 2023). Academic research and expert analysis play a crucial role in informing the formulation of effective policies to address the root causes of economic crises:

o *In-Depth Understanding of Causes*: Academic researchers delve into the complexities of economic issues and crises, conducting rigorous analyses to identify the underlying causes. Their in-depth studies provide policymakers with a solid understanding of the multifaceted factors contributing to the crisis.
o *Data-Driven Insights*: Researchers use data analysis to identify trends, correlations, and patterns that can shed light on the factors leading to the crisis. These data-driven insights guide policymakers in making informed decisions.

o *Evidence-Based Policy Formulation*: Academic research provides empirical evidence that policymakers can use to evaluate the potential impacts of different policy options. Evidence-based policies are more likely to be effective in addressing the root causes of a crisis.

o *Modeling and Forecasting*: Economists and researchers use modeling and forecasting techniques to project the potential outcomes of various policy interventions. This helps policymakers anticipate the effects of their decisions and adjust their strategies accordingly.

o *Policy Recommendations*: Academics often publish policy papers and reports that offer well-reasoned recommendations for addressing economic challenges guiding policymakers toward effective solutions.

o *Cross-Disciplinary Insights*: Economic crises often have social, political, and environmental dimensions. Academic research draws on various disciplines to provide a holistic understanding of the crisis, enabling policymakers to craft comprehensive solutions.

o *Long-Term Perspective*: Academic research takes a long-term perspective, examining historical trends and structural issues that might contribute to economic crises. This perspective helps policymakers avoid short-term fixes that may exacerbate underlying problems.

o *Risk Assessment*: Researchers can assess the potential risks associated with different policy options. This helps policymakers understand potential pitfalls and design strategies to mitigate negative consequences.

o *International Comparisons*: Comparative studies across countries and regions provide insights into successful policy approaches and cautionary examples. Policymakers can learn from these comparisons when designing their own solutions.

o *Public Awareness and Support*: Research findings can be communicated to the public through media and public engagement efforts. Informed citizens are more likely to support policies that are grounded in expert analysis and research.

o *Policy Evaluation*: After policies are implemented, researchers can assess their effectiveness and provide feedback to policymakers. This iterative process allows for adjustments and refinements based on real-world outcomes.

o *Interactions with Policymakers*: Engaging academics in dialogues with policymakers fosters collaboration and ensures that research findings are translated into practical policy recommendations: in many instances, academics can be change-makers (Holthaus & Stockmann, 2020).

o *Policy Innovation*: Academic research often uncovers innovative approaches to addressing economic challenges. These novel ideas can inspire policymakers to consider creative solutions that might not have been initially apparent (Aver et al., 2021).

o *Transparency & Accountability*: Relying on academic research promotes transparency in policy formulation. Policymakers can explain their decisions based on solid research, enhancing accountability to the public.

By incorporating insights from academic research and expert analysis, policymakers can develop well-informed and comprehensive strategies to address the root causes of economic crises. Collaboration between researchers, policymakers, and stakeholders enhances the likelihood of designing effective policies that promote economic stability and resilience.

For instance, several European universities played a role in addressing the challenges posed by the financial crisis of 2008.

– Researchers from the *London School of Economics and Political Science* (LSE) conducted studies and provided insights into the causes and consequences of the financial crisis. The Centre for Economic Performance at LSE produced research on various aspects of economic policy and the impacts of the crisis.
– The *University of Barcelona* conducted research on economic policies and offered expertise on addressing the economic challenges facing Spain during the financial crisis. Scholars at the university contributed to discussions on the impact of the crisis on labor markets and social welfare.
– German universities, including *Freie Universität Berlin*, were actively involved in economic research and policy discussions during the crisis. Economists and researchers provided analyses on the effects of the crisis on the German economy and contributed to policy debates.
– *Sciences Po* in Paris engaged in research on economic and social policies, providing analysis and recommendations for addressing the consequences of the financial crisis. The university's scholars contributed to discussions on the role of the state in economic recovery.
– Irish universities, including *University College Dublin*, were involved in researching the impact of the financial crisis on the Irish economy. Academics provided insights into economic policies and offered recommendations for addressing the challenges facing Ireland.

These examples showcase how universities across Europe contributed to understanding the economic crisis, offering policy recommendations, and engaging with the broader community to navigate the challenges that arose during and after the 2008 financial crisis.

Moreover, numerous European universities have been actively contributing to dealing with the COVID-19 crisis (Estermann et al., 2020; Steel et al., 2020; Alite & Zvirbule, 2020; Grek & Landri, 2021; Kapilan et al., 2021; Bularca et al., 2022):

- Research & Vaccine Development: European universities such as the *University of Oxford* in the United Kingdom played a pivotal role in the development of the Oxford-AstraZeneca COVID-19 vaccine. Researchers at Oxford were involved in early clinical trials, and the university collaborated with pharmaceutical companies for the production and distribution of the vaccine.
- Epidemiological Studies & Modeling: Several universities across Europe engaged in epidemiological research and modeling to understand the spread of the virus. *Imperial College London*, for instance, conducted modeling studies that influenced public health policies.
- Testing & Diagnosis: European universities collaborated with healthcare institutions to establish testing centers and diagnostic facilities. They were involved in the development and improvement of testing methods. For example, *Charité- Universitätsmedizin Berlin* in Germany was actively involved in diagnostic efforts.
- Public Health Policy & Communication: European universities provided expertise to governments and international organizations in shaping public health policies. They also contributed to public communication efforts to disseminate accurate information about the virus. Public Health England collaborated with academic institutions to inform the UK's response.
- Medical Training & Support: Medical schools and European universities with healthcare faculties contributed by training medical professionals and providing support to overwhelmed healthcare systems. *King's College London*, for instance, engaged in medical training and research related to COVID-19.
- Technological Solutions: European universities collaborated on technological solutions, such as contact-tracing apps and data analysis tools. *ETH Zurich* and EPFL (*École polytechnique fédérale de Lausanne*) in Switzerland were involved in technological initiatives related to the pandemic.
- Psychological Support and Mental Health Research: European universities recognized the impact of the pandemic on mental health and conducted research in this area. They also provided psychological support services to students and the community. The *University of Amsterdam*, for example, focused on mental health research and support.

These examples illustrate the diverse ways in which European universities have contributed to addressing the COVID-19 crisis.

Universities in Europe and economic diplomacy have a complex and ever-changing relationship. Through a variety of means, European universities have contributed significantly to economic development: they are centers of innovation and research, and they have helped the creation of novel goods, services, and technologies that can improve economic competitiveness. Knowledge transfer and the commercialization of research findings are frequently the results of collaboration between European academic institutions and business sectors. In order to educate and train skilled professionals, European universities are essential. Economic growth and innovation depend on a workforce that is highly educated and skilled. Universities in Europe offer instruction in a range of subjects, such as business, science, technology, and engineering. Initiatives and programs that encourage entrepreneurship are available at many European universities. They support researchers and students who want to launch their own companies with funding, resources, and mentorship. This promotes an innovative culture and helps the startup ecosystem expand. Additionally, they frequently work with other universities and research centers around the globe in partnerships and other international collaborations. These partnerships can result in knowledge sharing, cooperative research initiatives, and the creation of international networks that support economic diplomacy. Finally, European universities have played a pivotal role in addressing economic crises by leveraging their research capabilities, fostering innovation, providing skill development, supporting startups, influencing policy decisions, engaging with communities, collaborating internationally, and embracing the digital transformation. By capitalizing on their unique strengths, universities contribute significantly to Europe's resilience and capacity to overcome economic challenges. Policymakers and stakeholders should recognize the importance of sustaining and strengthening the role of universities as key partners in facing economic crises and building a prosperous future.

Bibliography

Economic Diplomacy: Historical Milestones

Ancient Trade and Diplomacy (Pre-modern Era)

Altman, A. (2010). How Many Treaty Traditions Existed in the Ancient Near East?. *Pax Hethitica: Studies on the Hittites and Their Neighbours in Honour of Itamar Singer* (51), 17.

Amin, M. A. (1970). Ancient Trade and Trade Routes between Egypt and the Sudan, 4000 to 700 BC. *Sudan Notes and Records*, 51, 23–30.

Auwers, M. (2013). The Gift of Rubens: Rethinking the Concept of Gift-Giving in Early Modern Diplomacy. *European History Quarterly*, 43(3), 421–441.

Borza, E. N. (1987). Timber and Politics in the Ancient World: Macedon and the Greeks. *Proceedings of the American Philosophical Society*, 131(1), 32–52.

Chandra, M. (1977). *Trade and Trade Routes in Ancient India*. Abhinav Publications.

Charlesworth, M. P. (2016). *Trade-Routes and Commerce of the Roman Empire*. Cambridge University Press.

Cohen, R., & Westbrook, R. (Eds.). (2000). *Amarna Diplomacy: The Beginnings of International Relations*. JHU Press.

Feldman, M. H. (2006). Diplomacy by Design: Luxury Arts and an" international style" in the Ancient Near East, 1400–1200 BCE. University of Chicago Press.

Harrower, M. J., & Dumitru, I. A. (2017). Digital Maps Illuminate Ancient Trade Routes. *Nature*, 543(7644), 188–189.

Kolb, R. (2018). The Basis of Obligation in Treaties of Ancient Cultures–Pactum Est Servandum?. In *International Law and Islam* (pp. 110–126). Brill Nijhoff.

Lambert, W. G. (1988). *The God-List in the Treaty between Hannibal and Philip V of Macedonia: A Study in Light of the Ancient Near Eastern Treaty Tradition*.

Lauinger, J. (2016). Approaching Ancient Near Eastern Treaties, Laws, and Covenants. *Journal of American Oriental Society*, 136(1), 125–134.

McLaughlin, R. (2010). *Rome and the Distant East: Trade Routes to the Ancient Lands of Arabia, India and China*. Bloomsbury Publishing.

Melville, S. C. (2020). *Royal Women and the Exercise of Power in the Ancient Near East. A Companion to the Ancient Near East*, 97–110.

Ptak, R. (2011). Asia. Sino-Malay Trade and Diplomacy from the Tenth Through to the Fourteenth Century. By Derek Heng. Athens: Ohio University Press, 2009. pp. xvi, 286. Maps, Plates (some coloured), Notes, Bibliography, Index. *Journal of Southeast Asian Studies*, 42(2), 341–344.

Sasson, J. M. (1983). Mari Dreams. *Journal of the American Oriental Society*, 103(1), 283–293.

Sasson, J. M. (2001). *On reading the Diplomatic Letters in the Mari Archives*.

Schulman, A. R. (1979). Diplomatic Marriage in the Egyptian New Kingdom. *Journal of Near Eastern Studies*, 38(3), 177–193.

Sen, T. (2006). The Yuan Khanate and India: Cross-Cultural Diplomacy in the Thirteenth and Fourteenth Centuries. *Asia Major*, 299–326.

Tremml-Werner, B., Hellman, L., & Van Meersbergen, G. (2020). Introduction. Gift and Tribute in Early Modern Diplomacy: Afro-Eurasian Perspectives. *Diplomatica*, 2(2), 185–200.

West, A. B. (1923). The Early Diplomacy of Philip II of Macedon Illustrated by His Coins. *The Numismatic Chronicle and Journal of the Royal Numismatic Society*, 169–210.

Wizarat, T. A. (2014). Reviving Historical Trade Routes. *Strategic Studies*, 34, 18–34.

Wilson, J. A. (1927). The Texts of the Battle of Kadesh. *The American Journal of Semitic Languages and Literatures*, 43(4), 266–287.

Ancient Egypt and Nubia (3rd Millennium BCE – 4th c. CE)

Abo-Eleaz, M. E. E. (2023). The Harsh Life of Diplomatic Messengers in Egypt in the Late Bronze Age. *The Ancient Near East Today*.

Adams, W. Y. (1984). The First Colonial Empire: Egypt in Nubia, 3200–1200 B.C. *Comparative Studies in Society and History*, 26(1), 36–71.

Avruch, K. (2000). Reciprocity, Equality, and Status-Anxiety in the Amarna Letters. In Cohen, R., & Westbrook, R. (Eds.), *Amarna Diplomacy: The Beginnings of International Relations*. Baltimore, MD: Johns Hopkins University Press.

Cohen, R. (2000). Intelligence in the Amarna Letters. In Cohen, R., & Westbrook, R. (Eds.), *Amarna Diplomacy International Relations*. Baltimore: M University Press.

Cohen, R., & Westbrook, R. (Eds.). (2000). *Amarna Diplomacy: The Beginnings of Inte Baltimore*. MD: Johns Hopkins University Press.

Jha, L. K., & Jha, N. K. (1998). Chanakya: The Pioneer Economist of the World. *International Journal of Social Economics*, 25(2–4), 267–282.

Manzo, A. (2022). *Ancient Egypt in its African Context: Economic Networks, Social and Cultural Interactions*. Cambridge University Press.

Meurer, G. (1996). *Nubier in Egypten bis zum Beginn des Neuen Reiches Titelzusatz: zur Bedeutung der Stele Berlin 14753* (*Nubians in Egypt until the Beginning of the New Kingdom Title Supplement: On the Significance of the Stele Berlin 14753*). Berlin

Norbo'tayev, S. T. (2022). The Concept of Diplomacy and the History of its Development, Ancient East Diplomacy. *Central Asian Journal of Literature, Philosophy and Culture*, 3(5), 16–18.

O'Connor, D. (1993). *Ancient Nubia: Egypt's Rival in Africa*. Philadelphia: The University Museum, University of Philadelphia.

Olivelle, P. (2013). *King, Governance, and Law in Ancient India: Kauṭilya's Arthaśāstra*. Oxford, UK: Oxford University Press.

Perlman, S. (1985). Greek Diplomatic Tradition and the Corinthian League of Philip of Macedon. *Historia: Zeitschrift für Alte Geschichte*, 34(2), 153–174.

Schulman, A. R. (1979). Diplomatic Marriage in the Egyptian New Kingdom. *Journal of Near Eastern Studies*. The University of Chicago Press, 38(3).

Sihag, B. S. (2007). Kautilya on Institutions, Governance, Knowledge, Ethics and Prosperity. *Humanomics*, 23(1), 5–28.

Tisdell, C. (2003). *A Western Perspective of Kauṭilya's Arthashastra: Does It Provide a Basis for Economic Science? Economic Theory, Applications, and Issues Working Paper No. 18*. Brisbane: School of Economics, The University of Queensland.

Waldauer, C., Zahka, W. J., & Pal, S. (1996). Kauṭilya's Arthashastra: A Neglected Precursor to Classical Economics. *Indian Economic Review*, XXXI(1), 101–108.

Wang, Z. (2023). *Intercultural Communication and Miscommunication: Egyptian Diplomacy in the New Kingdom Period* (Doctoral dissertation, The University of Chicago).

The Babylonian and Assyrian Empires in Mesopotamia (2nd & 1st Millennia BCE)

Beckman, G. (1996). *Hittite Diplomatic Texts*. Adanta, GA: Scholars Press.

Bell, C. (1992). *Ritual Theory, Ritual Practice*. Oxford University Press.

Black, J., George, A., & Postgate, N. (1999). *A Concise Dictionary of Akkadian*. Wiesbaden: Harrassowitz Verlag.

Radner, K. (2013*). Representing Assyrian Interests in the Vassal States' Assyrian Empire Builders*. University College London.

Sasson, J. M. (b. 1841). *Mari Archives: An Anthology of Old Babylonian Letters*.

Soldt, Wilfred H. van. (2012). Akkadian as a Diplomatic Language. In Stefan Weninger (Ed.), *The Semitic Languages: An International Handbook*, ch. 16 (pp. 405–415). Berlin, Boston: De Gruyter Mouton.

Caravan Cities

Dien, A. E. (2004). Palmyra as a Caravan City. *The Silk Road Newsletter*, 2(1), 21–28.

Gawlikowski, M. (1994). Palmyra as a Trading Centre. *Iraq*, 56, 27–33.

Gawlikowski, M. (2016). *Trade across Frontiers: Foreign Relations of a Caravan City* (Eds., Jørgen Christian Meyer, Eivind Seland, & Nils Anfinset, pp. 19–28).

Millar, F. (1998). Caravan Cities: The Roman Near East and Long-Distance Trade by Land. *Bulletin of the Institute of Classical Studies*. Supplement, 119–137.

Rostovtzeff, M. (2011). *Caravan Cities*. Read Books Ltd.

Rostovtzeff, M. I. (1932). The Caravan-Gods of Palmyra. *The Journal of Roman Studies*, 22(1), 107–116.

Phoenician and Greek City-States Diplomacy (8th–4th c. BCE).

Adcock, F. E., & Mosley, D. J. (1975). *Diplomacy in Ancient Greece*. London: Thames and Hudson.

Allison, G. (2017). The Thucydides' Trap. *Foreign Policy*, 9(6).

Bonner, R. J., & Smith, G. (1943). Administration of Justice in the Delphic Amphictyony. *Classical Philology*, 38(1), 1–12.

Bowden, H. (2003). The Functions of the Delphic Amphictyony before 346 BCE. *Scripta Classica Israelica*, 22, 67–83.

Brown, N. O. (1947). *Hermes the Thief: The Evolution of a Myth*. Madison: University of Wisconsin Press.

Chen, Y., Ioannides, Y. M., & Rauch, F. (2022). *Asymmetric Trading Costs and Ancient Greek Cities*. University of Oxford.

Demetriou, D. (2013). The Practice of Diplomacy: Sidonian Kings and Greek States in the Fourth Century BCE. In *Empires, Kingdoms, and Leagues in the Ancient Greek World*, 37.2, 146 Annual Meeting, January 8–11, New Orleans, LA.

Demetriou, D. (2018). Hellenizing Barbarians or Romanizing the World? The Worship of Artemis of Ephesos in Iberia and Gaul. AAH Meeting.

Demetriou, D. (2018). Trading Diplomats: Phoenician Trade Associations in the Mediterranean World. *UC San Diego-Fudan University Biannual Conference on Greco-Roman Antiquity*, May.

Demetriou, D. (2023). *Phoenicians among Others: Why Migrants Mattered in the Ancient Mediterranean*. Oxford Academic Books.

Dubois, M. (1885). *Les ligues Étolienne et Achéenne: leur histoire et leurs institutions, nature et durée de leur antagonisme*. E. Thorin.

French, A. (1988). The Guidelines of the Delian Alliance. *Antichthon*, 22, 12–25.

Hornblower, S. (2007). Did the Delphic Amphiktiony Play a Political Role in the Classical Period?. *Mediterranean Historical Review*, 22(1), 39–56.

Irad, M. (2013). *A Small Greek World: Networks in the Ancient Mediterranean.* Oxford University Press.

Jones, C. P. (1999). *Kinship Diplomacy in the Ancient World.* Cambridge, MA: Harvard University Press.

Jönsson, C., & Hall, M. (2003). Communication: An Essential Aspect of Diplomacy. *International Studies Perspectives*, May, 4(2), 195–210.

Lee, J. (2019). Did Thucydides Believe in Thucydides' Trap? The History of the Peloponnesian War and Its Relevance to US-China Relations. *Journal of Chinese Political Science*, 24(1), 67–86.

Markoe, G. (2000). *Phoenicians* (Vol. 2). Univ of California Press.

Mendels, D. (1979). Polybius and the Constitution of the Achaean League: A Note. *Scripta Classica Israelica*, 5, 85–93.

Mosley, J. D. (1973). Envoys and Diplomacy in Ancient Greece. *Historia: Zeitschrift für alte Geschichte, Einzelschriften*, Heft 22. Wiesbaden: Franz Steiner Verlag.

Sealey, R. (1976). *A History of the Greek City States, 700–338 BC* (Vol. 165). University of California Press.

Zuchtriegel, G. (2020). *Colonization and Subalternity in Classical Greece: Experience of the Nonelite Population.* Cambridge University Press.

Ancient and Middle Age China Diplomacy

Bagchi, P. C. (2011). *India and China: Interactions through Buddhism and Diplomacy; a Collection of Essays.* Anthem Press.

Boettke, P. J. (1990). The Theory of Spontaneous Order and Cultural Evolution in the Social Theory of FA Hayek. *Cultural Dynamics*, 3(1), 61–83.

Boykin, S. A. (2010). Hayek on Spontaneous Order and Constitutional Design. *The Independent Review*, 15(1), 19–34.

Carrai, M. A. (2021). History of International Law and China: Eurocentrism, Multinormativity, and the Politics of History. In *The Routledge Handbook of Chinese Studies* (pp. 234–249). Routledge.

Dale, G. (2018). 'Our world was made by nature': Constructions of Spontaneous Order. *Globalizations*, 15(7), 924–940.

Feng, Z. (2009). Rethinking the 'tribute system': Broadening the Conceptual Horizon of historical East Asian Politics. *Chinese Journal of International Politics*, 2(4), 545–574.

Hodgson, G. M. (1994). Hayek, Evolution, and Spontaneous Order. Chap, 16, 408–47.

Kang, D. C. (2010). Hierarchy and Legitimacy in International Systems: The Tribute System in Early Modern East Asia. *Security Studies*, 19(4), 591–622.

Khalimovich, O. N., Rasuljanovna, I. N., & Shakarovich, G. I. (2020). The Purpose and Outcome of Diplomatic Missions in the II-I Centuries between Central Asia and China. *Journal of Critical Reviews*, 7(9), 126–128.

Lee, J. Y. (2021). The Tribute System and the World Imagined in Early Modern East Asia. *Millennium*, 50(1), 256–266.

Luban, D. (2020). What Is Spontaneous Order?. *American Political Science Review*, 114(1), 68–80.

Mancall, M. (1968). The Ch'ing Tribute System: An Interpretive Essay. In *The Chinese World Order: Traditional China's Foreign Relations* (pp. 63–89). Harvard University Press.

Munn-Rankin, J. M. (1956). *Diplomacy in Western Asia in the Early Second Millennium B.C. Iraq XVIII*, part 1:68–110. The British School of Archeology in Iraq.

Raphals, L. (1994). Skeptical Strategies in the "zhuangzi" and "theaetetus". *Philosophy East and West*, 44(3), 501–526.

Tian, X., & Amado Mendes, C. (2021). Rethinking Tribute System and Chinese Foreign Aid from a Relational Perspective. *Relações Internacionais*.

Van Norden, B. W. (2004). *Mengzi: With Selections from Traditional Commentaries*. Hackett Publishing.

Wang, Y. K. (2013). Explaining the Tribute System: Power, Confucianism, and War in Medieval East Asia. *Journal of East Asian Studies*, 13(2), 207–232.

Zijun, W. (2019, September). Reconsideration on Foreign Trade Relations in Ancient China – Centered on the Silk Road and Tribute System. In *2019 Asia-Pacific Forum on Economic and Social Development* (Vol. 2, pp. 16–21). The Academy of Engineering and Education.

Ancient India Diplomacy

Roy, G. J. (1981). *Diplomacy in Ancient India*. New Delhi: Janaki Prakashan.

Sen, T. (2001). In Search of Longevity and Good Karma: Chinese Diplomatic Missions to Middle India in the Seventh Century. *Journal of World History*, 12(1), 1–28.

Silk Road Diplomacy (2nd c. BCE – 14th c. CE)

Baipakov, K. M., & Pidayev, S. R. (Eds.). (2011). *Prominent Archaeological Sites of Central Asia on the Great Silk Road*. Samarkand: ICAS

Blaydes, L., & Paik, C. (2021). Trade and Political Fragmentation on the Silk Roads: The Economic Effects of Historical Exchange between China and the Muslim East. *American Journal of Political Science*, 65(1), 115–132.

Dani, A. H. (2002). Significance of Silk Road to Human Civilization: Its Cultural Dimension. *Journal of Asian Civilizations*, 25(1), 72–79.

Frey, L. S., & Frey, M. L. (1999). *The History of Diplomatic Immunity*. Columbus: Ohio State University Press.

Khalimovich, O. N., Rasuljanovna, I. N., & Shakarovich, G. I. (2020). The Purpose and Outcome of Diplomatic Missions in the II-I Centuries between Central Asia and China. *Journal of Critical Reviews*, 7(9), 126–128.

Lewis, M.E. (2007). *The Early Chinese Empires: Qin and Han*.

Qin, Y. (2020). Diplomacy as Relational Practice. *The Hague Journal of Diplomacy*, 15(1–2), 165–173.

Sen, T. (2014). *Silk Road Diplomacy–Twists, Turns and Distorted History*. YaleGlobal Online.

Wilkinson, D. (2002). Civilizations as Networks: Trade, War, Diplomacy, and Command-Control. *Complexity*, 8(1), 82–86.

Wright, M. C. (1958). The Adaptability of Ch'ing Diplomacy. *The Journal of Asian Studies*, 17(3), 363–381.

Roman Diplomacy and Pax Romana (27 BCE–3rd c. CE)

Canepa, M (2008). Distant Displays of Power: Understanding Cross-Cultural Interaction Among the Elites of Rome, Sasanian Iran, and Sui-Tang China. *Ars orientalis*, 38, 121–154.

Paterson, J. (1998). *Trade and Traders in the Roman World: Scale, Structure and Organisation*. In Parkins, H., & Smith, C. (Eds.), *Trade, Traders and the Ancient City* (pp. 149–167). London: Routledge.

Schwarz, F. F. (1974). Pliny the Elder on Ceylon. *Journal of Asian History*, 8(1), 21–48.

Starr, Ch.G. (1956). The Roman Emperor and the King of Ceylon. *Classical Philology*, 51(1), 27–30.

Székely, M. (2005). Pliny the Elder and the Problem of Regnum Hereditarium. *Chronica*. Annual of the Institute of History. *University of Szeged*, 5(1), 3–14.

West, A.B. (1923). The Early Diplomacy of Philip II of Macedón Illustrated by His Coins. *Numismatic Chronicle*, Fifth Series, Vol. I.

Ancient African City-States

Anfray, F. (1981). The Civilization of Aksum from the First to the Seventh Century. *General History of Africa* II, 362.

Bathily, A. (1975). A Discussion of the Traditions of Wagadu with Some Reference to Ancient Ghana. *Bulletin de l'Institut Fondamental d'Afrique Noire*, Série B: Sciences Humaines, 37(1), 1–94.

Canós-Donnay, S. (2019). *The Empire of Mali*.

Cartwright, M., & ten Brink, C. (2020). *Mali Empire. Ancient History Encyclopedia*. Ancient History Encyclopedia.

Fage, J. D. (1957). Ancient Ghana: A Review of the Evidence. *Transactions of the Historical Society of Ghana*, 3(2), 3–24.

Fontein, J. (2016). *The Silence of Great Zimbabwe: Contested Landscapes and the Power of Heritage* (Vol. 37). Routledge.

Hall, R. N. (1905). The Great Zimbabwe. *Journal of the Royal African Society*, 4(15), 295–300.

Jansen, J. (2018). Beyond the Mali Empire – A New Paradigm for the Sunjata Epic. *The International Journal of African Historical Studies*, 51(2), 317–340.

Jones, C. P. (1999). *Kinship Diplomacy in the Ancient World* (Vol. 12). Harvard University Press.

Kusimba, C. M., Kim, N. C., & Kusimba, S. B. (2017). Trade and State Formation in Ancient East African Coast and Southern Zambezia. *Feast, Famine or Fighting? Multiple Pathways to Social Complexity*, 61–89.

Kusimba, C., & Walz, J. R. (2021). Debating the Swahili: Archaeology since 1990 and into the Future. *Archaeologies*, 1–41.

Ly-Tall, M. (1984). The Decline of the Mali Empire. *General History of Africa*, IV, 172–86.

Meyerowitz, E. L. (1952). A Note on the Origins of Ghana. *African Affairs*, 51(205), 319–323.

Mugane, J. M. (2015). *The Story of Swahili*. Ohio University Press.

Munnik, M. (1987). The Mali Empire. *Africa Insight*, 17(2), 136–137.

Munson, P. J. (1980). Archaeology and the Prehistoric Origins of the Ghana Empire. *The Journal of African History*, 21(4), 457–466.

Phillips, J. (1997). Punt and Aksum: Egypt and the Horn of Africa. *The Journal of African History*, 38(3), 423–457.

Phillipson, D. (2003). Aksum. *Azania: Archaeological Research in Africa*, 38(1), 1–68.

Phillipson, D. W. (2012). *Foundations of an African Civilization: Aksum & the Northern Horn, 1000 BC–1300 AD*. Boydell & Brewer Ltd.

Pikirayi, I. (2013). Great Zimbabwe in Historical Archaeology: Reconceptualizing Decline, Abandonment, and Reoccupation of an Ancient Polity, AD 1450–1900. *Historical Archaeology*, 47, 26–37.

Willis, J. R. (1975). *Ancient Ghana and Mali*.

Middle Ages' Diplomacy

Brough, G. (2018). Welsh-French Diplomacy in the Middle Ages. *The Welsh and the Medieval World: Travel, Migration and Exile*, 175–214.

Citarella, A. O. (1968). Patterns in Medieval Trade: The Commerce of Amalfi before the Crusades. *The Journal of Economic History*, 28(4), 531–555.

Cohen, R. (2001). The Great Tradition: The Spread of Diplomacy in the Ancient World. *Diplomacy and Statecraft*, 12(1), 23–38.

Crisp, R. P. (2003). *Marriage and Alliance in the Merovingian Kingdoms* (pp. 481–639). The Ohio State University.

Dahl, G. (2000). *Trade, Trust, and Networks: Commercial Culture in Late Medieval Italy*.

De Wulf, M. (2008). *Philosophy and Civilization in the Middle Ages*. Wipf and Stock Publishers.

Devries, K. (2002). Medieval – Espionage. In *A Cumulative Bibliography of Medieval Military History and Technology* (pp. 262–262). Brill.

Edgington, S. B. (2016). Espionage and Military Intelligence during the First Crusade, 1095–99. In *Crusading and Warfare in the Middle Ages* (pp. 75–86). Routledge.

Egenfeldt-Nielsen, S. (2012). Europa Universalis II: Conquest, Trading, Diplomacy from the Middle Ages to Napoleon. *Well Played*, 1(3).

Emerton, E. (1898). *The Beginnings of the Feudal System*.

Jucker, M. (2008). Trust and Mistrust in Letters: Late Medieval Diplomacy and Its Communication Practices. In *Strategies of Writing: Studies on Text and Trust in the Middle Ages: Papers from "Trust in Writing in the Middle Ages"(Utrecht, 28–29 November 2002)* (pp. 213–236).

Jussen, B. (2000). *Spiritual Kinship as Social Practice: Godparenthood and Adoption in the Early Middle Ages*. University of Delaware Press.

Lieber, A. E. (1968). Eastern Business Practices and Medieval European Commerce. *The Economic History Review*, 21(2), 230–243.

MacDonald, A. J. (2006). Did Intelligence Matter? Espionage in Later Medieval Anglo-Scottish Relations. *Historical Studies*, 25, 3–16.

Mattingly, G. (1937). The First Resident Embassies: Mediaeval Italian Origins of Modern Diplomacy. *Speculum*, 12(4), 423–439.

Molho, A. (1994). *Marriage Alliance in Late Medieval Florence* (Vol. 114). Harvard University Press.

The Diplomacy of the Byzantine Empire (4th-15th c.)

Bibicou, H. (1959). Une page d'histoire diplomatique de Byzance au xi e siècle: Michel VII Doukas, Robert Guiscard et la pension des dignitaires. *Byzantion*, 29, 43–75.

Diebler, S. (1995). Les hommes du Roi: Sur la représentation souveraine dans les relations diplomatiques entre Byzance et les Sassanides d'après les historiens byzantins du sixième siècle. *Studia Iranica*, 24(2), 187–218.

Drocourt, N. (2008). La diplomatie médio-byzantine et l'Antiquité. *Anabases. Traditions et réceptions de l'Antiquité*, (7), 57–87.

Drocourt, N. (2016). *Au nez et à la barbe de l'ambassadeur. Cheveux, poils et pilosité dans les contacts diplomatiques entre Byzance et l'Occident* (VIe–XIIe s.).

Drocourt, N. (2018). Byzantine Diplomacy. *The Encyclopedia of Diplomacy*, 1–16.

Drocourt, N., & Malamut, É. (2020). *La diplomatie byzantine, de l'Empire romain aux confins de l'Europe (Ve-XVe s.)* (Vol. 123). Brill.

Köhler, M. (2013). *Alliances and Treaties between Frankish and Muslim Rulers in the Middle East: Cross-Cultural Diplomacy in the Period of the Crusades. Translated by Peter M. Holt. Revised, edited and introduced by Konrad Hirschler* (Vol. 1). Brill.

Moulet, B. (2019). La Diplomatie à Byzance. À propos d'un ouvrage récent. *Le Moyen Âge*, 125(2), 425–430.

Shepard, J., & Franklin, S. (1992). Byzantine diplomacy. *Hampshire*.

Wozniak, F. E. (1979). Byzantine Diplomacy and the Lombard-Gepidic Wars. *Balkan Studies*, 20(1), 139–158.

Muslim Diplomacy

Drocourt, N. (2010). Christian-Muslim Diplomatic Relations. An Overview of the Main Sources and Themes of Encounter (600–1000). *Christian-Muslim Relations. A Bibliographical History. Volume 2 (900–1050)*, 29–72.

Knobler, A. (1996). Pseudo-Conversions and Patchwork Pedigrees: The Christianization of Muslim Princes and the Diplomacy of Holy War. *Journal of World History*, 181–197.

Köhler, M. (2013). *Alliances and Treaties between Frankish and Muslim Rulers in the Middle East: Cross-Cultural Diplomacy in the Period of the Crusades.*

Translated by Peter M. Holt. Revised, edited and introduced by Konrad Hirschler (Vol. 1). Brill.

Van Gelder, M., & Krstić, T. (2015). Introduction: Cross-Confessional Diplomacy and Diplomatic Intermediaries in the Early Modern Mediterranean. *Journal of Early Modern History, 19*(2–3), 93–105.

Venetian Diplomacy

Beverley, T. (1999). *Venetian Ambassadors 1454–94: An Italian elite* (Doctoral dissertation, University of Warwick).

Clark, C., & Pinder, D. (1999). Naval Heritage and the Revitalisation Challenge: Lessons from the Venetian Arsenale. *Ocean & Coastal Management, 42*(10–11), 933–956.

Dario, G. (1992). *22 Dispacci da Constantinopoli al Doge Giovanni Mocenigo.* Traduzione e commenti di Giuseppe Cabo. Introduzione di Alvise Zorzi. Venezia.

Dotson, J. E. (2001). Foundations of Venetian Naval Strategy from Pietro II Orseolo to the Battle of Zonchio, 1000–1500. *Viator, 32*, 113–126.

Dursteler, E. R. (2001). The Bailo in Constantinople: Crisis and Career in Venice's Early Modern Diplomatic Corps. *Mediterranean Historical Review, 16*(2), 1–30.

Foscari, F. (1844). Dispacci al senato Veneto di Francesco Foscari ed di altri oratori presso l'imperatore Massimiliano I nel 1496. *Archivio Storico Italian, 7*, 721–948

Greene, M. (2001). Ruling an Island Without a Navy. A Comparative View of Venetian and Ottoman Crete. *Oriente Moderno, 20*(1), 193–207.

Hocquet, J. C. (1995). Productivity Gains and Technological Change. Venetian Naval Architecture at the End of the Middle Ages. *Journal of European Economic History, 24*(3), 537.

Lane, F. C. (1934). Venetian Naval Architecture about 1550. *The Mariner's Mirror, 20*(1), 24–49.

Nicol, D. M. (1992). *Byzantium and Venice: A Study in Diplomatic and Cultural Relations.* Cambridge University Press.

Pedani, M. P. (2000). Safiye & Aposs Household and Venetian Diplomacy. *Turcica, 32*, 9–32.

Pirillo, D. (2016). Venetian Merchants as Diplomatic Agents: Family Networks and Cross-Confessional Diplomacy in Early Modern Europe. *Early Modern Diplomacy, Theatre and Soft Power: The Making of Peace,* 183–203.

Shaw, C. (2018). Venetian Diplomacy. The Encyclopedia of Diplomacy, 1–7.

Colonialism and Mercantilism (16th -18th Centuries)

Azzolini, M., & Lazzarini, I. (2017). *Italian Renaissance Diplomacy: A Sourcebook.* Durham.

Eltis, D., & Richardson, D. (1995). Productivity in the Transatlantic Slave Trade. *Explorations in Economic History,* 32(4), 465–484.

Fletcher, C. (2015). *Diplomacy in Renaissance Rome: The Rise of the Resident Ambassador.* Cambridge University Press.

Geggus, D. (2001). The French Slave Trade: An Overview. *The William and Mary Quarterly,* 58(1), 119–138.

Lazzarini, I. (2015). *Communication and Conflict: Italian Diplomacy in the Early Renaissance, 1350–1520.* OUP Oxford.

Lundell, R. (2016). Renaissance Diplomacy and the Limits of Empire: Eustace Chapuys, Habsburg Imperialisms, and Dissimulation as Method. In *The Limits of Empire: European Imperial Formations in Early Modern World History* (pp. 205–222). Routledge.

Mallett, M. (2001). Italian Renaissance Diplomacy. *Diplomacy and Statecraft,* 12(1), 61–70.

Mattingly, G. (1988). *Renaissance Diplomacy.* Courier Corporation.

McKee, S. (2008). Domestic Slavery in Renaissance Italy. *Slavery and Abolition,* 29(3), 305–326.

Perbi, A. (1992). The Relationship between the Domestic Slave Trade and the External Slave Trade in Pre-Colonial Ghana. *Research Review,* 8(1–2), 64.

Postma, J. M. (2008). *The Dutch in the Atlantic Slave Trade, 1600–1815.* Cambridge University Press.

Trade, S., Renaissance, B., & Back, F. (2005). African American. *The Journal of American History.*

Imperialism and Geopolitical Rivalries (19th Century)

Chamberlain, M. E. (2014). *The Scramble for Africa.* Routledge.

Chen, S. C. (2017). *Merchants of War and Peace: British Knowledge of China in the Making of the Opium War.* Hong Kong University Press.

Curli, B. (Ed.). (2022). *Italy and the Suez Canal, from the Mid-Nineteenth Century to the Cold War: A Mediterranean History.* Springer Nature.

Griffiths, I. (1986). The Scramble for Africa: Inherited Political Boundaries. *The Geographical Journal,* 152(2), 204–216.

Hoskins, H. L. (1940). Suez Canal Problems. *Geographical Review, 30*(4), 665–671.

Keevak, M. (2017). *Embassies to China: Diplomacy and Cultural Encounters before the Opium Wars*. Springer.

Kunz, D. B. (1991). *The Economic Diplomacy of the Suez Crisis*. Univ of North Carolina Press.

Lammers, D. N. (1967). Britain, Russia, and the Revival of "Entente Diplomacy": 1934. *Journal of British Studies*, 6(2), 99–123.

Michalopoulos, S., & Papaioannou, E. (2016). The Long-Run Effects of the Scramble for Africa. *American Economic Review*, 106(7), 1802–1848.

Pakenham, T. (2015). *The Scramble for Africa*. Hachette UK.

Schmitt, B. E. (1924). Triple Alliance and Triple Entente, 1902–1914. *The American Historical Review*, 29(3), 449–473.

Šedivý, M. (2022). Metternich and the Suez Canal: Informal Diplomacy in the Interests of Central Europe. *Central European History*, 55(3), 372–389.

Stevenson, D. (1997). Militarization and Diplomacy in Europe before 1914. *International Security*, 22(1), 125–161.

Stinchcombe, A. L. (1994). Class Conflict and Diplomacy: Haitian Isolation in the 19th-Century World System. *Sociological Perspectives*, 37(1), 1–23.

Tomaszewski, F. K. (2002). *A Great Russia: Russia and the Triple Entente, 1905 to 1914*. Bloomsbury Publishing USA.

Waley, A. (2013). *The Opium War Through Chinese Eyes* (Vol. 33). Routledge.

White, J. A. (2002). *Transition to Global Rivalry: Alliance Diplomacy and the Quadruple Entente, 1895–1907*. Cambridge University Press.

Interwar Period and Economic Nationalism (1919–1939)

Anievas, A. (2014). International Relations between War and Revolution: Wilsonian Diplomacy and the Making of the Treaty of Versailles. *International Politics*, 51, 619–647.

Boemeke, M. F., Feldman, G. D., & Gläser, E. (Eds.). (1998). *The Treaty of Versailles: A Reassessment after 75 Years*. Cambridge University Press.

Burk, K. (1981). Economic Diplomacy Between the Wars. *The Historical Journal*, 24(4), 1003–1015.

Eichengreen, B., & Irwin, D. A. (1995). Trade Blocs, Currency Blocs and the Reorientation of World Trade in the 1930s. *Journal of International Economics*, 38(1–2), 1–24.

Eichengreen, B., & Irwin, D. A. (2010). The Slide to Protectionism in the Great Depression: Who Succumbed and Why?. *The Journal of Economic History*, 70(4), 871–897.

Gatch, L. (2008). Local Money in the United States during the Great Depression. *Essays in Economic & Business History*, 26, 47–62.

Hayford, M., & Pasurka Jr, C. A. (1992). The Political Economy of the Fordney-McCumber and Smoot-Hawley Tariff Acts. *Explorations in Economic History*, 29(1), 30–50.

Heilperin, M. A. (2010). *Studies in Economic Nationalism* (No. 35). Ludwig von Mises Institute.

Malygina, A. A. (2019). *The Treaty of Versailles as a Milestone in the History of arms Control Diplomacy*.

Rosen, E. A. (2005). *Roosevelt, the Great Depression, and the Economics of Recovery*. University of Virginia Press.

Sharp, A. (2013). The Enforcement of the Treaty of Versailles, 1919–1923. In *After the Versailles Treaty* (pp. 5–20). Routledge.

Wallis, J. J. (1987). Employment, Politics, and Economic Recovery during the Great Depression. *The Review of Economics and Statistics*, 516–520.

Yellen, J. A. (2019). *The Greater East Asia Co-Prosperity Sphere: When Total Empire Met Total War*. Cornell University Press.

Post-World War II and Bretton Woods (1944)

Azevêdo, R. (2015). *A History of Law and Lawyers in the GATT/WTO: The Development of the Rule of Law in the Multilateral Trading System*. Cambridge University Press.

Bainbridge, T. (2000). A Brief History of the OECD. *OECD Observer*, 111–111.

Burns, K., Corrigan, B., Sanders, F., & Burns, K. (2017). *The Vietnam War*. Penguin Random House Audio Publishing Group.

Copeland, D. C. (1999). Trade Expectations and the Outbreak of Peace: Détente 1970–74 and the End of the Cold War 1985–91. *Security Studies*, 9(1–2), 15–58.

Cull, N. J. (2009). The Cold War and the United States Information Agency: American Propaganda and Public Diplomacy, 1945–1989. *Naval War College Review*, 62(2), 14.

Cumings, B. (2010). *The Korean War: A History* (Vol. 33). Modern Library.

DeLong, J. B., & Eichengreen, B. (1991). *The Marshall Plan: History's Most Successful Structural Adjustment Program*. National Bureau of Economic Research.

Dobson, A. P. (2002). *US Economic Statecraft for Survival, 1933–1991: of Sanctions, Embargoes and Economic Warfare* (Vol. 18). Routledge.

Drain, P. K., & Barry, M. (2010). Fifty Years of US Embargo: Cuba's Health Outcomes and Lessons. *Science*, 328(5978), 572–573.

Eastwood Jr, L. S. (1992). Secession: State Practice and International Law after the Dissolution of the Soviet Union and Yugoslavia. *Duke Journal of Comparative & International Law*, 3, 299.

Fascell, D. B. (1979). The Helsinki Accord: A Case Study. *The Annals of the American Academy of Political and Social Science*, 442(1), 69–76.

Gaddis, J. L. (1989). Intelligence, Espionage, and Cold War Origins. *Diplomatic History*, 13(2), 191–212.

Ghizoni, S. K. (2013). Nixon Ends Convertibility of US Dollars to Gold and Announces Wage/Price Controls. *Federal Reserve History*, 22, 2013.

Gowan, P. (1990). Western Economic Diplomacy and the New Eastern Europe. *New Left Review*, 182(77), 1989–1992.

Gray, C. S. (1971). The Arms Race Phenomenon. *World Politics*, 24(1), 39–79.

Head, K., Mayer, T., & Ries, J. (2010). The Erosion of Colonial Trade Linkages after Independence. *Journal of International Economics*, 81(1), 1–14.

Hogan, M. J. (1987). *The Marshall Plan: America, Britain and the Reconstruction of Western Europe, 1947–1952*. Cambridge University Press.

Hufbauer, G. C., Schott, J. J., & Elliott, K. A. (1990). *Economic Sanctions Reconsidered: History and CURRENT policy* (Vol. 1). Peterson Institute.

Hutchings, R. L. (1997). *American Diplomacy and the End of the Cold War: An Insider's Account of US Diplomacy in Europe, 1989–1992*. Woodrow Wilson Center Press.

Kaplowitz, D. R. (1998). *Anatomy of a Failed Embargo: US Sanctions against Cuba*. Lynne Rienner Publishers.

Mason, H. L. (2013). *The European Coal and Steel Community: Experiment in Supranationalism*. Springer.

Morgan, M. C. (2018). *The Final Act: The Helsinki Accords and the Transformation of the Cold War* (Vol. 26). Princeton University Press.

Schmidt, G. (Ed.). (2001). *A History of NATO: The First Fifty Years* (Vol. 3). Basingstoke: Palgrave.

Schuler, K., & Bernkopf, M. (2014). Who Was at Bretton Woods?. *Center for Financial Stability*, 1–31.

Seaborg, G. T. (1981). *Kennedy, Khrushchev, and the Test Ban*. Berkeley, Los Angeles and London: University of California Press.

Siddiqi, A. A. (2000). *Challenge to Apollo: the Soviet Union and the Space Race, 1945–1974* (Vol. 1). US National Aeronautics & Space Administration.

Smith, M. (2016). *European Union Diplomacy*. CM Constantinou, P. Kerr, & P. Sharp, The SAGE Handbook of Diplomacy, 308–316.

Spaulding, R. M. (1997). *Osthandel and Ostpolitik: German Foreign Trade Policies in Eastern Europe from Bismarck to Adenauer* (Vol. 1). Berghahn Books.

Trahair, R. C. (2004). *Encyclopedia of Cold War Espionage, Spies, and Secret Operations.* Bloomsbury Publishing USA.

Westad, O. A. (1997). *The Fall of Détente. Soviet-American Relations during the Carter Years.*

Zelizer, J. E. (2009). Détente and Domestic Politics. *Diplomatic History*, 33(4), 653–670.

Zubok, V. (2008). The Soviet Union and Détente of the 1970s. *Cold War History*, 8(4), 427–447.

Globalization and Trade Liberalization (Late 20th Century)

Abdel Wahaab, R. (2003). Sustainable Development and Environmental Impact Assessment in Egypt: Historical Assessment. *Environmentalist*, 23, 49–70.

Abdenur, A. E. (2014). China and the BRICS Development Bank: Legitimacy and Multilateralism in South–South Cooperation. *IDS Bulletin*, 45(4), 85–101.

Abdenur, A. E., & Folly, M. (2015). The New Development Bank and the Institutionalization of the BRICS. *BRICS-Studies and Documents*, 77–111.

Abdul Razaq, C. (2022). Economic Protectionist State Policy: An Analysis of Its Enduring Practices in the Contemporary International Trade Relations. *Journal of Social and Political Sciences*, 5(3).

Aggestam, K. (2004). Conflict Prevention: Old Wine in New Bottles?. In *Mitigating Conflict* (pp. 12–23). Routledge.

Aiping, Z., & Zhan, S. (2018). Origin, Achievements, and the Prospects of the Forum on China-Africa Cooperation. *China International Studies*, 72, 88.

Allen, B., Chan, K. K., Milne, A., & Thomas, S. (2012). Basel III: Is the Cure Worse Than the Disease?. *International Review of Financial Analysis*, 25, 159–166.

Amadei, B. (2019). Engineering for Peace and Diplomacy. *Sustainability*, 11(20), 5646.

Amuzegar, J. (1975). The North-South Dialogue: From Conflict to Compromise. *Foreign Affairs*, 54, 547.

Amuzegar, J. (1977). A Requiem for the North-South Conference. *Foreign Affairs*, 56, 136.

Andersen, E. (2022). 11. Non-Governmental Organizations as International Law's Diplomats. *Research Handbook on Law and Diplomacy*, 183, 191.

Anton, A. (2022a). Conceptual Pathways to Civil Society Diplomacy. *Diplomacy, Organisations and Citizens: A European Communication Perspective*, 81–98.

Anton, A. (2022b). Profiling a Niche Actor of Civil Society Diplomacy: The Unattached Diplomat. *Journal of Communication Management*, 27(2), 191–206.

Arel-Bundock, V., Atkinson, J., & Potter, R. A. (2015). The Limits of Foreign Aid Diplomacy: How Bureaucratic Design Shapes aid Distribution. *International Studies Quarterly*, 59(3), 544–556.

Arieti, S. A. (2005). The role of MERCOSUR as a Vehicle for Latin American Integration. *Chicago Journal of International Law*, 6, 761.

Arner, D. W., & Taylor, M. W. (2009). The Global Financial Crisis and the Financial Stability Board: Hardening the Soft Law of International Financial Regulation?. *University of New South Wales Law Journal, The*, 32(2), 488–513.

Arner, D. W., Panton, M. A., & Lejot, P. (2010). Central Banks and Central Bank Cooperation in the Global Financial System. *Pacific McGeorge Global Business & Development Law Journal*, 23, 1.

Arnopoulos, P. (1975). Consultation and Conciliation. *International Journal*, 30(1), 102–126.

Baciu, C., & Kotzé, K. (2022). Mimesis and Status-Seeking in the Global Order. BRICS Summit Diplomacy and Performative Practices. *Defence Studies*, 22(4), 709–735.

Barnett, R. M. (1993). Exchange Rate Arrangements in the International Monetary Fund: The Fund as Lawgiver, Adviser, and Enforcer. *Temple International & Comparative Law Journal*, 7, 77.

Bartels, L. (2001). Applicable Law in WTO Dispute Settlement Proceedings. *Journal of World Trade*, 35(3).

Basu Das, S. (2015). The Regional Comprehensive Economic Partnership: New Paradigm or Old Wine in a New Bottle?. *Asian-Pacific Economic Literature*, 29(2), 68–84.

Bayne, N. (1997). History of the G7 Summit: The Importance of American Leadership. N.Bain. https://tspace.library.utoronto.ca/html/1807/4806/document.Html

Benedick, R. E. (1998). The Montreal Protocol as a New Approach to Diplomacy. In *Protecting the Ozone Layer: Lessons, Models, and Prospects* (pp. 81–89). Boston, MA: Springer US.

Benedick, R. E. (2009, May). Science Inspiring Diplomacy: The Improbable Montreal Protocol. In *Twenty Years of Ozone Decline: Proceedings of the SYMPOSIUM for the 20th Anniversary of the Montreal Protocol* (pp. 13–19). Dordrecht: Springer Netherlands.

Bergsten, C. F., & Green, R. A. (Eds.). (2016). *International Monetary Cooperation: Lessons from the Plaza Accord after Thirty Years*. Peterson Institute for International Economics. 82702 29441

Besada, H., & Tok Ph D, E. (2014). South Africa in the BRICS: Soft Power Balancing and Instrumentalization. *Journal of International and Global Studies*, 5(2), 5.

Besada, H., Winters, K., & Tok, E. (2013). South Africa in the BRICS: Opportunities, Challenges and Prospects. *Africa Insight*, 42(4), 1–15.

Biziwick, M., Cattaneo, N., & Fryer, D. (2015). The Rationale for and Potential Role of the BRICS Contingent Reserve Arrangement. *South African Journal of International Affairs*, 22(3), 307–324.

Blowers, A. (1993). Environmental Policy: The Quest for Sustainable Development. *Urban Studies*, 30(4–5), 775–796.

Blundell-Wignall, A., & Atkinson, P. (2010). Thinking beyond Basel III: Necessary Solutions for Capital and Liquidity. *OECD Journal: Financial Market Trends*, 2010(1), 9–33.

Bond, P. (2020). BRICS Banking and the Demise of Alternatives to the IMF and World Bank. *International Development Assistance and the BRICS*, 189–218.

Borio, C. E., & Toniolo, G. (2006). *One Hundred and Thirty Years of Central Bank Cooperation: A BIS Perspective.*

Bouillaud, C. (2016). *International Summitry and Global Governance. The Rise of the G7 and the European Council, 1974–1991.* Cold War History Series.

Bowler, S., Indridason, I. H., Bräuninger, T., & Debus, M. (2016). Let's Just Agree to Disagree: Dispute Resolution Mechanisms in Coalition Agreements. *The Journal of Politics*, 78(4), 1264–1278.

Bradford, C. I., & Linn, J. F. (2012). A History of G20 Summits: The Evolving Dynamic of Global Leadership. *Journal of Globalization and Development*, 2(2).

Bunte, J. B., Giray, B., & Shea, P. (2022). *Repaying Debt with Land: Debt Diplomacy, Domestic Politics, and Land Transactions.*

Burlinova, N. V. (2022). The Role of NGOs in International Relations and Public Diplomacy. *Journal Of International Analytics*, 13(1).

Büthe, T. (2008). The Globalization of Health and Safety Standards: Delegation of Regulatory authority in the SPS Agreement of the 1994 Agreement Establishing the World Trade Organization. *Law and Contemporary Problems*, 71(1), 219–255.

Cagé, J., & Gadenne, L. (2018). Tax Revenues and the Fiscal Cost of Trade Liberalization, 1792–2006. *Explorations in Economic History*, 70, 1–24.

Carrai, M. A. (2018). It Is Not the End of History: The Financing Institutions of the Belt and Road Initiative and the Bretton Woods System. In *The Belt and Road Initiative* (pp. 107–145). Brill Nijhoff.

Cattaneo, N., Biziwick, M., & Fryer, D. (2015). The BRICS Contingent Reserve Arrangement and Its Position in the Emerging Global Financial Architecture. *Policy Insights*, 10.

Chakraborty, S. (2018). Significance of BRICS: Regional Powers, Global Governance, and the Roadmap for Multipolar World. *Emerging Economy Studies*, 4(2), 182–191.

Chan, S. I., & Song, W. (2020). Telling the China Story Well: A Discursive Approach to the Analysis of Chinese Foreign Policy in the "belt and road" Initiative. *Chinese Political Science Review*, 5(3), 417–437.

Charnovitz, S. (1997). A Critical Guide to the WTO's Report on Trade and Environment. *Arizona Journal of International and Comparative Law*, 14, 341.

Cheong, I., & Tongzon, J. (2013). Comparing the Economic Impact of the Trans-Pacific Partnership and the Regional Comprehensive Economic Partnership. *Asian Economic Papers*, 12(2), 144–164.

Chin, G. T. (2015). The State of the Art: Trends in the Study of the BRICS and Multilateral Organizations. *Rising Powers and Multilateral Institutions*, 19–41.

Chiu, K. S. (2011). China's Multilateral Diplomacy in Its Surrounding Areas: Theory and Practice. *Prospect Journal*, (6), 1–24.

Chiyemura, F. (2014). *South Africa in BRICS: Prospects and Constraints* (Doctoral dissertation).

Cohen, S. D. (1981). Forgiving Poverty: The Political Economy of the International Debt Relief Negotiations. International Affairs (*Royal Institute of International Affairs* 1944–), 58(1), 59–77.

Conti, J. (2010). *Between Law and Diplomacy: The Social Contexts of Disputing at the World Trade Organization*. Stanford University Press.

Cooper, A. F. (2014). The G20 and Contested Global Governance: BRICS, Middle Powers and Small States. *Caribbean Journal of International Relations and Diplomacy*, 2(3).

Cooper, A. F. (2017). The BRICS' New Development Bank: Shifting from Material Leverage to Innovative Capacity. *Global Policy*, 8(3), 275–284.

Cooper, A. F., & Cornut, J. (2019). The Changing Practices of Frontline Diplomacy: New Directions for Inquiry. *Review of International Studies*, 45(2), 300–319.

Correa, C. (2020). *Trade-Related Aspects of Intellectual Property Rights: A Commentary on the TRIPS Agreement*. Oxford University Press.

Cosimano, T. F., & Hakura, D. (2011). *Bank Behavior in Response to Basel III: A Cross-Country Analysis*.

Cottier, T. (2005). The Agreement on Trade-Related Aspects of Intellectual Property Rights. In *The World Trade Organization: Legal, Economic and Political Analysis* (pp. 1041–1120). Boston, MA: Springer US.

Dadush, U. (2009). *Resurgent Protectionism: Risks and Possible Remedies.* Carnegie Endowment for International Peace.

Daldegan, W., & Carvalho, C. E. (2022). BRICS as a Dynamic and in Process Phenomenon of Global Planning: An Analysis Based on the 2009–2020 Annual Summit Declarations. *Estudos Internacionais: revista de relações internacionais da PUC Minas,* 10(1), 117–147.

Davey, W. J. (2005). The WTO Dispute Settlement System: The First Ten Years. *Journal of International Economic Law,* 8(1), 17–50.

Davis, P. A. (1999). *The art of Economic Persuasion: Positive Incentives and German Economic Diplomacy.* University of Michigan Press.

Dean, J. W. (2001). The Asian Financial Crisis: Causes, Contagion and Consequences.

Delikat, M., & Kleiner, M. M. (2003). An Empirical Study of Dispute Resolution Mechanisms: Where Do Plaintiffs Better Vindicate Their Rights?. *Dispute Resolution Journal,* 58(4), 56.

Depledge, J. (2016). Climate Change Negotiations: Pushing Diplomacy to Its Limits. In *The New Economic Diplomacy* (pp. 294–315). Routledge.

Dimitrov, R. S. (2015). Climate Diplomacy. *Research Handbook of Climate Governance,* 97–108.

Dinan, D. (2004). *Europe Recast: A History of European Union* (Vol. 373). Basingstoke: Palgrave Macmillan.

Dizioli, A. G., & van Roye, B. (2018). The Resurgence of Protectionism: Potential Implications for Global Financial Stability. *Financial Stability Review,* 2.

Dobson, H. (2006). *The Group of 7/8.* Routledge.

Dollar, D., & Levin, V. (2006). The Increasing Selectivity of Foreign Aid, 1984–2003. *World Development,* 34(12), 2034–2046.

Dolzer, R., & Stevens, M. (1995). *Bilateral Investment Treaties.* Martinus Nijhoff Publishers.

Duggan, N. (2015). BRICS and the Evolution of a New Agenda Within Global Governance. *The European Union and the BRICS: Complex Relations in the Era of Global Governance,* 11–25.

Dyson, K. (1999). The Franco-German Relationship and Economic and Monetary Union: Using Europe to 'Bind Leviathan'. *West European Politics,* 22(1), 25–44.

Dyson, K. H., & Featherstone, K. (1999). *The Road to Maastricht: Negotiating Economic and Monetary Union*. Oxford University Press.

Eccleston, R. (2013). *The Dynamics of Global Economic Governance*. Books.

Edwards, S. (1983). Floating Exchange Rates, Expectations and New Information. *Journal of Monetary Economics*, 11(3), 321–336.

Egli, G. (2006). Don't Get Bit: Addressing ICSID's Inconsistent Application of Most-Favored-Nation Clauses to Dispute Resolution Provisions. *Pepper Law Reviews*, 34, 1045.

Esaka, T. (2000). The Louvre Accord and Central Bank Intervention: Was There a Target Zone?. *Japan and the World Economy*, 12(2), 107–126.

Everts, S. (1999). Economic and Monetary Union: A Test for US-European Relations. *The International Spectator*, 34(4), 21–27.

Fenwick, A. (1984). Evaluating China's Special Economic Zones. *International Tax & Business Law*, 2, 376.

Ferdinand, P. (2014). Rising Powers at the UN: An Analysis of the Voting Behaviour of BRICS in the General Assembly. *Third World Quarterly*, 35(3), 376–391.

Fewsmith, J. (2001). The Political and Social Implications of China's Accession to the WTO. *The China Quarterly*, 167, 573–591.

Fisher, E. C. (2006). *Beyond the Science/Democracy Dichotomy: The World Trade Organisation Sanitary and Phytosanitary Agreement and Administrative Constitutionalism*.

Flach, L., Hildenbrand, H. M., & Teti, F. (2021). The Regional Comprehensive Economic Partnership Agreement and Its Expected Effects on World Trade. *Intereconomics*, 56, 92–98.

Flandreau, M. (1997). Central Bank Cooperation in Historical Perspective: A Sceptical View. *Economic History Review*, 735–763.

Frankel, J. (2015). *The Plaza Accord, 30 Years Later* (No. w21813). National Bureau of Economic Research.

Freymann, E. (2022). One Belt One Road: Chinese Power Meets the World. In *One Belt One Road*. Harvard University Asia Center.

Gabler, M. (2010). Norms, Institutions and Social Learning: An Explanation for Weak Policy Integration in the WTO's Committee on Trade and Environment. *Global Environmental Politics*, 10(2), 80–117.

Gadinis, S. (2012). The Financial Stability Board: The New Politics of International Financial Regulation. *Texas International Law Journal*, 48, 157.

Gardini, G. (2010). *The Origins of Mercosur: Democracy and Regionalization in South America*. Springer.

Gardini, G. L. (2007). Who Invented Mercosur?. *Diplomacy and Statecraft*, 18(4), 805–830.

Gardini, G. L. (2012). In Defense of Oral History: Evidence from the Mercosur Case. *Journal of Politics in Latin America*, 4(1), 107–133.

Gertz, G. (2018). Commercial Diplomacy and Political Risk. *International Studies Quarterly*, 62(1), 94–107.

Gianviti, F. (2000). The Reform of the International Monetary Fund (Conditionality and Surveillance). In *International Law* (Vol. 34, p. 107).

Gillingham, J. (2003). *European Integration, 1950–2003: Superstate or New Market Economy?*. Cambridge University Press.

Glasson, J., & Therivel, R. (2013). *Introduction to Environmental Impact Assessment*. Routledge.

Glowka, L., Burhenne-Guilmin, F., Synge, H., McNeely, J. A., & Gündling, L. (1994). *A Guide to the Convention on Biological Diversity*.

Goh, E. (2004). *Constructing the US Rapprochement with China, 1961–1974: From'Red Menace'to'Tacit Ally'*. Cambridge University Press.

Goldberg, P. K. (2023). *The Unequal Effects of Globalization*. MIT Press.

Goldstein, M. M., & Crockett, M. A. (1987). *Strengthening the International Monetary System: Exchange Rates, Surveillance, and Objective INDICATORS*. International Monetary Fund.

Gottardi, P., & Mezzetti, C. (2022). *Shuttle Diplomacy*.

Gould, D. M. (1998). Has NAFTA Changed North American Trade?. *Economic Review-Federal Reserve Bank of Dallas*, 12–23.

Gowan, R. (2016). Asymmetrical Multilateralism: The BRICS, the US, Europe and the Reform of Global Governance (2005–2011). In *The European Union and Emerging Powers in the 21st Century* (pp. 165–183). Routledge.

Green, R. A., Papell, D. H., & Prodan, R. (2015). *Why Was the Plaza Accord Unique?*

Griffith-Jones, S. (2014). *A BRICS Development Bank: A Dream Coming True?* (No. 215). United Nations Conference on Trade and Development.

Guerrero, M. G. (2022). A Neo Institutionalist Proposal to Study the BRICS. *Contexto Internacional*, 44.

Gulrajani, N., Mawdsley, E., & Roychoudhury, S. (2020). The New Development Diplomacy in Middle-Income Countries. Retrieved February 5, 2023.

Guohua, Y., & Jin, C. (2001). The Process of China's Accession to the WTO. *Journal of International Economic Law*, 4(2), 297–328.

Guzman, A. T. (2002). The Cost of Credibility: Explaining Resistance to Interstate Dispute Resolution Mechanisms. *The Journal of Legal Studies*, 31(2), 303–326.

Hajnal, P. I. (2019). *The G20: Evolution, Interrelationships, Documentation* (p. 342). Taylor & Francis.

Halverson, K. (2004). China's WTO Accession: Economic, Legal, and Political Implications. *Boston College International and Comparative Law Review*, 27, 319.

Harrison, P. (2014). *South Africa in the BRICS*.

Heindl, J. A. (2006). Toward a History of NAFTA's Chapter Eleven. *Berkeley Journal of International Law* (BJIL), 24, 672.

Helleiner, E. (2010a). *The Financial Stability Board and International Standards*.

Helleiner, E. (2010b). What Role for the New Financial Stability Board? The Politics of International Standards after the Crisis. *Global Policy*, 1(3), 282–290.

Henning, C. R., & Destler, I. M. (1988). From Neglect to Activism: American Politics and the 1985 Plaza Accord. *Journal of Public Policy*, 8(3–4), 317–333.

Heymann, D. (2001). *Regional Interdependencies and Macroeconomic Crises: Notes on MERCOSUR*. ECLAC.

Hjertholm, P., & White, H. (2000). *Foreign aid in Historical Perspective. Foreign Aid and Development: Lessons Learnt and Directions for the Future*. New York: Routledge, 59–77.

Hodson, D. (2011). Governing the Euro Area in Good Times and Bad. *Oxford University Press*.

Hoekman, B. (2002). *The WTO: Functions and Basic Principles. Development, Trade, and the WTO: A Handbook* (pp. 41–50). Washington, DC: World Bank.

Hottinger, J. T. (2005). The Relationship Between Track One and Track Two Diplomacy. *Accord: an International Review of Peace Initiatives*, 16, 56–59.

Hutton, J., & Dickson, B. (2000). *Endangered Species Threatened Convention. The Past, Present and Future of CITES, the Convention on International Trade in Endangered Species of Wild Fauna and Flora*. Routledge.

Iida, K. (2004). Is WTO Dispute Settlement Effective. *Global Governance*, 10, 207.

Iqbal, B. A., & Rahman, M. N. (2016). BRIC (S) as an Emerging Block?. In *The Challenge of BRIC Multinationals* (Vol. 11, pp. 227–245). Emerald Group Publishing Limited.

Irwin, D. A. (2013). The Nixon Shock after Forty Years: The Import Surcharge Revisited. *World Trade Review*, 12(1), 29–56.

Johnston, S. (1997). The Convention on Biological Diversity: The Next Phase. *Review of European Community and International Environmental Law*, 6, 219.

Kahler, M. (2023). Global Governance in the Twenty-First Century: End of the Bretton Woods Moment?. *Contestation and Polarization in Global Governance: European Responses*, 17.

Kahn, M. J. (2011). The BRICs and South Africa as the Gateway to Africa. *Journal of the Southern African Institute of Mining and Metallurgy*, 111(7), 493–496.

King, P., & Tarbert, H. (2011). Basel III: An Overview. *Banking & Financial Services Policy Report*, 30(5), 1–18.

Kirton, J., & Larionova, M. (2022). The First Fifteen Years of the BRICS. *Vestnik Mezhdunarodnykh Organizatsii-International Organisations Research Journal*, 17(2).

Kondonassis, A. J., & Malliaris, A. G. (1996). NAFTA: Old and New Lessons from Theory and Practice with Economic Integration. *The North American Journal of Economics and Finance*, 7(1), 31–41.

Kuznetsov, A. (2023). *The Phenomenology of Globalization. In Polycentric World Order in the Making* (pp. 103–123). Singapore: Springer Nature Singapore.

Lafferty, W. M., & Meadowcroft, J. (2000). *Implementing Sustainable Development: Strategies and Initiatives in High Consumption Societies*. OUP Oxford.

Lancaster, C. (2008). *Foreign Aid: Diplomacy, Development, Domestic Politics*. University of Chicago Press.

Larionova, M. (2022). A Brief History of the G20 Institutional Dynamics (2008–21). *Dynamics*, 2008(21), 1.

Lateef, N. (1981). Parliamentary Diplomacy and the North-South Dialogue. *Georgia Journal of International & Comparative Law*, 11, 1.

Lawson, M. L. (2013). *Foreign Aid: International Donor Coordination of Development Assistance*.

Le Prestre, P. G. (Ed.). (2017). *Governing Global Biodiversity: The Evolution and Implementation of the Convention on Biological Diversity*. Routledge.

Lee, C. (Ed.). (2017). *Asia-Europe Cooperation after the 1997–1998 Asian Turbulence*. Routledge.

Lee, D., & Hocking, B. (2010). Economic Diplomacy. In *Oxford Research Encyclopedia of International Studies*.

Lee, M. J., Ostry, M. J. D., Prati, M. A., Ricci, M. L. A., & Milesi-Ferretti, M. G. (2008). *Exchange Rate Assessments: CGER Methodologies*. International Monetary Fund.

Lee, S. M. (2006). *ASEAN: Brief History and Its Problems*.

Leguey-Feilleux, J. R. (2017). *Global Governance Diplomacy: The Critical Role of Diplomacy in Addressing Global Problems*. Rowman & Littlefield.

Lim, T. W., Lim, W. X., Chan, H. H. L., & Tseng, K. H. Y. (2016). *China's One Belt One Road Initiative*. World Scientific.

Lop, G. V. (2017). Commercial Diplomacy in a Globalized World. *Przegląd Strategiczny*, 7(10), 367–382.

Mahbubani, K., & Mahbubani, K. (2022). Multilateral Diplomacy. *The Asian 21st Century*, 231–245.

Mar'I, M., Seraj, M., & Tursoy, T. (2023). The Role of Fiscal Policy in G20 Countries in the Context of the Environmental Kuznets Curve Hypothesis. *Energies*, 16(5), 2215.

Marchetti, J. A., & Mavroidis, P. C. (2011). The Genesis of the GATS (General Agreement on Trade in Services). *European Journal of International Law*, 22(3), 689–721.

Martin, J. (2022). *The Meddlers: Sovereignty, Empire, and the Birth of Global Economic Governance*. Harvard University Press.

Mattoo, A. (2003). China's Accession to the WTO: The Services Dimension. *Journal of International Economic Law*, 6(2), 299–339.

Matveev, A. (2015). Investor-state Dispute Settlement: The Evolving Balance between Investor Protection and State Sovereignty. *University of Western Australia Law Review*, 40, 348.

Mazenda, A., & Ncwadi, R. (2016). The Rise of BRICS Development Finance Institutions: A Comprehensive Look into the New Development Bank and the Contingency Reserve Arrangement. *African East-Asian Affairs*, (3).

Medeiros, E. S., & Fravel, M. T. (2003). China's New Diplomacy. *Foreign Affairs*, 82, 22.

Metzl, J. F. (2001). Network Diplomacy. *Georgetown Journal of International Affairs*, 77–87.

Mihajlovic, A. K. (2019). *The Role of the New Development Bank and BRICS Contingent Reserve Arrangement in the International Monetary and Financial System*.

Moomaw, W. R. (2018). Scientist Diplomats or Diplomat Scientists: Who Makes Science Diplomacy Effective?. *Global Policy*, 9, 78–80.

Moore, R. J. (1984). *Third-World Diplomats in Dialogue with the First World: The New Diplomacy*. Springer.

Mukhtar, H., & Hongdao, Q. (2017). A Critical Analysis of China Pakistan Free Trade Agreement: Learning Experiences for Pakistan with Respect to Its Future FTAs. *Global Journal of Politics and Law Research*, 5(6), 63–74.

Muller, M. H. (1981). Compensation for Nationalization: A North-South Dialogue. *Columbia Journal of Transnational Law*, 19, 35.

Muñoz, S., & Soler, P. (2017). Basel III End Game. *Regulation*, 1.

Mussa, M. (1997). IMF Surveillance. *The American Economic Review*, 87(2), 28–31.

Naray, O. (2008, October). Commercial Diplomacy: A Conceptual Overview. In *7th world conference of TPOs* (pp. 1–16).

Naray, O. (2011). Commercial Diplomats in the Context of International Business. *The Hague Journal of Diplomacy*, 6(1–2), 121–148.

Narine, S. (2008). Forty Years of ASEAN: A Historical Review. *The Pacific Review*, 21(4), 411–429.

Obergassel, W., Arens, C., Hermwille, L., Kreibich, N., Mersmann, F., Ott, H. E., & Wang-Helmreich, H. (2015). *Phoenix from the Ashes: An Analysis of the Paris Agreement to the United Nations Framework Convention on Climate Change; Part 1.*

Obstfeld, M., Cooper, R. N., & Krugman, P. R. (1985). Floating Exchange Rates: Experience and Prospects. *Brookings Papers on Economic Activity*, 1985(2), 369–464.

Orbie, J., Martens, D., Oehri, M., & Van den Putte, L. (2016). Promoting Sustainable Development or Legitimising Free Trade? Civil Society Mechanisms in EU Trade Agreements. *Third World Thematics: A TWQ Journal*, 1(4), 526–546.

Ortolano, L., & Shepherd, A. (1995). Environmental Impact Assessment: Challenges And Opportunities. *Impact Assessment*, 13(1), 3–30.

Osakwe, C. (2015). Contributions and Lessons from WTO Accessions: The Present and Future of the Rules-Based Multilateral Trading System. *WTO Accession and Trade Multilateralism: Case Studies and Lessons from the WTO at Twenty* (pp. 119–148). Cambridge: Cambridge University Press.

Pamment, J. (2016). *Intersections between Public Diplomacy & International Development: Case Studies in Converging Fields.* CPD Perspectives.

Pant, H. V. (2013). The BRICS Fallacy. *The Washington Quarterly*, 36(3), 91–105.

Pattanshetty, S., & Brand, H. (2022). Leveraging Health Diplomacy in Achieving AMR Policy Coherence. In *Antimicrobial Resistance* (pp. 165–176). CRC Press.

Pauwelyn, J. (1999). The WTO Agreement on Sanitary and Phytosanitary (SPS) Measures as Applied in the First Three SPS Disputes. EC-Hormones, Australia-Salmon and Japan-Varietals. *Journal of International Economic Law*, 2(4), 641–664.

Penttilä, R. (2013). *The Role of the G8 in International Peace and Security.* Routledge.

Perez del Castillo, S. (1993). MERCOSUR: History and Aims. *International Labour Review*, 132, 639.

Petropoulos, S. (2015). Opportunities, Challenges and Prospects of South Africa in the BRICS. *The European Union and the BRICS: Complex Relations in the Era of Global Governance*, 161–180.

Philippi, C. (2004). Between "Washington Consensus" and "Asian Way" Japanese Newspaper Authors Discussing the East Asian Financial and Economic Crisis of 1997/1998. *Japanstudien*, 15(1), 281–314.

Phlipot, C. (2010). Economic Diplomacy: Views of a Practitioner. *US Army War College Guide to National Security Issues Vol. 1: Theory of War and Strategy*.

Piros, S., & Koops, J. (2020). Towards a Sustainable Approach to EU Education Diplomacy? The Case of Capacity-Building in the Eastern Neighborhood. *Cultural Diplomacy in Europe: Between the Domestic and the International*, 113–138.

Poletti, A., Sicurelli, D., & Yildirim, A. B. (2021). Promoting Sustainable Development Through Trade? EU Trade Agreements and Global Value Chains. Italian Political Science *Review/Rivista Italiana Di Scienza Politica*, 51(3), 339–354.

Potter, P. B. (2001). The Legal Implications of China's Accession to the WTO. *The China Quarterly*, 167, 592–609.

Poulsen, L. N. S., & Aisbett, E. (2016). Diplomats Want Treaties: Diplomatic Agendas and Perks in the Investment Regime. *Journal of International Dispute Settlement*, 7(1), 72–91.

Prodi, R. (2016). Global Governance and Global Summits from the G8 to the G20: History, Opportunities and Challenges. *China & World Economy*, 24(4), 5–14.

Qi, C., & Zhang, J. X. (2018). The Economic Impacts of the China-Australia Free Trade Agreement-A General Equilibrium Analysis. *China Economic Review*, 47, 1–11.

Radulescu, I. G., Panait, M., & Voica, C. (2014). BRICS Countries Challenge the World Economy New Trends. *Procedia Economics and Finance*, 8, 605–613.

Ramos, L., Garcia, A., Pautasso, D., & Rodrigues, F. C. R. (2018). A Decade of Emergence: The brics'institutional Densification PROCESS. *Journal of China and International Relations*, 1–15.

Ravenhill, J. (2016). The Political Economy of an" Asian" Mega-FTA: The Regional Comprehensive Economic Partnership. *Asian Survey*, 56(6), 1077–1100.

Ray, S., Jain, S., Thakur, V., & Miglani, S. (2023). *Global Cooperation and G20: Role of Finance Track*. Springer.

Reich, A. (1996). From Diplomacy to Law: The Juridicization of International Trade Relations. *Northwestern Journal of International Law and Business*, 17, 775.

Reinhart, C. M. (2000). The Mirage of Floating Exchange Rates. *American Economic Review*, 90(2), 65–70.

Richter, R. (1989). The Louvre Accord from the Viewpoint of the New Institutional Economics. *Journal of Institutional and Theoretical Economics (JITE)/Zeitschrift für die gesamte Staatswissenschaft*, 704–719.

Richter, R., & Schmidt-Mohr, U. (1992). An Institutional-Economic Analysis of the Louvre Accord. In *Money, Trade, and Competition: Essays in Memory of Egon Sohmen* (pp. 59–86). Berlin, Heidelberg: Springer Berlin Heidelberg.

Risse, T., Engelmann-Martin, D., Knope, H. J., & Roscher, K. (1999). To Euro or Not to Euro? The EMU and Identity Politics in the European Union. *European Journal of International Relations*, 5(2), 147–187.

Sachs, J. D. (1989). Conditionality, Debt Relief, and the Developing Country Debt Crisis. In *Developing Country Debt and Economic Performance, Volume 1: The International Financial System* (pp. 255–296). University of Chicago Press.

Sander, F. E. (1985). Alternative Methods of Dispute Resolution: An Overview. *University of Florida Law Review*, 37, 1.

Saner, R. (2006). Development Diplomacy by Non-State Actors: An Emerging Form of Multistakeholder Diplomacy. *Multistakeholder Diplomacy: Challenges and Opportunities*, 93–105.

Saner, R., & Yiu, L. (2008). Business – Government – NGO Relations: Their Impact on Global Economic Governance. In *Global Governance and Diplomacy: Worlds Apart?* (pp. 85–103). London: Palgrave Macmillan UK.

Sarma, K. M., & Andersen, S. O. (2011). Science and Diplomacy: Montreal Protocol on Substances that Deplete the Ozone Layer. *Science Diplomacy: Antarctica, Science, and the Governance of International Spaces*.

Sauvé, P. (1995). Assessing the General Agreement on Trade in Services. *J. World Trade*, 29, 125.

Scott, A. (2011). The Nixon Shocks: The Opening to China and New Economic Policy. In *Allies Apart: Heath, Nixon and the Anglo-American Relationship* (pp. 50–79). London: Palgrave Macmillan UK.

Sebastião, S. P., & de Carvalho Spínola, S. (2022). *Diplomacy, Organisations and Citizens*. Springer International Publishing.

Shah, S. H., Kamal, M. A., & Yu, D. L. (2022). Did China-Pakistan Free Trade Agreement Promote Trade and Development in Pakistan?. *International Journal of Finance & Economics*, 27(3), 3459–3474.

Shakdwipee, P., & Mehta, M. (2017). From Basel I to Basel II to Basel III. *International Journal of New Technology and Research* (IJNTR), 3(1), 66–70.

Shaw, T. M. (2015). African Agency? Africa, South Africa and the BRICS. *International Politics*, 52(2), 255–268.

Shelton, G., & Paruk, F. (2008). The Forum on China-Africa Cooperation: A Strategic Opportunity. *Institute for Security Studies Monographs*, 2008(156), 222.

Shubin, V. (2015). South Africa in the BRICS: Last But Not Least. *International Organisations Research Journal*, 10(2), 171–183.

Siméon, N., Li, X., & Xiao, S. (2022). China's Agricultural Assistance Efficiency to Africa: Two Decades of Forum for China-Africa Cooperation Creation. *Journal of Agriculture and Food Research*, 9, 100329.

Simonin, B. L. (2008). Nation Branding and Public Diplomacy: Challenges and Opportunities. *Fletcher Forum of World Affairs*, 32, 19.

Singh, S. (2013). Future of Golden BRICS. *Strategic Analysis*, 37(4), 393–397.

Singh, S., & Dube, M. (2014). *BRICS and the World Order: A Beginner's Guide*. Available at SSRN 2443652.

Sinha, M. (2013). An Evaluation of the WTO Committee on Trade and Environment. *Journal of World Trade*, 47(6).

Slaughter, S. (2013). Debating the International Legitimacy of the G20: Global Policymaking and Contemporary International Society. *Global Policy*, 4(1), 43–52.

Slaughter, S. (2015). The G20's Role in Legitimating Global Capitalism: Beyond Crisis Diplomacy?. *Contemporary Politics*, 21(4), 384–398.

Slovik, P., & Cournède, B. (2011). *Macroeconomic Impact of Basel III*.

Smith, G. (2011). *G7 to G8 to G20: Evolution in Global Governance*.

Streltsov, D. (2019). 'Nixon shocks' and Their Implications for the Japanese Diplomacy. Vostok. *Afro-Aziatskie obshchestva: istoriia i sovremennost*, (2), 158–171.

Swanson, T. (2013). *Global Action for Biodiversity: An International Framework for Implementing the Convention on Biological Diversity*. Routledge.

Tänzler, D. (2018). Climate Diplomacy and Peace. In *Routledge Handbook of Environmental Conflict and Peacebuilding* (pp. 295–305). Routledge.

Tarasofsky, R. G. (1999). The WTO Committee on Trade and Environment: Is It Making a Difference?. *Max Planck Yearbook of United Nations Law Online*, 3(1), 471–488.

Taylor, I. (2010). *The Forum on China-Africa Cooperation* (FOCAC) (Vol. 48). Routledge.

Toye, J. (2003). The International Monetary Fund (IMF) and the World Bank (WB). In Michie, Jonathan (Ed.), *The Handbook of Globalisation* (pp. 358–369).

Trachtman, J. P. (1999). Domain of WTO Dispute Resolution. *Harvard International Law Journal*, 40, 333.

Troitskiy, M. (2015). BRICS Approaches to Security Multilateralism. *ASPJ Africa & Francophonie*, 2, 76–88.

Tucker, A. L., & Madura, J. (1991). Impact of the Louvre Accord on Actual and Anticipated Exchange Rate Volatilities. *Journal of International Financial Markets, Institutions & Money*, 1(2), 43–59.

Vandevelde, K. J. (2010). *Bilateral Investment Treaties: History, Policy, and Interpretation*. Oxford University Press.

Victor, D. G. (2016). What the Framework Convention on Climate Change Teaches Us about Cooperation on Climate Change. *Politics and Governance*, 4(3), 133–141.

Vijayakumar, N., Sridharan, P., & Rao, K. C. S. (2010). Determinants of FDI in BRICS Countries: A Panel Analysis. *International Journal of Business Science & Applied Management* (IJBSAM), 5(3), 1–13.

Waibel, M. (2010). *The Diplomatic Channel*.

Wang, H. (2019). The New Development Bank and the Asian Infrastructure Investment Bank: China's Ambiguous Approach to Global Financial Governance. *Development and Change*, 50(1), 221–244.

Wang, Y., & Li-Ying, J. (2014). How Do the BRIC Countries Play Their Roles in the Global Innovation Arena? A Study Based on USPTO Patents during 1990–2009. *Scientometrics*, 98, 1065–1083.

Ward, W. R. (1995). Man or Beast: The Convention on Biological Diversity and the Emerging Law of Sustainable Development. *Vanderbilt Journal of Transnational Law*, 28, 823.

Warner, G. (2007). Nixon, Kissinger and the Rapprochement with China, 1969–1972. *International Affairs*, 83(4), 763–781.

Weiss, T. G. (1985). Alternatives for Multilateral Development Diplomacy: Some Suggestions. *World Development*, 13(12), 1187–1209.

Weiss, T. G. (1986). *Multilateral Development Diplomacy in UNCTAD: The Lessons of Group Negotiations, 1964–84*. Springer.

Whitesides, G. (2020). Learning from Success: Lessons in Science and Diplomacy from the Montreal Protocol. *Science & Diplomacy*, 9(2), 1–13.

Woody, K. (1995). The World Trade Organization's Committee on Trade and Environment. *Georgetown Environmental Law Review*, 8, 459.

Woolcock, S., & Bayne, N. (Eds.). (2013). *The New Economic Diplomacy: Decision-Making and Negotiation in International Economic Relations*. Ashgate Publishing Ltd.

Würdemann, A. I. (2018). The BRICS Contingent Reserve Arrangement: A Subversive Power Against the IMF's Conditionality?. *The Journal of World Investment & Trade*, 19(3), 570–593.

Xiang, H., Kuang, Y., & Li, C. (2017). Impact of the China–Australia FTA on Global Coal Production and Trade. *Journal of Policy Modeling*, 39(1), 65–78.

Yao, X., Yasmeen, R., Li, Y., Hafeez, M., & Padda, I. U. H. (2019). Free Trade Agreements and Environment For Sustainable Development: A Gravity Model Analysis. *Sustainability*, 11(3), 597.

Young, J. H. (1977). Surveillance over Exchange Rate Policies. *Finance and Development*, 14(3), 17–19.

Zahrnt, V. (2011). Transparency of Complex Regulation: How Should WTO Trade Policy Reviews Deal with Sanitary and Phytosanitary Policies?. *World Trade Review*, 10(2), 217–247.

Zeiler, T. W. (2013). Requiem for the Common Man: Class, the Nixon Economic Shock, and the Perils of Globalization. *Diplomatic History*, 37(1), 1–23.

Zhou, P. (2001). North-South Dialogue. *Tiempo: Global Warming and the Third World*, 40(41), 1–7.

Zhu, J., & Wei, F. (2022). Overview of the Role of the Party's Scientific Authority in Implementation of Convention on International Trade in Endangered Species of Wild Fauna and Flora. *Bulletin of Chinese Academy of Sciences* (Chinese Version), 37(11), 1614–1622.

Zhu, Y., & Webber, M. (2016). The Impact of Western Economics on China's Reforms from the Late 1970s to the Present: An Overview. *The Diffusion of Western Economic Ideas in East Asia*, 364–375.

The 21st Century

Akhtar, S. I. (2023). US-EU Trade and Economic Relations. *Current Politics and Economics of Europe*, 34(2/3), 249–254.

Alexandra-Cristina, D. I. N. U. (2023, May). Cyber Diplomacy and Artificial Intelligence: Opportunities and Challenges. In *Proceedings of the International Conference on Cybersecurity and Cybercrime-2023* (pp. 86–93). Asociatia Romana pentru Asigurarea Securitatii Informatiei.

Alvstam, C. G., & Kettunen, E. (2019). The EU-Japan Economic Partnership Agreement: Second Best Option or New Generation of Preferential Trade Arrangements?. In *CESifo Forum* (Vol. 20, No. 02, pp. 3–9). München: ifo Institut–Leibniz-Institut für Wirtschaftsforschung an der Universität München.

Attatfa, A., Renaud, K., & De Paoli, S. (2020). Cyber Diplomacy: A Systematic Literature Review. *Procedia Computer Science*, 176, 60–69.

Bendiek, A., & Stürzer, I. (2022). *Advancing European Internal and External Digital Sovereignty: The Brussels Effect and the EU-US Trade and Technology Council*.

Biedenkopf & Petri (2021). The European External Action Service and EU Climate Diplomacy: Coordinator and Supporter in Brussels and Beyond. *European Foreign Affairs Review*, 26.1.

Biedenkopf, K., & Petri, F. (2019). EU Delegations in European Union climate Diplomacy: The Role of Links to Brussels, Individuals and Country Contexts. *Journal of European Integration*, 41(1), 47–63.

Bocse, A. M. (2019). EU Energy Diplomacy: Searching for New Suppliers in Azerbaijan and Iran. *Geopolitics*, 24(1), 145–173.

Bongardt, A. (2023). EU Trade Policy and Climate Change1. *The Political Economy of Europe's Future and Identity*, 94.

Bossman, A., Gubareva, M., & Teplova, T. (2023). Asymmetric Effects of Geopolitical Risk on Major Currencies: Russia-Ukraine Tensions. *Finance Research Letters*, 51, 103440.

Bovan, A., Vučenović, T., & Peric, N. (2020). Negotiating Energy Diplomacy and Its Relationship with Foreign Policy and National Security. *International Journal of Energy Economics and Policy*, 10(2), 1–6.

Bulmer, S. (2022). Germany, the Eurozone Crisis and the Covid-19 Pandemic: Failing Forward or Moving On?. *Comparative European Politics*, 20(2), 166–183.

Burri, M., & Polanco, R. (2020). Digital Trade Provisions in Preferential Trade Agreements: Introducing a New Dataset. *Journal of International Economic Law*, 23(1), 187–220.

Buti, M., & Fabbrini, S. (2023). Next Generation EU and the Future of Economic Governance: Towards a Paradigm Change or Just a Big One-Off?. *Journal of European Public Policy*, 30(4), 676–695.

Cabral, L., Haucap, J., Parker, G., Petropoulos, G., Valletti, T. M., & Van Alstyne, M. W. (2021). *The EU Digital Markets Act: A Report From A Panel of Economic Experts* (Eds., Cabral, L., Haucap, J., Parker, G., Petropoulos, G., Valletti, T., & Van Alstyne, M.). Luxembourg: The EU Digital Markets Act, Publications Office of the European Union.

Cardwell, P. J., & Moret, E. (2023). The EU, Sanctions and Regional Leadership. *European Security*, 32(1), 1–21.

Catsoulis, I. M. (2022). *The Impact of the EU-Japan Economic Partnership Agreement (EPA) on Government Procurement*.

Champimpi, M. (2023). *Economic and Trade Diplomacy: USA, China and European Union* (Doctoral dissertation, University of Piraeus (Greece))

Chattu, V. K., & Chami, G. (2020). Global Health Diplomacy Amid the COVID-19 Pandemic: A Strategic Opportunity for Improving Health, Peace, and Well-Being in the CARICOM Region – A Systematic Review. *Social Sciences*, 9(5), 88.

Chattu, V. K., Singh, B., Kaur, J., & Jakovljevic, M. (2021). COVID-19 Vaccine, TRIPS, and Global Health Diplomacy: India's Role at the WTO Platform. *BioMed Research International*, 2021.

Cheikh, N. B., & Zaied, Y. B. (2023). Investigating the Dynamics of Crude Oil and Clean Energy Markets in Times of Geopolitical Tensions. *Energy Economics*, 124, 106861.

Cohen, J. (2023). The Rise of Geopolitical Swing States. *Godman Sachs Intelligence*, 15 May.

Conconi, P., Herghelegiu, C., & Puccio, L. (2021). EU Trade Agreements: To Mix Or Not to Mix, That Is the Question. *Journal of World Trade*, 55(2).

Culpepper, P. D. (2019). *Creating Cooperation: How States Develop Human Capital in Europe.* Cornell University Press.

Dadush, U. (2022). *Deglobalisation and Protectionism.* Bruegel.

De Grauwe, P., & Ji, Y. (2022). The Fragility of the Eurozone: Has It Disappeared?. *Journal of International Money and Finance*, 120, 102546.

de Paula, N. (2021). Planetary Health Diplomacy: A Call to Action. *The Lancet Planetary Health*, 5(1), e8–e9.

Dennison, S., & Engström, M. (2023). *Decarbonisation Nations: How EU Climate Diplomacy Can Save the World. Policy Brief.* Berlin: European Council on Foreign Relations (ECFR).

Donnelly, S. (2023). Bank Supervision Between Risk Reduction and Economic Renewal. *Journal of European Integration*, 45(1), 59–77.

Duina, F. (2022). What's in My Sandwich?: Trade, Values, and the Promise of Deeper Integration. In *Transatlantic Relations* (pp. 119–138). Routledge.

Earsom, J., & Delreux, T. (2021). Evaluating EU Responsiveness to the Evolution of the International Regime Complex on Climate Change. *International Environmental Agreements: Politics, Law and Economics*, 21(4), 711–728.

Eisl, A., & Rubio, E. (2022). What Makes Economic Differentiation Effective? Insights from the EU Energy Sector, Banking Union and Third-Country Access to the Single Market. *The International Spectator*, 57(1), 90–106.

Fahey, E., & Wieczorek, I. (2022). The European Parliament as a Defender of EU Values in EU-Japan Agreements: What Role for Soft Law and Hard Law Powers?. *European Law Review*, 47(3).

Fan, J. H., Omura, A., & Roca, E. (2023). Geopolitics and Rare Earth Metals. *European Journal of Political Economy*, 78, 102356.

Felbermayr, G., Kimura, F., Okubo, T., & Steininger, M. (2019). Quantifying the EU-Japan Economic Partnership Agreement. *Journal of the Japanese and International Economies*, 51, 110–128.

Fileva, M. (2021). The Impact of Globalization and the Interconnectedness with the Comprehensive Economic and trade Agreement between Canada and the European Union. *Journal of Liberty and International Affairs*, 7(1), 106–119.

Fonseca, L. M., & Azevedo, A. L. (2020). COVID-19: Outcomes for Global Supply Chains. Management & Marketing. *Challenges for the Knowledge Society*, 15(s1), 424–438.

Free, C., & Hecimovic, A. (2021). Global Supply Chains after COVID-19: The End of the Road for Neoliberal Globalisation?. *Accounting, Auditing & Accountability Journal*, 34(1), 58–84.

Friel, S., Schram, A., & Townsend, B. (2020). The Nexus between International Trade, Food Systems, Malnutrition and Climate Change. *Nature Food*, 1(1), 51–58.

García, M. J. (2022). Sanctioning Capacity in Trade and Sustainability Chapters in EU Trade Agreements: The EU–Korea Case. *Politics and Governance*, 10(1), 58–67.

Gereffi, G., Lim, H. C., & Lee, J. (2021). Trade Policies, Firm Strategies, and Adaptive Reconfigurations of Global Value Chains. *Journal of International Business Policy*, 1–17.

Gheyle, N. (2022). Evading Vetoes: Exiting the Politicized Decision Trap in EU Trade Policy. JCMS: *Journal of Common Market Studies*, 60(6), 1723–1740.

Giordani, P. E., & Mariani, F. (2022). Unintended Consequences: Can the Rise of the Educated Class Explain the Revival of Protectionism?. *Journal of Economic Theory*, 200, 105385.

Goldsmith, B. E., Horiuchi, Y., & Matush, K. (2021). Does Public Diplomacy Sway Foreign Public Opinion? Identifying the Effect of High-Level Visits. *American Political Science Review*, 115(4), 1342–1357.

Graz, J. C., & Hauert, C. (2019). Translating Technical Diplomacy: The Participation of Civil Society Organisations in International Standardisation. *Global Society*, 33(2), 163–183.

Gurtu, A., & Johny, J. (2021). Supply Chain Risk Management: Literature Review. *Risks*, 9(1), 16.

Henry, M. G. (2019). Keeping the Peace: Gender, Geopolitics and Global Governance Interventions. *Conflict, Security & Development*, 19(3), 263–268.

Hervé, A. (2021). *The European Union and Its Model to Regulate International Trade Relations*. Fondation Robert Schuman.

Hopewell, K. (2022a). Emerging Powers, Leadership, and South–South Solidarity: The Battle over Special and Differential Treatment at the WTO. *Global Policy*, 13(4), 469–482.

Hopewell, K. (2022b). Heroes of the Developing World? Emerging Powers in WTO Agriculture Negotiations and Dispute Settlement. *The Journal of Peasant Studies*, 49(3), 561–584.

Hucker, D. (2020). *Public Opinion and Twentieth-Century Diplomacy: A Global Perspective*. Bloomsbury Publishing.

Hufbauer, G. C., & Jung, E. (2020). What's New in Economic Sanctions?. *European Economic Review*, 130, 103572.

Hufbauer, G. C., & Jung, E. (2021). Economic Sanctions in the Twenty-First Century. *Research Handbook on Economic Sanctions*, 26–43.

Huijgh, E. (2019). Changing Tunes for Public Diplomacy: Exploring the Domestic Dimension. In *Public Diplomacy at Home* (pp. 32–51). Brill Nijhoff.

Jaursch, J. (2023). Regional Mobilization in International Trade Policy: The US States in Transatlantic Trade Negotiations. *Regional & Federal Studies*, 33(1), 47–67.

Javed, S., & Chattu, V. K. (2020). Strengthening the COVID-19 Pandemic Response, Global Leadership, and International Cooperation Through Global Health Diplomacy. *Health Promotion Perspectives*, 10(4), 300.

Justinek, G. (2022). From One Crisis to Another. *International Journal of Diplomacy and Economy*, 8(2), 109.

Keijzer, N., Burni, A., Erforth, B., & Friesen, I. *The Rise of the Team Europe Approach in EU Development Cooperation*.

Kenkel, K., & Destradi, S. (2019). Explaining Emerging Powers' Reluctance to Adopt Intervention Norms: Normative Contestation and Hierarchies of Responsibility. *Revista Brasileira de Política Internacional*, 62.

Kettunen, E., & Alvstam, C. G. (2023). The EU-Japan Era and the Question of Forman and the Question of Formal and Informal Trade Barriers for European Businesses in Japan. *Trames: A Journal of the Humanities & Social Sciences*, 27(3).

Kholmuradovich, K. B. (2022). "People's Diplomacy"-An Important Factor for the Development of Regional Cooperation. *The Peerian Journal*, 6, 71–74.

Kickbusch, I., & Liu, A. (2022). Global Health Diplomacy – Reconstructing Power and Governance. *The Lancet*, 399(10341), 2156–2166.

Kim, R. E. (2020). Is Global Governance Fragmented, Polycentric, or Complex? The State of the Art of the Network Approach. *International Studies Review*, 22(4), 903–931.

Kimura, C. (2022). Negotiating Capital and the EU-Japan Economic Partnership Agreement. *Cuadernos Europeos de Deusto*, (05), 33–49.

Kirchberger, S., Sinjen, S., & Woermer, N. (2022). *Russia-China Relations: Emerging Alliance or Eternal Rivals?* (p. 315). Springer Nature.

Klimes, M., Michel, D., Yaari, E., & Restiani, P. (2019). Water Diplomacy: The Intersect of Science, Policy and Practice. *Journal of Hydrology*, 575, 1362–1370.

Korosteleva, E. A., & Flockhart, T. (2020). Resilience in EU and International Institutions: Redefining Local Ownership in a New Global Governance Agenda. *Contemporary Security Policy*, 41(2), 153–175.

Li, Z., & Li, T. (2022). Economic Sanctions and Regional Differences: Evidence from Sanctions on Russia. *Sustainability*, 14(10), 6112.

Limna, P., Kraiwanit, T., & Siripipatthanakul, S. (2022). The Growing Trend of Digital Economy: A Review Article. *International Journal of Computing Sciences Research*, 6, 1–11.

Linsenmaier, T., Schmidt, D. R., & Spandler, K. (2021). On the Meaning (s) of Norms: Ambiguity and Global Governance in a Post-hegemonic World. *Review of International Studies*, 47(4), 508–527.

Liu, F., Feng, J., Zhai, G., & Razzaq, A. (2022). Influence of Fiscal Decentralization and Renewable Energy Investment on Ecological Sustainability in EU: What Is the Moderating Role of Institutional Governance?. *Renewable Energy*, 200, 1265–1274.

Livada, A., Papastamou, A., & Boulieris, P. (2023). *Income Inequality in Western Balkans. SITES 2023 Annual Conference: Persistence and Change: The New Challenges for Economic Development*. Naples, Italy, 14 September, https://www.conftool.net/sites-2023/sessions.php

Lohmann, S. (2019, July). Diplomats and the Use of Economic Sanctions. In *New Realities in Foreign Affairs* (pp. 23–32). Nomos Verlagsgesellschaft mbH & Co. KG.

Manfredi-Sánchez, J. L., & Smith, N. R. (2023). Public Diplomacy in an Age of Perpetual Crisis: Assessing the EU's Strategic Narratives Through Six Crises. *Journal of Communication Management*, 27(2), 241–258.

Markopoulou, D., Papakonstantinou, V., & De Hert, P. (2019). The New EU Cybersecurity Framework: The NIS Directive, ENISA's Role and the General Data Protection Regulation. *Computer Law & Security Review*, 35(6), 105336.

Martin, J. (2022). *The Meddlers: Sovereignty, Empire, and the Birth of Global Economic Governance*. Harvard University Press.

Martínez, J. E. B. (2022). Emerging Middle Powers Versus Peripheral Leadership. *Handbook of Regional Conflict Resolution Initiatives in the Global South*, 267.

Meunier, S., & Nicolaidis, K. (2019). The Geopoliticization of European Trade and Investment Policy. *Journal of Common Market Studies*, 57, 103.

Miroudot, S. (2020). Reshaping the Policy Debate on the Implications of COVID-19 for Global Supply Chains. *Journal of International Business Policy*, 3, 430–442.

Moloney, N. (2023). *EU Securities and Financial Markets Regulation*. Oxford University Press.

Morgan, T. C., Syropoulos, C., & Yotov, Y. V. (2023). Economic Sanctions: Evolution, Consequences, and Challenges. *Journal of Economic Perspectives*, 37(1), 3–29.

Morita, K. (2020). Recent Development in the European Union Regarding Investment Dispute Settlement Mechanism-An Analysis of the Comprehensive Economic and Trade Agreement: CETA. *Hitotsubashi Journal of Law and Politics*, 48, 69–77.

Nagabhatla, N., Cassidy-Neumiller, M., Francine, N. N., & Maatta, N. (2021). Water, Conflicts and Migration and the Role of Regional Diplomacy: Lake Chad, Congo Basin, and the Mbororo Pastoralist. *Environmental Science & Policy*, 122, 35–48.

Narlikar, A. (2022). How Not to Negotiate: The Case of Trade Multilateralism. *International Affairs*, 98(5), 1553–1573.

Năstase, E. A. (2022). An Approach to the European Union's Energy Diplomacy. *Euro-Atlantic Studies*, (5), 141–171.

Neuwahl, N. (2021). Brexit and Canada: Stopgap Solutions for the EU–Canada Comprehensive Economic and Trade Agreement (CETA) or a New Beginning?. *International Studies*, 58(2), 248–264.

Nye, J. S. (2019). Soft Power and Public Diplomacy Revisited. *The Hague Journal of Diplomacy*, 14(1–2), 7–20.

Oosthuizen, M. E. (2022). *The Changing Nature of Diplomacy in the 21st Century: from Diplomatic Generalists to Four Types of Specialists* (Doctoral dissertation, University of Johannesburg).

Orsini, A., Le Prestre, P., Haas, P. M., Brosig, M., Pattberg, P., Widerberg, O., … & Chandler, D. (2020). Complex Systems and International Governance. *International Studies Review*, 22(4), 1008–1038.

Özkaragöz Doğan, E., Uygun, Z., & Akçomak, İ. S. (2021). Can Science Diplomacy Address the Global Climate Change Challenge?. *Environmental Policy and Governance*, 31(1), 31–45.

Panetta, F. (2023). United We Stand: European Integration as a Response to Global Fragmentation. *European Central Bank*, 24 April.

Pastukhova, M., Pepe, J. M., & Westphal, K. (2020). *Beyond the Green Deal: Upgrading the EU's energy diplomacy for a New Era* (No. 31/2020). SWP Comment.

Peksen, D. (2019). When Do Imposed Economic Sanctions Work? A Critical Review of the Sanctions Effectiveness Literature. *Defence and Peace Economics*, 30(6), 635–647.

Pereira, P. S. (2019). The EU–Japan Economic Partnership Agreement from the European Parliament's Perspective: A Landmark Agreement beyond Trade. *Journal of Inter-Regional Studies: Regional and Global Perspectives* (JIRS), 2, 16.

Petri, F. (2020). Revisiting EU Climate and Energy Diplomacy: A Starting Point for Green Deal Diplomacy. *Egmont European Policy Brief*, 65, 1–9.

Porter, P. (2019). Advice for a Dark Age: Managing Great Power Competition. *The Washington Quarterly*, 42(1), 7–25.

Prantl, J. (2022). Reuniting Strategy and Diplomacy for 21st Century Statecraft. *Contemporary Politics*, 28(1), 1–19.

Ridley, W., Luckstead, J., & Devadoss, S. (2022). Wine: The Punching Bag in Trade Retaliation. *Food Policy*, 109, 102250.

Roederer-Rynning, C., & Greenwood, J. (2020). Black Boxes and Open Secrets: Trilogues as 'politicised diplomacy'. *West European Politics*, 44(3), 485–509.

Roger, C. B. (2020). *The Origins of Informality: Why the Legal Foundations of Global Governance Are Shifting, and Why It Matters*. Oxford University Press.

Rong, K. (2022). Research Agenda for the Digital Economy: an IBCDE Framework. *Journal of Digital Economy*.

Ruffini, P. B. (2020). Collaboration and Competition: The Twofold Logic of Science Diplomacy. *The Hague Journal of Diplomacy*, 15(3), 371–382.

Sama, L. M., Stefanidis, A., & Casselman, R. M. (2022). Rethinking Corporate Governance in the Digital Economy: The Role of Stewardship. *Business Horizons*, 65(5), 535–546.

Sanskar. (2023). The Impact of Protectionist Policies on Global Trade. *Indian Journal of Integrated Research in Law*, 3, 1.

Sharma, S. K., Srivastava, P. R., Kumar, A., Jindal, A., & Gupta, S. (2023). Supply Chain Vulnerability Assessment for Manufacturing Industry. *Annals of Operations Research*, 326(2), 653–683.

Shrestha, S. B., Parajuli, L. K., & Shrestha, M. V. (2022). Science Diplomacy: An Overview in the Global and National Context. *Journal of Foreign Affairs*, 2(01), 41–51.

Singh, J. P. (2020). Trade Negotiations at the (Possible) End of Multilateral Institutionalism. *International Negotiation*, 25(1), 31–52.

Smith, M. (2022). How Much of a New Agenda? International Structures, Agency, and Transatlantic Order. *Politics and Governance*, 10(2), 219–228.

Solana, J. (2020). The Case for 'Human Diplomacy'. *The Hague Journal of Diplomacy*, 15(4), 670–680.

Stephen, M. D., & Parízek, M. (2019). New Powers and the Distribution of Preferences in Global Trade Governance: From Deadlock and Drift to Fragmentation. *New Political Economy*, 24(6), 735–758.

Tirole, J. (2023). Competition and the Industrial Challenge for the Digital Age. *Annual Review of Economics*, 15, 573–605.

Usherwood, S. (2023). UK-EU Relations After the Windsor Framework. *Political Insight*, 14(2), 12–15.

Van Bergeijk, P. A. (2022a). Economic Sanctions and the Russian War on Ukraine: a Critical Comparative Appraisal. *International Institute of Social Studies*. Available online: https://www.iss.nl/en/news/economic-sancti ons-and-russian-war-ukraine-critical-comparative-appraisal-peter-ag-van-bergeijk

Van Bergeijk, P. A. (2022b). Sanctions Against the Russian War on Ukraine: Lessons from History and Current Prospects. *Journal of World Trade*, 56(4).

Van der Harst, J. (2023). The European Commission and the "Europeanisation" of EU Trade Diplomacy: The Case of EU-China Relations, 1999–2021. *Asia Europe Journal*, 1–15.

Veale, M., & Zuiderveen Borgesius, F. (2021). Demystifying the Draft EU Artificial Intelligence Act – Analysing the Good, the Bad, and the Unclear Elements of the Proposed Approach. *Computer Law Review International*, *22*(4), 97–112.

Weiss, T. G., & Wilkinson, R. (2019). *Rethinking Global Governance*. John Wiley & Sons.

Xu, Z., Elomri, A., Kerbache, L., & El Omri, A. (2020). Impacts of COVID-19 on Global Supply Chains: Facts and Perspectives. IEEE *Engineering Management Review*, 48(3), 153–166.

Yazdi-Feyzabadi, V., Amini-Rarani, M., & Delavari, S. (2020). The Health Consequences of Economic Sanctions: Call for Health Diplomacy and International Collaboration. *Archives of Iranian Medicine*, 23(pecial), S51.

Yueh, L. (2020). *Economic Diplomacy in the 21st Century: Principles and Challenges*. LSE Ideas, August.

Zwarts, H., Du Toit, J., & Von Solms, B. (2022, June). A Cyber-Diplomacy and Cybersecurity Awareness Framework (CDAF) for Developing Countries. In *European Conference on Cyber Warfare and Security* (Vol. 21, No. 1, pp. 341–349).

How Safe Are We? Shaping European Economy by Geopolitical Shocks

Acharyya, R., & Kar, S. (2014). *International Trade and Economic Development.* USA: Oxford University Press.

Adler, G., Cubeddu, L., & Gopinath, G. (2021). Taming the Currency Hype. *Exchange.*

Aggestam, K. (2016). *18 Diplomatic Mediation.* The SAGE Handbook of Diplomacy.

Agoraki, M. E. K., Kouretas, G. P., & Laopodis, N. T. (2022). Geopolitical risks, uncertainty, and stock market performance. *Economic and Political Studies,* 10(3), 253-265.

Akram, Q. F. (2020). Oil Price Drivers, Geopolitical Uncertainty and Oil Exporters' Currencies. *Energy Economics,* 89, 104801.

Al Mamun, M., Uddin, G. S., Suleman, M. T., & Kang, S. H. (2020). Geopolitical Risk, Uncertainty and Bitcoin Investment. *Physica A: Statistical Mechanics and Its Applications,* 540, 123107.

Al-Marashi, I., & Causevic, A. (2020). NATO and Collective Environmental Security in the MENA. *Journal of Strategic Security,* 13(4), 28–44.

Alperovitch, D. (2022). The Case for Cyber-Realism: Geopolitical Problems Don't Have Technical Solutions. *Foreign Affairs,* 101, 44.

Altman, D., & Lee, M. M. (2022). Why Territorial Disputes Escalate: The Causes of Conquest Attempts since 1945. *International Studies Quarterly,* 66(4), 076.

Ang, A., & Chen, J. (2002). Asymmetric correlations of equity portfolios. *Journal of financial Economics,* 63(3), 443–494.

Anser, M. K., Syed, Q. R., Lean, H. H., Alola, A. A., & Ahmad, M. (2021). Do Economic Policy Uncertainty and Geopolitical Risk Lead to Environmental Degradation? Evidence from Emerging Economies. *Sustainability,* 13(11), 5866.

Antonakakis, N., Gupta, R., Kollias, C., & Papadamou, S. (2017). Geopolitical Risks and the Oil-Stock Nexus Over 1899–2016. *Finance Research Letters,* 23, 165–173.

Aras, B., & Ozbay, F. (2008). The Limits of the Russian–Iranian Strategic Alliance: Its History and Geopolitics, and the Nuclear Issue. *The Korean Journal of Defense Analysis,* 20(1), 47–62.

Armao, F. (2004). Why Is Organized Crime So Successful?. In *Organised Crime and the Challenge to Democracy* (pp. 25–35). Routledge.

Atapattu, S. (2020). Climate Change and Displacement: Protecting 'Climate Refugees' Within a Framework of Justice and Human Rights. *Journal of Human Rights and the Environment,* 11(1), 86–113.

Atar, E., Hossain, F., & Ullah, A. A. (2023). Syrian Refugees in Turkey: Exploring the Role of I/NGOs in Refugee Crisis. *Third World Quarterly, 44*(2), 231–245.

Auerswald, D. P. (2020). Arctic Narratives and Geopolitical Competition. In *Handbook on Geopolitics and Security in the Arctic: The High North Between Cooperation and Confrontation* (pp. 251–271).

Aven, T., & Zio, E. (2021). Globalization and Global Risk: How Risk Analysis Needs to Be Enhanced to Be Effective in Confronting Current Threats. *Reliability Engineering & System Safety, 205*, 107270.

Avram, C. (2012). Choke Points-The Geopolitical Importance for the Global Era. In *International Scientific Conference" Strategies XXI"* (Vol. 1, p. 69). "Carol I" National Defence University.

Balcilar, M., Demirer, R., & Hammoudeh, S. (2019). Quantile relationship between oil and stock returns: Evidence from emerging and frontier stock markets. *Energy Policy, 134*, 110931.

Baldwin, R. E. (1979). Determinants of trade and foreign investment: Further evidence. *The Review of Economics and Statistics*, 40–48.

Barnard-Wills, D. (2013). Security, Privacy and Surveillance in European Policy Documents. *International Data Privacy Law, 3*(3), 170–180.

Barnett, M., & Duvall, R. (2023). International Organizations and the Diffusion of Power. In *International Organization and Global Governance* (pp. 46–58). Routledge.

Bashir, M. F., Shahbaz, M., Malik, M. N., Ma, B., & Wang, J. (2023). Energy Transition, Natural Resource Consumption and Environmental Degradation: The Role of Geopolitical Risk in Sustainable Development. *Resources Policy, 85*, 103985.

Baur, D. G., & Smales, L. A. (2020). Hedging geopolitical risk with precious metals. Journal of Banking & Finance, 117, 105823.

Bekkers, E., & Góes, C. (2022). The Impact of Geopolitical Conflicts on Trade, Growth, and Innovation: An Illustrative Simulation Study. *Global Economic Consequences of the War in Ukraine Sanctions, Supply Chains and Sustainability.*

Bercovitch, J. (1996). Understanding Mediation's Role in Preventive Diplomacy. *Negotiation Journal, 12*(3), 241–258.

Berkman, P. A., & Vylegzhanin, A. N. (Eds.). (2012). *Environmental Security in the Arctic Ocean.* Springer.

Berzina, K., & Soula, E. (2020). Conceptualizing Foreign Interference in Europe. *Alliance for Securing Democracy, German Marshall Fund of the United States*, 19.

Bhagwati, J. (1958). International Trade and Economic Expansion. *The American Conomic Review, 48*(5), 941–953.

Black, F. (1976). The pricing of commodity contracts. *Journal of financial economics*, 3(1-2), 167–179.

Blanchard, J. M. F. (2005). Linking Border Disputes and War: An Institutional-Statist Theory. *Geopolitics*, 10(4), 688–711.

Blanchard, O. (2021). Currency Wars, Coordination, and Capital Controls. In *The Asian Monetary Policy Forum: Insights for Central Banking* (pp. 134–157).

Blank, L. (2023). Disarmament, Non-Proliferation, and Arms Control. In *International Conflict and Security Law* (pp. 36–54). Edward Elgar Publishing.

Boguslavskaya, Y. (2016). NATO and Environmental Security. *Central European Journal of International & Security Studies*, 10(3).

Bouoiyour, J., Selmi, R., Hammoudeh, S., & Wohar, M. E. (2019). What Are the Categories of Geopolitical Risks that Could Drive Oil Prices Higher? Acts or Threats?. *Energy Economics*, 84, 104523.

Bouras, C., Christou, C., Gupta, R., & Suleman, T. (2019). Geopolitical risks, returns, and volatility in emerging stock markets: Evidence from a panel GARCH model. *Emerging Markets Finance and Trade*, 55(8), 1841–1856.

Braem, Y. (2007). Managing Territories with Rival Brothers: The Geopolitical Stakes of Military–Humanitarian Relations. In *Civil-Military Cooperation in Post-Conflict Operations* (pp. 49–69). Routledge.

Brighi, E., & Giusti, S. (2023). Italian Diplomacy and the Ukrainian Crisis: The Challenges (and Cost) of Continuity. *Contemporary Italian Politics*, 15(2), 190–204. https://doi.org/10.1080/23248823.2023.2195776

Brinkerhoff, D. W., & Brinkerhoff, J. M. (2004). Partnerships between International Donors and Non-Governmental Development Organizations: Opportunities and Constraints. *International Review of Administrative Sciences*, 70(2), 253–270. https://doi.org/10.1177/0020852304044254

Buchanan, Ben. (2020). *The Hacker and the State: Cyber-Attacks and the New Normal of Geopolitics*. Harvard University Press.

Caldara, D., & Iacoviello, M. (2022). Measuring Geopolitical Risk. *American Economic Review*, 112(4), 1194–1225.

Cao, C., Li, X., & Liu, G. (2023). Does Geopolitical Risk Matter for Corporate Investment Decisions? Evidence from Cross-Border Acquisitions. *Economics & Politics*.

Chatterjee, C. (2020). *Economic Diplomacy and Foreign Policy-Making*. Palgrave Macmillan.

Chen, N., Imbs, J., & Scott, A. (2009). The Dynamics of Trade and Competition. *Journal of International Economics*, 77(1), 50–62.

Cheng, C. H. J., & Chiu, C. W. J. (2018). How Important Are Global Geopolitical Risks to Emerging Countries?. *International Economics*, 156, 305–325.

Chesney, M., Reshetar, G., & Karaman, M. (2011). The impact of terrorism on financial markets: An empirical study. *Journal of banking & finance*, 35(2), 253–267.

Chitakornkijsil, P. (2009). Smes, Entrepreneurship and Development Strategies. *International Journal of Organizational Innovation*, 1(4).

Chortane, S. G., & Pandey, D. K. (2022). Does the Russia-Ukraine War Lead to Currency Asymmetries? A US Dollar Tale. *The Journal of Economic Asymmetries*, 26, e00265.

Dalby, S. (2003). Geopolitical Identities: Arctic Ecology and Global Consumption. *Geopolitics*, 8(1), 181–202.

Dalby, S. (2014a). Critical Geopolitics and the Control of Arms in the 21st Century. In *Reconceptualising Arms Control* (pp. 38–54). Routledge.

Dalby, S. (2014b). Environmental Geopolitics in the Twenty-First Century. *Alternatives*, 39(1), 3–16.

Das, D., Kannadhasan, M., & Bhattacharyya, M. (2019). Do the emerging stock markets react to international economic policy uncertainty, geopolitical risk and financial stress alike?. *The North American Journal of Economics and Finance*, 48, 1–19.

Demczuk, A. M. (2023). Joe Biden, Ukraine, Russia, Military Buildup, the Ed States of America, Hard Power, Soft Power, Coercive Diplomacy. *TEKA of Political Science and International Relations*, 17(1), 23–36.

Demidov, V., Mokhorov, D., Mokhorova, A., & Askarov, Z. (2021). International Legal Problems of Fighting Corruption in the Context of Geopolitical Integration. In *Proceedings of Topical Issues in International Political Geography* (pp. 313–326). Springer International Publishing.

Demir, E., & Danisman, G. O. (2021). The Impact of Economic Uncertainty and Geopolitical Risks on Bank Credit. *The North American Journal of Economics and Finance*, 57, 101444.

Dempsey, K. E., & McDowell, S. (2019). Disaster Depictions and Geopolitical Representations in Europe's Migration 'Crisis'. *Geoforum*, 98, 153–160.

Der Derian, J. (1987). Mediating Estrangement: A Theory for Diplomacy. *Review of International Studies*, 13(2), 91–110.

Devanny, J., Martin, C., & Stevens, T. (2021). On the Strategic Consequences of Digital Espionage. *Journal of Cyber Policy*, 6(3), 429–450.

Di Nicola, A. (2022). Towards Digital Organized Crime and Digital Sociology of Organized Crime. *Trends in Organized Crime*, 1–20.

Dijink, G. (2002). *National Identity and Geopolitical Visions: Maps of Pride and Pain*. Routledge.

Dolven, B., Lawrence, S. V., & O'Rourke, R. (2021). China Primer: South China Sea Disputes. *Congressional Research Service,* February corr2.

Donaubauer, J., Glas, A., Meyer, B., & Nunnenkamp, P. (2018). Disentangling the Impact of Infrastructure on Trade Using a New Index of Infrastructure. *Review of World Economics*, 154, 745–784.

Douzet, F., Pétiniaud, L., Salamatian, L., Limonier, K., Salamatian, K., & Alchus, T. (2020, May). Measuring the Fragmentation of the Internet: The Case of the Border Gateway Protocol (BGP) during the Ukrainian Crisis. In *2020 12th International Conference on Cyber Conflict (CyCon)* (Vol. 1300, pp. 157–182). IEEE.

Ellis, P., & Pecotich, A. (2001). Social Factors Influencing Export Initiation in Small and Medium-Sized Enterprises. *Journal of Marketing Research*, 38(1), 119–130.

Elsayed, A. H., & Helmi, M. H. (2021). Volatility transmission and spillover dynamics across financial markets: the role of geopolitical risk. *Annals of Operations Research*, 305(1), 1–22.

Esmailzadeh, Y. (2023). Defining Terrorism: Debates, Challenges, and Opportunities. *Challenges, and Opportunities (May 27, 2023)*.

Evans, O. (2019). The Effects of US-China Trade War and Trumponomics. In *Forum Scientiae Oeconomia* (Vol. 7, No. 1, pp. 47–55). Wydawnictwo Naukowe Akademii WSB.

Falk, R. (1995). The Complexities of Humanitarian Intervention: A New World Order Challenge. *Michigan Journal of International Law*. 17, 491.

Falkenmark, M. (1989). Middle East Hydropolitics: Water Scarcity and Conflicts in the Middle East. *Ambio: A Journal of Environment and Society,* 18(6), 350–352.

Fang, S., & Li, X. (2020). Historical Ownership and Territorial Disputes. *The Journal of Politics*, 82(1), 345–360.

Feenstra, R. C. (2010). *Product Variety and the Gains from International Trade*. Cambridge, MA: MIT Press.

Feenstra, R., & Kee, H. L. (2004). On the Measurement of Product Variety in Trade. *American Economic Review*, 94(2), 145–149.

Ferreira, C., Cardoso, C., Travassos, M., Paiva, M., Pestana, M., Lopes, J. M., & Oliveira, M. (2021). Disorders, Vulnerabilities and Resilience in the Supply Chain in Pandemic Times. *Logistics*, 5(3), 48.

Fey, M., & Ramsay, K. W. (2010). When Is Shuttle Diplomacy Worth the Commute? Information Sharing Through Mediation. *World Politics*, 62(4), 529–560.

Fisher, A. (2010). Mapping the Great Beyond: Identifying Meaningful Networks in Public Diplomacy. *CPD Perspectives on Public Diplomacy*, 2, 1–87.

Forbes, K. J., & Rigobon, R. (2002). No contagion, only interdependence: measuring stock market comovements. *The journal of Finance*, 57(5), 2223–2261.

Forum on Microbial Threats. *Board on Global Health; Institute of Medicine; National Academies of Sciences, Engineering, and Medicine. Global Health Risk Framework: Governance for Global Health: Workshop Summary.* Washington, DC: National Academies Press (US); 2016 May 11. 4, Challenges for Fragile States. Available from: https://www.ncbi.nlm.nih.gov/books/NBK362968/

Free, C., & Hecimovic, A. (2021). Global Supply Chains after COVID-19: The End of the Road for Neoliberal Globalisation?. *Accounting, Auditing & Accountability Journal*, 34(1), 58–84.

Fung, C. J. (2023). Rising Powers and Normative Resistance: China, India, and the Responsibility to Protect. *Journal of Contemporary China*, 32(141), 386–398.

Funke, M., & Ruhwedel, R. (2001). Product Variety and Economic Growth: Empirical Evidence for the OECD Countries. *IMF Staff Papers*, 48(2), 225–242.

Funke, M., Schularick, M., & Trebesch, C. (2020). *Populist Leaders and the Economy.*

Furfari, S. (2012). *Energy Politics and Geopolitics. An Analysis of the International Tensions in the 21st Century*; Politique et géopolitique de l'énergie: Une analyse des tensionsinternationales au XXIesiècle. Politique et géopolitique de l'énergie. Editions Technip.

Gaibulloev, K., & Sandler, T. (2023). Common Myths of Terrorism. *Journal of Economic Surveys*, 37(2), 271–301.

Gereffi, G., Humphrey, J., & Sturgeon, T. (2005). The Governance of Global Value Chains. *Review of International Political Economy*, 12(1), 78–104.

Glosten, L. R., Jagannathan, R., & Runkle, D. E. (1993). On the relation between the expected value and the volatility of the nominal excess return on stocks. *The journal of finance*, 48(5), 1779–1801.

Graham, M. A., & Ramiah, V. B. (2012). Global terrorism and adaptive expectations in financial markets: Evidence from Japanese equity market. *Research in International Business and Finance*, 26(1), 97–119.

Grossman, G. M. (1983). *International trade, foreign investment, and the formation of the entrepreneurial class* (No. w1174). National Bureau of Economic Research.

Godefroidt, A. (2023). How Terrorism Does (and Does Not) Affect Citizens' Political Attitudes: A Meta-Analysis. *American Journal of Political Science*, 67(1), 22–38.

Guan, A. C. (2000). The South China Sea Dispute Revisited. *Australian Journal of International Affairs*, 54(2), 201–215.

Gupta, R., Gozgor, G., Kaya, H., & Demir, E. (2019). Effects of Geopolitical Risks on Trade Flows: Evidence from the Gravity Model. *Eurasian Economic Review*, 9, 515–530.

Gupta, V., Gupta, C., Rubalcaba, L., Duc, A. N., Wang, X., & Butlewski, M. (2023). Foreign Embassies Internationalization support for Small and Medium-Sized Enterprises: Need to Balance Innovation Strategy & Innovation Support Policies. *IEEE Engineering Management Review*.

Gustafsson, P., & Segerstrom, P. (2010). North–South Trade with Increasing Product Variety. *Journal of Development Economics*, 92(2), 97–106.

Gustafsson, P., & Segerstrom, P. S. (2011). North–South Trade with Multinational Firms and Increasing Product Variety. *International Economic Review*, 52(4), 1123–1155.

Habib, M. M., & Stracca, L. (2015). Is There a Global Safe Haven?. *International Finance*, 18(3), 281–298.

Haddadin, M. J. (2001). Water Scarcity Impacts and Potential Conflicts in the MENA Region. *Water International*, 26(4), 460–470.

Hall, D. (2013). *Land*. John Wiley & Sons.

Hallgren, A., & Hansson, A. (2021). Conflicting Narratives of Deep Sea Mining. *Sustainability*, 13(9), 5261.

Hamdaoui, M., & Maktouf, S. (2019). Overall Effects of Financial Liberalization: Financial Crisis Versus Economic Growth. *International Review of Applied Economics*, 33(4), 568–595.

Hammi, B., Zeadally, S., & Nebhen, J. (2023). Security Threats, Countermeasures, and Challenges of Digital Supply Chains. *ACM Computing Surveys*.

Hanson, F., O'Connor, S., Walker, M., & Courtois, L. (2019). *Hacking Democracies: Cataloguing Cyber-Enabled Attacks on Elections*.

Hedström, A., Zelander, N., Junttila, J., & Uddin, G. S. (2020). Emerging market contagion under geopolitical uncertainty. *Emerging Markets Finance and Trade*, 56(6), 1377–1401.

Hinšt, D. (2021). Disinformation as Geopolitical Risk for Transatlantic Institutions. *International Studies*, 21(2), 89–111.

Hochman, G., Tabakis, C., & Zilberman, D. (2013). The Impact of International Trade on Institutions and Infrastructure. *Journal of Comparative Economics*, 41(1), 126–140.

Hoffman, D. A. (2011). Mediation and the Art of Shuttle Diplomacy. *Negotiation Journal*, 27(3), 263–309.

Hussain, Z., Wang, Z., Wang, J., Yang, H., Arfan, M., Hassan, D., ... & Faisal, M. (2022). A Comparative Appraisal of Classical and Holistic Water Scarcity Indicators. *Water Resources Management*, 36(3), 931–950.

Ioannides, I. (2022). What European Union in the "age of uncertainty"? Weathering the Geopolitical Storms in a World of Perpetual Crises. *Intereconomics*, 57(6), 363–367.

Irion, K., Kaminski, M. E., & Yakovleva, S. (2023). Privacy Peg, Trade Hole: Why We (Still) Shouldn't Put Data Privacy in Trade Law. *University of Chicago Law Review Online*, 1.

Iwanicz-Drozdowska, M., Rogowicz, K., Kurowski, Ł., & Smaga, P. (2021). Two decades of contagion effect on stock markets: Which events are more contagious?. *Journal of Financial Stability*, 55, 100907.

James, N., Menzies, M., Chok, J., Milner, A., & Milner, C. (2023). Geometric Persistence and Distributional Trends in Worldwide Terrorism. *Chaos, Solitons & Fractals*, 169, 113277.

Jaspal, R., Nerlich, B., & Lemańcyzk, S. (2014). Fracking in the Polish Press: Geopolitics and National Identity. *Energy Policy*, 74, 253–261.

Jaud, M., Kukenova, M., & Strieborny, M. (2018). Finance, Comparative Advantage, and Resource Allocation. *Review of Finance*, 22(3), 1011–1061.

Jenne, E. K. (2021). Populism, Nationalism and Revisionist Foreign Policy. *International Affairs*, 97(2), 323–343.

Jinji, N. (2006). International Trade and Terrestrial Open-Access Renewable Resources in a Small Open Economy. *Canadian Journal of Economics/Revue canadienne d'économie*, 39(3), 790–808.

Johnson, J. E., & Haug, P. (2021). Modifications to Global Supply Chain Management Strategies Resulting from Recent Trade Disruptions: An Exploratory Study. *Journal of Global Operations and Strategic Sourcing*, 14(4), 701–722.

Jones, R. W., & Dei, F. (1983). International trade and foreign investment: A simple model. *Economic Inquiry*, 21(4), 449.

Jones, K. (2023). Populism, Globalization, and the Prospects for Restoring the WTO. *Politics and Governance*, 11(1), 181–192.

Kamal, J. B., Wohar, M., & Kamal, K. B. (2022). Do Gold, Oil, Equities, and Currencies Hedge Economic Policy Uncertainty and Geopolitical Risks During Covid Crisis?. *Resources Policy*, 78, 102920.

Kamenopoulos, S. N., & Agioutantis, Z. (2020). Geopolitical Risk Assessment of Countries with Rare Earth Element Deposits. *Mining, Metallurgy & Exploration*, 37(1), 51–63.

Kathman, J. D. (2011). Civil War Diffusion and Regional Motivations for Intervention. *The Journal of Conflict Resolution*, 55(6), 847–876. http://www.jstor.org/stable/23208008

Keller, W., & Utar, H. (2023). International Trade and Job Polarization: Evidence at the Worker Level. *Journal of International Economics*, 145, 103810.

Khan, K., Khurshid, A., & Cifuentes-Faura, J. (2023). Investigating the Relationship Between Geopolitical Risks and Economic Security: Empirical Evidence from Central and Eastern European Countries. *Resources Policy*, 85, 103872.

Kluver, R., & Fu, W. (2004). The Cultural Globalization Index. *Foreign Policy*, 10.

Kojima, K. (1973). A macroeconomic approach to foreign direct investment. *Hitotsubashi Journal of economics*, 14(1), 1–21.

Kotcharin, S., & Maneenop, S. (2020). Geopolitical Risk and Shipping Firms' Capital Structure Decisions in Belt and Road Initiative Countries. *International Journal of Logistics Research and Applications*, 23(6), 544–560.

Krušković, B. D., & Maričić, T. (2015). Empirical Analysis of the Impact of Foreign Exchange Reserves to Economic Growth in Emerging Economies. *Applied Economics and Finance*, 2(1), 102–109.

Kurecic, P. (2015). Geoeconomic and Geopolitical Conflicts: Outcomes of the Geopolitical Economy in a Contemporary World. *World Review of Political Economy*, 6(4), 522–543.

Kusen, A., & Rudolf, M. (2019). Feedback Trading: Strategies during Day and Night with Global Interconnectedness. *Research in International Business and Finance*, 48, 438–463.

Lachininskii, S., & Xiaoling, L. (2021). The Geopolitical Risks and Prospects for Russia-Western Relations in the Baltic Region. *Pskov Journal of Regional Studies*, 4, 3–15.

Le, A. T., & Tran, T. P. (2021). Does Geopolitical Risk Matter for Corporate Investment? Evidence from Emerging Countries in Asia. *Journal of Multinational Financial Management*, 62, 100703.

Lee, A. C., Khaw, F. M., Lindman, A. E., & Juszczyk, G. (2023). Ukraine Refugee Crisis: Evolving Needs and Challenges. *Public Health*, 217, 41–45.

Lee, C. C., Olasehinde-Williams, G., & Akadiri, S. S. (2021). Are Geopolitical Threats Powerful Enough to Predict Global Oil Price Volatility?. *Environmental Science and Pollution Research*, 28, 28720–28731.

Lee, F., & Falco, G. (2023). *The Vulnerabilities Less Exploited: Cyberattacks on End-of-Life Satellites* (No. 9839). EasyChair.

Lenzen, M., Moran, D., Bhaduri, A., Kanemoto, K., Bekchanov, M., Geschke, A., & Foran, B. (2013). International Trade of Scarce Water. *Ecological Economics*, 94, 78–85.

Li, K., Cui, Y., Li, W., Lv, T., Yuan, X., Li, S., ... & Dressler, F. (2022). When Internet of Things Meets Metaverse: Convergence of Physical and Cyber Worlds. *IEEE Internet of Things Journal*, 10(5), 4148–4173.

Li, K., Qiu, J., & Wang, J. (2019). Technology Conglomeration, Strategic Alliances, and Corporate Innovation. *Management Science*, 65(11), 5065–5090.

Libiszewski, S. (1991). What Is an Environmental Conflict. *Journal of Peace Research*, 28(4), 407–422.

Liu, X., Ahmad, S. F., Anser, M. K., Ke, J., Irshad, M., Ul-Haq, J., & Abbas, S. (2022). Cyber Security Threats: A Never-Ending Challenge for E-Commerce. *Frontiers in Psychology*, 13, 927398.

Long, H., Zaremba, A., Zhou, W., & Bouri, E. (2022). Macroeconomics matter: Leading economic indicators and the cross-section of global stock returns. *Journal of Financial Markets*, 61, 100736.

Lorz, O. (2020). Investment in Trade Facilitating Infrastructure: A Political-Economy Analysis. *European Journal of Political Economy*, 65, 101928.

Lubinski, C., & Wadhwani, R. D. (2020). Geopolitical Jockeying: Economic Nationalism and Multinational Strategy in Historical Perspective. *Strategic Management Journal*, 41(3), 400–421.

Macaraig, C. E., & Fenton, A. J. (2021). Analyzing the Causes and Effects of the South China Sea Dispute. *The Journal of Territorial and Maritime Studies*, 8(2), 42–58.

Marcucci, S., Alarcon, N. G., Verhulst, S. G., & Wullhorst, E. (2023). Mapping and Comparing Data Governance Frameworks: A Benchmarking Exercise to Inform Global Data Governance Deliberations. *preprint archive:2302.13731*.

Martin, D. (2003). What Do Foreign Trade Offices Do Best?. *International Journal of Commerce and Management*, 13(2), 54–73.

Maulana, Y. I., & Fajar, I. (2023). Analysis of Cyber Diplomacy and its Challenges for the Digital Era Community. *IAIC Transactions on Sustainable Digital Innovation (ITSDI)*, 4(2), 169–177.

McDonnell, D. (2016). Populist Leaders and Coterie Charisma. *Political Studies*, 64(3), 719–733.

McMillan, M., & Verduzco, Í. (1986). New Evidence on Trade and Employment: an Overview. *Trade and Employment*, 1994, 23.

McSherry, P. M. (2015). *Post-Cold War East Asia: A Geopolitical Overview With Recommendations for US Force Posture*. Air Command and Staff College.

Mehrabi, Z., Delzeit, R., Ignaciuk, A., Levers, C., Braich, G., Bajaj, K., ... & You, L. (2022). Research Priorities for Global Food Security Under Extreme Events. *One Earth*, 5(7), 756–766.

Melitz, M. J., & Redding, S. J. (2021). *Trade and Innovation* (No. w28945). National Bureau of Economic Research.

Metcalfe-Hough, V. (2015). The Migration Crisis? Facts, Challenges and Possible Solutions. *Taken from* https://www. odi. org/sites/odi. org. uk/files/odi-assets/publicationsopinion-files/9913. pdf on, 14, 2016.

Metzl, J. F. (2001). Network Diplomacy. *Georgetown Journal of International Affairs*, 77–87.

Mohapatra, N. K. (2021). *Geopolitics of the Black Sea Region (Bsr) and Russia-Nato Strategic Game: India's Policy Options*. Available at SSRN 3957968.

Montagna, C. (2001). Efficiency Gaps, Love of Variety and International Trade. *Economica*, 68(269), 27–44.

Moons, S. J., & van Bergeijk, P. A. (2017). Does Economic Diplomacy Work? A Meta-Analysis of Its Impact on Trade and Investment. *The World Economy*, 40(2), 336–368.

Morariu, J., & Brennan, K. (2009). Effective Advocacy Evaluation: The Role of Funders. *The Foundation Review*, 1(3), 100–108. https://doi.org/10.4087/foundationreview-d-09-00031.1

Naray, O., & Bezençon, V. (2017). Management and Business Research on Commercial Diplomacy: Examining Trends and Themes. *The International Trade Journal*, 31(4), 332–359.

Naray, O. (2008, October). Commercial Diplomacy: A Conceptual Overview. In *7th World Conference of TPOs* (pp. 1–16).

Naray, O. (2011). Commercial Diplomats in the Context of International Business. *The Hague Journal of Diplomacy*, 6(1–2), 121–148.

Nazir, U. (2023). The Winds of Change Are Blowing: Globalization's Impact on Renewable Energy and Environmental Challenges. *Archives of the Social Sciences: A Journal of Collaborative Memory*, 2(1), 78–93.

Novelli, M. (2010). The New Geopolitics of Educational Aid: From Cold Wars to Holy Wars?. *International Journal of Educational Development*, 30(5), 453–459.

Nygaard, A. (2023). The Geopolitical Risk and Strategic Uncertainty of Green Growth after the Ukraine Invasion: How The Circular Economy Can Decrease The Market Power of and Resource Dependency on Critical Minerals. *Circular Economy and Sustainability*, 3(2), 1099–1126.

O'Connor, S., Hanson, F., Currey, E., & Beattie, T. (2020). *Cyber-Enabled Foreign Interference In Elections and Referendums* (Vol. 28). Canberra: Australian Strategic Policy Institute.

Ohlin, J. D. (2020). *Election Interference: International Law and the Future of Democracy*. Cambridge University Press.

O'Reilly, G. (2019). *Aligning Geopolitics, Humanitarian Action and Geography in Times of Conflict* (pp. 64–70). Springer.

Osuna, A. M. A. (2013). *International Trade and Infrastructure Development: Interactions Between Geneva and the Developing World*. University of Geneva Faculty of Economic and Social Sciences.

Pacheco, L. M., & Matos, A. P. (2022). Foreign Presence and Export Performance: The Role of Portuguese Commercial Diplomacy. *The International Trade Journal*, 36(2), 147–169.

Pan, L., Wang, Y., Sun, X., & Sadiq, M. (2023). Natural Resources: A Determining Factor Of Geopolitical Risk in Russia? Revisiting Conflict-Based Perspective. *Resources Policy*, 85, 104033.

Papakyriakou, P., Sakkas, A., & Taoushianis, Z. (2019). The impact of terrorist attacks in G7 countries on international stock markets and the role of investor sentiment. *Journal of International Financial Markets, Institutions and Money*, 61, 143–160.

Papastamou, A. (2023a). How Safe Are We? Shaping European Economy by Geopolitical Shocks. *Actual Problems of Economics* (Актуальні проблеми економіки), March, 3(261), 43–50. https://www.doi.org/10.32752/1993-6788-2023-1-261-43-50

Papastamou, A. (2023b). The Conundrum of European Economic Diplomacy: Trade, Development Aid & Democracy. *International Journal of Latest Research in Humanities and Social Science* (IJLRHSS), 06(07), 344–348.

Pappas, T. S. (2016). Are Populist Leaders "charismatic"? The Evidence from Europe. *Constellations*, 23(3), 378–390.

Peele, R. B. (1997). The Importance of Maritime Chokepoints. *The US Army War College Quarterly: Parameters*, 27(2), 8.

Peterson, D., & Hoffman, S. (2022). Geopolitical Implications of AI and Digital Surveillance Adoption. *Brookings Institution*.

Piattoeva, N., Viseu, S., & Wirthová, J. (2023). Introduction to the Special Issue 'Return of the Nation: Education in an Era of Rising Nationalism and Populism'. *European Educational Research Journal*, 22(5), 595–606.

Pilgun, E. V. (2022). Political Manipulation via Crisis Ideologization. *Political Science*, *1*(2).

Qin, M., Su, C. W., Umar, M., Lobonţ, O. R., & Manta, A. G. (2023). Are Climate and Geopolitics the Challenges to Sustainable Development? Novel Evidence from the Global Supply Chain. *Economic Analysis and Policy*, 77, 748–763.

Raddant, M., & Kenett, D. Y. (2021). Interconnectedness in the Global Financial Market. *Journal of International Money and Finance*, 110, 102280.

Randall, C. (2010). Geopolitical Conditions of Internationalism, Human Rights, and world law. *Journal of Globalization Studies*, *1*(1), 29–45.

Regan, P. M., & Kim, H. (2020). Water Scarcity, Climate Adaptation, and Armed Conflict: Insights from Africa. *Regional Environmental Change*, *20*, 1–14.

Rehmann, J. (2013). *Theories of Ideology: The Powers of Alienation and subjection* (Vol. 54). Brill.

Roberts, A., Choer Moraes, H., & Ferguson, V. (2019). Toward a geoeconomic order in international trade and investment. *Journal of International Economic Law*, 22(4), 655–676.

Robinson, R. E. (2023). The Excentric Idea of Imperialism, With or Without Empire. In *Imperialism*. Routledge.

Rodrigue, J. P. (2004). Straits, Passages and Chokepoints: A Maritime Geostrategy of Petroleum Distribution. *Cahiers de géographie du Québec*, 48(135), 357–374.

Roger, C., & Rowan, S. (2023). The New Terrain of Global Governance: Mapping Membership in Informal International Organizations. *Journal of Conflict Resolution*, 67(6), 1248–1269.

Rotberg, R. I. (2003). Failed States, Collapsed States, Weak States: Causes And Indicators. *State Failure and State Weakness in a Time of Terror*, 1, 25.

Ruta, M., & Venables, A. J. (2012). International Trade in Natural Resources: Practice and Policy. *Annual Revie of Resource Economics*, 4(1), 331–352.

Saeed, S., Altamimi, S. A., Alkayyal, N. A., Alshehri, E., & Alabbad, D. A. (2023). Digital Transformation and Cybersecurity Challenges for Businesses Resilience: Issues and Recommendations. *Sensors*, 23(15), 6666.

Saez, P. (2022). *Navigating Humanitarian Dilemmas in the Ukraine Crisis*. Humanitarian Policy Group (HPG).

Safitri, D., & Hotimah, O. (2022, November). Rhetoric in Polarization by Public Relations on Social Media. In *ICHELSS: International Conference on Humanities, Education, Law, and Social Sciences* (Vol. 2, No. 1, pp. 127–135).

Salisu, A. A., Ogbonna, A. E., Lasisi, L., & Olaniran, A. (2022). Geopolitical Risk and Stock Market Volatility in Emerging Markets: A GARCH–MIDAS Approach. *The North American Journal of Economics and Finance*, 62, 101755.

Scheffran, J. (2020). The Geopolitical Impact of Climate Change in the Mediterranean Region: Climate Change as a Trigger of Conflict and Migration. *Mediterranean Yearbook*.

Scherer, F. M. (2002). International Trade and Competition Policy. In *Competition and Trade Policies* (pp. 10–25). Routledge.

Segal, U. A. (2019). Globalization, Migration, and Ethnicity. *Public Health*, 172, 135–142.

Selmi, R., Bouoiyour, J., & Wohar, M. E. (2022). "Digital Gold" and Geopolitics. *Research in International Business and Finance*, 59, 101512.

Sharif, A., Aloui, C., & Yarovaya, L. (2020). COVID-19 Pandemic, Oil Prices, Stock Market, Geopolitical Risk and Policy Uncertainty Nexus in the US Economy: Fresh Evidence from the Wavelet-Based Approach. *International Review of Financial Analysis*, 70, 101496.

Shen, L., & Hong, Y. (2023). Can Geopolitical Risks Excite Germany Economic Policy Uncertainty: Rethinking in the Context of the Russia-Ukraine Conflict. *Finance Research Letters*, 51, 103420.

Shiquan, D., Deyi, X., Yongguang, Z., & Keenan, R. (2023). Critical Mineral Sustainable Supply: Challenges and Governance. *Futures*, 103101.

Shishodia, A., Sharma, R., Rajesh, R., & Munim, Z. H. (2023). Supply Chain Resilience: A Review, Conceptual Framework and Future Research. *The International Journal of Logistics Management*, 34(4), 879–908.

Siamagka, N. T., & Brouthers, K. D. (2020). *25 International Market Entry and Expansion*. The Routledge Companion to Strategic Marketing, 53.

Sikkink, K. (2009). The Power of Networks in International Politics. *Networked Politics: Agency, Power, and Governance*, 228–247.

Singh, T. (2010). Does International Trade Cause Economic Growth? A Survey. *The World Economy*, 33(11), 1517–1564.

Smales, L. A. (2021). Policy uncertainty in Australian financial markets. *Australian Journal of Management*, 46(3), 523–547.

Sohrbeck, A. J., Yadong, S., & Zeuthen, J. W. (2023). *Global Data Governance: The Global Fragmented Data Regulatory Framework and Digital Technology's Role in International Relations Theory*.

Sommerville, M., Essex, J., & Le Billon, P. (2014). The 'global food crisis' and the Geopolitics of Food Security. *Geopolitics*, 19(2), 239–265.

Stivas, D. (2023). Greece's Response to the European Refugee Crisis: A Tale of Two Securitizations. *Mediterranean Politics*, 28(1), 49–72.

Storey, I. (2020). *The South China Sea Dispute in 2020–2021*. ISEAS-Yusof Ishak Institute.

Stuenkel, O. (2017). *Post-Western World: How Emerging Powers Are Remaking Global Order*. John Wiley & Sons.

Swain, A. (2008). Mission Not Yet Accomplished: Managing Water Resources in the Nile River Basin. *Journal of International Affairs*, 201–214.

Swain, A. (2011). Challenges for Water Sharing in the Nile Basin: Changing Geo-Politics and Changing Climate. *Hydrological Sciences Journal*, 56(4), 687–702.

Tanchum, M. (2020). How Did the Eastern Mediterranean Become the Eye of a Geopolitical Storm?. *Foreign Policy*, 18.

Terman, R., & Byun, J. (2022). Punishment and Politicization in the International Human Rights Regime. *American Political Science Review*, 116(2), 385–402.

Therme, C. (2021). The Iran-Russia Geopolitical Encounter: A Marriage of Convenience Rather Than a Strategic Alliance. *Turkey, Russia and Iran in the Middle East: Establishing a New Regional Order*, 153–166.

Thrall, C. (2023). Informational Lobbying and Commercial Diplomacy. Working Paper. *Niehaus Center for Globalization and Governance, Princeton University*. Available at: https://www.calvinthrall.com/assets/amcham_adst_0.5.0.pdf

Trad, A. (2022, December). Entity Transformation Projects: The Extreme Crisis Strategy (XCS). In *Proceedings of 15th SCF International Conference on "Economic, Social, and Environmental Sustainability in the Post Covid-19 World"* (p. 209).

Tuathail, G. Ó. (1999). Understanding Critical Geopolitics: Geopolitics and Risk Society. *The Journal of Strategic Studies*, 22(2–3), 107–124.

Tuathail, G. Ó. (2000). *The Postmodern Geopolitical Condition: States, Statecraft, and Security at the Millennium*. Taylor & Francis.

Unfried, K., Kis-Katos, K., & Poser, T. (2022). Water Scarcity and Social Conflict. *Journal of Environmental Economics and Management*, 113, 102633.

Vakulchuk, R., Overland, I., & Scholten, D. (2020). Renewable Energy and Geopolitics: A Review. *Renewable and Sustainable Energy Reviews*, 122, 109547.

Van Camp, C., & Peeters, W. (2022). A World Without Satellite Data as a Result of a Global Cyber-Attack. *Space Policy*, 59, 101458.

Van Ha, H., & Tran, T. Q. (2017). International Trade and Employment: A Quantile Regression Approach. *Journal of Economic Integration*, 531–557.

Van Wessel, M., Schulpen, L., Hilhorst, T., & Biekart, K. (2017). Mapping the Expectations of the Dutch Strategic Partnerships for Lobby and Advocacy. The Netherlands Ministry of Foreign Affairs' Social Development Department/ Civil Society Organisations Division (DSO/MO). Available at: https://edepot. wur.nl/410800

Vargas-Hernández, J. G. (2023). Relocation Strategy of Global Supply Chain and Value Chain under Deglobalization. In *Managing Inflation and Supply Chain Disruptions in the Global Economy* (pp. 62–80). IGI Global.

Väyrynen, R. (2023). International Stability and Risky States: The Enforcement of Norms. In *Raimo Väyrynen: A Pioneer in International Relations, Scholarship and Policy-Making: With a Foreword by Olli Rehn and a Preface by Allan Rosas* (pp. 369–390). Cham: Springer International Publishing.

Vogel, J. M., Longo, C., Spijkers, J., Palacios-Abrantes, J., Mason, J., Wabnitz, C. C., ... & Fujita, R. (2023). Drivers of Conflict and Resilience in Shifting Transboundary Fisheries. *Marine Policy*, 155, 105740.

Wang, K. H., Su, C. W., & Umar, M. (2021). Geopolitical Risk and Crude Oil Security: A Chinese Perspective. *Energy*, 219, 119555.

Wang, L., Li, C., Chen, X., & Zhu, L. (2020). Causal Relationship Between the Spread of the COVID-19 and Geopolitical Risks in Emerging Economies. *Frontiers in Public Health*, 8, 626055.

Wernick, D. (2006). Terror Incognito: International BUSINESS in an Era of Heightened Geopolitical Risk. *Corporate Strategies under International Terrorism and Adversity*, 59–82.

Whyte, C., & Mazanec, B. M. (2023). *Understanding Cyber-Warfare: Politics, Policy and Strategy*. Taylor & Francis.

Wibowo, A. R. R. (2022). The Importance of Global Effort to Secure Space Sector from Cyberattack. *Intermestic: Journal of International Studies*, 7(1), 298–315.

Wiebe, K. (2001). The Nile River: Potential for Conflict and Cooperation in the Face of Water Degradation. *Natural Resources Journal*, 731–754.

Winter, T. (2015). Heritage Diplomacy. *International Journal of Heritage Studies*, 21(10), 997–1015.

Wood, W. B. (1994). Forced Migration: Local Conflicts and International Dilemmas. *Annals of the Association of American Geographers*, 84(4), 607–634.

Woodland, A. D. (1982). International Trade and Resource Allocation. (No Title).

Wulf, W. A., Haimes, Y. Y., & Longstaff, T. A. (2003). Strategic Alternative Responses to Risks of Terrorism. *Risk Analysis: An International Journal*, 23(3), 429–444.

Yakop, M., & Van Bergeijk, P. A. (2009). The Weight of Economic and Commercial Diplomacy. *International Institute of Social Studies (ISS) Working Paper*, (478).

Yoo, J. (2011). Fixing Failed States. *California Law Review*, 99(1), 95–150. http://www.jstor.org/stable/23014430

Young, J. C., Young, J. R., & Aubert, B. A. (2022). Insights from Diplomacy for the Prevention and Resolution of Conservation Conflicts. *Conservation Letters*, 15(5), e12891.

Yu, P. (2012). Resource-Allocation Advantage and International Trade. Available at SSRN 2209454.

Zalnieriute, M. (2015). An International Constitutional Moment for Data Privacy in the Times of Mass-Surveillance. *International Journal of Law and Information Technology*, 23(2), 99–133.

European Economy & Institutional Liberalism: Post-War Reconstruction of Ukraine

Abbott, K., Keohane, R., Moravcsik, A., Slaughter, A., & Snidal, D. (2000). The Concept of Legalization. *International Organization, 54*(3), 401–419. doi:10.1162/002081800551271

Aligica, P. D. (2023). Reconstructing the Postwar Black Sea Region, 4 January, https://www.gisreportsonline.com/r/black-sea-postwar/

Bason, C., Conway, R., Hill, D., & Mazzucato, M. (2020). A New Bauhaus for a Green Deal. November.[Online] Available at: ucl. ac. uk/bartlett/public-purpose/sites/public-purpose/files/new_bauhaus_cb_rc_dh_mm_0.   pdf [Accessed 20 March 2021].

Baylis, J., & Smith, S. (Ed.) (2005). *The Globalization of World Politics: An Introduction to International Relations*. Oxford: Oxford University Press.

Bennett, V. (2023). EBRD Outlines a View of a Successful Ukraine Reconstruction, https://www.ebrd.com/news/2023/ebrd-outlines-a-view-of-a-successful-ukraine-reconstruction.html#

Brinkley, D., & Facey-Crowther, D. R. (Eds.). (1994). *The Atlantic Charter*. New York: Palgrave Macmillan.

Bull, H. (1977). *The Anarchical Society: A Study of Order in World Politics*. Basingstoke: Macmillan.

Charap, S., Geist, E., Frederick, B., Drennan, J. J., Chandler, N., & Kavanagh, J. (2021). *Russia's Military Interventions: Patterns, Drivers, and Signposts*. Santa

Monica, CA: RAND Corporation, https://www.rand.org/pubs/research_repo rts/RRA444-3.html

Chupilkin, M., & Kóczán, Z. (2022). The Economic Consequences of War: Estimates Using Synthetic Controls. *EBRD Working Paper* 271.

Danichev, A. (2022). What Would Be Signs Protests in Russia Are Making a Difference? *The Harvard Gazette*, https://news.harvard.edu/gazette/story/2022/03/here-are-signs-protests-in-russia-are-making-difference/

Donahue, J., & Nye, J. (Ed.) (2000). *Governing in a Globalized World*. Washington, D.C.: Brookings Institution Press.

European Bank for Reconstruction and Development (EBRD) (2023). Regional Economic Prospects, May.

European Commission. (2023). "RebuildUkraine". New European Bauhaus: Call for Projects to Help Rebuild Ukraine and Foster Sustainable Construction Skills in Europe. Press Release, 18 April.

European Investment Bank. (2023). Italy Provides €100 Million to Support the EIB EU for Ukraine Initiative. Press Release, 26 April, https://www.eib.org/en/press/news/italy-provides-eur100-million-to-support-the-eib-eu-for-ukraine-initiative

Evans, G. (2008). *The Responsibility to Protect: Ending Mass Atrocity Crimes Once and For All*. Washington D.C.: Brooking Institution Press.

Fedorenko, V., & Fedorenko, M. (2022). Russia's Military Invasion of Ukraine in 2022: Aim, Reasons, and Implications. *Krytyka Prawa. Niezależne studia nad prawem*, 14(1), 7–42.

Glazer, S. G. (1971). The Brezhnev Doctrine. *International Lawyer*, 5#1, 169–179.

Gorodnichenko, Y., Sologoub, I., & di Mauro, B. W. (2022). *Rebuilding Ukraine: Principles and Policies*. Centre for Economic Policy Research.

Grieco, J. M. (1988). Anarchy and the Limits of Cooperation: A Realist Critique of the Newest Liberal Institutionalism. *International Organization*, 42(3), 485–507.

Hoffman, S. (1999). The Crisis of Liberal Internationalism. *Foreign Policy*, 98, Spring.

Hughes, G. (2008). The Soviet–Afghan War, 1978–1989: An Overview. *Defence Studies*, 8(3), 326–350.

Ikenberry, G. John. (2001). *After Victory: Institutions, Strategic Restraint, and the Rebuilding of Order After Major Wars*. Princeton University Press.

IMF. (2023a). IMF Executive Board Approves US$15.6 Billion under a New Extended Fund Facility (EFF) Arrangement for Ukraine as part of a US$115 Billion Overall Support Package. Press Release 23/101.

IMF. (2023b). Statement by IMF Managing Director Kristalina Georgieva at the Conclusion of Her Visit to Ukraine, Press Release, 23/48, February 21.

Izzeldin, M., Muradoğlu, Y. G., Pappas, V., Petropoulou, A., & Sivaprasad, S. (2023). The Impact of the Russian-Ukrainian War on Global Financial Markets. *International Review of Financial Analysis*, 87.

Józwiak, A., Górnikiewicz, M., & Bielawski, R. (2023). *Summary and Conclusions: Russian Interactions of "hard power" and "soft power" as the Elements of the Mechanics of Russian Influence on Ukraine. Influence of Russian Activities: Middle East Europe, the Visegrad Group Countries and Ukraine*, 441.

James III, W. M. (2020). *A Political History of the Civil War in Angola, 1974–1990*. Routledge.

Kappner, K., Szumilo, N., & Constantinescu, M. (2022). Estimating the Short-Term Impact of War on Economic Activity in Ukraine. *VoxEU.org*, 21 June.

Keohane, R., & Nye, J. (1977). *Power and Interdependence: World Politics in Transition*. Boston: Little, Brown & Company.

Keohane, R. O. (2012). Twenty Years of Institutional Liberalism. *International Relations*, 26(2), 125–138.

Kimball, J. P. (1997). Russia's Vietnam War. *Reviews in American History*, 25(1), 157–162.

Kyiv School of Economics. (2023). Russia's War Has Caused over $138 Billion in Damages in Ukraine. *News Feed*, 23 March, https://kyivindependent.com/ kyiv-school-of-economics-russias-war-has-caused-over-138-billion-in-dama ges-to-ukraines-infrastructure/

Lamt, S. (2005). Contemporary Mainstream Approaches: Neo-Realism and Neo-Liberalism. In Baylis, J., & Smith, S. (Eds.), *The Globalization of World Politics: An Introduction to International Relations*. Oxford: Oxford University Press.

Liadze, I., Macchiarelli, C., Mortimer-Lee, P., & Sanchez Juanino, P. (2023). Economic Costs of the Russia-Ukraine War. *The World Economy*, 46(4), 874–886.

Mac Ginty, R., & Richmond, O. (2007). Myth or Reality: Opposing Views on the Liberal Peace and Post-war Reconstruction. *Global Society*, 21(4), 491–497.

Mac Sweeney, N. (2009). *Private-Sector Development in Post-Conflict Countries*. Donor Committee for Enterprise Development.

Mearsheimer, John J. (1994). The False Promise of International Institutions. *International Security*, 19(3), 5–49.

Mills, R., & Fan, Q. (2006). *The Investment Climate in Post-Conflict Situations*. World Bank Policy Research Working Paper.

Mordowanec, N. (2023). Putin's War in Ukraine Has a Trillion-Dollar Price Tag. *Newsweek*, 23 February, https://www.newsweek.com/russia-spending-trilli ons-rubles-ukraine-war-1783463

OECD. (2023). *National Accounts Data Files*.

Ouimet, M. J. (2003). *The Rise and Fall of the Brezhnev Doctrine in Soviet Foreign Policy*. New Cold War History. The University of North Carolina Press.

Parrish, S. D., & Narinsky, M. D. (1994). New Evidence on the Soviet Rejection of the Marshall Plan, 1947: Two Reports. Woodrow Wilson International Center for Scholars, Working Paper No. 9.

Peschka, M. P. (2011). *The Role of the Private Sector in Fragile and Conflict-Affected States*. World Development Report Background Paper.

Remnek, Richard B. (1992). Translating 'New Soviet Thinking' into Practice: The Case of Ethiopia. In George W. Breslauer (Ed.), *Soviet Policy in Africa: From the Old to the New Thinking*. Berkeley, CA: University of California at Berkeley.

Rosado-García, M. J., Kubus, R., Argüelles-Bustillo, R., & García-García, M. J. (2021). A New European Bauhaus for a Culture of Transversality and Sustainability. *Sustainability*, 13(21), 11844.

Ruggie, J.G. (1982). International Regimes, Transactions, and Change: Embedded Liberalism in the Postwar Economic Order. *International Organization*, 36(2), 379–415.

Siang, N.Q. (2023). What Happens When the Guns Fall Silent? *The Edge*, 9 February, https://www.theedgesingapore.com/news/geopolitics/what-happ ens-when-guns-fall-silent

Thakur, R., & Weiss, T. (2009). R2P: From Idea to Norm-and Action? *Global Responsibility to Protect*, Vol. 1.

The World Bank. (2023). *National Accounts Data*, https://data.worldbank.org/ indicator/Ny.Gdp.Mktp.Cd?most_recent_value_desc=true

The World Bank. (2023). Russia's Invasion of Ukraine and Cost-of-Living Crisis Dim Growth Prospects in Emerging Europe and Central Asia. Press Release, 6 April, https://www.worldbank.org/en/news/press-release/2023/04/06/russ ian-invasion-of-ukraine-and-cost-of-living-crisis-dim-growth-prospects-in-emerging-europe-and-central-asia

The World Bank, the Government of Ukraine, the European Union, and the United Nations. (2023). Ukraine Rapid Damage and Needs Assessment: February 2022 – February 2023, March.

Trautman, L. J., & McFarlin, M. (2023). Putin, Russia And Ukraine: International Human Rights Violations, War Crimes, & Future Implications. *War Crimes, & Future Implications* (March 20, 2023).

U.S. State Department Executive Agreement. (1941). Atlantic Charter. Series No. 236

Ukraine Recovery Conference, URC. (2022). 'Lugano Declaration', Lugano, 4–5 July, https://uploads-ssl.webflow.com/621f88db25fbf24758792dd8/62c68 e41bd53305e8d214994_URC2022%20Lugano%20Declaration.pdf

UkraineInvest. (2023). Investment prospects in Ukraine: Ministry of Economy of Ukraine and J.P. Morgan Signed a Memorandum of Understanding, https:// ukraineinvest.gov.ua/news/09-02-2023-3/

UN General Assembly. (2023). General Assembly Overwhelmingly Adopts Resolution Demanding Russian Federation Immediately End Illegal Use of Force in Ukraine, Withdraw All Troops. 11th Emergency Special Session, 5th & 6th Meetings, 2 March, https://press.un.org/en/2022/ga12407.doc.htm

UNCHR. (2023). Operational Data Portal. https://data2.unhcr.org/en/sit uations/ukraine US State Department Bulletin, September 27, 1941, Washington, DC: Government Printing Office, 1941, https://avalon.law.yale. edu/wwii/interall.asp

Von Stein, J. (2005). Do Treaties Constrain or Screen? Selection Bias and Treaty Compliance. *The American Political Science Review*, 99 (4): 611–622.

Watier, M. A., & United States Army School of the Americas Fort Benning Ga Fort Benning United States. (2017). *Russia Foreign Policy in Latin America – Case Study of Nicaragua* (Doctoral dissertation, Fort Benning, GA: WHINSEC).

WTO. (2023a). *One year of war in Ukraine: Assessing the impact on global trade and development.*

WTO. (2023b). *Global Trade Outlook and Statistics.*

Trade, Development Aid & Democracy

Armstrong, K. A. (2006). Inclusive Governance? Civil Society and the Open Method of Co-Ordination. *Civil Society and Legitimate European Governance. Cheltenham: Edward Elgar*, 42–67.

Baracani, E. (2008). EU Democratic Rule of Law Promotion. In *International Actors, Democratization and the Rule of Law* (pp. 69–102). Routledge.

Barbé, E., & Johansson-Nogués, E. (2008). The EU as a Modest 'force for good': The European Neighbourhood Policy. *International Affairs*, 81–96.

Barry, F., King, M., & Matthews, A. (2010). Policy Coherence for Development: Five Challenges. *Irish Studies in International Affairs*, 21(1), 207–223.

Bartels, L. (2013). Human Rights and Sustainable Development Obligations in EU Free Trade Agreements. *Legal Issues of Economic Integration*, 40(4).

Batmanghelidj, E., & Hellman, A. (2018). Europe, Iran, and Economic Sovereignty: a New Banking Architecture in Response to US Sanctions. *European Leadership Network*, 7.

Bekemans, L. (2018). Citizens' Participation and Participatory Governance in the EU. *Studia Europejskie-Studies in European Affairs*, 22(4 (88)), 47–70.

Bergeijk, P. A. G., Okano-Heijmans, M., & Melissen, J. (2011). *Economic Diplomacy: Economic and Political Perspectives*. Martinus Nijhoff Publishers.

Bertoldi, P., Economidou, M., Palermo, V., Boza-Kiss, B., & Todeschi, V. (2021). How to Finance Energy Renovation of Residential Buildings: Review of Current and Emerging Financing Instruments in the EU. *Wiley Interdisciplinary Reviews: Energy and Environment*, 10(1), e384.

Bodenstein, T., & Faust, J. (2017). Who Cares? European Public Opinion on Foreign Aid and Political Conditionality. *JCMS: Journal of Common Market Studies*, 55(5), 955–973.

Boehmer, H. M., & Zaytsev, Y. K. (2019). Raising Aid Efficiency with International Development Aid Monitoring and Evaluation Systems. *Journal of MultiDisciplinary Evaluation*, 15(32), 28–36.

Boonstra, J., & Shapovalova, N. (2012). *Thinking Security, Doing Development? The Security-Development Nexus in European Policies Towards Tajikistan* (Vol. 12). EUCAM Working Paper.

Börzel, T. A. (2017). The Noble West and the Dirty Rest? Western Democracy Promoters and Illiberal Regional Powers. In *Democracy Promotion and the Challenges of Illiberal Regional Powers* (pp. 149–166). Routledge.

Börzel, T. A., & Risse, T. (2004, October). One Size Fits All! EU Policies for the Promotion of Human Rights, Democracy and the Rule of Law. In *Workshop on Democracy Promotion* (Vol. 4, No. 5). Stanford: Stanford University.

Bosse, G. (2012). The EU and Belarus: Perpetual Tango All over Again. *European Policy Centre*, 24.

Bouyala Imbert, F. (2017). *EU Economic Diplomacy Strategy*. European Commission, Directorate General for External Policy Department, March, https://www.europarl.europa.eu/RegData/etudes/IDAN/2017/570483/EXPO_IDA(2017)570483_EN.pdf

Browning, C. S., & Joenniemi, P. (2008). Geostrategies of the European Neighbourhood Policy. *European Journal of International Relations*, 14(3), 519–551.

Carbone, M. (2013). Mission Impossible: The European Union and Policy Coherence for Development. In *Policy Coherence and EU Development Policy* (pp. 1–20). Routledge.

Carbone, M., & Keijzer, N. (2016). The European Union and Policy Coherence for Development: Reforms, Results, Resistance. *The European Journal of Development Research*, 28, 30–43.

Carleton University European Union Centre of Excellence & Canada-Europe Transatlantic Dialogue (CETD). (2015). *Workshop: Strategic Partnership as an Instrument of EU Foreign Policy*, 13 April.

Cortright, D., Seyle, C., & Wall, K. (2017). *Governance for Peace: How Inclusive, Participatory and Accountable Institutions Promote Peace and Prosperity.* Cambridge University Press.

Crawford, P. W. (2004). *Aiding Aid: A Monitoring & Evaluating Framework To Enhance International Aid Effectiveness* (Doctoral dissertation).

Cuyvers, L. (2014). The Sustainable Development Clauses in Free Trade Agreements of the EU with Asian Countries: Perspectives for ASEAN?. *Journal of Contemporary European Studies*, 22(4), 427–449.

Derlukiewicz, N., Mempel-Śnieżyk, A., Mankowska, D., Dyjakon, A., Minta, S., & Pilawka, T. (2020). How Do Clusters Foster Sustainable Development? An Analysis of EU Policies. *Sustainability*, 12(4), 1297.

Duke, S. (2013). The European External Action Service and Public Diplomacy. In *European Public Diplomacy: Soft Power at Work* (pp. 113–136). New York: Palgrave Macmillan US.

Dür, A., & Gastinger, M. (2023). Spinning a Global Web of EU External Relations: How the EU Establishes Stronger Joint Bodies Where They Matter Most. *Journal of European Public Policy*, 30(6), 1072–1091.

EPRS. (2018). Democracy Support in EU External Policy, Ionel Zamfir, February.

EPRS. (2019). Peace and Security Outlook, Peace and Security in 2019: Overview of EU Action and Outlook for the Future, Elena Lazarou and Others, May.

European Commission (2019). 2019 EU Report on Policy Coherence for Development. Brussels, 28 January, SWD(2019) 20 final, https://internatio nal-partnerships.ec.europa.eu/system/files/2019-09/swd-2019-20-pcdreport _en.pdf

European Commission, Directorate-General for International Cooperation and Development. (2018). *An Introduction to the European Union's International Cooperation and Development Policy*. Publications Office, https://data.europa. eu/doi/10.2841/008349

European Commission. (2015). Towards a New European Neighbourhood Policy: the EU Launches a Consultation on the Future of Its Relations with Neighbouring Countries. 4 March, https://ec.europa.eu/commission/pres scorner/detail/en/IP_15_4548

European Commission. European Development Policy, https://international-partnerships.ec.europa.eu/policies/european-development-policy_en

European Union External Action. (2021). Economic Relations, Trade and Sustainability, https://www.eeas.europa.eu/eeas/economic-relations-trade-and-sustainability_en

European Union Global Strategy. (2016). Shared Vision, Common Action: A Stronger Europe. *A Global Strategy for the European Union's Foreign and Security Policy*, https://www.eeas.europa.eu/sites/default/files/eugs_revie w_web_0.pdf

Fagan, A. (2011). EU Assistance for Civil Society in Kosovo: A Step Too Far for Democracy Promotion?. *Democratization*, 18(3), 707–730.

Fiedlschuster, M. (2016). Democratizing EU Democracy Assistance? The EU's Perspective on Civil Society. In *European Neighbourhood Policy: Geopolitics between Integration and Security* (pp. 71–91). London: Palgrave Macmillan UK.

Forster, J., & Stokke, O. S. (Eds.). (2013). *Policy Coherence in Development co-Operation*. Routledge.

Frank, R. (2002). EU-North Korean Relations: No Effort Without Reason. *International Journal of Korean Unification Studies, Seoul: Korea Institute of National Unification*, 87–119.

Fumagalli, M. (2007). Tajikistan and the EU: From Post-Conflict Reconstruction to Critical Engagement. *CEPS Policy Briefs*, (1–12), 1–6.

Gammage, C. (2018). A Critique of the Extraterritorial Obligations of the EU in Relation to Human Rights Clauses and Social Norms in EU Free Trade Agreements. *Europe and the World: A law review*, 2(1), 1–20.

Gómez Isa F. et al. (2016). Challenges to the Effectiveness of EU Human Rights and Democratisation Policies. FRAME Deliverable No 12.3.

Góra, M., Styczynska, N., & Zubek, M. (Eds.). (2020). *Contestation of EU Enlargement and European Neighbourhood Policy. Actors, Arenas, and Arguments*. Copenhagen: Djøf Forlag.

Haas, Ernst B. (1978). *Global Evangelism Rides Again: How to Protect Human Rights Without Reall Trying*. Berkeley, California: Institute of International Studies.

Hackenesch, C. (2019). Aid, Political Conditionality, and Other International Efforts to Support Democracy in Africa. In *Oxford Research Encyclopedia of Politics*.

Hall, M. (2007). The EU and Uzbekistan: Where to go from here?. *CEPS Policy Briefs*, (1–12), 1–6.

Haukkala, H. (2008). The European Union as a Regional Normative Hegemon: The Case of European Neighbourhood Policy. *Europe-Asia Studies*, 60(9), 1601–1622.

Ismailov, S., & Jarabik, B. (2009). The EU and Uzbekistan: Short-Term Interests Versus Long-Term Engagement. *EUCAM Policy Brief*, 8, 1.

Justinek, G. (2023). State of Economic Play: European Union and Economic Diplomacy. *Inder Science* Online, January 31, pp. 81–92, https://doi.org/10.1504/IJDIPE.2023.128807

Keukeleire, S., & Delreux, T. (2022). *The Foreign Policy of the European Union*. Bloomsbury Publishing.

Killian, P. M. E. (2021). Economic Diplomacy as A Subject and Research Agenda: Practical, Conceptual and Methodological Issue. *Global Strategis*, 15(1), 51, 2442–9600.

Koch, S. (2015). A Typology of Political Conditionality Beyond Aid: Conceptual Horizons Based on Lessons from the European Union. *World Development*, 75, 97–108.

Kurki, M. (2011). Governmentality and EU Democracy Promotion: The European Instrument For Democracy and Human Rights and the Construction of Democratic Civil Societies. *International Political Sociology*, 5(4), 349–366.

Kusek, J. Z., & Rist, R. C. (2004). *Ten Steps to a Results-Based Monitoring and Evaluation System: A Handbook for Development Practitioners*. World Bank Publications.

Lane, D. (2010). Civil Society in the Old and New Member States: Ideology, Institutions and Democracy Promotion. *European Societies*, 12(3), 293–315.

Lee, J. S. (2005). The Two Faces of EU-North Korea Relations. *The Korean Journal of Defense Analysis*, 17(1), 33–52.

Liubkina, O., Murovana, T., Magomedova, A., Siskos, E., & Akimova, L. (2019). *Financial Instruments of Stimulating Innovative Activities of Enterprises and Its Improvements*.

Luong, P. J., & Weinthal, E. (1999). The NGO Paradox: Democratic Goals and Non-Democratic Outcomes in Kazakhstan. *Europe-Asia Studies*, 51(7), 1267–1284.

Marchi, L. (2014). Obstinate and Unmovable? The EU vis-à-vis Myanmar via EU-ASEAN. *Australian and New Zealand Journal of European Studies*, 6(1), 55–73.

Marková, J. (2019). The Importance of Economic Diplomacy in the Further Development of the EU. *International Journal of Public Administration, Management and Economic Development*, 4(1).

Mehtap, S. (2014). An EU-Arab Partnership to Foster Entrepreneurship Education in the Middle East: The ASPIRE Program. *International Proceedings of Economics Development and Research*, 81, 124.

Migliorelli, M., & Dessertine, P. (2018). Time for New Financing Instruments? A Market-Oriented Framework to Finance Environmentally Friendly Practices in EU Agriculture. *Journal of Sustainable Finance & Investment*, 8(1), 1–25.

Moens, B., & Aarup, S.A. (2023). EU's Trade Ideals Face 'economic security' Reality Check. *Politico*, 19 June, https://www.politico.eu/article/eu-trade-economic-security-strategy-us-china-competition-tariffs/

Montinola, G. R. (2010). When Does Aid Conditionality Work?. *Studies in Comparative International Development*, 45, 358–382.

Mudida, R. (2012). Emerging Trends and Concerns in the Economic Diplomacy of African States. *International Journal of Diplomacy and Economy*, 1(1), 95–109.

Papastamou, A. (2022). Economic Diplomacy and Human Rights: In search of a Democratic Framework. *Rocznik Administracji Publicznej*, (8), 443–463.

Pardo, R. P. (2017). *The EU and the Korean peninsula: Diplomatic Support, Economic Aid and Security Cooperation*. Istituto Affari Internazionali (IAI).

Pavlićević, D. (2022). Contesting China in Europe: Contextual Shift in China-EU Relations and the Role of "China Threat". In *The China Question: Contestations and Adaptations* (pp. 67–92). Singapore: Springer Nature Singapore.

Perlin, G. C. (2003). *International Assistance to Democratic Development: A Review*. Institute for Research on Public Policy.

Perulli, A. (2018). The Perspective of Social Clauses in International Trade. In *Rapporto al Congresso ISLSSL di Torino, ora in* Casale, G., & Treu, T. (Eds.), *Transformation at Work: Challenges for the National Systems of Labour Law and Social Security*. Torino, Giappichelli.

Petiteville, F.(2003). Exporting "values". EU External Cooperation as a Soft Diplomacy. In Knodt, M., & Princen, S. (Eds.), *Understanding the European Union's External Relations*. Routledge

Picciotto, R. (2005). The Evaluation of Policy Coherence for Development. *Evaluation*, 11(3), 311–330.

Raik, K. (2006). *Promoting Democracy Through Civil Society: How to Step Up the EU's Policy towards the Eastern Neighbourhood* (No. 237). CEPS.

Rose, R., & Mishler, W. (2002). Comparing Regime Support in Non-Democratic and Democratic Countries. *Democratization*, 9(2), 1–20.

Rudloff, B., & Laurer, M. (2016). The EU as Global Trade and Investment Actor – The Times They Are a-Changin'. *Working Paper, Research Division EU/Europe*,

Stiftung Wissenschaft und Politik, German Institute for International, and Security Affairs, https://www.swp-berlin.org/publications/products/arbeits papiere/IO_trade_EU.pdf

Sanchez Salgado, R. (2014). Rebalancing EU Interest Representation? Associative Democracy and EU Funding of Civil Society Organizations. *JCMS: Journal of Common Market Studies*, 52(2), 337–353.

Santiso, C. (2002). Promoting Democracy by Conditioning Aid? Towards a More Effective EU Development Assistance. *Internationale Politik und Gesellschaft*, (3), 107–134.

Schimmelfennig, F. (2007). European Regional Organizations, Political Conditionality, and Democratic Transformation in Eastern Europe. *East European Politics and Societies*, 21(1), 126–141.

Segone, M. (2008). Evidence-Based Policy Making and the Role of Monitoring And Evaluation Within the New Aid Environment. *The Role of Monitoring and Evaluation in Evidence-Based Policy Making*, 16.

Sianes, A. (2017). Shedding Light on Policy Coherence for Development: A Conceptual Framework. *Journal of International Development*, 29(1), 134–146.

Sicurelli, D. (2017). The Conditions for Effectiveness of EU Human Rights Promotion in Non-Democratic States. A Case Study of Vietnam. *Journal of European Integration*, 39(6), 739–753.

Siitonen, L. (2016). Theorising Politics Behind Policy Coherence for Development (PCD). *The European Journal of Development Research*, 28, 1–12.

Skelcher, C., & Torfing, J. (2010). Improving Democratic Governance Through Institutional Design: Civic Participation and Democratic Ownership in Europe. *Regulation & Governance*, 4(1), 71–91.

Smith, K. E. (1998). Use of Political Conditionality in the EU's Relations with Third Countries: How Effective. *European Foreign Affairs Review*, 3, 253.

Smith, K. E. (2005). The Outsiders: the European Neighbourhood Policy. *International Affairs*, 81(4), 757–773.

Snow, N. (2020). Rethinking Public Diplomacy in the 2020s. In *Routledge Handbook of Public Diplomacy* (pp. 3–12). Routledge.

Spence, D. (2012). The Early Days of the European External Action Service: A Practitioner's View. *The Hague Journal of Diplomacy*, 7(1), 115–134.

Stokke, O. (1995). Aid and Political Conditionality: Core Issues and State of the Art. *Aid and Political Conditionality*, 82, 1–87.

Strupczewski, J. (2023). EU Executive Proposes New Withholding Tax Rules to Attract Investors. *Reuters*, 19 June, https://www.reuters.com/markets/europe/ eu-exec-proposes-new-withholding-tax-rules-attract-investors-2023-06-19/

Titievskaia, J. (2023). *The Commission's 2015 'Trade for all' Strategy*. European Parliament Members' Research Service. Legislative Train, June, https://www.europarl.europa.eu/legislative-train/carriage/trade-for-all-strategy/report?sid=7101

Tsereteli, M. (2018). The Economic Modernization of Uzbekistan. *Uzbekistan's New Face*, 82.

Tvevad, J. (2017). EU-Cuba Relations: A New Chapter Begins. *European Parliament Directorate General for External Policies, Policy Department*.

Van den Putte, L. (2015). EU bilateral Trade Agreements and the Surprising Rise of Labour Provisions. *International Journal of Comparative Labour Law and Industrial Relations*, 31(3).

Van Vooren, B. (2011). A Legal-Institutional Perspective on the European External Action Service. *Common Market Law Review*, 48(2).

Vanhoonacker, S., & Pomorska, K. (2013). The European External Action Service and Agenda-Setting in European Foreign Policy. *Journal of European Public Policy*, 20(9), 1316–1331.

Vasilescu, L. (2014). Accessing Finance for Innovative EU SMES Key Drivers and Challenges. *Economic Review: Journal of Economics and Business*, 12(2), 35–47.

Vatta, A. (2018). The Social Clauses in EU Trade Agreements: Contents and Prospects. *Poliarchie/Polyarchies*, 2018(2), 286–306.

Vogelgesang, S. (1979). Diplomacy of Human Rights. *International Studies Quarterly*, 23(2), 216–245. https://doi.org/10.2307/2600243

Von Soest, C., & Grauvogel, J. (2015). *How Do Non-Democratic Regimes Claim Legitimacy?* Comparative Insights from Post-Soviet Countries.

Youngs, R. (2012). 18 Democratic Conditionality. *Routledge Handbook of Democratization*.

Zaharioaie, M. (2012). Appropriate Financial Instruments for Public-Private Partnership in European Union. *Procedia Economics and Finance*, 3, 800–805.

Zanger, S. C. (2000). Good Governance and European Aid: The Impact of Political Conditionality. *European Union Politics*, 1(3), 293–317.

Zimmer, A., & Obuch, K. (2022). If Not for Democracy, for What? Civil Society Organisations in Non-Democratic Settings. *Realities, Challenges, Visions? Towards a New Foreign Cultural and Educational Policy*, 4, 77.

Organizing Competitive Postgraduate Programs on Economic Diplomacy

Aksoy, M., & Çiçek, A. (2018). Redefining Diplomacy in the 21st Century. *MANAS Sosyal Araştırmalar Dergisi*, 7(3).

Blechman, B. M., Pickering, T. R., & Gingrich, N. (2009). Final Report of the State Department in 2025 Working Group. *Advisory Committee on Transformational Diplomacy.* https://2001-2009.state.gov/documents/organization/99879.pdf

Bokhan, A., & Zalizniuk, V. (2022). Economic Diplomacy in New Projections of Activation. *Baltic Journal of Economic Studies*, 8(4), 19–25. https://doi.org/10.30525/2256-0742/2022-8-4-19-25

Bolewski, W. (2007). *Diplomacy and International Law in Globalized Relations.* Springer Science & Business Media.

Booth, K., & Erskine, T. (Eds.). (2016). *International Relations Theory Today.* John Wiley & Sons.

Bull, H., Kingsbury, B., & Roberts, A. (Eds.). (1990). *Hugo Grotius and International Relations.* Clarendon Press.

Cantwell, J., & Krug, R. (2017). Bridging Theory and Practice: The Role of Practitioners in Economic Diplomacy Education. *International Studies Quarterly*, 61(2), 324–337.

Cederman, L. E., & Girardin, L. (2023). Computational Approaches to Conflict Research from Modeling and Data to Computational Diplomacy. *Journal of Computational Science*, 72, 102112.

Chaban, N. (2023). Collaborative Settings of Co-Creation: Knowledge Diplomacy and Pedagogical Thinking in Communication. *Journal of Technical Writing and Communication.* https://doi.org/10.1177/00472816231188652

Charles, V., & Emrouznejad A. (Eds.) (2022). *Modern Indices for International Economic Diplomacy.* Palgrave Macmillan Cham. https://doi.org/10.1007/978-3-030-84535-3

Cirnu, C. E., & Vasile, P. C. (2022). A Blockchain-Based Application as Part of a Digital Diplomacy Approach to Facilitate and Advance Cyber Diplomacy. *International Journal of Cyber-Diplomacy*, 3, 51–60.

Cohen, M. (2019). Experiential Learning in Economic Diplomacy: Simulations and Case Studies. *Diplomatic Studies Review*, 24(3), 412–428.

Constantinou, C. M. (2015). In pursuit of crisis diplomacy. *The Hague Journal of Diplomacy*, 10(1), 29–34.

Cooper, E. (2020). Technology Integration in Economic Diplomacy Education. *Journal of Economic Diplomacy*, 15(1), 58–72.

Da Vinha, L. (2018). Maps of War and Peace: Rethinking Geography in International Affairs. *Brown Journal of World Affairs*, 25, 73.

Doole, F. T., Littin, S., Myers, S. A., Somasekhar, G., Steyaert, J. C., & Lansey, K. (2022). Workshop Review: Experiential Learning for Training Future Science Policy and Diplomacy Experts. *Journal of Science Policy & Governance*, 21(01), October 17.

Faizullaev, A. (2022). Diplomacy for Professionals and Everyone. Series: *Diplomatic Studies*, 20, Chapter 6: Diplomatic Methods, Skills and Mindset. E-Book ISBN: 9789004517356.

Fels, E., & Weiss, L. (2001). Adapting Postgraduate Economic Diplomacy Programs to Global Trends. *Global Affairs Quarterly*, 26(4), 521–536.

Gilboa, E. (2001). Cultural Sensitivity in Economic Diplomacy: Building Cross-Cultural Competence. *Diplomacy and Culture Journal*, 10(2), 187–204.

Gregory, B. (2008). Public Diplomacy and Governance: Challenges for Scholars and Practitioners. In *Global Governance and Diplomacy: Worlds Apart?* (pp. 241–256). London: Palgrave Macmillan UK.

Grewe, W. G. (1999). The Role of International Law in Diplomatic Practice. *Journal of the History of International Law*, 1, 22.

Gribincea, A., & Gribincea, C. (2014). Economic Diplomacy as a Tool for Achieving National Interests. *Studii Economice*, (1), 35–45.

Henrikson, A. (2004). The Geography of Diplomacy. *The Geography of War and Peace: From Death Camps to Diplomats*, 369–395.

Hofius, M. (2022). Diplomats on the Frontlines: Knowing and Ordering in Crisis. *The Hague Journal of Diplomacy*, 18(1), 1–34. https://doi.org/10.1163/1871191x-bja10142

Jazbec, M. (2013). The Sociology of Diplomacy: A General Outline with Some Aspects and Dilemmas. *Perspectives: Review of International Affairs*, 1, 87–108.

Kamin, M. (2013). *Soft Skills Revolution: A Guide for Connecting with Compassion for Trainers, Teams, and Leaders*. John Wiley & Sons.

Knight, J. (2022). *Knowledge Diplomacy in International Relations and Higher Education*. Springer Nature.

Knutsen, T. L. (2008). A Lost Generation? IR Scholarship before World War I. *International Politics*, 45, 650–674.

Krein, A. T. (2023). Model United Nations: (Didactic) Module Content. In *Model United Nations*. Springer Texts in Political Science and International Relations. Springer, Cham. https://doi.org/10.1007/978-3-031-13524-8_4

Lieber, K. A. (2007). The New History of World War I and What It Means for International Relations Theory. *International Security*, 32(2), 155–191.

Makinda, S. M., & Higgott, R. A. (2002). International Collaboration in Economic Diplomacy Education. *Global Studies in Higher Education*, 18(3), 345–362.

Manor, I. (2023). The Road Not Taken: Why Digital Diplomacy Must Broaden Its Horizons. *Place Branding and Public Diplomacy*, 19(2), 206–210.

McCarthy, Mary M. (2018). *Routledge Handbook of Japanese Foreign Policy*. Routledge.

Melissen, J. (2005). The New Public Diplomacy: Between Theory and Practice. In *The New Public Diplomacy: Soft Power in International relations* (pp. 3–27). London: Palgrave Macmillan UK.

Mesot, J. (2022). Science Diplomacy: Showcasing New Multidisciplinary Approaches. Chapter 14, In Cauce, Ana Mari, Flückiger, Yves & van der Zwaan, Bert (Eds.), *Universities as the Fifth Power? Risks and Strategies*. Geneva, Switzerland: Association Glion Colloquium.

Narlikar, A., & Watson, A. (2014). Multidisciplinary Approaches to Economic Diplomacy Education. *International Relations Education Journal*, 9(1), 76–90.

Niklasson, B. (2020). The Gendered Networking of Diplomats. *The Hague Journal of Diplomacy*, 15(1–2), 13–42. https://doi.org/10.1163/1871191X-BJA10005

Paquette, P., Lu, Y., Bocco, S. S., Smith, M., Satya, O.-G., Kummerfeld, J. K, Pineau, J., Singh, S., & Courville, A. C. (2019). No-Press Diplomacy: Modeling Multi-Agent Gameplay. In *Advances in Neural Information Processing Systems* (pp. 4476–4487).

Pawar, R., & Singh, I. (2023). *The Virtual Vanguards: Exploring the Evolution of Digital Diplomacy*. Pencil.

Phlipot, C., & Bartholomees, J. B. (2012). Economic Diplomacy Views of a ctitioner. In Volume I: Theory of War and Strategy (pp. 193–204). Strategic Studies Institute, US Army War College. http://www.jstor.org/stable/resrep12116.18

Schweizer, K. W., & Schumann, M. J. (2008). The Revitalization Of Diplomatic History: Renewed Reflections. *Diplomacy and Statecraft*, 19(2), 149–186.

Sinkovics, R. R., & Sinkovics, N. (2009). Professional Development and Networking in Economic Diplomacy Programs. *Journal of Economic Diplomacy*, 14(2), 210–224.

Smith, R. F. (2011). *The Craft of Political Analysis for Diplomats* (Vol. 48). Potomac Books, Inc.

Snow, N. (2020). Rethinking Public Diplomacy in the 2020s. In *Routledge Handbook Of Public Diplomacy* (pp. 3–12). Routledge.

Strange, S. (1970). International Economics And International Relations: A Case Of Mutual Neglect. *International Affairs (Royal Institute of International Affairs 1944)*, 304–315.

Trachtman, J. P. (2019). Faculty Expertise and Postgraduate Economic Diplomacy Education. *Diplomacy and International Relations Journal*, 30(4), 2–548.

Van Bergeijk, P. A., Yakop, M., & de Groot, H. L. (2011). The Economic Effectiveness of Diplomatic Representation: An Economic Analysis of Its Contribution to Bilateral Trade. *The Hague Journal of Diplomacy*, 6(1–2), 101–120.

van Bergeijk, P. A., Okano-Heijmans, M., & Melissen, J. (2011). Introduction Economic Diplomacy: The Issues. In *Economic Diplomacy*. Leiden, The Netherlands: Brill | Nijhoff. https://doi.org/10.1163/9789004209619_002

van Bergeijk, P. A. G., Moons, S. J. V., & Martincus, C. V. (Eds.). (2018). The Future of Economic Diplomacy Research. In *Research Handbook on Economic Diplomacy: Bilateral Relations in a Context of Geopolitical Change*. Edward Elgar Publishing.

Vienne, E. D., & Nahum-Claudel, C. (2020). Anthropology and Diplomacy. Is Another Form Of Diplomacy Possible?[Introduction]. *Terrain. Anthropologie & Sciences Humaines*, (73).

Vucetic, S. (2013). Ethical Dimensions of Economic Diplomacy Education: Case Studies and Pedagogical Approaches. *Ethics in International Affairs Review*, 22(3), 318–335.

Weisbrode, K. (2013). *Old Diplomacy Revisited: A Study in the Modern History of Diplomatic Transformations*. Springer.

Bridges of Diplomacy and Prosperity: The Dual Role of European Universities

Adedoyin, O. B., & Soykan, E. (2023). Covid-19 Pandemic and Online Learning: The Challenges and Opportunities. *Interactive Learning Environments*, 31(2), 863–875. https://doi.org/10.1080/10494820.2020.1813180

Alali, Dr Walid Y. (2022). The Contribution of Education to Economic Development, December 5. SSRN: https://ssrn.com/abstract=4293524. http://dx.doi.org/10.2139/ssrn.4293524

Aleffi, C., Tomasi, S., Ferrara, C., Santini, C., Paviotti, G., Baldoni, F., & Cavicchi, A. (2020). Universities and Wineries: Supporting Sustainable Development in Disadvantaged Rural Areas. *Agriculture*, 10(9), 378. https://doi.org/10.3390/agriculture10090378

Allan, D. (2015). The Universities and the Scottish Enlightenment. *The Edinburgh History of Education in Scotland*, 97–113.

Altbach, P. G., & Salmi, J. (Eds.). (2011). *The Road to Academic Excellence: The Making of World-Class Research Universities*. World Bank Publications.

Amiano Bonatxea, I., Gutiérrez-Goiria, J., Vazquez-De Francisco, M. J., & Sianes, A. (2022). Is the Global Reporting Initiative Suitable to Account for University Social Responsibility? Evidence from European Institutions. *International Journal of Sustainability in Higher Education*, 23(4), 831–847.

Assunção, M. A., & Moreira, G. O. (2020). Addressing Societal Issues: Need for a New University Culture and a Transformation of Academic Practices. In *Sustainable Pedagogical Research in Higher Education* (pp. 41–52). Routledge.

Astigarraga, J. (Ed.). (2015). *The Spanish Enlightenment Revisited* (pp. 169–181). Oxford: Voltaire Foundation.

Aston, N. (2023). *Enlightened Oxford: The University and the Cultural and Political Life of Eighteenth-Century Britain and Beyond*. Oxford University Press.

Auricchio, Laura (2014). *The Marquis: Lafayette Reconsidered*. Vintage.

Aver, B., Fošner, A., & Alfirević, N. (2021). Higher Education Challenges: Developing Skills to Address Contemporary Economic and Sustainability Issues. *Sustainability*, 13(22), 12567. https://doi.org/10.3390/su132212567

Bacian, I. C., & Eisele, K. (2023). Early Implementation of four 2021–2027 EU Programmes: Erasmus +, Creative Europe, European Solidarity Corps and Citizens, Equality, Rights and Values (Strand 3). *EPRS: European Parliamentary Research Service*. Belgium. https://policycommons.net/artifacts/4511432/early-implementation-of-four-2021-2027-eu-programmes/5321142/

Ball, A. F. (2012). To Know Is Not Enough: Knowledge, Power, and the Zone of Generativity. *Educational Researcher*, 41, 283–293. https://doi.org/10.3102/0013189x12465334

Bamakan, S.M.H., Nezhadsistani, N., Bodaghi, O. et al. (2022). Patents and Intellectual Property Assets As Non-Fungible Tokens; Key Technologies and Challenges. *Scientific Reports*, *12* (2178). https://doi.org/10.1038/s41598-022-05920-6

Banks, J. A. (2009). Multicultural Education: Dimensions and Paradigms. In *The Routledge International Companion to Multicultural Education* (pp. 9–32). Routledge.

Becker, A. H. (2006). *Fear of God and the beginning of Wisdom: the School of Nisibis and the Development of Scholastic Culture in late Antique Mesopotamia*. University of Pennsylvania Press.

Becker, Garry S. (1964). *Human Capital; A Theoretical And Empirical Analysis, With Special Reference To Education*. New York: National Bureau of Economic Research. Columbia University Press.

Beerkens, M., & Vossensteyn, H. (2011). The Effect of the ERASMUS Programme on European Higher Education: The Visible Hand of Europe. In *Reform of Higher Education in Europe* (pp. 45–62). Brill.

Bell, M., & Lewis Jr, N. (2023). Universities Claim To Value Community-Engaged Scholarship: So Why Do They Discourage It?. *Public Understanding of Science*, 32(3), 304–321.

Benke, M. (2022). Apprenticeship in Dual and Non-Dual Systems. Between Tradition and Innovation. *Hungarian Educational Research Journal*, 12(3), 361–366. https://doi.org/10.1556/063.2022.00171

Benneworth, P., & Kuhlmann, C. S., & Rip, A. (2014). The Challenge of Addressing Grand Challenges. *EU Commission*. unha, J. (2015). Universities' Contributions to Social Innovation: Reflections in Theory & Practice. *European Journal of Innovation Management*, 18(4), 508–527.

Benneworth, P., & Jongbloed, B. (Eds.). (2010). *Who Matters to Europe's Universities? A Study of System Diversity, Change and Performance in Higher Education*. Springer.

Bergan, S. (2019). The European Higher Education Area: A Road to the Future or at Way's End?. *Tuning Journal for Higher Education*, 6(2), 23–49.

Biskup, T. A University for Empire? The University of Göttingen and the Personal Union 1737–1837. *The Hanoverian Dimension in British History 1714–1837*.

Bleich, E. (2002). Integrating Ideas into Policy-Making Analysis: Frames and Race Policies in Britain and France. *Comparative Political Studies*, 35(9), 1054–1076. https://doi.org/10.1177/001041402237506

Bohm, A., Koeper-Saul, V., & Mossmann, C. (2019). The European University Tandem Project–an Integrated Online Platform to Foster Intercultural Language Exchanges across Europe (and beyond). *Innovative Language Teaching and Learning at University: A Look at New Trends*, 53–61.

Bonaccorsi, A., & Daraio, C. (Eds.). (2007). *Universities and Strategic Knowledge Creation: Specialization and Performance in Europe*. Edward Elgar Publishing.

Borg, S. (1994). Language Awareness as Methodology: Implications for Teachers and Teacher Training. *Language Awareness*, 3, 61–71. https://doi.org/10.1080/09658416.1994.9959844

Boucher, G., Conway, C., & Van Der Meer, E. (2003). Tiers of Engagement by Universities in Their Region's Development. *Regional Studies*, 37(9), 887–897.

Bracht, O. et al. (2006). The Professional Value of ERASMUS Mobility. Final Report to the European Commission. https://www.academia.edu/download/39400080/The_Professional_Value_of_ERASMUS_Mobili20151024-5819-ebzkdi.pdf

Bréhier, L. (1926). Notes sur l'histoire de l'enseignement supérieur à Constantinople. *Byzantion*, 3(1), 73–94.

Brighton, D. (2015). *Successful Innovations?: Efficient Knowledge and Technology Transfer and International Collaboration*.

Brown, J. S., Collins, A., & Duguid, P. (1989). Situated Cognition and the Culture of Learning. *Educational Researcher*, 18, 32–42. https://doi.org/10.3102/0013189x018001032

Browning, R. (1978). Literacy in the Byzantine World. *Byzantine and Modern Greek Studies*, 4, 39–54.

Bularca, M. C., Nechita, F., Sargu, L., Motoi, G., Otovescu, A., & Coman, C. (2022). Looking for the Sustainability Messages of European Universities' Social Media Communication During the Covid-19 Pandemic. *Sustainability*, 14(3), 1554.

Bulgakova, A. (2022). 10 Top-Tier European University Accelerator Programmes. *EU Startups*, September.

Cai, Y. (2023). Towards a New Model of EU-China Innovation Cooperation: Bridging Missing Links between International University Collaboration and International Industry Collaboration. *Technovation,* 119.

Carayannis, E. G., & Morawska-Jancelewicz, J. (2022). The Futures of Europe: Society 5.0 and Industry 5.0 as Driving Forces of Future Universities. *Journal of the Knowledge Economy*, 13, 3445–3471. https://doi.org/10.1007/s13132-021-00854-2

Cardozier, V. R. (1993). *Colleges and Universities in World War II*. Bloomsbury Publishing USA.

Cardwell, D. S., & Jones, R. V. (1975). Science and World War I. *Proceedings of the Royal Society of London. A. Mathematical and Physical Sciences*, 342(1631), 447–456.

Carlsson, B., Acs, Z. J., Audretsch, D. B., & Braunerhjelm, P. (2009). Knowledge Creation, Entrepreneurship, and Economic Growth: A Historical Review. *Industrial and Corporate Change*, 18(6), 1193–1229.

Castiaux, J. H. A. (2007). Knowledge Creation through University-Industry Collaborative Research Projects. *Electronic Journal of Knowledge Management*, 5(1), 43–54.

Čeginskas, V. L., & Lähdesmäki, T. (2023). Dialogic Approach in the EU's International Cultural Relations: Joint EUNIC-EU Delegation Projects as Heritage Diplomacy. *International Journal of Cultural Policy*, 29(1), 34–50.

Chan, Y. E., & Farrington, C. J. T. (2018). Community-Based Research: Engaging Universities in Technology-Related Knowledge Exchanges. *Information and Organization*, 28(3), 129–139, https://doi.org/10.1016/j.infoandorg.2018.08.001.

Chatterton, P. (2000). The Cultural Role of Universities in the Community: Revisiting the University-Community Debate. *Environment and Planning A*, 32(1), 165–181.

Clarysse, B., Wright, M., Lockett, A., Van de Velde, E., & Vohora, A. (2005). Spinning Out New Ventures: A Typology of Incubation Strategies from European Research Institutions. *Journal of Business Venturing*, 20(2), 183–216.

Compagnucci, L., & Spigarelli, F. (2020). The Third Mission of the University: A Systematic Literature Review on Potentials and Constraints. *Technological Forecasting and Social Change*, 161, 120284.

Comsa, M. T., Conroy, M., Edelstein, D., Edmondson, C. S., & Willan, C. (2016). The French Enlightenment Network. *The Journal of Modern History*, 88(3), 495–534.

Comunian, R., Taylor, C., & Smith, D. N. (2014). The Role of Universities in the Regional Creative Economies of the UK: Hidden Protagonists and the Challenge of Knowledge Transfer. *European Planning Studies*, 22(12), 2456–2476.

Curaj, A., Deca, L., & Pricopie, R. (2020). *European Higher Education Area: Challenges for a New Decade* (p. 596). Springer Nature.

Dakowska, D. (2019). Higher Education Policy in the European Union. In *Oxford Research Encyclopedia of Politics*.

Dalmarco, G., Hulsink, W., & Blois, G. V. (2018). Creating Entrepreneurial Universities in an Emerging Economy: Evidence from Brazil. *Technological Forecasting and Social Change*, 135, 99–111.

De la Croix, D., Docquier, F., Fabre, A., & Stelter, R. (2020). *The Academic Market and the Rise of Universities in Medieval and Early Modern Europe (1000–1800)*.

De Vita, M. G. (2007). Fostering Intercultural Learning Through Multicultural Group Work. In *Teaching International Students* (pp. 87–95). Routledge.

De Wit, H. (2016). Internationalisation and the Role of Online Intercultural Exchange. *Online Intercultural Exchange: Policy, Pedagogy, Practice*, 4, 69–82.

De Wit, H. (Ed.). (2015). *European Higher Education at the Crossroads: Between the Bologna Process and National Reforms*. Springer.

Deissinger, T. (2022). The Standing of Dual Apprenticeships in Germany: Institutional Stability and Current Challenges. In Billett, S., Stalder, B. E., Aarkrog, V., Choy, S., Hodge, S., & Le, A. H. (Eds.), *The Standing of Vocational Education and the Occupations It Serves. Professional and Practice-based Learning* (Vol. 32). Cham: Springer. https://doi.org/10.1007/978-3-030-96237-1_5

Di Cagno, D., Fabrizi, A., & Meliciani, V. (2014). The Impact of Participation in European Joint Research Projects on Knowledge Creation and Economic Growth. *The Journal of Technology Transfer*, 39, 836–858.

Dimier, V. (2006). Three Universities and the British Elite: A Science of Colonial Administration in the UK. *Public Administration*, 84(2), 337–366.

Dooley, B. (1989). Social Control and the Italian Universities: From Renaissance to Illuminismo. *The Journal of Modern History*, 61(2), 206–239.

Dornbusch, F., & Brenner, T. (2013). *Universities as Local Knowledge Hubs Under Different Technology Regimes: New Evidence from Academic Patenting* (No. R6/2013). Arbeitspapiere Unternehmen und Region.

Drijvers, H. J. (1995). The School of Edessa: Greek Learning and Local Culture. In *Centres of Learning* (pp. 49–59). Brill.

EHEARome2020. (2020). *Rome Ministerial Communiqué*. 19 November 2020.

Empire, B. (2020). Monasteries, Society. *The Oxford Handbook of Christian Monasticism*, 155.

Erdoğan, V. (2019). Integrating 4C Skills of 21st Century into 4 Language Skills in EFL Classes. *International Journal of Education and Research*, 7 (11) November.

Estermann, T., Bennetot Pruvot, E., Kupriyanova, V., & Stoyanova, H. (2020). *The Impact of the Covid-19 Crisis on University Funding in Europe*. Brussels, Belgium: European University Association asbl.

European Commission. (2020). *Erasmus+ Programme Guide*. Brussels.

European Commission. (2022a). *Higher Education: Making EU's Universities Ready for the Future through Deeper Transnational Cooperation*. Strasbourg: Press Release.

European Commission. (2022b). *European Strategy for Universities*.

European Commission. (2022c). 10 Unique Study Programmes in Europe. https://education.ec.europa.eu/news/10-unique-study-programmes-in-europe

European Commission. (2022d). *European Education Area. 50 European Universities to Cooperate across Borders and Disciplines*.

European Commission. (2022e). *Social Economy and Inclusive Entrepreneurship – Social Entrepreneurship*. https://ec.europa.eu/social/main.jsp?catId=952&intPageId=2914&langId=en

European Parliament. (2023). The European Universities Initiative: first Lessons, Main Challenges and Perspectives. *Policy Department for Structural and Cohesion Policies Directorate-General for Internal Policies*, PE733.105.

European University Foundation. (2023). Let Us Experience Together! How to Provide Educational Offers for Senior Citizens on the University Campus. 31 March.

Fabricius, A. H., Mortensen, J., & Haberland, H. (2017). The Lure of Internationalization: Paradoxical Discourses of Transnational Student Mobility, Linguistic Diversity and Cross-Cultural Exchange. *Higher Education*, 73(4), 577–595.

Fabrizi, A., Guarini, G., & Meliciani, V. (2016). Public Knowledge Partnerships in European Research Projects and Knowledge Creation Across R&D Institutional Sectors. *Technology Analysis & Strategic Management*, 28(9), 1056–1072.

Fattori, N. (2013). *The Policies of Nikephoros II Phokas in the Context of the Byzantine Economic Recovery* (Master's Thesis, Middle East Technical University).

Fischer, G., Rohde, M., & Wulf, V. (2007). Community-Based Learning: The Core Competency of Residential, Research-Based Universities. *Computer Supported Learning*, 2, 9–40, https://doi.org/10.1007/s11412-007-9009-1

Foray, D., & Lundvall, B. (1996). The Knowledge-Based Economy: From the Economics of Knowledge to the Learning Economy. In OEDC (Ed.), *Employment and Growth in the Knowledge-Based Economy*. Paris: The Organisation.

Gál, Z., & Ptáček, P. (2019). The Role of Mid-Range Universities In Knowledge Transfer and Regional Development: The Case of Five Central European Regions. *Handbook of Universities and Regional Development* (pp. 279–300). Cheltenham, UK: Edward Elgar Publishing.

Garben, S. (2012). The Future of Higher Education in Europe: The Case for a Stronger Base in EU Law. *LEQS Paper*, (50).

Gascoigne, J. (2002). *Cambridge in the Age of the Enlightenment: Science, Religion and Politics from the Restoration to the French Revolution*. Cambridge University Press.

Gaston, P. L. (2023). *The Challenge of Bologna: What United States Higher Education Has to Learn from Europe, and Why It Matters That We Learn It*. Taylor & Francis.

Gavroglu, K. (2001). *The Sciences in the European Periphery During the Enlightenment*.

Goddard, J., & Puukka, J. (2008). The Engagement of Higher Education Institutions in Regional Development: An Overview of the Opportunities and challenges. *Higher Education Management and Policy*, 20(2), 11–41.

González-Pernía, J. L., Kuechle, G., & Peña-Legazkue, I. (2013). An Assessment of the Determinants of University Technology Transfer. *Economic Development Quarterly*, 27(1), 6–17.

Gottlieb, W. W. (2021). *Studies in Secret Diplomacy: During the First World War*. Taylor & Francis.

Greenwood, D., & Levin, M. (2001). Re-organizing Universities and 'Knowing How': University Restructuring and Knowledge Creation for the 21st Century. *Organization*, 8(2), 433–440.

Grek, S., & Landri, P. (2021). Education in Europe and the COVID-19 Pandemic. *European Educational Research Journal*, 20(4), 393–402.

Grendler, P. F. (2002). *The Universities of the Italian Renaissance*. JHU Press.

Grendler, P. F. (2003). Renaissance Humanism, Schools, and Universities. In *L'étude de la renaissance nunc et cras: Actes du colloque de la Fédération internationale des sociétés et instituts d'étude de la Renaissance. FISIER*.

Grendler, P. F. (2004). The Universities of the Renaissance and Reformation. *Renaissance Quarterly*, 57(1), 1–42.

Grendler, P. F. (2022). Paul Oskar Kristeller on Renaissance Universities. In *Humanism, Universities, and Jesuit Education in Late Renaissance Italy* (pp. 153–193). Brill.

Guo, S., & Jamal, Z. (2007). Nurturing Cultural Diversity in Higher Education: A Critical Review of Selected Models. *Canadian Journal of Higher Education*, 37(3), 27–49.

Gupta, R. K. (2023). Does University Entrepreneurial Ecosystem and Entrepreneurship Education Affect the Students' Entrepreneurial Intention/ Startup Intention? In: Chakrabarti, A., Suwas, S., & Arora, M. (Eds.), *Industry 4.0 and Advanced Manufacturing. Lecture Notes in Mechanical Engineering*. Singapore: Springer. https://doi.org/10.1007/978-981-19-0561-2_32

Hagen, S. (2008). From Tech Transfer to Knowledge Exchange: European Universities in the Marketplace. *Wenner-Gren International Series*, 84, 103–117.

Haldon, J. (2020). *Warfare, State and Society in the Byzantine World 565–1204*. Routledge.

Hayek, F. (1937). Economics and Knowledge. *Economica*, IV, http://www.haye kcenter.org/friedrichhayek/hayek.html

Hayek, F. (1945). The Use of Knowledge in Society. *American Economic Review*, XXXV(4), 519–530. http://www.hayekcenter.org/friedrichhayek/hayek.html

Hazelkorn, E. (Ed.). (2015). *Global Rankings and the Geopolitics of Higher Education: Understanding the Influence and Impact of Rankings on Higher Education, Policy and Society*. Routledge.

Heitor, M. (2015). How University Global Partnerships May Facilitate a New Era of International Affairs and Foster Political and Economic Relations. *Technological Forecasting and Social Change*, 95, 276–293.

Herbermann, C. (Ed.). (1913). *"Joseph-Marie, Comte de Maistre"* . *Catholic Encyclopedia*. New York: Robert Appleton Company.

Herbst, M. T. (2019). Bureau of Barbarians. *The Byzantine Empire: A Historical Encyclopedia [2 volumes]*, 11.

Herrmann, D. G. (1997). *The Arming of Europe and the Making of the First World War*. Princeton University Press.

Hidayati, M., Kartika, D., Widiati, U., Suharyadi, Wulyani, A. N., & Basthomi, Y. (2023). *Proceedings of the International Seminar on Language, Education, and Culture (ISoLEC 2022)*.

Highman, L., Marginson, S., & Papatsiba, V. (2023). Higher Education and Research: Multiple Negative Effects and No New Opportunities after Brexit. *Contemporary Social Science*, 1–19.

Hilde de Ridder-Symoens (Ed.). (1992). *A History of the University in Europe*, Vol. I: *Universities in the Middle Ages*. Cambridge University Press.

Hill, C., & Vanhoonacker-Kormoss, S. (2023). *International Relations and the European Union*. Oxford University Press.

Hillerbrand, R., & Werker, C. (2019). Values in University–Industry Collaborations: The Case of Academics Working at Universities of Technology. *Science &i Engineering Ethics* 25, 1633–1656. https://doi.org/10.1007/s11 948-019-00144-w

Holloran, J. R. (2000). *Professors of Enlightenment at the University of Halle, 1690–1730*. University of Virginia.

Holmes, A. F., Webb, K. J., & Albritton, B. R. (2022). Connecting Students to Community: Engaging Students Through Course Embedded Service-Learning Activities. *The International Journal of Management Education*, 20(1), https://doi.org/10.1016/j.ijme.2022.100610.

Holthaus, L., & Stockmann, N. (2020). Who Makes the World? Academics and (Un)cancelling the Future. *New Perspectives*, 28(3), 413–427. https://doi.org/10.1177/2336825X20935246

Hook, A., & Sher, R. B. (Eds.). (2001). *The Glasgow Enlightenment*. Birlinn Ltd.

Horne, J., & Pietsch, T. (2016). Universities, Expertise and the First World War. *History of Education Review*, 45(2), 142–150.

Irish, T. (2015). From international to Inter-Allied: Transatlantic University Relations in the Era of the First World War, 1905–1920. *Journal of Transatlantic Studies*, 13, 311–325.

Jaeck, E. G. (1917). A Few Notes on Goethe-Bibliography. *The Journal of English and Germanic Philology*, 16(2), 241–49.

Jansen, S., Van De Zande, T., Brinkkemper, S., Stam, E., & Varma, V. (2015). How Education, Stimulation, and Incubation Encourage Student Entrepreneurship: Observations from MIT, IIIT, and Utrecht University. *The International Journal of Management Education*, 13(2), 170–181.

Johansson, J. (2007). *Learning to Be (Come) a Good European: A Critical Analysis of the Official European Union Discourse on European Identity and Higher Education* (Doctoral dissertation, Linköping University Electronic Press).

Jongbloed, B., Enders, J., & Salerno, C. (Eds.). (2008). *Higher Education and Its Communities: Interconnections, Interdependencies and a Research Agenda.* Sense Publishers.

Kaldellis, A. (2012). *Procopius of Caesarea: Tyranny, History, and Philosophy at the End of Antiquity.* University of Pennsylvania Press.

Kapilan, N., Vidhya, P., & Gao, X. Z. (2021). Virtual Laboratory: A Boon to the Mechanical Engineering Education during COVID-19 Pandemic. *Higher Education for the Future*, 8(1), 31–46.

Kaspar, K., Burtniak, K., & Rüth, M. (2023). Online Learning during the COVID-19 Pandemic: How University Students' Perceptions, Engagement, and Performance Are Related to Their Personal Characteristics. *Current Psychology*, 20 March, https://doi.org/10.1007/s12144-023-04403-9

Kavak, E. B. (2020). Eternal Peace: The First Diplomatic Contact Between Justinian and Chosroes Anushirvan. *Cedrus*, 8, 581–591.

Kazhdan, A. P., & Wharton, A. J. (1985). *Change in Byzantine Culture in the Eleventh and Twelfth Centuries.* University of California Press.

Khapaev, V. V., & Glushich, A. M. (2020). *The Book of Ceremonies by Constantine VII Porphyrogennetos on the Organization of Competitions at the Hippodrome of Constantinople.*

Killick, D. (2017). *Developing Intercultural Practice: Academic Development in a Multicultural and Globalizing World.* Routledge.

Klofsten, M., Fayolle, A., Guerrero, M., Mian, S., Urbano, D., & Wright, M. (2019). The Entrepreneurial University as Driver for Economic Growth and Social Change – Key Strategic Challenges. *Technological Forecasting and Social Change* 141, 149–158. https://doi.org/10.1016/j.techfore.2018.12.004

Knobel, M., Patricia Simões, T., & Henrique de Brito Cruz, C. (2013). International Collaborations Between Research Universities: Experiences and Best Practices. *Studies in Higher Education*, 38(3), 405–424.

Kruse, M. (2018). *Economic Thought and Ideology in Procopius of Caesarea.* (Eds., Greatrex, G., & Janniard, S., pp. 39–54).

Kunoff, H. (1972). *The Enlightenment and German University Libraries: Leipzig, Jena, Halle, and Göttingen Between 1750 and 1813.* Indiana University.

Kwiek, M. (2021). What Large-Scale Publication and Citation Data Tell Us about International Research Collaboration in Europe: Changing National Patterns in Global Contexts. *Studies in Higher Education*, 46(12), 2629–2649.

Kwok, L. (2022). Labor Shortage: A Critical Reflection and a Call for Industry-Academia Collaboration. *International Journal of Contemporary Hospitality Management*, 34(11), 3929–3943. https://doi.org/10.1108/IJCHM-01-2022-0103

Kyriakis, M. J. (1971). The University: Origin and Early Phases in Constantinople. *Byzantion*, 41, 161–182.

Laleva, T. (2019). Saint Methodius: Life and Canonization. *Studia Ceranea. Journal of the Waldemar Ceran Research Centre for the History and Culture of the Mediterranean Area and South-East Europe*, (9), 27–37.

Lazzarini, I. (2022). Drocourt, N., & Malamut, É. (Eds.). (2020). La diplomatie byzantine, de l'Empire romain aux confins de l'Europe (Ve–XVe s.). *Diplomatica*, 4(1), 145–148.

Lebeau, Y., & Papatsiba, V. (2016). Conceptions and Expectations of Research Collaboration in the European Social Sciences: Research Policies, Institutional Contexts and the Autonomy of the Scientific Field. *European Educational Research Journal*, 15(4), 377–394.

Lebrun, Richard A. (1967). Joseph de Maistre, How Catholic a Reaction? *CCHA Study Sessions*, 34, 29–45.

Lendner, C. (2007). University Technology Transfer Through University Business Incubators and How They Help Start-Ups. *Handbook of Research on Techno-entrepreneurship*, 163–169.

Lillington-Martin, C. (2009). Procopius, Belisarius and the Goths. *Journal of the Oxford university History Society*, (7), 1–17.

Lillington-Martin, C. (Ed.). (2017). *Procopius of Caesarea: Literary and Historical Interpretations*. Taylor & Francis.

Lind, F., Styhre, A., & Aaboen, L. (2013). Exploring University-Industry Collaboration in Research Centres. *European Journal of Innovation Management*, 16(1), 70–91.

Link, A. N., John T. Scott, J. T., & Siegel, D. S. (2003). The Economics Of Intellectual Property at Universities: An Overview of the Special Issue. *International Journal of Industrial Organization*, 21(9), 1217–1225. https://doi.org/10.1016/S0167-7187(03)00080-8

Lobkowicz, N. (1987). The German University Since World War II. *History of European Ideas*, 8(2), 147–154.

Lugard, L. (1933). Colonial Administration. *Economica*, (41), 248–263.

Machlup, F. (1962). *The Production and Distribution of Knowledge in the United States*. Princeton, NJ: Princeton University Press.

Machlup, F. (1970). *Education and Economic Growth*. Lincoln: University of Nebraska Press.

Machlup, F. (1980). *Knowledge and Knowledge Production*. Princeton, NJ: Princeton University Press.

Maes, K., Debackere, K., & van Dun, P. (2011). Universities, Research and the "Innovation Union". *Procedia-Social and Behavioral Sciences*, 13, 101–116.

Magdalino, P. (1978). Manuel Komnenos and the Great Palace. *Byzantine and Ern Greek Studies*, 4, 101–114.

Magdalino, P. (2002). *The Empire of Manuel I Komnenos, 1143–1180*. Cambridge University Press.

Magistretti, S., Dell'Era, C., Verganti, R., & Bianchi, M. (2022). The Contribution of Design Thinking to the R of R&D in Technological Innovation. *R&D Management*, 52, 108–125. https://doi.org/10.1111/radm.12478

Mäkinen, K., Lähdesmäki, T., Kaasik-Krogerus, S., Čeginskas, V. L., & Turunen, J. (2023). EU Heritage Diplomacy: Entangled External and Internal Cultural Relations. *International Journal of Cultural Policy*, 29(1), 9–22.

Marginson, S. (Ed.). (2016). *Higher Education and the Common Good*. Routledge.

Markopoulos, A. (2008). Education. In Jeffreys, E., Haldon, John F., & Cormack, R. (Eds.), *The Oxford Handbook of Byzantine Studies*. Oxford Handbooks in Classics and Ancient History, Oxford: Oxford University Press.

Marra, Mita (2022). Productive Interactions in Digital Training Partnerships: Lessons Learned for Regional Development and University Societal Impact Assessment. *Evaluation and Program Planning*, 95.

Maassen, P., Andreadakis, Z., Gulbrandsen, M., & Stensaker, B. (2019). The place of universities in society: characteristics, changes, and challenges. *The Place of Universities in Society*, 104.

Mathisen, R. (1986). *Patricians as Diplomats in Late Antiquity*.

Mattsson, P., Laget, P., Vindefjärd, A. N., & Sundberg, C. J. (2010). What Do European Research Collaboration Networks in Life Sciences Look Like?. *Research Evaluation*, 19(5), 373–384.

Morris, P. S. (2022). Innovation Diplomacy. *Intellectual Property and the Law of Nations, 1860–1920*, 58, 99.

Munari, F., Pasquini, M., & Toschi, L. (2015). From the Lab to the Stock Market? The Characteristics and Impact of University-Oriented Seed Funds in Europe. *Journal of Technology Transfer*, 40, 948–975. https://doi.org/10.1007/s10961-014-9385-4

Musselin, C. (Ed.). (2018). *Research and Innovation in Higher Education: Understanding the Contradictions*. Springer.

Ndou, Valentina (2021). Social Entrepreneurship Education: A Combination of Knowledge Exploitation and Exploration Processes. *Administrative Sciences,* 11(4), 112. https://doi.org/10.3390/admsci11040112

Nicol, Donald M. (1968). The Byzantine Family of Kantakouzenos (Cantacuzenus), ca. 1100–1460: A Genealogical and Prosopographical Study. *Dumbarton Oaks Studies* 11. Washington, DC: Dumbarton Oaks Center for Byzantine Studies.

Ņikitina, T., Lapiņa, I., Ozoliņš, M., Irbe, M. M., Priem, M., Smits, M., & Nemilentsev, M. (2020). Competences for Strengthening Entrepreneurial Capabilities in Europe. *Journal of Open Innovation: Technology, Market, and Complexity,* 6(3), 62.

OECD (1996). *The Knowledge*-based *Economy.* Paris: The Organisation.

Olcay, G. A., & Bulu, M. (2017). Is Measuring the Knowledge Creation of Universities Possible?: A Review of University Rankings. *Technological Forecasting and Social Change,* 123, 153–160.

Oliver, W. H. (2015). The Heads of the Catechetical School in Alexandria. *Verbum et Ecclesia,* 36(1), 1–14.

Osborne, J. (1999). Politics, Diplomacy and the Cult of Relics in Venice and the Northern Adriatic in the First Half of the Ninth Century. *Early Medieval Europe,* 8(3), 369–386.

Osorno-Hinojosa, R., Mikko, Koria & Delia del Carmen Ramírez-Vázquez. (2022). Open Innovation with Value Co-Creation from University–Industry Collaboration. *Journal of Open Innovation: Technology, Market, and Complexity,* 8(1), 32. https://doi.org/10.3390/joitmc8010032

Panayiotou, S. (2019). Arab-Byzantine Seafaring in the Balkans and Eastern Mediterranean: The Portrait of Leo of Tripoli and Damian of Tyre Through Primary Sources. *Bulgarian e-Journal of Archaeology Supplements| Българско е-Списание за Археология Supplementa,* 7, 333–345.

Papastamou, A. (2018). In the Shadow of the European Economic Crisis: Best Practices for Continuing Education, In Szpaderski, A., & Urick, M. J. (Eds.), *Management and Welfare: Applications and Theories of Leadership for the Economy, State, and Healthcare.* HPL Publications, Inc., Douglassville 2018, ISBN: 978-1-61305-018-7.

Papastamou, A. (2023). The Role of European Universities in Addressing The Economic Crisis. *European Journal of Development Studies,* 3(5). https://doi.org/10.24018/ejdevelop.2023.3.5.316

Pearton, M. (1984). *Diplomacy, War, and Technology Since 1830.* Studies in Government & Public.

Peset, J. L. (2006). Enlightenment and Renovation in the Spanish University. In *Universities and Science in the Early Modern Period* (pp. 231–239). Dordrecht: Springer Netherlands.

Peters, M. A. (2001). National Education Policy Constructions of the 'Knowledge Economy': Towards a Critique. *Journal of Educational Enquiry*, 2(1), http://www.education.unisa.edu.au/JEE/

Peters, M. A. (2002a). *Education Policy in the Age of Knowledge Capitalism. Keynote address to the World Comparative Education Forum, Economic Globalization and Education Reforms.* 14–16 October. Beijing Normal University. *Policy Futures in Education*, 1(2).

Peters, M. A. (2002b). Universities, Globalisation and the Knowledge Economy. *Southern Review*, 35(2).

Peters, M. A. (2002c). New Zealand as the 'Knowledge Society': Universities, the Foresight Project and the Tertiary White Paper. *Leading and Managing*, 6(2), 16–32.

Peters, M. A. (2002d). The University in the Knowledge Economy. *Arena Journal*, 17, 1–11. [Google Scholar].

Peters, M. A. (2003a). Poststructuralism and Marxism: Education as Knowledge Capitalism. *Journal of Education Policy*, 18(2), 115–130. Taylor & Francis [Online, Web of Science ®].

Peters, M. A. (2003b). *Building Knowledge Cultures: Education in an Age of Knowledge Capitalism.* Lanham: Rowman & Littlefield.

Peters, M. A. (2003c). Classical Political Economy and the Role of Universities in the New Knowledge Economy. *Globalisation, Societies and Education*, 1(2), 153–168.

Purcell, W. M., Henriksen, H., & Spengler, J.D. (2019). Universities as the Engine of Transformational Sustainability toward Delivering the Sustainable Development Goals: "Living labs" for Sustainability. *International Journal of Sustainability in Higher Education*, 20(8), 1343–1357, https://doi.org/10.1108/IJSHE-02-2019-0103

Radko, N., Belitski, M., & Kalyuzhnova, Y. (2023). Conceptualising the Entrepreneurial University: The Stakeholder Approach. *The Journal of Technology Transfer*, 48, 955–1044.

Ragusa, A., Caggiano, V., Ramos, R. T., González-Bernal, J. J., Gentil-Gutiérrez, A., Bastos, S. A. M. C., González-Santos, J., & Santamaría-Peláez, M. (2022). High Education and University Teaching and Learning Processes: Soft Skills. *International Journal of Environmental Research and Public Health*, 19(17), 10699. https://doi.org/10.3390/ijerph191710699

Rance, P. (2005). Narses and the Battle of Taginae (Busta Gallorum) 552: Procopius and Sixth-Century Warfare. *Historia: Zeitschrift für Alte Geschichte*, (H. 4), 424–472.

Reichert, S. (2006). *The Rise of Knowledge Regions: Emerging Opportunities and Challenges for Universities* (p. 59). Brussels: European University Association.

Ricci, R., Colombelli, A., & Paolucci, E. (2019). Entrepreneurial Activities and Models of Advanced European Science and Technology Universities. *Management Decision*, 57(12), 3447–3472.

Rietbergen, P. (1998). *Europe: A Cultural History*. Routledge.

Ritzen, Jo. (2015). European Universities during the Crisis: A Public Policy Perspective, with a Brief Excursion to the US. *IZA Policy Paper* (107), September.

Rosser, John H. (2001). *Historical Dictionary of Byzantium*. Scarecrow Press.

Rothman, E. N. (2021). *The Dragoman Renaissance: Diplomatic Interpreters and the Routes of Orientalism* (p. 402). Cornell University Press.

Rüegg, W. (Ed.). (2004). *A History of the University in Europe: Volume 3, Universities in the Nineteenth and Early Twentieth Centuries (1800–1945)* (Vol. 3). Cambridge University Press.

Sanchez-Caballe, A., Gisbert-Cervera, M., & Esteve-Mon. F. (2020). The Digital Competence of University Students: A Systematic Literature Review. *Aloma: Revista de Psicologia, Ciències de l'Educació i de l'Esport*, 38(1), 63–74.

Sarantis, A. (2009). War and Diplomacy in Pannonia and the Northwest Balkans during the Reign of Justinian: The Gepid Threat and Imperial Responses. *Dumbarton Oaks Papers*, 63, 15–40.

Sarantis, A. (2018). Diplomatic Relations between the Eastern Roman Empire and the "barbarian" Successor States, 527–565. *History Compass*, 16(11), e12498.

Schaeffer, V., & Matt, M. (2016). Development of Academic Entrepreneurship in A Non-Mature Context: The Role of the University as a Hub-Organisation. *Entrepreneurship & Regional Development*, 28(9–10), 724–745.

Schor, A. M. (2007). Theodoret on the "School of Antioch": A Network Approach. *Journal of Early Christian Studies*, 15(4), 517–562.

Schultz, Theodore W. (1963). *The Economic Value of Education*. New York: Columbia University Press.

Shepard, J., & Franklin, S. (1992). *Byzantine Diplomacy*. Hampshire.

Sim, M. S. C., Galloway, J. E., Ramos, H. M., & Mustafa, M. J. (2023). University's Support for Entrepreneurship and Entrepreneurial Intention: The Mediating

Role of Entrepreneurial Climate. *Journal of Entrepreneurship in Emerging Economies*, 15(2), 360–378.

Smith, S., Smith, Taylor-Smith, E., Fabian, K., & Kotz, D. (2023). The Practice of Apprenticeships as Work-Integrated Learning. In Zegwaard, K. E., & Pretti, T. J. (Eds.), *The Routledge International Handbook of Work-Integrated Learning*. Taylor & Francis.

Spada, I., Chiarello, F. Barandoni, F. S., Ruggi, G., Martini, A., & Fantoni, G. (2022). Are Universities Ready to Deliver Digital Skills And Competences? A Text Mining-Based Case Study of Marketing Courses in Italy. *Technological Forecasting and Social Change*, 182. https://doi.org/10.1016/j.techfore.2022.121869.

Stathakopoulos, D. (2023). A Short History of the Byzantine Empire. *A Short History of the Byzantine Empire*, 1–256.

Steel, J. J., Sitko, J. C., Adkins, M. G., Hasstedt, S. C., Rohrer, J. W., & Almand, E. A. (2020). Empowering Academic Labs and Scientists to Test for COVID-19. *Biotechniques*, 69(4), 245–248.

Stephen, J. C., Hernandez, M. E., Roman, M., Graham, A. C., & Scholz, R. W. (2008). Higher Education as a Change Agent for Sustainability in Different Cultures and Contexts. *International Journal of Sustainability in Higher Education*, 9(3), 317–338. https://doi.org/10.1108/14676370810885916.

Stiglitz, Joseph E. (1999a). Knowledge as a Global Public Good. https://www.researchgate.net/profile/Eugenio-Bobenrieth/publication/46440722_The_Political_Economy_of_International_Environmental_Cooperation/links/55ddb07308ae79830bb531ed/The-Political-Economy-of-International-Environmental-Cooperation.pdf#page=346

Stiglitz, Joseph E. (1999b). *Public Policy For a Knowledge Economy*. 27 January, London: Department for Trade and Industry and Center for Economic Policy Research. http://www.worldbank.org/html/extdr/extme/jssp012799a.htm

Stirling, S., Maxey, L., & Luna, H. (2013). *The Sustainable University*. Abingdon: Routledge.

Stöckmann, J. (2020). The First World War and the Democratic Control of Foreign Policy. *Past & Present*, 249(1), 121–166.

Stoilova, V. (2020). The First World War and the Institutionalization of International Relations as an Academic Discipline. *Балканистичен Форум*, (2), 58–64.

Sullivan, D. F. (2012). Siege warfare, Nikephoros II Phokas, relics and personal piety. In *Byzantine Religious Culture* (pp. 395–409). Brill.

Tadjer, H., Lafifi, Y., Seridi-Bouchelaghem, H., & Gülseçen, S. (2022). Improving Soft Skills Based on Students' Traces in Problem-Based Learning Environments. *Interactive Learning Environments*, 30(10), 1879–1896. https://doi.org/10.1080/10494820.2020.1753215

Teixeira, P., & Shin, J. C. (Eds.). (2019). *Encyclopedia of International Higher Education Systems and Institutions*. Springer.

Thi Ngoc Ha, N., Spittle, M., Watt, A., & Van Dyke, N. (2023). A Systematic Literature Review of Micro-Credentials in Higher Education: A Non-Zero-Sum Game. *Higher Education Research & Development*, 42:6, 1527–1548, https://doi.org/10.1080/07294360.2022.2146061

Tomy, S., & Pardede, E. (2020). An Entrepreneurial Intention Model Focusing on Higher Education. *International Journal of Entrepreneurial Behavior & Research*, 26(7), 1423–1447. https://doi.org/10.1108/IJEBR-06-2019-0370

Trencher, G., Yarime, M., McCormick, K. B., Doll, C. N., & Kraines, S. B. (Eds.). (2013). *Urban Sustainability Transitions: Policy-Making and Research in Cities in the Global South*. Routledge.

Trencher, G., Yarime, M., McCormick, K., Doll, C., & Kraines, S. (2014). Beyond the Third Mission: Exploring the Emerging University Function of Co-Creation For Sustainability. *Science and Public Policy*, 41(2), 151–179.

Turquois, E., & Turquois, E. (2013). *Envisioning Byzantium: Materiality and Visuality in Procopius of Caesarea* (Doctoral dissertation, Oxford University, UK).

Ursić, L., Baldacchino, G., Bašić, Ž., Sainz, A. B., Buljan, I., Hampel, M., … & Markić, L. V. (2022). Factors Influencing Interdisciplinary Research and Industry-Academia Collaborations at Six European Universities: A Qualitative Study. *Sustainability*, 14(15), 9306.

Valencia-Arias, A., Arango-Botero, D., & Sánchez-Torres, J. A. (2022). Promoting Entrepreneurship Based on University Students' Perceptions of Entrepreneurial Attitude, University Environment, Entrepreneurial Culture and Entrepreneurial Training. *Higher Education, Skills and Work-Based Learning*, 12(2), 328–345.

Van Vught, F. A., & Ziegele, F. (Eds.). (2011). *Multidimensional Ranking: The Design and Development of U-Multirank*. Springer.

Van Weele, M., van Rijnsoever, F. J., Eveleens, C. P., Steinz, H., van Stijn, N., & Groen, M. (2018). Start-EU-Up! Lessons from International Incubation Practices to Address the Challenges Faced by Western Start-Ups. *The Journal of Technology Transfer*, 43, 1161–1189.

Verger, J. (1973). *Les universités au Moyen Âge*. Paris: Presses Universitaires de France.

Vetoshkina, L., Lamberg, L., Ryymin, E., Rintala, H., & Paavola, S. (2023). Innovation Activities in a University of Applied Sciences: Redefining Applied Research. *Journal of Applied Research in Higher Education*, 15(2), 289–302.

Vollmuth, R., & Keil, G. (2003). Steadiness and Progress. Medicine in Würzburg in the Mirror of the Centuries-A Contribution to the Foundation of the University of Würzburg 600 Years Ago. *Wurzburger Medizinhistorische Mitteilungen*, 22, 7–20.

Vowell, S. (2015). *Lafayette in the Somewhat United States*. Riverhead.

Wang, Q., Cheng, Y., & Liu, N. C. (2012). Building World-Class Universities: Different Approaches to a Shared Goal. In *Building World-Class Universities* (pp. 1–10). Brill.

Watts, E. (2004). Justinian, Malalas, and the End of Athenian philosophical Teaching in AD 529. *The Journal of Roman Studies*, 94, 168–182.

Woods, D. (2012). Theophilus of Edessa-(RG) Hoyland (trans.) Theophilus of Edessa's Chronicle and the Circulation of Historical Knowledge in Late Antiquity and Early Islam.(Translated Texts for Historians 57.) Pp. vi+ 368, maps. Liverpool: Liverpool University Press, 2011. Paper,£ 19.99 (Cased,£ 65). ISBN: 978-1-84631-698-2 (978-1-84631-697-5 hbk). *The Classical Review*, 62(2), 473–475.

World Bank. (1998). *World Development Report: Knowledge For Development*. Oxford: Oxford University Press.

Wright, T. S. A. (2002). Definitions and Frameworks for Environmental Sustainability in Higher Education. *International Journal of Sustainability in Higher Education*, 3(3), 203–220, https://doi.org/10.1108/1467637021 0434679

Youtie, J., & Shapira, P. (2008). Building an Innovation Hub: A Case Study of the Transformation of University Roles in Regional Technological and Economic Development. *Research Policy*, 37(8), 1188–1204.

Zalite, G. G., & Zvirbule, A. (2020). Digital Readiness and Competitiveness of the EU Higher Education Institutions: The COVID-19 Pandemic Impact. *Emerging Science Journal*, 4(4), 297–304.

Zhao, M. Q., & Allen, R. (2023). Training Problem-Solvers by Using Real World Problems as Case Studies. In Daimi, K., & Al Sadoon, A. (Eds.), *Proceedings of the Second International Conference on Innovations in Computing Research (ICR'23). Lecture Notes in Networks and Systems* (Vol. 721). Cham: Springer. https://doi.org/10.1007/978-3-031-35308-6_36

Zmuidzinaite, R., Zalgeviciene, S., & Uziene, L. (2021). Factors Influencing the Performance of Technology Transfer Offices: The Case of the European Consortium of Innovative Universities. *Inžinerinė ekonomika – Engineering Economics*. Kaunas: KTU, 32(3), 221–233.